Input Matters in SLA

personal property of

Keith FAULKNER

PEFC
PEFC/16-33-111
CATG-PEFC-052
www.pefc.org

SECOND LANGUAGE ACQUISITION
Series Editor: Professor David Singleton, *Trinity College, Dublin, Ireland*

This series brings together titles dealing with a variety of aspects of language acquisition and processing in situations where a language or languages other than the native language is involved. Second language is thus interpreted in its broadest possible sense. The volumes included in the series all offer in their different ways, on the one hand, exposition and discussion of empirical findings and, on the other, some degree of theoretical reflection. In this latter connection, no particular theoretical stance is privileged in the series; nor is any relevant perspective – sociolinguistic, psycholinguistic, neurolinguistic, etc. – deemed out of place. The intended readership of the series includes final-year undergraduates working on second language acquisition projects, postgraduate students involved in second language acquisition research, and researchers and teachers in general whose interests include a second language acquisition component.

Full details of all the books in this series and of all our other publications can be found on http://www.multilingual-matters.com, or by writing to Multilingual Matters, St Nicholas House, 31-34 High Street, Bristol BS1 2AW, UK.

SECOND LANGUAGE ACQUISITION
Series Editor: David Singleton, Trinity College, Dublin, Ireland

Input Matters in SLA

Edited by

Thorsten Piske and
Martha Young-Scholten

MULTILINGUAL MATTERS
Bristol • Buffalo • Toronto

Library of Congress Cataloging in Publication Data
A catalog record for this book is available from the Library of Congress.
Input Matters in SLA
Edited by Thorsten Piske and Martha Young-Scholten.
Second Language Acquisition: 35
Includes bibliographical references.
1. Second language acquisition. 2. Psycholinguistics.
I. Piske, Thorsten. II. Young-Scholten, Martha.
P118.2.I55 2008
401'.93–dc22 2008026642

British Library Cataloguing in Publication Data
A catalogue entry for this book is available from the British Library.

ISBN-13: 978-1-84769-110-1 (hbk)
ISBN-13: 978-1-84769-109-5 (pbk)

Multilingual Matters
UK: St Nicholas House, 31-34 High Street, Bristol BS1 2AW, UK.
USA: UTP, 2250 Military Road, Tonawanda, NY 14150, USA.
Canada: UTP, 5201 Dufferin Street, North York, Ontario M3H 5T8, Canada.

The policy of Multilingual Matters/Channel View Publications is to use papers that are natural, renewable and recyclable products, made from wood grown in sustainable forests. In the manufacturing process of our books, and to further support our policy, preference is given to printers that have FSC and PEFC Chain of Custody certification. The FSC and/or PEFC logos will appear on those books where full certification has been granted to the printer concerned.

Typeset by Techset Composition Ltd., Salisbury, UK.
Printed and bound in Great Britain by MPG Books Ltd.

Contents

Contributors

Benedetta Bassetti, Laurea, University of Rome; MA, Birkbeck, University of London; PhD, University of Essex, is a Visiting Research Associate at the Institute of Education, University of London. She is interested in the acquisition and use of additional languages and writing systems. She is founding co-editor of the journal *Writing Systems Research*.

Werner Bleyhl, PhD University of Tübingen, is professor emeritus at the University of Education Ludwigsburg, Germany. He was a Fulbright scholar in 1980. His research and numerous publications focus on foreign language learning and teaching of adults and young learners, taking into account the research findings of developmental psychology, language acquisition and brain research. Bleyhl advocates a broad and flexible approach to language teaching which should – both theoretically and practically – come to grips with the principles of non-linearity and self-organization that so clearly determine the complex processes of language learning.

Ocke-Schwen Bohn, Dr.phil. Kiel University, is professor and Chair of English Linguistics at Aarhus University. With funding from the German DFG, the Danish SHF/FKK, and in collaboration with American, Canadian, and Australian colleagues, Bohn's research focuses on cross-language and second language speech perception, foreign-accented speech, and infant speech perception.

Rikke Louise Bundgaard-Nielsen, MA, Aarhus University, Denmark, is currently a PhD student at MARCS Auditory Laboratories, University of Western Sydney, Australia. Her research focuses on second language speech perception and production, as well as native and cross-dialect speech perception.

Kees de Bot graduated from the University of Nijmegen in General Linguistics and Applied Linguistics. His research concerns a number of topics including foreign language attrition, language and dementia in multilingual settings, maintenance and shift of minority languages and the psycholinguistics of bilingual language processing, early and late forms of bilingual education and immersion and the application of Dynamic Systems Theory in SLA and multilingualism.

He is Chair of Applied Linguistics and director of the Research School for Behavioral and Cognitive Neurosciences (BCN) at the University of Groningen.

Nel de Jong, MA Free University Amsterdam; PhD, University of Amsterdam is currently an assistant professor at Queens College of the City University of New York. De Jong's work focuses on second language acquisition and aims to characterize the changes in knowledge and processing mechanisms that are brought about by specific teaching methods.

James E. Flege, PhD retired in 2006 from the Speech & Hearing Division, University of Alabama. For 25 years he conducted research examining the development of speech in a second language under the auspices of grants from the National Institutes of Health (NIH). The results of this research is available at www.jimflege.com

Stephen Krashen is best known for developing the first comprehensive theory of second language acquisition, introducing the concept of sheltered subject matter teaching, and as the co-inventor of the Natural Approach. He has also contributed to theory and application in the areas of bilingual education, and reading. He was the 1977 Incline Bench Press champion of Venice Beach and holds a black belt in Tae Kwon Do. His current books are Summer Reading: Program and Evidence (with Fay Shin, published by Allyn and Bacon), English Learners in American Classrooms (with Jim Crawford, published by Scholastic), and English Fever (Crane Publishing Company, Taipei).

Wander Lowie graduated from the University of Amsterdam in English and speech science. His PhD research focused on the acquisition of interlanguage morphology. He is currently employed at the University of Groningen, where he works in the Departments of English and Applied Linguistics. His research has focused on the development of morphology, phonology and the lexicon in a second language, more recently from the perspective of dynamic systems theory. Together with Marjolijn Verspoor, Kees the Bot he has published several articles on the application of dynamic systems theory to second language development in, among others, Bilingualism and The Modern Language Journal.

Alene Moyer is Associate Professor of Germanic Studies and Second Language Acquisition in the School of Languages, Literatures and Cultures at the University of Maryland, College Park, where she teaches graduate and undergraduate courses in sociolinguistics, second language acquisition, German linguistics, and foreign language teaching methods. Her research explores the experiential and socio-psychololgical factors relevant to accent in a second language. She is currently working on a book on the social implications of foreign accent in the USA.

Andreas Rohde, PhD and German 'Habilitation', Kiel University, is a professor in linguistics and second language teaching at Cologne University. Rohde's research focuses on second/foreign language acquisition in bilingual programmes at kindergarten and primary school level.

Anja K. Steinlen, University of Kiel, PhD University of Aarhus, is currently working as a researcher in a COMENIUS "Lifelong Learning Project" at the English Department, University of Kiel. Her interests lie in psycholinguistics and her research focuses on the acquisition of native and nonnative sounds by children and adults as well as on the acquisition of nonnative grammatical and lexical structures in an immersion kindergarten and school context.

John Stephenson, BA, University of Manchester; MA, University of Durham, teaches English and linguistics at Mie University, Japan. His research interests include second language acquisition of phonology and comprehension-based language-learning methodologies.

Bill VanPatten (PhD, University of Texas) is Professor and Director of the Graduate Program in Applied Linguistics and Second Language Studies at Texas Tech University. He has published widely in the areas of input processing and processing instruction. He is currently conducting research on ambiguity resolution with second language learners, looking specifically at the issues of transfer and ultimate attainment. He also writes fiction and sometimes performs standup comedy.

Marjolijn Verspoor (MA Louisiana State University; PhD University of Leiden) is Senior Lecturer in the Departments of English Language and Culture and Applied Linguistics at the University of Groningen. Her main research interests are second language acquisition and English linguistics within a cognitive linguistic framework.

Henning Wode is a professor emeritus at the English Department of Kiel University, Germany. A large part of his work has been concerned with the psycholinguistics of language acquisition including L1, L2, re-acquisition, and foreign language teaching. Amongst other things, he figures among the pioneers who established L2 acquisition research as a scientific discipline during the early 1970s. Since the 1990s he has been very much engaged in introducing immersion teaching in Germany by adapting Canadian immersion to the German/European scenario.

Acknowledgements

Our thanks to the following reviewers:
Mamiko Akita – Waseda University, Japan
Nancy Faux – Virginia Commonwealth University, USA
Susan Foster-Cohen – University of Canterbury, New Zealand
Julia Herschensohn – University of Washington, USA
Randal Holme – Hong Kong Institute of Education, Hong Kong
Georgette Ioup – University of New Orleans, USA
Steve Kirk – Durham University, UK
Bede McCormack – Hunter College, USA
Mike Sharwood Smith – Heriot Watt University, UK
Elaine Tarone – University of Minnesota, USA
Ineke van de Craats – Radboud University Nijmegen, Netherlands
Melinda Whong – Leeds University, UK

Without the tireless support of our editorial assistant Clare Wright, who juggled her Newcastle University PhD, you would not be holding this book in your hands.

Introduction

Considering the Matters of Why and How Input Matters

That INPUT[1] matters comes as no surprise to second language practitioners, but the issue of exactly how input affects SECOND LANGUAGE ACQUISITION (SLA) is another matter. Second language acquisition researchers who see the SECOND LANGUAGE LEARNER as capable of unconsciously converting what is heard into a linguistic system take it for granted: as long there is input, acquisition will occur. One of the aims of this chapter is to elucidate the place of input in current SLA research. An ancillary aim is to provide to the outside observer a general account of the state of the art with respect to SLA research, in particular its relation to the classroom and the second language teacher.

Let us start with a central issue that remains unresolved in research circles. We know from casual observation as well as systematic research that under normal circumstances the route of development in both first and second language acquisition does not vary nearly as much as rate of development. When we consider the END STATE of second language acquisition, variation is rife, particularly among those individuals who begin to learn a second language after childhood. One learner might end up indistinguishable from a NATIVE SPEAKER, whereas another who has spent just as long in that country might demonstrate only basic oral proficiency. For those researchers who maintain that second language acquisition is driven by innate linguistic mechanisms, mere exposure to input from other speakers is all that is necessary for acquisition to take place. When the focus is on internal linguistic properties, little attention is paid to the possibility that variation in external factors such as input might influence anything, apart perhaps from rate (when there is a meager amount of input, for example). Authors represented in this book both consider whether input matters with respect to route and end state, as well as look at some highly specific matters relating to input.

Despite decades of research into the cognitive, psycho-social and environmental factors responsible for the variation observed in second language acquisition, surprisingly little can be stated conclusively. When it comes to the specific environmental factor with which this book is concerned, namely INPUT, we cannot easily point to just what in the language the learner hears influences rate, route or end state. It is therefore useful to step back and consider from a variety of perspectives what we do know about input. The next 13 chapters build on the reader's basic knowledge about second language acquisition, converting this knowledge into specific expectations about learners, but always in relation to input. These expectations apply to learners whose exposure to a second language is not predigested through explanation of grammar or error correction or manipulated through form-focused exercises, drills and memorization. Reports by a range of established and up-and-coming researchers about their own work results in a reader's tour through fertile terrain where the guiding thread is second language input the learner receives.

A vast amount of published information on second language acquisition is now widely available; rather than competing for shelf space with the numerous high-quality overviews of second language acquisition that have appeared in textbook, handbook and encyclopedia form, our edited volume is intended to complement such books. Familiarity with any one of these will help in two ways. First, knowledge of SLA research is useful for making sense of much of what will be discussed in the 13 subsequent chapters. Second, knowledge of SLA is the starting point in an exploration of the influence of input. Unless you are an active researcher, you probably struggle to make sense of current reports of studies which treat abstract linguistic issues. If your only contact with SLA research occurred (or is occurring) while fulfilling degree requirements (and you were not drawn into the world of research), you likely find current publications inaccessible, particularly compared to those written three or four decades ago. For reasons we will detail below, many SLA researchers are nowadays far less concerned with pedagogical relevance than was the case 40 years ago, and where information from researchers to non-researchers once flowed freely, there is often now but a trickle. The expansion of research in SLA has also resulted in a parallel increase in specialised terminology. Although such terms will be elaborated on in the text in which they appear in this volume, we nonetheless include a glossary at the back of the book. You may have already noticed the terms and abbreviations that appear in SMALL CAPS. These are made salient in this manner upon first use in the book, and each term is defined in the glossary as understood by the contributors in the context of their chapters.

To make best use of this book, a grasp of the basics of SLA research is essential. We assume the introductory level of knowledge gained from Lightbown and Spada (2006), but as as a send-off on your tour, we provide you with a brief (re-)orientation in this chapter. We will also make explicit the conceptual underpinnings of those comprehension methods of teaching whose aim is to simply provide the second language learner with everyday, unadulterated input.

Theory and Practice

Those who work on first or second language acquisition would readily agree that these are truly exciting times in research. Humans are intensely curious about what *Homo sapiens* excels at; that is, language. Since the early 1980s there has been a worldwide explosion of formal linguistics-based research which addresses the issue of how the human mind represents and constructs linguistic COMPETENCE. But, as with any line of inquiry into the mind, researchers have not always been in agreement, and if one probes further, one finds that ideas on how humans develop language have differed not only for decades but at least for centuries. In recent history, views on human language began to diverge in the 1950s when Noam Chomsky first challenged prevailing opinion, arguing that rather than the product of interaction with the environment, as claimed by the Behaviorists and Piagetians, human language is the product of an innate faculty for language. On the language side of things, Chomsky went beyond the traditional description and classification of languages where he and his followers adopted the aim of accounting for the native speaker's unconscious linguistic knowledge along with explaining how that knowledge is acquired.

This dual aim is not necessarily the aim of all those who study language acquisition. Several decades ago Lightbown and White (1987: 483) pointed to the situation that has persisted over the last 50 years where 'the relationship between linguistics and acquisition research has at times been very close and at other times practically nonexistent'. The same holds for the relationship between linguistics and pedagogy. In the early 1970s, Diller (1971: 5) expressed his scepticism about pedagogical developments, noting that it was historically not the case that 'the faults of one method were corrected by a new method'. Yet surprisingly, that same decade marks the heyday of the confluence of formal linguistics and second language pedagogy. From the mid-1960s into the 1970s fresh ideas about the latter were developing in relation to new directions in the former. At the time, Chomsky's talk at the 1966 Northeast Language Teachers' Association was only the most recent example of the traditional partnership between linguists and language teachers. In the early 20th century this included such luminaries as Leonard Bloomfield (1942), Dwight Bolinger (1960) and Otto Jespersen (1904), and centuries ago thinkers such as Comenius (1654) who in the 17th century advocated use of aural input and pictures to teach Czech, German, Hungarian and Latin.

Chomksy's (1966) address might well mark the end of this partnership, but his final words to teachers remain relevant today. He encourages awareness of four aspects of linguistic theory: (1) the creative aspect of language use; (2) the abstractness of linguistic representations; (3) the universality of underlying linguistic structure; and (4) the role of intrinsic organization in cognitive processes. The idea that creative language use is based on abstract, universally-constrained linguistic representations points to the practical advice that teachers need only surround their learners with the appropriate linguistic environment (input) to enable these cognitive processes to do their work.

At the mid-century mark the area of inquiry known as SLA barely existed. Newmeyer and Weinberger (1988) trace its roots to the then-dominant STRUCTURALISM-based contrastive analysis in Europe (see e.g. Fisiak, 1980) and in North America, where Lado's (1957) Contrastive Analysis Hypothesis bridged structural linguistics, Behaviorism and second language teaching. Starting in 1967, inspired by Corder's positive stance towards ERRORS, the focus shifted from method and teacher to learner. Learners' errors became a legitimate object of inquiry and the field of SLA as we now know it was born. The same year, Lenneberg (1967) published his work on the CRITICAL PERIOD Hypothesis, putting forward the idea that the brain becomes less flexible around puberty when the two hemispheres have completed their lateralization, that is, when the dominant hemisphere (the left hemisphere for most right-handers) is specialized for language. In his 1973 paper, Krashen presented his critical examination of the same sort of brain trauma recovery evidence Lenneberg considered. Challenging the assumed biological basis for child–adult differences in language acquisition and pathological language loss, Krashen argued that signs of hemispheric specialization are already present at birth and that lateralization is complete by age five. For many, the biological basis for a critical period thus disappeared.[2]

Four decades hence, with systematic inquiry in second language acquisition having become as vigorous as inquiry into first language acquisition, the objective observer can rightfully expect that research will have yielded myriad implications and applications for second language teaching. Programmes aimed at providing future and experienced language teachers with background knowledge typically include coverage of this ever-expanding body of research. For example, in the 1990s, a common goal in the programs for second language teachers reviewed by Uber Grosse (1991) was familiarity with SLA research and attendant pedagogical applications. More recently, Pica (2003) writes that an understanding of second language learners' systematic development informs teaching. However, expectations that new lines of research in formal linguistics introduced from the 1960s onwards would lead to a deeper understanding of how best to teach second languages have not been met. Then and now many (e.g. Kramsch, 2003) have expressed disillusionment with the confusion regarding the nature of SLA as a field of inquiry and its contribution to pedagogy. Chaudron (2001) demystifies the situation somewhat in his examination of over 80 years' of publications on classroom instruction in *The Modern Language Journal*. Among the limitations he points to of the studies published in that journal is failure to base research questions on what is known about second language acquisition along with failure to describe what actually happens in the classroom. Chaudron's conclusions can be read as an appeal for close bidirectional cooperation between SLA researchers and teachers. When it comes to basic second language acquisition research, such cooperation is now far less common than was the case three or four decades ago. In 1982, Krashen (1982b) was already noting low levels of interaction between the domains of SLA research and pedagogy. This trend is typified by SLA research which is carried out independently of pedagogical concerns, where results are shared with like-minded readers and audiences without reference to classroom implications. Who is at fault? Researchers are neither loathe to share their research findings with non-researchers nor are they dismissive of classroom learners; in fact, a good many researchers collect their data from such learners. The causes of the current situation lie deeper and relate to the aims of linguistic theory, which have, in turn, become the aims of much of SLA research. Let us examine these factors more closely.

Several decades ago, Newmeyer (1982) pointed out that although the possibilities for applying Chomskyan theory were optimistically seized upon in the 1960s, soon after these ideas were presented, disillusion set in. Newmeyer (1982: 90) traces this to a basic misunderstanding of the primary goal of GENERATIVE LINGUISTICS, which is to account for the native speaker's linguistic competence, manifested as a grammar with non-variable and non-fuzzy categories and rules, and with general, universal structural properties not based on cognitive, contextual or sociological factors. PERFORMANCE is irrelevant. That is, neither implicit nor explicit in the goal of generative linguistics is a speaker's actual linguistic behavior, where a number of non-linguistic factors ranging from anxiety to memory capacity conspire to determine what actually comes out of that particular person's mouth (Chomsky, 1965: 4).

The quest to develop a theory of linguistic competence translated into an interest in PROPERTY THEORIES whose relevance for language acquisition lies in accounting for 'the specific innate abilities that make this achievement possible' (Chomsky, 1965: 27). In their 1987 paper, Lightbown and White note that disappointment with the failure of these theories to provide explanations of language development began, in the 1960s, to lead some child language researchers away from theory-driven investigation back to the type of data-driven or descriptive work that had previously dominated child language research. Lightbown and White argue that the recruitment of ideas from outside of linguistics in building a comprehensive theory of language acquisition has not diminished the need for a linguistic theory of language acquisition as the essential basis of the theory.

The same misunderstandings of the aims of the generative linguistics enterprise have tended to carry over to second language acquisition research where the split of SLA research from teaching was unfortuitously triggered at the 1966 teachers' conference by a remark often taken out of context. Newmeyer (1982) notes that while Chomsky is widely cited for an expression of scepticism towards the pedagogical relevance of both linguistic theory and psychology, these following additional remarks are often neglected:

> Surely the teacher of language would do well to keep informed of progress and discussion in these fields, and the efforts of linguists and psychologists to approach the problems of language teaching from a principled point of view are extremely worthwhile. (Chomsky, 1966/1970: 52)

Newmeyer (1982: 92) adds that although actual applications of generative linguistics to teaching have been (and still are) few, implications 'were immediate and have been profound'. As an example he cites Spolsky's (1970) 10 anti-Behaviorist generalizations, which had, before the introduction of generative linguistics, been highly controversial but in the 1970s were welcomed with enthusiasm. The misunderstanding Newmeyer described in the early 1980s has persisted into the 21st century, where one is just as likely to find a comment such as Pica's (2003) about the value of SLA research for second language teachers as one is to hear remarks such as Kramsch's (2003) revealing frustration with the relation of SLA research to pedagogy. Diametrically opposing views stem not only from the diverging paths described above which SLA researchers and teachers have taken, but also to a great extent from the issues that SLA research has focused on over the last several decades. Work has revolved around arriving at a PROPERTY THEORY to account for the second language learner's abstract linguistic knowledge. This may be precisely where SLA research has not quite yielded enough grist for teachers to form all the expectations of their learners they would like.

Property Theories

Parallel to a good majority of the studies in first language acquisition, the bulk of studies in second language acquisition address the properties of the learner's underlying system, most aspects of which are hidden from learner, teacher as well as researcher. Since its inception, much of the work in SLA has focused on the ARCHITECTURE of the learner's INTERLANGUAGE where researchers have focused on developing a property theory of acquisition. In arriving at a theory of second language acquisition, the crucial first step is arriving at a deep and sophisticated understanding of the learner's abstract underlying system. As already noted above, the researcher can not consider the many linguistic and non-linguistic factors that might conspire to move the learner from one stage of acquisition to the next until there is a clear account of the properties of each given stage. It has been this property-theory-based work in SLA research that largely informs teaching practice, in Pica's words, by translating findings into the set of expectations based on the general characteristics of L2 development that Lightbown (1985) first enumerated.[3]

In the last several decades, there have been important advances in this respect. In first language acquisition research up until the 1980s, the child was viewed as a HYPOTHESIS TESTER who evaluated any number of potential GRAMMARS based on evidence from the input. Highly specific ideas put forward in the 1980s about possible grammars considerably narrowed the child's HYPOTHESIS SPACE. A current central assumption in generative linguistics is that a speaker's linguistic competence ends up being far more complex than the input available (Chomsky, 1981). For example, the input to which children are exposed is primarily other speakers' performance; as such this will include false starts and slips of the tongue and also be largely devoid of comprehensive corrections. In addition, the input also fails in the first place to reveal underlying linguistic structure. When compared with the individual's resulting grammar, the input exhibits a POVERTY OF THE STIMULUS. Syntactic examples cited are from English wh-questions such as the one shown in (1). Children, who are well known to make a range of errors as they acquire their first language, simply do not make errors like the one in (2) when they begin to produce sentences like the one in (1). Hence they would never have the opportunity to be corrected.

(1)   What did Jane say that Mary believes that John saw?
(2)   *What did Mary believe the rumour that John had won?

In relation to a grammar that allows (1), yet excludes (2), the input contains no information that (2) is ungrammatical, only that the fronting of a wh-word is possible, on the basis of (1). Children are able to overcome the poverty of the stimulus in syntax because innate universal structural constraints applying to the distribution of elements are hard-wired, as in UNIVERSAL GRAMMAR (UG) (Chomsky, 1981). These constraints translate into a smaller set of conjectures about wh-question formation in English than children might possibly entertain. The cognitive load is thus reduced when the young child need not consider the infinity of possible languages the input might lead to. Hence the otherwise cognitively immature child is able to acquire language in a remarkably short period of time. Numerous studies since the 1960s up to the present have demonstrated how children's development in a given language exhibits common non-adult patterns (i.e. ERRORS) whose systematicity points to the operation of innate constraints on the ideas children develop (i.e. their non-adult grammars) based on the input they receive. Where generative linguists argue that the negative evidence children do receive in the form of correction is unreliable, note again that children do not even commit errors as in (2) with regard to the many CONSTRUCTIONS they master. All together this has led to the proposal that acquisition occurs in response only to POSITIVE EVIDENCE, that is, the language that the learner hears in his/her surrounding, ambient environment.[4]

The variation that exists across human languages is built into the learner's innate predispostion in the form of expectations about possible languages (under Universal Grammar, as PARAMETER SETTINGS). How this applies can be illustrated with reference to languages that allow subjects to be empty, for example, when they are not emphasized. In languages such as English, pronominal subjects (i.e. 'I' or 'he') are unstressed when not emphasized in the discourse. The omission of pronominal subjects is widely attested (see, e.g. Hyams, 1986) in data from children regardless of whether they are learning English, French or German (languages that do not allow empty subjects) or Arabic, Japanese or Spanish (languages that do). But children exposed to English, French and German eventually figure out that subjects cannot be empty and children exposed to Arabic, Japanese and Spanish figure out that they can be. What in the input causes the learner to move from one stage to the next? In both first and second language acquisition, this is a question to which there are many possible answers, none of them conclusive.

In their discussion of the 20th century relationship between generative linguistic theory and language acquisition research, Lightbown and White (1987) point out how the idea of a mental grammar (linguistic competence) has guided language acquisition research since its inception. From the 1980s onwards, researchers have taken seriously the idea that linguistic theory should explain 'how it is possible for children to acquire language' (Lightbown & White, 1987: 484), and what the constraints are that govern how the learner revises his/her conjectures in response to the input (Bertolo, 2001: 2). Importantly, the issue at stake is not how children do so in real time, but how humans are capable in the first place of INTERNALIZING the formal linguistic properties of language.

Since then, debate among generative language acquisitionists has continued apace on whether linguistic theory can be applied in the same way to adult L2 acquisition, that is, whether Universal Grammar constrains the acquisition of additional languages throughout the lifespan. Studies of second language learners indeed reveal similar systematic grammars. White (1989, 2003) details a range of studies pointing to the conclusion that not only are young children's developing grammars UG-constrained, but that both younger and older second language learners' interlanguages are also.[5] With respect to older second language learners, some of the most compelling studies are of learners whose exposure to the TARGET LANGUAGE was wholly NATURALISTIC, where they heard only PRIMARY LINGUISTIC DATA from the start and throughout development but received no classroom instruction. Well-known work includes studies of immigrant Italian, Portuguese and Spanish speakers (Clahsen *et al.*, 1983) and Korean and Turkish speakers (Vainikka & Young-Scholten, 1994) who were learning German without any formal instruction. Such studies escape the problem of determining whether a second language learner is drawing on innate linguistic mechanisms or on the sort of general cognitive mechanisms[6] whose additional use is typical in an instructed context [as in Krashen's (1985) ACQUISITION VS. LEARNING].

Input under property theories in first language acquisition

The idea that humans are equipped to acquire language from birth in the form of the universals proposed by Chomsky (1981) has sometimes been taken to mean that input is wholly irrelevant. Certainly biological predisposition counts for nought when no input at all is available; this we know from unintentional experiments where children have been completely deprived of input as in the famous case of WILD CHILD Genie discussed in Curtiss (1982). Over the last several decades, the study of deaf children has begun to uncover just what the predisposition for language enables children to do with minimal input. Deaf children growing up in hearing families have at their disposal input in the form of paralinguistic gestures from their family members. In her book, Goldin-Meadow (2005) shows how the close study of such children's use of gestures reveals that – unlike their family members' gestures – the children's gestures represent a linguistic system now known as HOMESIGN. Further evidence along similar lines shows that deaf children are able to take signed input from adult users of a rudimentary PIDGIN sign language and create a full language, as documented in the recent case of Nicaraguan Sign Language (Senghas *et al.*, 2004).[6] Because there was no sign language in Nicaragua prior to the 1970s, linguists were able to document in detail the differences in sign language structure across generations of users to identify the contributions made by the children through their innate hard-wiring for language.

Chomsky challenged two further assumptions about language acquisition [see Piatelli-Palmirini's (1979) transcripts of his debate with Piaget]: that the physical manipulation of objects in the real world and the cognitive milestones seen as essential by Piagetians are irrelevant to the acquisition of language. With respect to physical factors, most celebrated (from the film *My Left Foot*) is the case of Christy Brown (1954) who, despite cerebral palsy, was able to move the toe of his left foot to type an autobiography (and a number of other literary works) revealing his complete acquisition of linguistic competence in the language to which he was exposed, English. With respect to cognitive factors, Smith and Tsimpli (1995) have shown in their study of a young man with very low IQ that not only is his native English comparable to that of speakers of normal IQ, but his ability to acquire second languages is exceptional. Bishop and Mogford's (1988) collection of reports of studies provides more evidence from the full spectrum of exceptional circumstances, indicating a developmental dissociation of general cognitive mechanisms from core linguistic properties such as those involved in syntax. It seems that children in exceptional circumstances typically acquire language unexceptionally.

As we pointed out above, when it comes to second language acquisition, the operation of innate mechanisms can be more difficult to examine if the data under consideration are from learners who have received instruction.[7] Methodological challenges have not prevented researchers from arriving at a number of very precise ideas about L2 learners' internal grammars. The most fruitful line of research looks at features of L2 learners' INTERLANGUAGE GRAMMARS that bear no direct relation to their NATIVE LANGUAGE or to what they have been taught or otherwise exposed to in order to search for evidence of the operation of UG [see White's (1989) description of the methodology employed, which is not yet outdated].

Where does this leave us with respect to how a learner moves from one developmental stage to the next when acquiring a particular language? Even the best property theory will not translate into an account of the learner's transition from one stage to the next during the process of actually acquiring a language. In first language acquisition, we know that there is something in the input that results in a child exposed to English arriving at a grammar that, for example, disallows empty subjects and rules out ungrammatical wh-questions such as the one in (2) above. Researchers working within a generative linguistic framework refer to the information in the input that prompts syntactic development as a TRIGGER. As Bertolo (2001: 5) puts it, the history of work on the interaction between parametric linguistics and the child's ability to learn language is based on the assumption that humans do not learn by enumeration of probabilities or hypotheses about previous grammars; in other words, children are not just hypothesis testers. But, both the specific triggers for syntactic development and a greater role for input in general is still widely debated. This now takes us from the idea of property theory to TRANSITION THEORY.

Transition Theories

More than a decade ago Wesche (1994) noted that the UG approach to SLA had not been helpful in explaining the observed variation in the rate at which L2 learners progress or the level of attainment they finally reach.

Ten years later in their textbook, Mitchell and Myles (2004: 12) still offer a hypothetical statement: 'If we become better at explaining the learning process [...] there will be a payoff' for teachers and all their learners. Linguistic theory has yielded rich accounts of the properties of inter-language, but there has been far less attention devoted to what accounts for transitions between stages of development (see White, 1996). In this sense Ellis (2005: 209) is accurate in his assertion that SLA is still 'a very young field of study'. Sharwood Smith and Truscott (2005: 205) acknowl-edge the confusion that property-driven work arouses when studies show that learners 'do not jump neatly from one discrete stage to another, but undergo periods of optionality, sometimes quite long ones, where both new and old forms occur in learner performance'. The two authors empha-size the need for work in second language acquisition that goes beyond the properties of the learner's interlanguage to consider 'how the L2 sys-tem grows over time in response to the language user's continued experi-ence with the language. Only recently have attempts been made to propose theoretical accounts in terms compatible with property theories' (Sharwood Smith & Truscott, 2005: 204). This need is widely accepted, but there has been much less research over the decades devoted to arriving at a theory of second language acquisition that would include a transition component.

Input and transition theories

That there is far less known about the transitions L2 learners make than the properties of their interlanguage grammars is not to say that the input that might account for such transitions has not been systematically stud-ied. Indeed, there have been numerous studies on the effect of classroom methods and techniques on second language learners. One thriving line of research has long involved exploring classroom learners' responses to various means of instruction, where input is manipulated in various ways. Studies involving input also look at the second language learner's notic-ing of mismatches 'between what he or she produces/knows and what is produced by speakers of the second language (Gass, 1988: 202). But as Pica (2003) rightly notes, generative SLA researchers dismiss consideration of input from this perspective, where cognitive processes associated with conscious learning such as attention, awareness and practice lie outside the domain of linguistic competence. Thus investigations contributing to a transition theory in SLA entail considering the second language learn-er's unconscious, UG-driven acquisition of language in relation only to the primary linguistic data received.

Another line of investigation has considered input in connection with interaction (see, e.g. chapters in Gass & Madden, 1985). Under the view of language acquisition where internal linguistic mechanisms equip the learner to make sense of the primary linguistic data, interaction with adult or native-speaking interlocutors (including modifications these speakers might be prompted to make in response to the learner's output) plays a minor role. At odds with UG-driven language acquisition, this Piagetian-based research program has led to hundreds of studies both on L1 and L2 development which document the modifications proficient speakers make when addressing less proficient speakers. The conclusion is often that modifcation enhances comprehension or brings specific information to learners' attention (Ellis, 1990). Research has confirmed the existence of registers variably referred to as caretakerese (with respect to children), foreigner talk and teacher talk, and details regarding the modifications which native and non-native speakers make have been well discussed (see, e.g. Wesche, 1994 for a description of these registers).[8] However, it is possible that input modifications only influence rate of acquisition, as documented in Newport *et al.*'s (1977) first language acquisition study (see Ellis, 1985 on L2 acquisition). If modified input or negotiation of meaning drive development, research to date has not illuminated how such processes account for the learner's transition from one stage of development to the next. As Lightbown and White (1987) noted two decades ago, interactionist hypotheses fail to address the problem of how children arrive at the actual linguistic properties of ADULT GRAMMAR, and how L2 learners acquire the abstract properties they have been shown to acquire, even if they do not attain native competence. Studies since the 1970s have shown that both children's and adults' initial L2 grammars undergo UG-constrained development as a result of further exposure to target language input. Property-theoretic work has revealed this, but as discussed above, such work has largely ignored what accounts for movement from one stage to the next, including how input factors might be involved.[9] We also know that LATE STARTERS/LEARNERS do not invariably CONVERGE on the target language. Many studies have confirmed what Johnson and Newport's (1989) study of immigrants in the USA indicated: those whose first exposure to the target language is after the age of puberty may FOSSILIZE at a non-native end-state (Selinker, 1972), and with considerable variation.[10] Here we have a condundrum. If the consensus among SLA researchers is that L2 acquisition at any age is an unconscious process guided by innate linguistic mechanisms, how can the observed variation with respect to the end-state be explained? Researchers have long grappled with this problem from a variety of perspectives, but it is only recently that input has begun to receive consideration from SLA quarters.[11]

If the development of linguistic competence in a second language can be traced to the dual sources of a genetically transmitted language capacity and to the socially transmitted knowledge of a specific language, it is important to understand more about the latter in the terms of the contribution of input. Among first language acquisition researchers working within a generative framework, that input can have an effect on route is often ignored. One might consider, as does Kempen (1998), examining the input before drawing conclusions about syntactic development. Kempen further suggests that among the causes of heterogeneous learning trajectories claimed to exist for younger vs. older first or second language learners are input characteristics.

At the most basic level, we do not know how much input second language learners actually get. There is, in fact, no consensus on how much exposure a learner requires (Carroll, 2001; Wode, 1994c). With respect to classroom learners, Lightbown (2000: 449) gives as the prime cause of incomplete acquisition of a foreign language limited contact with the target language. Learners in immersion settings can be expected to enjoy far more contact with the target language, yet when studies of such learners address age and ultimate attainment, they usually do so in terms of learners' LENGTH OF RESIDENCE in the target language country to draw conclusions regarding exposure. It is unlikely that an average adult living in a new language country initially receives anything comparable to the 9000 hours of input a child has received by the age of five (Sharwood Smith, 1994a). For those adults who are immigrants (rather than, say, university students) the amount of input can be severely limited due to few opportunities for oral interaction with native speakers outside their immigrant community (see e.g. Flege & Liu, 2001). In the extreme case where the learner's level of education is low, input will be more limited without access to print (VanPatten, 1988). It is very likely that this state of affairs results in adult immigrants' failure to progress beyond the rudimentary system of communication Klein and Perdue (1997) refer to as the BASIC VARIETY.[12] One might reasonably ask whether second language learners (especially adults) crucially differ from children learning their first language when it comes to input. While the average child hears thousands of hours of speech by age five, recall those children discussed above who manage to use whatever is available (e.g. paralinguistic gestures) to create language-like systems from their hard-wired linguistic capacity. There are no known accounts of older learners exhibiting similar abilities; note the failure of adolescent wild child Genie to develop beyond early stage syntax despite considerable post-discovery exposure.

If our theory of SLA is one under which the learner acquires language unconsciously, we need to consider how he or she gets from the continous speech stream – essentially 'noise' – to the construction of a mental grammar for that L2. However, the raw material from which learners learn is 'one of the most under-researched and under-theorised aspects of second language acquisition' (Carroll, 2001: 1). Carroll points out that there is no consensus on how learners initially process the sounds they hear, how they then encode what they hear and then construct the representations which characterize the complex systems we know learners arrive at (based on the many property-theory-driven studies). It is worth keeping an eye on Carroll's ongoing work (e.g. Carroll, 2004a) on the interface between the initial acoustic signal and the linguistic mechanisms in the mind that segment the speech stream into processable chunks. One related and growing line of inquiry typically employs experimentation to determine how second language learners process input in real time (see e.g. Towell & Hawkins, 2004).

But transition theory building is very much work underway. When results from current and future studies produce a set of robust findings, SLA theory will yield clearer implications for classroom teachers. While we await the finished theory, we offer a book on input. The volume you are about to read concerns the language to which second language learners are directly exposed and the effect this language might have on their linguistic development. Before we discuss the volume's contents, let us first look at how input has been considered under various approaches to second language teaching.

Input in L2 Pedagogy

If – as in first language acquisition – second language acquisition 'is by its nature a self-regulatory process' (Jordens, 1996: 407), to what extent is the acquisition process subject to external influences? There are two approaches to second language teaching that see the learner as being guided by an in-built syllabus. The first, the European-based COMMUNICATIVE LANGUAGE TEACHING (CLT – Munby, 1978; Van Ek, 1975; Wilkins, 1972), is not directly aligned with SLA research, unlike the second, the COMPREHENSION APPROACH (CPA). Although both CLT and CPA are equally learner-centered, the former focuses on the learner as communicator and the latter on the learner as language system generator. More importantly, the former assumes language acquisition is driven by the meaningful interaction we refer to as communication. Under a comprehension approach, such communicative exchanges are not strictly required because the meaningful work is carried out as a response to input by the learner's internal linguistic mechanisms.

Approaches that involve reception of aural input are variations on ideas that date back to Comenius in the 17th century, carrying through to the development of the Direct Method in the latter half of the 19th century and to 20th century comprehension methods. The comprehension approach is associated with Palmer (1917) at the start of that century and then from the second half onwards with names such as Asher (1969), Burling (1978), Krashen (1976), Nida (1958), Postovsky (1970) and, Winitz and Reeds (1973). Comprehension approach adherents such as Postovsky echo what SLA researchers take for granted:

> In the natural learning process, development of recognition would precede, not follow, the development of retrieval of knowledge [where

for the former] the learner has to store linguistic information in his auditory short-term memory for a brief period of time until it is further processed and matched with the information stored in his long-term memory. (Postovsky, 1982: 67)

The favorable position of an approach to teaching involving reception of input is still evident among SLA theorists such as Sharwood Smith and Truscott (2005: 211) who write that linguistic competence is 'driven by comprehension rather than PRODUCTION because the former imposes constraints on the processors that are not found in the latter'.

When considering L2 pedagogy, both the comprehension approach (where acquisition is internally driven) and the COMMUNICATIVE APPROACH where acquisition is externally driven) prioritise understanding of the meaning of utterances over the grammatical form of these utterances. But unlike the communicative approach, the comprehension approach enjoys a certain agnosticism with respect to the social functions of language. If the learner is on center stage in both approaches, it is for quite different reasons. For the communicative approach, the learner's needs as a social user of language dictate what happens in the classroom, while for the comprehension approach, it is the learner's in-built syllabus that does so. This leaves those teachers – not to mention materials developers – who favor a comprehension approach in a difficult position. Social functions can and do appear on syllabi. But, it has been notoriously difficult to develop methods and materials that exploit how linguistic mechanisms impose order on the noise that we refer to as input. With no fully developed transition theory to guide the teacher, what remains is to consider the input itself in greater detail.

Input

Consider how the following two statements relate to each other. The first is from one of the developers of a method to teaching which holds that exposure to input is sufficient, and the second is from one of the foremost property theory researchers. When comprehension approach advocate Postovsky (1982: 68) notes that 'the student learns essentially what he hears', this is not unlike SLA theorist White's (1996) suggestion that inappropriate input might impede the operation of UG. What, exactly, are we talking about when it comes to input? Cook (2001: 129) admonishes the teacher to be aware of the different sources of input, stressing the premise that language to which learners are exposed is one element of L2 success. In instructional terms, this translates into the provision of 'optimal samples of language for the learner to profit from'. Since the 1970s the task of the language teacher has been seen variously as creation of a 'rich and varied learning environment' (Blair, 1982: 7), the generation of good input

(Zobl, 1992), a 'rich sample of language materials [...] regardless of whether these represent normal communicative situations' (Jordens, 1996: 431, 444), and ever more input in the classroom (Dudley, 2004). There is an additional call for non-aural input; for example, Little *et al.* (1994: 46) argue for the use of authentic written texts to 'provide a richer linguistic diet [... which can contribute to replicating] the "language bath" in which the first language learner is immersed from birth'.

One might argue that meaningful, COMPREHENSIBLE INPUT is less important than native or NATIVE-LIKE input. Young-Scholten (1995) makes the point that the positive evidence provided in primary linguistic data can turn out to have negative consequences in, for example, the acquisition of the phonology of a second language if that input is non-native accented. In their study, Flege *et al.* (1999) note that, although extended exposure to a foreign language in a classroom context starting at primary school level is likely to have a positive effect on learners' acquisition of MORPHOSYNTAX, one should be aware that learners' success in learning a foreign language is also dependent on a substantial amount of target language input from native speakers (see also, Piske, 2007, 2008). Not only do foreign language students hear incorrect pronunciations and ungrammatical sentences from their classmates, but they may often receive such input from teachers (see Winitz & Yanes, 2002). Immigrants who spend most of their time with other non-native L2 speakers may also be exposed to a substantial amount of non-native-accented and ungrammatical input which may lead to the development of norms different from those of native speakers in the community (see Piske *et al.*, 2001).

Few of us have a deep or detailed understanding of what providing 'good', 'rich' or 'varied' input entails, and we lack awareness regarding the amount and nature of the input to which learners are exposed outside the classroom as well as within the classroom, from other learners. We hope that this volume will begin to remedy this state of affairs.

The Next 13 Chapters

The chapters in this book treat input at both a macro and a micro level, but the emphasis is generally not on the manipulation of input. Our reasons here are twofold. First, our starting point is a pedagogical approach that assumes what SLA research assumes, namely, that provision of unaltered input is all that is necessary, given the continued use of the language specific mechanisms that enabled the learner's acquisition of a first language. This further entails the assumption that language is special and that input relevant to the acquisition of language is also in a sense special because no manipulation of input is required. For example, Schwartz (1993) argues that if adult L2 learners use the same mechanisms as young children do in the acquisition of language, then – just as is the case for children – only exposure to ambient language will result in linguistic competence (in Krashen's terminology, acquired knowledge). She observes that the learner can produce language as the result of error correction, explanation of grammar, drilling and memorization, but argues that the source of this production is not the language specific mechanisms. Rather, it is the same sort of knowledge that the learner draws on to play chess or engage in any type of more general cognitive activity.[13] Our second reason for a de-emphasis on manipulation of input is the existence of a substantial body of research on issues relating to what normally falls under the category of classroom instruction [see, e.g. Ellis's (1990) summary]. However, the claims Schwartz makes generate a range of hypotheses, and we include in this book VanPatten's chapter, which exemplifies how one might take her ideas forward empirically.

What is the nature of the stimuli to which language learners are exposed? For Carroll (2001), use of the word *input* in disparate contexts masks what exactly is meant by the word. Where *input* is used to refer to a physical entity that affects the visual and auditory perceptual systems, that is, the 'stuff out there' (Carroll, 2001: 8), she suggests use of the word *stimuli* instead. However, we and the chapter authors use the term *input* in this book, and (as is the case in SLA research) in the various contexts in which it has been used.

The exploration of input in this volume is intended to shed at least some light on the question with which this chapter began: to what can we attribute variations in rate, route and end state in second language acquisition? The following chapters represent contributions from established and emerging researchers whose ongoing research programs treat topics which relate in various ways to what learners listen to and read, not only with respect to English as a second language but also with respect to Chinese, Danish, Dutch, German, Indonesian and Spanish, both in target and foreign language settings. Through the presentation of research that represents the spectrum of current thinking, we aim to build a bridge between SLA research and the classroom for the reader who asks what the usefulness of SLA research is.

The chapters in this book

Part 1: Matters of input

Part 1 starts with a chapter that addresses the acquisition of morphosyntax. In the three odd decades since Bailey *et al.* (1974) concluded that learners follow the same order in their development of grammatical morphemes in L2 English regardless of their age of initial exposure as well as their first language, there has been discussion of the source of this order. Andreas Rohde looks at one of the first morphemes to appear in learners' oral production *-ing* and considers whether four German children immersed in English for six months used this morpheme to mark the progressive aspect. Even though the most prominent function of *-ing* in the input the children received from their English-speaking peers was to mark the progressive, the children's development was not heavily influenced by any sort of input bias. Thus in this instance, input does not appear to matter very much with respect to route of acquisition.

In Chapter 2, Bill VanPatten turns to the classroom and looks at whether the processing of input can be pushed by certain techniques. Rather than addressing how linguistic competence develops, he is concerned with developing classroom techniques to force learners 'get data' from the input to develop this competence while they are engaged in comprehension. With examples from English speakers learning Spanish, he discusses his Input Processing Model, which is predicated on three major principles: (1) comprehension is effortful for learners and constrained by working memory properties; (2) comprehension is largely lexically driven, at least at early and intermediate stages; and (3) learners have particular processing strategies for relating nouns to verbs. These three principles have consequences for the linguistic data that learners get from the input at any given time in terms of how they accurately 'tag' the data as they hear them.

Marjolijn Verspoor, Wander Lowie and Kees de Bot, in Chapter 3, provide a conceptual discussion on the broader consideration of a range of possible influences on L2 development and on how input can be shaped to force the learner to process it more effectively. They include findings from an empirical study by Verspoor and Winitz (1997) that grouped the presentation of lexical items in fields (without explicit explanation) when these were presented to the learner. The authors discuss the findings from this study of intermediate learners in terms of their cognitive linguistics-based Dynamic Systems Theory, arguing that the development of linguistic competence in a second language is the result of the interaction of input with the internal reorganization of that system. At the end of their chapter, they put theory into practice by reporting on their own experiences in learning Indonesian using aural comprehension-based self-instruction materials.

Stephen Krashen's chapter provides an update on one of the major influences in second language pedagogy over the last 40 years. In discussing his Comprehension Hypothesis he covers his evidence for this hypothesis and against competing hypotheses that have attracted attention such as the Comprehensible Output Hypothesis and the Noticing Hypothesis. He reiterates his conclusion that more comprehensible input, in the form of reading, leads to better gains in reading comprehension, vocabulary, grammar and writing style. Taking Universal Grammar literally, he extends this idea beyond the confines of our solar system to the universe, where the testing of hypotheses will have to await recruitment of the relevant informants.

The next two chapters in Part 1 of this book critically address the comprehension approach. Nel de Jong, in Chapter 5, puts to the test a central assumption of some adherents of the comprehension approach: that delaying production will produce better results. She focuses on the idea that second language learners are often able to understand more than they can produce and pursues questions about the overlap between comprehension and production. On the basis of data from Dutch learners of Spanish, she questions whether it is necessary to delay production and whether comprehension training can, as claimed, pre-empt errors in production. Then, in Chapter 6, John Stephenson critically addresses the comprehension approach; in the process of detailing an American CPA-based method developed by Harris Winitz, *The Learnables* he takes the opportunity to compare and contrast CPA and CLT. Much of this chapter considers reactions to this method of learning Japanese by CLT-reared learners who were at the same time learning about SLA. Data from learner diaries point to frustration at being denied the usual means of measuring progress, that is, production. The implications here are the danger that learners and teachers will abandon comprehension approach methods if they do not fully understand the unconscious processes involved in language acquisition.

Werner Bleyhl closes Part 1 by criticising approaches to foreign language teaching based on the belief that consciousness raising through explicitly teaching grammatical rules plays a crucial role in successfully learning foreign languages. Bleyhl points out that the chronological sequence in which grammatical structures are acquired cannot be altered by classroom instruction or specially arranged input. This is why in Chapter 7 he argues that foreign language teachers should not try to force grammatical structures upon their students. Instead teachers should provide learners with relevant and motivating input that also serves as feedback, enabling them to find out which of their hypotheses about the foreign language are tenable and which ones are not.

Part 2: Input matters in phonology

Answers to the question of whether adults can also make use of innate linguistic mechanisms have been affirmative but qualified in the light of NON-CONVERGENCE on the target language. The case against the learner's continued use of linguistic mechanisms throughout the lifespan seems clearest when it comes to phonology. Kramsch (2003) points to the decline in interest in addressing the development of a second phonology in the classroom from when Long (1990) concluded that the critical period for a second language sound system starts to close at age six. This lack of general interest is a pity, given the amount of empirical evidence we now have which points to post-puberty learners' use of innate linguistic mechanisms in their acquisition of phonological competence [see, e.g. Ioup & Weinberger's (1987) collection of second language phonology studies, and Young-Scholten's (1996) assessment of several decades worth of findings]. Similar to what studies on syntactic acquisition have revealed, the phonology research indicates that L2 learners retain into adulthood the capacity to unconsciously develop a second phonology, and that they pass through interlanguage stages constrained by properties that are neither from their native nor the target language but from what we might refer to as Universal Phonology. Before we turn to an overview of the chapters in Part 2, we provide a brief orientation for the reader on research in L2 phonology.

High levels of attainment in L2 phonology are often considered to be less important than in morphology or syntax, based on the premise that non-native production with respect to phonology contributes less to communicative success than do morphology or syntax. Demoting the importance of phonology is actually quite problematic. To begin with, when the learner's goal is 'comfortable intelligibility' (Kenworthy, 1987) instead of production based on native-like competence, we find that those features contributing to intelligibility are often the same features with which learners persistently struggle. Sumdangdej's (2007) study of the whole age range of learners of English in Thailand provides but one example where comfortable intelligibility is beyond the grasp of even those whose initial exposure is in childhood. More important than intelligiblity in production is comprehension. We no longer assume that L2 phonology operates solely at the level of production (e.g. McAllister, 1995), or that the internal representations upon which they depend to decipher auditory stimuli are comparable to a native speaker's. This turns out to have wider repercussions. When we consider the very starting point of language acquisition, we realize that more is at stake than simply acquiring a good accent. As Sharwood Smith and Truscott (2005: 208) point out during their discussion of transition theories, once the L2 learner has auditorily processed environmental stimuli, the next step is assigning existing, native language phonological structures to these acoustic data. Studies addressing this issue reveal the details of how the learner's first language influences what is taken in as well as what is produced. A study by Matthews and Brown (2004) showed this in a particularly striking manner: Japanese learners of English actually heard non-existent vowels between consonants in English clusters which were the same as those they often insert in production.

Is it possible that input matters more than age? At least when it comes to phonology, two intriguing studies suggest that input may matter at least as much as age, particularly during the initial period of exposure. When Sumdangdej (2007) played audio recordings of British school children during Thai children's first semester of English, he found their production of syllables and stress was significantly better than that of children receiving the normal Thai-accented instruction. But when Akita (2001) tracked the progress of three Japanese university students who spent a year in the UK after having studied English for more than seven years at secondary and university level, she found only modest to good levels of improvement.

If the assignment of a phonological interpretation is the first port of call with respect to the input the learner receives, it is not surprising that studies are starting to show how a learner's non-native phonology leads to problems in the development of other aspects of the L2. In their study of a possible INTERFACE between phonology and morphology in L2 acquisition, Goad *et al.* (2003), for example, conclude that some of the problems Chinese-speaking learners have in the development of past tense in English can be attributed to influence from their native phonology, which does not allow the sort of syllables often created by past tense marking in English.

There are thus four reasons for devoting the entire second half of this book to phonology. First, anyone studying linguistics learns about sound systems and their operation. But if there is any study of acquisition, it's usually of children's, and not of second language learners'. The result is familiarity with babies' stages of babbling and knowledge about what children substitute for inter-dental fricatives, but lack of awareness that adult second language learners, in fact, do some of the same things children do. It should therefore come as a pleasant surprise that research points to the conclusion that post-puberty learners' tongues are not invariably directed by the facts of their native language sound systems (see in particular the research by James E. Flege and his colleagues).

The second reason is because mutual intelligibility hinges not only morphosyntax, but also phonology with respect to both the learner's production and perception. To wit, a recent exchange between neighbors. A is a native speaker; B is a university professor from an eastern European country.

A: Our other cat has just lost his collar again.
B: How do you explain that? Is it seasonal?
A: Well, it's regular. Both cats claw at them and they come off.
B: (Puzzled.) They come off?
A: Yes, we've put a new collar on this one and so far she's kept it.
B: Oh, collar! I thought you said 'color'.

B's identical pronunciation of 'collar' and 'color' reveals that he makes no phonemic distinction between /ɒ/ and /ʌ/. It is wishful thinking to imagine that second language speakers can understand and make themselves understood without having achieved close to a native phonological system on aspects of phonology such as phonemic distinctions, stress and syllable structure.

The third reason for an equal focus on phonology in input matters relates directly to the topic of this book. When it comes to morphology, syntax and LEXIS, the second language learner is, by definition, old enough to be literate, and hence has written input available. In some situations (e.g. the foreign language context), this may be the learner's main source of input. Written text certainly varies as well, but it will typically be in a standard variety, and fully grammatical. But when it comes to phonology, there is considerably more scope for variation. Learners in immersion settings may be exposed to a range of accents including the foreign accents of other non-native speakers; classroom learners are often primarily exposed to the latter. This exposure can be expected to have an effect on the second language learner's developing system, influencing not only end state, but also route of development.

The fourth and perhaps most important reason for inclusion of phonology is, as discussed above, because aural stimuli are the first port of call for language acquisition. If we consider that there is an interface between phonology and morphosyntax during acquisition where there is the potential for the learner to perceive and then store acoustic signals through a native language filter, it is important to know just what might be going on in the phonological domain in the first place.

The chapters in Part 2

Alene Moyer (Chapter 8) addresses one of the questions posed earlier: how much input is needed? She looks at second language learners of German to explore new understandings of the significance of input for long-term attainment. Taking a closer look at adults in a target-language immersion setting, she discusses her study of learners from various first language backgrounds to investigate in detail how they go about obtaining input. She describes how use of complex statistical instrumentation contributes to a complete picture of the role of the individual in obtaining input and she emphasises why input matters as much as age in the long run in terms of phonological attainment.

This topic is then taken up and extended in terms of methodological issues by Jim Flege in Chapter 9. The major purpose of Flege's chapter is to determine which role input plays in L2 speech learning and how input is related to other factors such as AGE OF ARRIVAL (AOA), LENGTH OF RESIDENCE (LOR) or amount of L1 and L2 use, whose importance is frequently discussed in the L2 literature. Flege presents various results showing that L2 input, and in particular input received from native speakers, does indeed have an influence on both EARLY and LATE LEARNERS' performance in an L2, and that the role of input in L2 speech learning should not be underestimated. However, Flege also points out that it is rather difficult to directly measure L2 input, and that future research should address the question of how better estimates of L2 input can be obtained.

Unlike children acquiring their first language, second language learners – especially older ones – are often exposed from the start to a form of input largely unaddressed in the introduction above: written text. Given that WRITING SYSTEMS represent linguistic units with different levels of transparency, spelling conversion rules and conventions, where orthographic representations have been shown to affect native speakers when they are performing metalinguistic tasks, we can predict that exposure to orthography will influence L2 learners. In Chapter 10, Benedetta Bassetti looks at the influence of the Roman alphabet PINYIN system on Chinese L2 learners and finds that it results in the non-target production of a range of segments which can neither be traced to L1 influence nor to developmental universals. This points to the influence ORTHOGRAPHIC INPUT can have on the route of development in L2 phonology.

Ocke-Schwen Bohn and Rikke Louise Bundgaard-Nielsen in Chapter 11 focus on English vowels; they argue that many studies of foreign-accented speech have been conducted in second language settings where learners receive input that is assumed to be relatively homogeneous. Foreign language learners, who learn an additional language in a setting where this language is not the primary medium of communication (in this case Danish L1 learners of English), are frequently exposed to a range of varieties of the target language which may differ considerably with respect to their sound systems. The authors discuss in detail how, in addition to the influence of the learner's L1 language, one must consider the issue of input heterogeneity.

Like Bohn and Bundgaard-Nielsen, Anja Steinlen (Chapter 12) also considers vowels, and like Bassetti, she focuses on the way in which they are represented. In this case, however, her consideration is of the International Phonetic Alphabet rather than a conventional writing system. She points out that when pronunciation is taught, teachers and learners often make use of the phonetic symbols of IPA to inform their articulation. But, she argues that this is an unrealistic filtering of the input. When pronunciation guides compare vowels cross-linguistically or when they predict non-native vowel production, they base their analysis on a comparison of phonetic symbols as a tool. Problems arise when identically transcribed segments have different acoustic qualities or differently transcribed segments have the same acoustic qualities. The implications here are that teacher and learner need to be aware of where the IPA fails to capture phonetic detail and where possible, to use information from acoustic analysis as well.

Moyer, Flege, Bohn and Bundgaard-Nielsen and Steinlen offer a different perspective on the study of second language learning from some of the more generative–linguistics-based accounts described in the previous section. These authors are mainly interested in the study of second language speech. By carrying out well-controlled experimental studies, researchers in this field examine how learning a second language is influenced by linguistic – in particular both phonetic and phonological factors – and by subject variables such as age of learning, quantity and quality of L2 input, gender or motivation. A recent collection of chapters providing a good survey of L2 speech research is Bohn and Munro (2007).

As Bleyhl closes Part 1 with a summary of what the research means for the classroom, so Henning Wode closes Part 2 by linking several issues, namely, the development of pronunciation in immersion programs, the nature of L1 transfer, and whether there is a sensitive/critical period in the biological sense (Chapter 13). The data derive from various kinds of immersion teaching current in Germany, as well as from non-tutored L2 acquisition and traditional foreign language teaching. As for immersion, the data indicate that immersion students can, and do, develop a remarkably good L2 pronunciation without any remedial teaching at all, but they tend to retain a slight non-native accent irrespective of the age of entry into the immersion program. Wode argues that there are no differences across the age range to warrant the conclusion that the way the L2 is processed and/or learned changes as a function of age in any biological sense. Even at 3;0 the substitutions parallel those familiar from older learners including adults. The only factor that can be identified to have an influence on the nature of the L2 substitutions is the state of development of the learner's L1 phonological system, because this is the basis from which transfer is generated. Wode concludes, whatever the nature of sensitive/critical periods, there is no direct biological basis for them in terms of developmental structures, in particular, in terms of the nature of transfer patterns. In addition to the obvious implications the immersion data have for immersion teaching and the training of teachers, Wode points out that the L2 regularities found across learners also account for the phonological peculiarities of contact varieties such as the New Englishes.

Dedication

We close this introductory chapter with a dedication to Professor Harris Winitz. The spark that ignited development of this book was our mutual respect for a thinker who has since the 1960s quietly been involved in the quest to understand the interplay between input, linguistic structure and SECOND LANGUAGE DEVELOPMENT. Harris Winitz prompted us in our own research and teaching to take another look at input, particularly in its relation to the development of a second phonology. One of his intriguing ideas, which although his own *Learnables* teaching program rests on this premise, has gone relatively unexamined, apart from Winitz *et al.* (1995). This is the claim that production from the start of L2 exposure influences the route of phonological development, ultimately resulting in an end state that is more distant from the target than would be the case were production delayed. Among the studies that the readers of this book might be roused to undertake, we hope that at at least one of you will take up the challenge to investigate whether an initial silent period does, in fact, ultimately lead to more native-like L2 phonology.

Notes

1. All terms and concepts that appear in SMALL CAPS in this book are defined in the glossary.
2. The age issue is still very much unresolved. While age differences in second language success are patently observable it remains unclear what the precise causes are; see Herschensohn (2007) for an enlightening discussion.
3. In her 2000 update of her 1985 article, Lightbown mentions the great increase since then in work on second language acquisition, particularly with respect to studies asking pedagogical questions. Although property-theory-driven SLA studies indeed exclude reference to pedagogical concerns, the bulk of pedagogy-driven and property-theory-driven research findings can nonetheless be distilled into the same set of expectations.
4. For those who are interested in the underpinnings of SLA in child language acquisition, Lust and Foley (2004) is a collection of those seminal, must-read papers that have influenced the thinking of child language acquisition researchers and theoretical linguists in the last half century.
5. Note that since the publication of this book there have been a number of books which discuss how Universal Grammar is held to operate in child first and second language language acquisition. In second language acquisition, this work also addresses the nature of the influence of the L1 during the acquisition of an L2.
6. See also Bickerton (1981) who earlier arrived at the same conclusions based on hearing children who had received spoken pidgin language input.
7. Jordens (1996) warns of the danger in assuming that because older learners can use general cognitive/metacognitive skills in instructed settings, this is how linguistic competence is acquired in an L2. It is a difficult but essential requirement for the researcher to at least attempt to determine the source of a learner's knowledge. Here see Schwartz (1993) for an elaboration on sources of knowledge akin to Krashen's learning vs. acquisition.
8. Research in this vein in child language acquisition has tended to revolve around documenting the corrections parents make to children's errors (such as overgeneralizations of past tense -ed as in 'goed') and the recasts they make of children's non-adult utterances (also proposed as a form of corrective feedback); see, for example, Marcus (1993) for a critical view. If either is shown to have an effect on children's emerging linguistic competence, this would give input a greater role. The verdict is, however, still out.
9. Books and articles on input published around the same time as the present volume are a harbinger of the general recognition of this need; see for example, Han (2007); Nizegorodcew (2007); Rast (2008).
10. The considerable variation with respect to that end state (ranging from close to quite considerable distance from target language norms) led Bley-Vroman (1990) to argue that post-puberty learners make use of general cognitive mechanisms whose use typically exhibits the same sort of variation in outcome as in mastery of a skill such as chess. Flege (personal communication) does

not consider it appropriate to apply the term 'fossilization' to L2 learners' developing sound systems. He points out that acoustic studies have repeatedly shown that both early and late starters' phonetic categories will always remain somewhat variable.

11. See Sorace (2000) and DeKeyser (2000) for several additional different perspectives on the end-state issue. Flege (this volume) also offers a different perspective where he has repeatedly criticized Dekeyser's views and does so in his chapter.

12. See Vainikka and Young-Scholten (2005), on the issue of whether learners' basic word order transfers from their L1.

13. Various other authors have questioned on both conceptual and empirical grounds the usefulness of explicit focus on forms for acquisition of linguistic competence, for example in the 1980s and 1990s Felix (1985), Felix and Weigl (1991), VanPatten (1988) and more recently Young-Scholten (2004).

Part 1

Matters of Input

Chapter 1

Input Frequency and the Acquisition of the Progressive

ANDREAS ROHDE

Introduction

The progressive form has proved to be very salient in native English-speaking INPUT so that it is generally expected to figure very early in L2 learner data. However, the fact that the progressive form has a number of different functions may render the acquisition process rather complex and the mere fact that the progressive is correctly formed in L2 acquisition does not entail that its uses are in fact target-like. In the first part of this chapter, the development of the progressive form is sketched for four German children acquiring English during a six-month stay in California. Two main functions of the progressive are under scrutiny: as a marker of grammatical aspect with both present and past reference, and as a marker of future tense without marking grammatical aspect. The data are compared with input data from American children the German children were in contact with. The distribution of the functions over the six months varies considerably, suggesting that each function of the progressive is tackled separately. In the second part, the focus is on LEXICAL ASPECT or AKTIONSART and the ASPECT HYPOTHESIS. In relation to the results of the first part, it is investigated to what extent the PRODUCTION data reflect the distribution of *–ing* inflected verb types in the input data with regard to the verbs' inherent verbal aspect.

The Role of Input in Second Language Acquisition

In the days of behaviourism, both L1 and L2 language acquisition[1] were mainly seen as a process of the learner's imitation (Lado, 1957; Skinner, 1957). This is why the input any language learner was exposed to was of primary importance. L2 learners' output was viewed as a more or less faithful mirror of the language which NATIVE SPEAKERS of the TARGET

LANGUAGE provided (Gass & Selinker, 2001: 259ff). Once language acquisition was increasingly regarded as a creative construction process (Dulay & Burt, 1974b), researchers became more interested in the internal mechanisms of the learner and in the developmental sequences that could be identified for linguistic structures (for L1 acquisition see Bloom, 1970; Brown, 1973; for L2 acquisition see Bailey *et al.*, 1974; Dulay & Burt, 1973, 1974a, 1974b; for L2 negation see Wode, 1976; for L2 questions see Wode, 1981). The input the learners received was only of marginal interest, all the more so because the POVERTY OF THE STIMULUS was and is regarded as a characteristic feature of the input, leading to the logical problem of language acquisition (White, 1989). But input (also known as PLD = PRIMARY LINGUISTIC DATA) has been considered essential by generative approaches for some time (see Carroll, 2001; Schwartz, 1993; Schwartz & Gubala-Ryzak, 1992). Non-generative approaches from the 1970s on have also considered input (and social exchange) as crucial (e.g. Krashen's INPUT HYPOTHESIS, Swain's OUTPUT HYPOTHESIS, Long's INTERACTION HYPO-THESIS, CONNECTIONISM – for an overview see Mitchell & Myles, 2004).

The present study's background is a functional non-generative approach to L2 acquisition, that is, it is not assumed that linguistic knowledge is available from the outset. Rather, this knowledge is determined by general learning mechanisms 'operating on the rich data provided by human interaction' (Ellis, 1994: 369). In this study, learner input proves to play a two-fold role. First, it will be shown that both input frequency and saliency trigger the use of the progressive form by German learners of English. Second, however, the polysemous nature of the progressive in the input makes it difficult for the learners to subconsciously attribute a clear-cut function to the progressive form, leading to a rather complex developmental sequence which does not lead to L2 mastery at the end of a six-month stay.

The Progressive Form in English

The progressive form in English has a number of different functions which range from marking grammatical aspect to marking future tense to expressing stylistic nuances.[2] In the following, two main functions of the progressive form in English are briefly discussed as they play a major role for the data these learners produce. The first concerns the progressive as a grammatical aspectual category, the second is the progressive's function as a marker for future tense.

The progressive as a marker of grammatical aspect

The prototypical and most frequent function of the progressive is to mark grammatical aspect, that is, give information about the internal structure of the action or event expressed. According to Quirk *et al.*, the main semantic features of the progressive are:

> *imperfectivity*: the action or event are not complete.
> *duration*: actions and events are not punctual.
> *boundedness*: the duration of states expressed in the progressive is limited. (Compare 'We are living in London' in contrast to 'We live in London'). (Quirk *et al.*, 1985)

As a grammatical aspectual category, the progressive can be used across all tenses. In the past tense, for example, the progressive is often used when the background of an event (1) or an implicit reference point is given (2):

(1) I was reading when the doorbell rang.
(2) She was writing her first novel at the time.

In connection with the present perfect, the progressive can be used to make subtle semantic differences which, however, are not important for the present study as this combination is not featured in the learner data used for the analysis.

The progressive as a marker of future tense

There are two uses of the progressive with future reference. The first one regards the periphrastic CONSTRUCTION *going to* + V, which expresses 'future fulfilment of present intention' (Quirk *et al.*, 1985: 214). This function is not discussed as it is a specific use where the *-ing* inflection appears in the contracted form *gonna*, which as frozen form is likely not analysed by the learner as *going to*.

(3) I'm going to see Deirdre in Berlin tomorrow.
(4) She's going to leave in a couple of days.

Accordingly, the second use of the progressive with future reference can be referred to as 'future arising from present arrangement, plan, or programme' (Quirk *et al.*, 1985: 215). Here, the progressive form is used without any additional verb:

(5) I'm finishing my work after dinner.
(6) Megan and I are leaving for Berlin tomorrow.

It will be shown that this latter use of the progressive for marking future tense is quite prominent in the learners' production discussed in this chapter. It has to be noted here that German, the L1 of the learners analysed in this chapter, does not mark grammatical aspect with an auxiliary. In German, the difference between habituality ('I read a book') and ongoing processes ('I am reading a book') is not marked morphologically. The context usually makes clear whether an action is habitual or in progress. If the difference has to be made explicit, temporal adverbs, such as *nun* (now) or *gerade* (just now) have to be added ('Ich lese ein Buch' vs. 'Ich lese gerade/nun ein Buch').

In the input, *-ing* is phonetically more SALIENT than the other verb inflections -s and *-ed*, as *-ing* (be it in its full form or as [IN])[3] always consists of two sounds, thus changing the prosodic structure of the verb. In addition, forms of the auxiliary *be* used with the present participle makes the progressive form apparently easy – that is, salient – for the learner to identify in the input. As a consequence, *-ing* figures very early in production data from learners. This observation has been supported by numerous studies, from the morpheme order studies of the 1970s (see Introduction above) to more recent studies in L2 PROCESSABILITY THEORY (Pienemann, 2006; Pienemann *et al.*, 2006). However, it cannot be concluded that the progressive form is target-like just because *-ing* inflected verbs occur in L2 data from early on. We will in fact see that the developmental sequence for the progressive form is a long drawn-out process.

The Aspect Hypothesis

As stated above, the progressive primarily represents a grammatical aspectual category in English. Grammatical aspect has to be clearly distinguished from the *lexical* or *inherent aspect* of the verb (this phenomenon is also referred to as *aktionsart* [*aktions* = action; *art* = manner'] (see Andersen & Shirai, 1994; Comrie, 1976). According to Vendler (1967), the following types of lexical aspect can be distinguished:

(i)   Achievement – that which takes place instantaneously, and is reducible to a single point in time, this point being the necessary endpoint or goal (e.g. *start, recognize, die, reach the summit*,[4] etc). These verbs or predicates are referred to as 'telic' (Greek *telos* = 'aim').

(ii) Accomplishment – that which has some duration, but has a necessary endpoint or goal (e.g. *run a mile, make a chair, build a house, write a book*, etc). These verbs and predicates are also referred to as 'telic'.

(iii) Activity – that which has duration, but without a necessary endpoint (e.g. *run, walk, play, sing*, etc). These verbs and predicates are referred to as atelic.

(iv) State – that which has no dynamics, and continues without additional effort or energy being applied (e.g. *see, love, hate, want*, etc). These verbs are referred to as atelic (Shirai & Kurono, 1998: 247 ff.) (see Table 1.1).

The Aspect Hypothesis (AH) predicts that verbal inflections in both early L1 and L2 acquisition redundantly mark the lexical aspect inherent in the verb or predicate rather than tense or grammatical aspect. These predictions of the AH have been shown in L2 acquisition for a variety of languages and

Table 1.1 Semantic features for the four categories of inherent lexical aspect

Semantic features	States	Activities	Accomplishments	Achievements
Punctual	–	–	–	+
Telic	–	–	+	+
Dynamic	–	+	+	+

language combinations (Andersen & Shirai, 1994; Rohde, 1997; Salaberry & Shirai, 2002).[5] This study will exclusively focus on the development of the progressive form, thus the other verbal inflections will be ignored.

In L2 English, the -ing inflection[6] is prototypically affiliated with activities and accomplishments whereas -ed is mainly found with achievements, and the 3rd person singular – s is predominantly associated with states (Housen, 2002; Rohde, 1996, 1997).

Data and Procedure

The data of four children, aged four to nine, are reviewed. These children spent six months in a small town in California and acquired English in naturalistic contexts without any formal instruction involved.[7] Their L2 development was documented in the form of diary data/spontaneous notes. Additional data come from selected tape recordings that were made to complement the diary data (Rohde, 1996, 1997; Wode, 1981). The input data discussed in this chapter are taken from seven selected tape recordings that have been exhaustively transcribed to include interlocutors. The data comprise spontaneous speech from nine American children aged six to nine.

Two developmental sequences will be shown for the German children's L2 acquisition of the progressive form with respect to its function. In the first part of the study, the development of the progressive form with its functions as both a grammatical aspectual category and as a means of marking future tense is presented. In the second sequence shown, the link between the -ing inflection and the highlighted lexical aspect is investigated within the framework of the Aspect Hypothesis. It will be shown that each function of the progressive form is tackled separately so that the learner data only reflect the input distribution to a limited extent. It will be suggested that due to the fact that the children highlight different functions of the progressive in each month of L2 exposure, the predictions for the developmental sequence of -ing inflected verbs according to the Aspect Hypothesis are not entirely met and may have to be slightly modified. The data will also be discussed with regard to the Distributional Bias Hypothesis (see later section), which makes predictions about the distribution of lexical aspect in L1 speech.

The Learners: The Development of Uses of the Progressive Form. Results and Discussion

In this section, the data of the six-month stay are presented in chrono-logical order divided into monthly samples of L2 exposure, starting with the second month as there are no instances of the progressive form docu-mented earlier.[8]

Month 2

(7) H/D I'm pitching really fast.[9]
(8) H/D I'm stealing (H is stealing a base in a baseball match).
(9) H/D It's car coming.[10]
(10) H/D Hey, look John. I'm riding my bike like this.
(11) L/T Heiko's sleeping.
(12) H/T Where are you kicking?
(13) H/T He play on your team.

In (7), the 9-year-old Heiko goes outside to practice pitching. Strictly speaking, this utterance refers to a future event, that is, something that the boy intends to do. (8) is taken from a baseball match where the form *stealing* had been heard in the input numerous times before. (9) gives an exam-ple of a verb that at first exclusively appears in the progressive. (10), (11) and (12) are examples which include typical verbs appearing in the pro-gressive. However, all three verbs are also used in their base forms in a target-like fashion. (13) is an instance where the progressive form would be appropriate but where the verb remains in its base form.

Month 3

(14) L/T You wanna … I'm helping.
(15) L/T No, I don't want playing.
(16) H/D For what you're looking?
(17) H/D What do you do? / What are you doing? (after a long pause)
(18) H/T I'm working on it.
(19) B/D I'm freezing.
(20) L/T I caught one. He swim.
(21) L/T I throw out.
(22) L/T He swim.

The examples above demonstrate a number of interesting tendencies. (14) suggests one of the first uses of the progressive with future reference as Lars announces his offer rather than commenting on his helping. In (15) the use of *-ing* may be influenced by the German infinitive and 1st/3rd person plural ending *-en* which is often pronounced as [ɪn]. Another interesting observation is the use of the verb *swim*. (20) and (22) as well as later instances (see below) suggest that the function of the progressive as a grammatical aspectual category has not been fully grasped yet. This is especially conspicuous for the verb *swim*. This is corroborated by (17) in which Heiko obviously is in doubt as to which form is the appropriate one in the context.

Month 4

(23) H/D   You can't jump this far. I was jumping that far.
(24) H/D   It start to raining.
(25) H/T   Yes, he was watching Inga. He likes to watch Inga.
(26) H/T   We was out bassfishing last night [...] caught a bass and then we was fixing our fishing poles and do that.
(27) H/T   I go up to Yellow Jacket when he mading the hamburger.
(28) L/T   Who's winning?
(29) L/T   This one is still swimming, too.
(30) L/T   It's not swimming any more, there it swims [...] there it swim.
(31) L/D   Why you not was keeping this little one over there, Henning?
(32) L/D   Inga swim. And you don't.

Lars' utterances containing the verb *swim* reveal that the present progressive is still causing problems for the learner. In (32), it remains uninflected. In (29), it is inflected. However, (29) is a reply to the utterance 'This one is still swimming' by a young American friend and is thus directly taken from the input. A couple of minutes later in the same situation (30), Lars again shows how uncertain he is when it comes to the appropriate inflection, producing -ing, -s and no inflection. The particular verb *swim* may be causing problems as it is very similar to the German 'schwimmen'. The inflected *swimming* resembles the German infinitive and 1st/3rd person plural forms 'schwimmen' and may lead Lars to leave the verb uninflected. Along the same lines, (24) may be a result of TRANSFER from German, too. Heiko inflects the verb *rain* as in German you would find the infinitive 'regnen' in this particular case. Again, -*ing* seems to be used as both a verb inflection to mark grammatical aspect and as an infinitive marker.

In the fourth month of L2 exposure, the progressive is extended to past contexts (23, 25, 26, 27, 31). However, rather than marking past progressive, the use of the progressive replaces simple past. In Rohde (1997) I have argued that the use of the progressive in these contexts may be more transparent for the learners than simple past. Past is encoded in the auxiliary and the verb receives the -*ing* inflection which is more salient than the realisations of -*ed*.[11] (26) suggests that Heiko gives a chronological account of the events, therefore, *fixing* is not target-like in this context.

Although, from a formal point of view, the use of the past progressive is transparent for the learners and is preferred to the simple past for some time (see month 5), it seems to further complicate the comprehension of what the target-like use of the 'progressive' indicates. One feature of the present progressive is to express actions or events which currently are in progress, which are taking place in the present and which are as yet incomplete. This seems to be the most conspicuous use of the progressive in the input – it is also the first use which is adopted by the young L2 learners. The problem, however, is that during the fourth month of L2 exposure, a time when the children are becoming increasingly proficient referring to past and future events, the progressive expresses yet another feature which seems to be difficult to grasp from the input: Ongoing actions and events are referred to in the past, generally being linked to a reference point which is expressed in the simple past ('I was cleaning the floor when I was hit by the vase').

Month 5

(33) L/T   I was using all the way two.
(34) L/T   You were fishing too, Henning.
(35) L/T   I was caughting two on one day and on the 'nother day one, too.
(36) L/T   No, Henning, I was driving the car.
(37) L/T   I think Birgit was kissing.
(38) L/T   He was gotting hundred dollars from Hoopa.
(39) L/T   You're not playing that what you want to do.
(40) I/D   Larsie is bluting.
(41) L/T   You're starting all the time.
(42) H/D   What does the bear right now?

A tendency which was first observed during the fourth month is now very prominent: the use of the past progressive in contexts where the simple past would be more target-like. (35) is especially interesting because the inflected verb *caught* very clearly refers to completed events in the past which do not require the progressive. (42) is remarkable because despite the use of *now* the verb is not inflected for present progressive as would be target-like. This utterance appears to be a case of transfer from the children's L1 German where there is no do-support in interrogation. (39) is another example where the progressive does not mark grammatical aspect but rather has future reference. (40) suggests lexical transfer from German 'bluten', however, the inflection is of course appropriate. (41) is the first use of a stylistic nuance expressed by the progressive (see above), which certainly does not make the progressive more transparent in general as 'start' as an achievement verb is in conflict with the function of expressing an ongoing event in the present and rather expresses a habitual state. It cannot be inferred from the tape recording whether this particular utterance is a repeated L1 utterance.

Month 6

(43) L/T I'm not giving all of mine.
(44) L/T I'm not fighting.
(45) H/T I'm not want my car back.
(46) I/D Henning, you wait for Mom?
(47) I/T I don't know what he do.
     (*answering the question 'What is he doing there?'*)

In the final month of L2 exposure, there are hardly any occurrences of the past progressive. (43) and (44) indicate that the present progressive with future reference is becoming more popular.[12] As for the youngest sibling, the four-year old Inga has clearly not fully grasped the concept of progressive as her two utterances suggest.

The question of whether the children have acquired the progressive form with its two main functions marking grammatical aspect and future tense at the end of their six-month stay in the United States cannot be conclusively answered. As we know from numerous other studies sketching developmental sequences [overviews in Ellis (1994) and Wode (1988/ 1993)], the main problem is a clear criterion for acquisition. This criterion cannot simply be the emergence of the progressive form in production. According to such a simplistic criterion, the progressive form as a means of marking grammatical aspect would be considered acquired in month 2 in the data analysed in this study. As has become clear in the morpheme order studies of the 1970s, the formal appearance of a morpheme cannot be equated with its full acquisition as this would imply mastery of both target-like form and function. For analyses which used the same data as in this study, Bahns (1983) showed that acquisition criteria are very problematic as they necessarily have to be arbitrary. He demonstrates that for the acquisition of modal auxiliaries, the point of acquisition can drastically differ when the criterion is modified: In Bahns (1981), the modal auxiliary *can* was regarded as acquired after occurring five times in the data in a sequence of 20 consecutive days. According to this criterion, Lars acquired *can* after an L2 exposure of one month and 16 days. However, Bahns (1981) ignored a number of instances of non-target-like uses of *can* during this time span. In a reanalysis of the L2 data, Bahns (1983: 61) defines a new criterion according to which '[a] modal auxiliary is considered acquired if it is used target-like in at least 90% of its total usages in three consecutive samples [one sample = 10 days], where there are at least five usages in each sample.[13] The point of acquisition is the first day of the first of the three consecutive samples'. This point now moved from 1;16 to 2;30, that is, one and a half months later.

From a formal point of view, it is true that the progressive form -*ing* occurs within the first L2 utterances by the learners, bearing out the old claim that its salience in the input leads to the learners picking it up very early on. From a functional point of view, it has been shown that even at the end of the six-month stay in the United States during which the learners had intensive contact with L1 speakers of English, the present progressive is not exclusively used in a target-like fashion, especially by the youngest learner. In addition, the past progressive is not fully mastered at the end of the stay.

The Distributional Bias Hypothesis

It is still unclear which factors are involved in the association of verbal inflections with inherent lexical aspect in language learners. The L1 and L1/L2 combination, learner age and rate of proficiency, to name but some, are apparently only of minor importance. It rather seems to be the question of whether the preferred coupling of aktionsart and verb inflection has its origin in cognitive operating principles or whether the association is mainly a characteristic of the input which is then more or less faithfully adopted by language learners (Andersen, 1993; Andersen & Shirai, 1994; Salaberry & Shirai, 2002).

The skewed distribution of verbal inflections in the input, that is, in the speech of native speakers, has come to be known as the Distributional Bias Hypothesis:[14] The unequal affiliation of verb and inflection is thus already given in the learners' target model: Activities primarily appear with the -*ing* inflection although this is only a statistical tendency (Andersen & Shirai, 1996: 548); in the input -*ing* can of course be found with other verbs than just activities. The Distributional Bias Hypothesis is by no means a claim of exclusivity where -*ing* *only* co-occurs with activity verbs. In addition, the degree to which the distribution of inflections is skewed strongly hinges on the discourse context. However, in L2 data, the skewed distribution, that is, the affiliation of verb inflection and lexical aspect, is stronger than in the input.

In their review, Andersen & Shirai (1996: 549–555) report on numerous studies supporting the DBH for various input-learner situations. Perhaps not surprisingly, learner-directed speech shows a stronger distributional bias than discourse among native speakers in which the potential possibilities of using verbs with more than one inflection seems to be more strongly exploited, especially in situations in which subtle meanings are expressed through the non-prototypical coupling of lexical aspect and the -*ing* inflection:

(48) You are always leaving me.
(49) I'm lovin' it.

In (48) the *-ing* inflected achievement *leave* occurs in a habitual context (marked by *always*) yielding a specific reading that is not accounted for in the grammar by Quirk *et al.* (1985). In (49) a state verb occurs in the progressive, a use which seems to be widespread in American English and which appears to yield a dynamic interpretation of the verb (see Gavis, 1998).

The affiliation of verb inflection and aktionsart in L2 acquisition is stronger than in the input, as stated above. However, even within L2 data, there can be strong variation. The following example for L1 Spanish/L2 English shows that the inflection is sometimes attached to a verb and remains on the verb even across different tenses: 'The one guy tell me, "I want to you *makin'* one pant ...", meaning something like "one guy might tell me, I want you to make me a pair of pants"' (Robison, 1990: 326). *Make* keeps the *-ing* inflection in this utterance although the infinitive would be target-like. The inherent aspect of duration is expressed by the L2 learner although this use is non-target-like. In this particular case the inherent lexical aspect of the verb determines the use of the verbal inflection added. Compare (24) above ('it start to rainin''), which is very similar: The inflection sticks to the verb although it is not used in the progressive with an auxiliary but as an infinitive.[15]

Input from Children's Peers: The Use of the Progressive Form and Inherent Lexical Aspect. Results and Discussion

In this section, the association of -ing with inherent lexical aspect is discussed for the two German boys[16] in comparison with the available input data. According to the Distributional Bias Hypothesis, the *-ing* inflection should be predominantly found on activity verbs (e.g. 'to write', 'to sing'), followed by accomplishments (e.g. 'to write a book', 'to build a house'; recall that both denote durative events with the former being atelic, the latter being telic). Achievements (e.g. 'to leave', 'to come', 'to win') are found in the progressive form, too, but to a lesser extent. Very often *-ing* inflected achievement verbs mark future tense (see above). Accordingly, the aspect hypothesis predicts that 'in languages that have progressive aspect, progressive marking begins with activities, then extends to accomplishments and achievements' (Bardovi-Harlig, 2002: 130). Thus, it is expected that the predominant association of inflection and lexical verb category follows the frequency of the associations in the input. The L2 verb tokens analysed for this study have been classified with the help of Robison's (1995) operational tests (see his appendix for a full description of the tests).

As the above analysis has shown, marking of future tense plays an important role for the German L2 learners of English, this is at least documented for some of the samples. Thus, it is possible that the use of *-ing* inflected verbs with future reference correlates with a different type of verb other than activities due to the fact that the duration of an event or an action is irrelevant when referred to in the future. Achievements, for example, are rare in the present progressive as they refer to events and actions of a limited duration and thus are atypical in the progressive. With future reference, however, achievements could be used in the progressive as the *-ing* inflection would no longer mark grammatical aspect but simply tense.

Figures 1.1 and 1.2 give the association of -ing inflected verb with the lexical aspectual class for the two boys, Lars and Heiko. The data are divided into five different samples, representing five months of L2 exposure. Figure 1.3 gives the percentages of total types for the two boys and the input data. The input data are not divided into different samples as they stem from nine different children altogether and do not represent a developmental sequence.

The input data reveal the expected distribution: Most of the inflected verbs are in fact activities, followed by accomplishments. Achievements play a minor role in the data. The L2 data reflect the same tendency as in

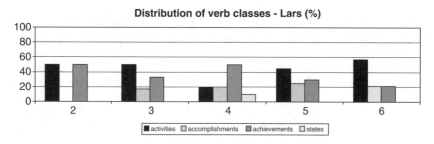

Figure 1.1 Distribution of *-ing* inflected verbs with the four types of inherent lexical aspect over the six-month stay – Lars (Months 2–6)

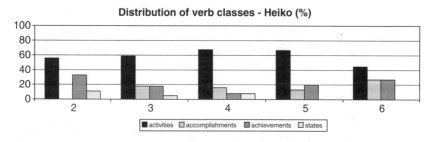

Figure 1.2 Distribution of *-ing* inflected verbs with the four types of inherent lexical aspect over the six-month stay – Heiko (Months 2–6)

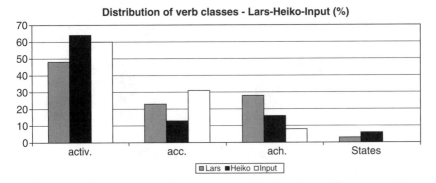

Figure 1.3 Distribution of -*ing* inflected verbs with the four types of inherent lexical aspect – Total types for Lars, Heiko and Input data

the input although, for Lars, the dominance of activities is not as pronounced as in the input. For Heiko, activities dominate from the beginning, but in contrast to the input data, achievements and states first appear in the progressive with accomplishments occurring in Month 3 for the first time. However, achievements and accomplishments are equally frequent. Lars shows a distribution of verb classes comparable to the L1 input at the end of the six-month stay. In Month 2, the number of activities and achievements is equally high, in Month 4, -*ing* inflected achievements are preferred over any other verb class.

States hardly play any role with regard to the progressive, which is predicted by the fact that state verbs such as *love, want, like, hear, smell*, etc. are simply incompatible with the progressive – at least in standard grammars. The few -*ing* inflected states which are recorded for Heiko are interesting (for a discussion of these see Housen, 2002: 172) but due to the low number of occurrences, they can be ignored.

Figures 1.4, 1.5 and 1.6 present an overview of the development of the progressive form for the two functions of grammatical aspect and future tense, the former being further divided into present and past reference. The data reveals that the distribution of the functions expressed by the progressive is only similar to the input distribution at times. In Month 5, for example, Lars' use of the past progressive is more frequent than the present progressive. In Month 3 the present progressive is followed by the use of the progressive with future reference. Both learners show that for each month-long sample there is mainly one function of the progressive which is preferred in its use. Heiko starts out focusing on the future function, then apparently reflecting the input distribution before he focuses on (mostly non-target-like) past marking (Month 4). For Lars, on the other hand, from Month 2 to 4, the present progressive with present

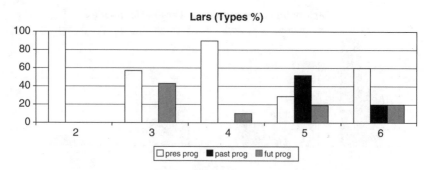

Figure 1.4 The occurrences of the progressive with three different grammatical functions for Lars over the six-month stay in the United States[17] (Months 2–6)

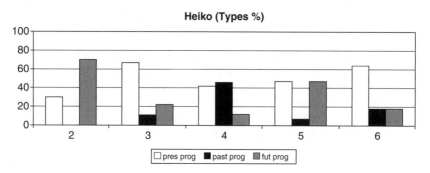

Figure 1.5 The occurrences of the progressive with three different grammatical functions for Heiko over the six-month stay in the United States (Months 2–6)

interpretation is the prevailing function before the past progressive dominates in Month 5.

Figure 1.6 reveals that, all types taken together over the six months, the two boys' use of -*ing* inflected verbs resembles the input quite closely. As stated above, this does not entail that all uses of the progressive are in fact target-like. Interestingly, the predominance of the progressive with present reference in the input is only reflected in six of the 10 learner samples (2 × 5 months). In the remaining four samples, the use of the progressive with future or past reference prevails or is equally frequent as the present progressive.

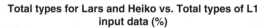

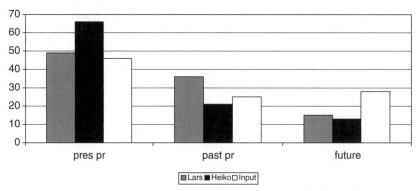

Figure 1.6 The occurrences of the progressive with three different grammatical functions for Lars and Heiko and L1 input data from nine American children

Conclusion

The two-part study reported on in this chapter investigated both the development of the progressive as a marker of both grammatical aspect and future tense on the one hand, and, the distribution of *-ing* inflected verbs with regard to the inherent lexical aspect of the verb, on the other. The input data analysed in this chapter show the expected scenario according to which the predominant use of the progressive is to mark ongoing events and actions in the present followed by marking future. The first part of the study shows that the different functions of the progressive are acquired in a piecemeal fashion with each of the different functions dominating for some time in the L2 data (present progressive > future tense > past progressive). The different samples show that the distribution of the three functions varies quite strongly, suggesting that the two boys prefer a particular function for specific periods of time during their six-month stay in the United States.

As for the study on lexical aspect, in line with the Distributional Bias Hypothesis, the most frequently used inherent lexical verb class in the L1 input is activities followed by accomplishments and a relatively low number of achievements. What is not supported in the L2 data studied here is the developmental sequence for lexical aspect predicted by for example, Bardovi-Harlig (2002: 130) according to which *-ing* is first used with activities, then extending to accomplishments and achievements. In fact, the L1 input distribution in this study would suggest exactly that sequence, with achievements being the last verb class to be inflected for progressive. The L2 data, however, clearly show a preference for achievements over accomplishments within the time span of six months – perhaps due to the fact that accomplishments very often require a verb plus object, whereas achievements do not (*cf.* 'I'm writing a letter' vs. 'I'm leaving'). It is possible, in line with Robison's (1995) findings, that the input distribution is more faithfully presented in interlanguage data with growing proficiency.

Implications for Second Language Teaching[18]

The implications of this study for L2 teaching are two-fold. Due to its frequency in the input, the progressive form must be given a prominent role in the input for language students. In both naturalistic and instructed L2 acquisition, at the beginning, learners tend to communicate about the 'here and now' so that the present progressive as a marker of grammatical aspect is the natural choice to start with. In the modern L2 classroom, the teacher could make sure, for example, through the selection of tasks, that the learners are given the opportunity to talk about ongoing actions/processes in the present. The learners then have to figure out the contrast between the present progressive and the simple present (the latter is less prominent in L1 English corpora – see Tesch, 2000).[19] For younger learners, such a contrast is preferably introduced through a FOCUS ON FORM approach (Ellis, 1994: 639 ff), which means that the learners' awareness of grammatical distinctions is raised without formal grammar teaching, which would make these distinctions explicit through the formulation of rules. At a later stage, when learners are introduced to means of expressing plans, actions and events in the future, the present progressive as a marker of future tense could be introduced separately. This may be more fruitful than presenting the progressive form as a multi-functional structure all at once. After all, learners prefer to associate one form with one function (the ONE-TO-ONE PRINCIPLE, see Andersen & Shirai, 1994). Classroom input can never be as rich as a naturalistic context which gives learners plenty of opportunities to work out any form's different functions.

As for lexical aspect, it can be useful to teach older learners the difference between *telic* and *atelic verbs* (see before). One possibility could be to give students the following test frame: 'If one was *verb*ing, but was interrupted while *verb*ing, has one *verb*ed?' (Dowty, 1979: 58 ff.; Garey, 1957: 105.). If, for example, *sleep* is substituted for *verb*, the answer has to be 'yes', *sleep* then is an atelic verb that does not contain an inherent aim or endpoint. On the other hand, if a verb such as *leave* is inserted, the answer must be 'no': if you are interrupted while leaving the house, you clearly have not left it. The verb *leave* therefore is telic.

This distinction can be particularly useful for understanding the present perfect progressive. German learners of English tend to have problems with the appropriate form of the verb for example, in questions such as 'Has it been raining?' or 'Have you been crying?', often thinking *'Has it rained?' or *'Have you cried?' are the correct constructions. Once they know that atelic verbs tend to appear with *-ing* in these questions (and the respective answers) and telic verbs with *-ed* or as irregular forms respectively, they have grasped a crucial characteristic of the present perfect progressive (this difference is usually not made in the available learner grammars). In general, input in the L2 classroom is unable to provide the learner with sufficient evidence to make the difference between present perfect and present perfect progressive.

Notes

1. In this chapter, I am not making the distinction between 'acquisition' and 'learning', thus using both terms interchangeably. Intuitively, the distinction may make sense in a number of contexts (e.g. to distinguish between naturalistic L2 acquisition and L2 classroom learning. However, this distinction is not testable and proves to be problematic in various contexts.
2. Compare 'You are always telling me that' with 'You always tell me that' or 'I'm seeing pink elephants' with 'I see pink elephants'.
3. The pronunciation of *-ing* as [In] is in fact very similar to the German infinitive and 1st/3rd person plural ending *-en*, which is also often pronounced as [In].
4. This example shows that lexical aspect or aktionsart is an inherent feature of each verb but can be modified by the direct object and thus is a matter of the predicate: Thus, *to write* would be classified as an activity as it is atelic, whereas *to write a book* would be telic and thus changes into an accomplishment.
5. More recent publications include: Al-Zidjali (2005) (L1 Arabic/L2 English); Gavruseva (2002) (L1 Russian/L2 English); Haznedar (2001) (L1 Turkish/L2 English).
6. In most instances, this concerns the use of the progressive form.
7. In fact, three of the four children attended school, however, there was no specific ESL instruction.
8. During the first half of the first month, the four children predominantly use their L1 German, apart from a number of socio-pragmatic utterances such as 'come on', 'hello', 'thank you' or 'bye bye'. In the second half they begin to mix English chunks and German, for example, 'It looks like is(t) gelandet' ('It looks like [the plane] has landed').
9. The initials H, L, B, I refer to the four children involved. D refers to diary data, T to tape data.
10. This example could be explained in terms of *holistic chunking* (Myles, 2004; Rohde, 1997). In fact, there are possibly two chunks here: On the one hand, the utterance could be based on the structure 'It's X' where X is an as yet unanalysed whole. 'Car coming', on the other hand, may be based on an input utterance such as 'There is a car coming', where the chunk 'car coming' has been memorised by the learner.
11. In fact, up to this point, the verbs which appear with the *-ed* inflection and past reference may be interpreted as memorised chunks.

12. The tape recording reveals that the utterance is Lars' announcement that he is not willing to fight about Lego pieces.
13. The criterion of 'at least five usages in each sample' is in addition to Brown's (1973) criterion of 90% in obligatory contexts over three consecutive samples. In contrast to Brown, however, Bahns rather counted usages than suppliance of modals in obligatory contexts.
14. A skewed distribution of verbal inflections in native speakers' production had also been reported by Bybee (1985) and Comrie (1976). Neither of the two, however, presented data to substantiate their claim (see Andersen & Shirai, 1996: 548 ff).
15. Note, however, that here the similarity between the German infinitive ending 'en' ('regnen' = *to rain*) may also contribute to the use of *raining*.
16. The data of the two girls are not considered here as a month-by-month analysis is not possible due to the paucity of the data.
17. Only verb types (not tokens) are included. However, when a verb is used with two or three different functions and/or when a different aktionsart is involved, two or three tokens of one verb are counted as two or three different verbs. This basically concerns high frequency verbs such as *go, do* and *come (up)*. As for tokens, there is a total of 104 tokens for Heiko, 89 for Lars, and 75 for the American children.
18. Usually the distinction is made between *second* and *foreign language teaching*. The term *foreign language* is normally used for an additional language which is learnt in an environment where this language is not the *ambient language* (e.g. French or German in England). This use is in contrast to *second language* which usually refers to a language which is additionally acquired to one's *first language* in an environment where the L2 is the ambient language, that is, where it is most people's NATIVE LANGUAGE (Ellis, 1994: 11 ff.). I am not making this difference here as it is irrelevant for the discussion.
19. Tesch (1993) suggests that the simple present should in fact be introduced before the present progressive as the latter is often overgeneralized by German learners of English. This seems all the more absurd as she otherwise proposes that the more frequent a form is in L1 input the earlier it should be taught.

Chapter 2

Processing Matters in Input Enhancement

BILL VANPATTEN

Introduction

As one might guess, INPUT matters in instructed SLA as much as it does in SLA more generally. The field of research in instructed SLA has increasingly moved toward the concept of 'input enhancement' as a way of describing how outside intervention might make a difference on the acquisition of formal properties of language (e.g. syntax, phonology, morphology and lexicon). Coined by Sharwood Smith (1993), input enhancement refers to any overt attempt to draw learners' attention to formal properties of language and comes in many varieties – and, as Sharwood Smith (1993: 177) points out, may come in positive and negative forms. Positive input enhancement 'would simply make more salient certain correct forms in the input. Negative input enhancement would flag given forms as incorrect, thus signaling to the learner they (*sic*) have violated the target norms'. Similarly, Long (1991: 45–46; and elsewhere) has used the term FOCUS ON FORM, which he takes to mean overtly drawing 'students' attention to linguistic elements as they arise incidentally in lessons whose overriding focus is on meaning or communication'. Both input enhancement and focus on form are grounded in the idea that work with formal properties of language for the purposes of fostering acquisition is best done if learner attention is simultaneously focused on meaning. This of course rules out a number of techniques in which attention is exclusively on form (see, e.g. Wong & VanPatten, 2003).

Falling within the parameters of input enhancement and focus on form are a number of techniques and approaches, most notably TEXT ENHANCEMENT, RECASTS, INPUT FLOOD, DICTOGLOSS and INPUT–OUTPUT CYCLES (see, e.g. Doughty & Williams, 1998; Wong, 2005). The focus of the present chapter is processing instruction (PI). The premise underlying processing instruction is deceptively simple. It goes like this:

- learners need input for acquisition;
- a major problem in acquisition might be the way in which learners process input;
- if we can understand how learners process input, then we might be able to devise effective input enhancement or focus on form to aid acquisition of FORMAL FEATURES of language.

The key here is PROCESSING. In stark contrast to more traditional approaches that do not consider how the learner's mind interacts with input – such as explanation plus oral practice – a processing approach may consider the linguistic nature of a grammatical form or property of language but not without asking at least the following questions:

(1) When a learner encounters something new in the input, how does he or she process it?
(2) What makes some things more difficult to process than others?
(3) In general, what might be the underlying problems in processing grammatical information in the input that impedes or delays acquisition in an L2 context?

The purpose of the present chapter is to briefly describe processing instruction and its underpinnings. To do so, I will first discuss the nature of (input) processing looking at it from various perspectives. I will then look at a test case (word order in Spanish) and follow this with a presentation of processing instruction. I will then do the same for a different grammatical structure (tense inflections). I will also touch upon the research on processing instruction as well as several major criticisms that have been leveled at it.

Processing Input

As learners are confronted with utterances in the L2, two things must simultaneously happen: (1) they must attempt to understand what the other person is saying and (2) their internal processors must map what was said (meaning) onto how it was said (form, i.e. the formal properties of language). This is a tremendous challenge. Imagine the beginning learner of Japanese (L1 can be any non-Eastern language) confronted with the following utterance: *Silvia wa ataka ga il dake zya naku, yoku benkyoo simasu.* Our fictional learner (although he or she surely exists somewhere in the world) must try to grasp that the speaker is saying 'Sylvia is not only intelligent, but also hardworking'. How does our learner do this? And when our learner does, what parts of the formal properties of language (e.g. case endings, tense markers, etc.) become data for acquisition if any? Clearly, just because a learner can make some sense of this sentence does not mean that all formal aspects contained in the utterance are fodder for acquisition. If this were the case for most utterances, acquisition would not be so exceedingly slow and generally incomplete (vis à vis NATIVE SPEAKER competence).

Research on processing has led to various perspectives, most of them complementary albeit different in scope. These perspectives are best found in the work of O'Grady, Carroll, and my own work. I will take each in turn.

In line with current perspectives, O'Grady (2003) takes the position that a good deal of acquisition problems stem from the challenges that learners face when processing utterances. Specifically, he refers to *computational complexity*. Computational complexity is based on structural distance between elements in an utterance that are co-referential in some way, structural distance in turn meaning the number of syntactic nodes that intervene between the coreference. A syntactic NODE is an abstract concept that basically means the 'dividing line' between major phrases, such as noun phrases (NP), verb phrases (VP), prepositional phrases (PP) and what we can call complementizer phrases (CP)–phrases that introduce a clause. O'Grady gives the example of relative clauses in Korean as in the following. Note that in Korean, relative clauses precede the noun they modify, unlike English:

(1) SUBJECT RELATIVE:
    [$_S$...namca-lul   cohaha-nun]   yeca
        man-ACC   like-RC.Prs.   woman[1]
        'The woman who likes the man ...'

(2) DIRECT OBJECT RELATIVE:
    [$_S$ Namca-ka   [$_{VP}$ ... cohaha-nun]]   yeca
        man-NOM   like-RC.Prs.   woman
        'The woman who the man likes ...'

In these examples, coreference involves the relationship between the RELATIVE CLAUSE MARKER *nun* and whether its coreferent HEAD NOUN (the noun it refers to) is an object or subject of the verb. In the subject relative, there is only one node that intervenes between the head noun *yeca* and the relative marker: [S, which stands for 'sentence']. With the object relative, there are two intervening nodes: [S] and [VP]. O'Grady uses this example to illustrate that structural distance is not the same as linear distance given that both nouns are 'adjacent' to the verb and thus linearly equidistant from it. In O'Grady *et al.* (2003), L1 speakers of English heard various sentences with relative clauses and were asked to match what they heard to a picture, their choice clearly indicating what noun they believed to be the head of the relative clause. What the researchers found was that participants were correct on subject relative clauses 73.2% of the time and correct on objects only 22.7%. Thus, object relatives were mistaken for subject relatives significantly more than subjects were mistaken for objects. O'Grady interprets this as evidence for computational complexity in processing as a source of problem in acquisition.

Carroll (2001; and elsewhere) has argued that acquisition is largely a PARSING problem. That is, learning proceeds because of changes in parsing. Parsing involves, minimally, categorizing words into appropriate lexical and functional categories, projecting a syntactic structure, and checking that coreferential or grammatically related features in an input string 'match'. (Carroll includes many more levels of processing that include phonology, semantics and other aspects of language but of relevance here are syntactic and morphological properties.) A parser is thus the formal mechanism that makes the computations that O'Grady refers to in his work. Where O'Grady and Carroll differ is their commitment to a generative approach to linguistics and the concept of an innate linguistic module (i.e. UNIVERSAL GRAMMAR or UG); Carroll is committed to it while O'Grady is not and is what is referred to as a 'general nativist'.

In Carroll's view of things, acquisition occurs when there is a parsing failure that signals to the learner that something has gone wrong.[2] Something goes wrong when how something is parsed does not match what the learner believes is the intended meaning *or* when features that are supposed to match do not match. In the example from Korean relative clauses, for acquisition to proceed in Carroll's view of things, the learner must parse a direct object relative as a subject relative and at the same time be confronted with real world information that this parse is incorrect; that is, the facts of what is being talked about reveal to the learner that the relative clause is not a subject relative clause (i.e. 'Oh, it's not the man liking the woman but the woman liking the man . . .'). This then signals to the parsing mechanism that something needs to be adjusted and this may happen immediately, it may happen later, or, in some cases, it may never happen.

Carroll's 'acquisition proceeds when there is a parsing failure' approach creates a dilemma for acquisition, which she acknowledges and suggests as the main source of non-learning: just how much 'noise' can go by without the L2 learner's parser detecting a failure? Learners can miss a lot of data in the input early on because their parsers either cannot handle the information or merely do not process it. This is one explanation for why gender of nouns is acquired late or not acquired at all by learners coming from languages in which gender and gender agreement is non-existent. For these learners, their L1 parsers do not have 'built in expectations' that nouns and adjectives have to agree and thus no parsing happens when, say, a feminine noun appears in the same sentence with a masculine adjective; their parsers do not check for matches. This may be compounded by prosodic/phonological properties of the L2, as in the case of French being learned by L1 speakers of, say, English. For example, the definite articles *le* (masculine) and *la* (feminine) are 'swallowed up' by the following noun, especially in fast speech. *Le* in particular is often only realised as *l'* such that *le livre* (the book) may sound like *l'liv*. Learners with English as L1 cannot transfer anything to help processing and a chicken-and-egg scenario is set up: in the case of gender and adjective agreement, how do you get something into the parser so there is a failure when you never detect it in the input to begin with? In the case of gender, unlike the example from Korean relative clauses, there is no real world information that provides any kind of feedback regarding correct parsing. For example, there is nothing about a table, the moon, or a house that in Spanish would suggest the adjective must be *blanca* and there is nothing about a horse, a book, and a car that suggests the adjective must be *blanco*. Key to Carroll's perspective, then, is the transfer of L1 parsing during L2 comprehension.

In my work (e.g. VanPatten, 1996, 2004a, 2007), input processing is defined as (1) making FORM-MEANING connections and (2) parsing sentences (who does what to whom). I draw from general tenets of COGNITIVE PSYCHOLOGY as well as some of the work on sentence processing and have established a set of principles that guide what learners do when confronted with input. The two most important principles are these:[3]

(i) LEXICAL PREFERENCE PRINCIPLE (LPP). If grammatical forms express a meaning that can also be encoded lexically (i.e. that grammatical marker is redundant), then learners will not initially process those grammatical forms until they have lexical forms (words) to which they can match them.[4]

(ii) The First Noun Principle. Learners tend to process the first noun or pronoun they encounter in a sentence as the subject.

The LPP suggests that one problem from an acquisition perspective is that parsers cannot make matches unless they have something to match to, thus speaking to one aspect of Carroll's processing dilemma for learners. For example, learners cannot parse tense markings until they have lexical forms to which these can be matched. Thus, learners' initial form-meaning connections will be lexical in nature: in the case of tense, these will be adverbial expressions (e.g. *yesterday, tomorrow, last week, right now*) and learners will simply 'miss' grammatical markers of tense. The idea here is that for some time, as learners build up a lexicon, many grammatical features that are redundant with the meanings of lexical items, will go unprocessed because the parser cannot match them to anything.[5] Such features include tense-aspect markers, person-number markers, adjective agreement markers, and many others.[6]

The First Noun Principle departs from Carroll's account of sentence processing in that the First Noun Principle claims that tagging the first noun as the subject is a universal processing procedure and not one derived from the L1. That is, regardless of whether a learner's first language is subject initial (dominant in the world's languages) or object initial, when attempting to learn a second language the learner's parsing mechanism will assume that the first noun or pronoun is a subject. This particular procedure accounts for many problems in acquisition for L2s like Spanish, Hungarian, and others that have flexible word order; that is, learners may readily encounter SVO, SOV, OVS and other orders in the input. When structures are 'frozen' in OVS patterns or if the language is NULL-SUBJECT – like Spanish – a good number of acquisition problems are created by this one parsing procedure. As in the case of Carroll, learners can only overcome this problem when the facts of the real world do not match the parsing.

Test Case: Word Order in Spanish

One particular learning difficulty in Spanish involves word order. Spanish is not a strict SVO language as is the case in English and other languages. As we will see with some examples in a minute, Spanish makes robust use of SVO, SOV and OVS (in addition to VOS under certain discourse conditions). In addition, Spanish makes frequent use of OV and VO (as well as plain V) given it is a null-subject language; that is, subject pronouns are not necessary (e.g. *hablo* = I speak, *llueve* = It's raining). The pronoun system thus presents a problem for learners. It takes some time for learners to construct an underlying MENTAL REPRESENTATION that not only includes the pronouns and what they mean, but the abstract syntactic constraints that govern movement of constituents. Let us examine the following sentences:

(3) Juan se levanta.
     John REFL-gets up.
     John gets up.
(4) Se levanta.
     REFL-gets up.
     He gets up.
(5) María lo ve.
     Mary him-ACC sees.
     Mary sees him.
(6) Lo ve María.
     him-ACC sees Mary.
     Mary sees him.
(7) A María le gusta mucho Juan.
     DAT-Mary her-DAT pleases much John.[7]
     Mary likes John a lot (lit: John pleases Mary a lot.)

Work on sentence processing has revealed that learners of Spanish – at least with English as L1 – rely on the first noun strategy to interpret all of these sentences. (1) and (3) present few to no problems whereas (2), (4) and (5) are typically processed incorrectly such that the object is taken to be the subject, resulting in misinterpretations and faulty form-meaning connections. Thus, *Se levanta* is processed as 'He (*se*) gets up' and the reflexive pronoun *se* becomes allomorphic with the pronoun *él* ('he'). The learner's system gets really scrambled when sentences like (4) enter the picture and then *lo* gets tagged as 'he' as well (as in 'He sees Mary'). In (5), the dative marker *a* seems to not get processed at all as learners mistakenly take Mary to be the subject. The result of this is that learners end up with a jumbled mess for the pronoun system and their mental representation has not yet uncovered that Spanish is not strictly SVO and that there are MOVEMENT RULES, some of which are obligatory. This can persist for some time in the INTERLANGUAGE GRAMMAR.

Carroll would account for this by saying the problem resides in the L1 parser kicking in to process Spanish sentences. The English parser expects an SVO sentence and thus proceeds accordingly. She might also agree with O'Grady that computational complexity compounds with L1 expectations. In my work I have accounted for this by saying the problem resides in the universal strategy of expecting first (pro)nouns to be subjects of sentences. O'Grady would argue that an OVS order involves a layer of processing complexity not found in SVO sentences. SVO sentences do not disrupt the UNDERLYING REPRESENTATION of the sentence; that is, linear order and underlying representation match. But OVS has moved elements resulting in a gap situation. The linear representation is OVS but according to O'Grady the underlying representation would be $[_S \ldots [_{VP}$ lo ve $\ldots]$ Maria] where the suspension points represent the gaps that exist from movement. The gap in sentence initial position, which is where the subject is expected, has to be checked later in the sentence when a noun is processed that can be the subject. In the meantime, a syntactic node has to be crossed: a VP. At the same time, a gap is created after the verb where the object is expected and this gap has to be checked against a noun or pronoun in order to satisfy the meaning and grammaticality of the sentence. Thus, there are two computations that have to be resolved in processing this sentence.

Clearly these accounts differ, although in the end they may be so compatible as to be fused into one model. For example, VanPatten's first noun strategy could be combined with O'Grady's computational complexity as well as Carroll's L1 parser transfer in the following way: Learners may transfer L1 processing procedures when attempting to process L2 input. If the L2 input string resembles universals of parsing, then a universal parsing procedure may kick in and override effects from the L1. In either case, acquisition difficulties increase as computational complexity is increased.

We will leave the resolution of these varying perspectives on processing for the time being because the end result – as indicated previously – is that the pedagogical intervention may very well be the same. The question that falls out from each of these perspectives is this: 'How do we get L2 learners to correctly process subjects and objects of sentences?'

Processing Instruction

Processing instruction is a pedagogical intervention in which learners are literally forced to process input correctly. In Carroll's terms, it induces failure in the parser and forces readjustment. How does it do this? Processing instruction uses what I have termed *structured input* (e.g. Lee & VanPatten, 2003; VanPatten, 1993, 1996, 2002a; see also Farley, 2005; Wong, 2004a). Structured input is input contained in activities in which learner attention is on meaning yet at the same time is manipulated in such a way as to force processing. To do this, there must be a processing problem that is identified. In the case of Spanish word order the problem is the First Noun Principle or an L1 parser-transfer problem and/or computational complexity. Once the processing problem is identified, input activities can be developed such that SVO, OVS and OV sentences alternate in what are called REFERENTIAL ACTIVITIES. Referential activities are activities that have right or wrong answers. For example, the first referential activity we might use to induce correct processing of subjects and objects might be a picture matching task. Learners would hear a mixture of SVO, OVS and OV sentences and be asked to match what they hear to one of several pictures. In the case of *Lo ve María* (him-ACC sees Mary-NOM) learners would see two pictures: one in which a boy is looking at Mary and another in which Mary is looking at a boy. If the learners take *lo* to be the subject and *María* to be the object, they will incorrectly select the first picture. When learners hear 'No, the correct answer is the second picture', the parser receives feedback that there is a problem: the real world referent (the picture) does not match how the sentence was parsed (as SVO). The parser is put on alert. Learners may next encounter another OVS sentence and the parser may make a mistake again. Then an SVO may come next and the parse will succeed. Maybe an OVS or an OV comes next and the parser may make a mistake again but start to 'pencil something in'.

It is important to remember two corollaries to the First Noun Principle when developing these activities. One corollary states that a learner's parser may rely on EVENT PROBABILITIES to interpret a sentence even if the word order says otherwise. Given the Spanish sentence *Al estudiante lo corrigió la profesora* (to the student-ACC him-ACC corrected the professor-NOM 'The professor corrected the student'), a learner may indicate that the professor is doing the correcting because this makes the most sense; in the real world, it is more probable that professors correct students and not the other way around. Another corollary says that learners may rely on LEXICAL SEMANTICS to interpret sentences. Given the sentence *Ese programa lo detesta Juan* ('John hates that program'), learners may use the semantics of the verb 'hate' to interpret the sentence. Hate requires an animate subject capable of experiencing emotion. Given programs are not animate and can not hate, the sentence must mean that John hates a program. In structured input activities, we are careful to make sure that all sentences have two nouns equally capable of being subjects and objects of the verb; that is, two animate nouns either of which is as likely as the other as being the subject of the verb. Otherwise, we are ignoring intervening processing issues that may undermine the intent of the activities.

How many trials does it take before the parser begins to attempt alternative parsing strategies? Fernández (2005) reports that for her group of learners, the mean number of trials before learners begin to consistently process sentences correctly regardless of the word order is 11.6 (STANDARD DEVIATION (SD) = 8.1, suggesting considerable INDIVIDUAL VARIATION). Her focus was word order and CLITIC OBJECT PRONOUNS, as in our example.

In typical processing instruction lessons, learners first work through several referential activities and then work through a string of AFFECTIVE ACTIVITIES. Affective activities do not have right or wrong answers but instead learners respond based on their opinions, personal experiences, and so on. A typical activity for the target structure at hand might be this one:

Select a female relative and write her name and relationship to you below. Then check off any statements that are true for you.

Nombre: _____ Relación: _____

  ❏ La admiro.[8]

  ❏ La respeto.

  ❏ La detesto.

  ❏ La llamo con frecuencia.

  ❏ La veo cuando puedo.

  ❏ La entiendo bien.

Now select a male relative and do the same.

Nombre: _____   Relación: _____

    ❑ Lo admiro.

    ❑ Lo respeto.

    ❑ Lo detesto.

    ❑ Lo llamo con frecuencia.

    ❑ Lo veo cuando puedo.

    ❑ Lo entiendo bien.

Compare your responses. With whom do you have a better relationship? Do you see these people

in the same way?

Unlike referential activities, there is no attempt to induce correct processing. Correct processing is inferred via the referential activities that preceded the affective activities. What happens in affective activities is continued and concentrated processing of OV and OVS sentences, structured in such a way that the learner will indeed continue to process the sentences correctly.

To summarize processing instruction then, we see the following characteristics:

- learners are engaged in structured input activities, not output activities;
- the input is structured to combat identified processing problems;
- referential activities force correct processing;
- affective activities reinforce correct processing;
- all activities involve a simultaneous focus on meaning and how that meaning is ENCODED FORMALLY.

Another Test Case: Inflections

Word order, pronouns, relative clauses, and so on are one thing, but what about 'simple' morphological inflections? What about such things as tense-markers, third-person -s and others? What are the processing problems here? Again, the problem depends on which account of processing the researcher follows.

O'Grady would say that the processing problems of inflections differ depending on computational complexity. If the inflection does not have to agree with anything, then it will be easier to process in the input compared with something that co-refers to something else, and that complexity is compounded when syntactic nodes must be crossed during sentence processing. In this view of things, something like progressive -*ing* in English is easier to process than a past-tense marker. The progressive marker does not have to agree with anything whereas the tense marker must agree with an adverbial or a time frame established in the discourse. This agreement crosses a VP node as in [$_S$ Yesterday John [$_{VP}$ dropped a plate . . .]. The adverb *yesterday* has been moved from its expected position inside the VP leaving a gap, as indicated by the suspension points. Agreement between the adverb and tense marker, then, must cross the VP node.

Carroll would most likely agree but would add that the issue is compounded by whether or not the L1 parser is built to handle such agreement features. For example, because Chinese does not mark tense on verbs, Chinese L1 speakers do not have this agreement check built into their parsers whereas Spanish speakers do. Thus, Spanish speakers should be able to process tense markers sooner than speakers of Chinese.

In my work, I would say that the Lexical Preference Principle is the problem. The progressive marker is easier than a past tense marker because it generally does not have to agree with any lexical item but the past tense marker has to agree with something inside or outside the sentence. Until the lexicon is sufficiently built up such that there is easy lexical retrieval during input processing, tense markers will be difficult to process (i.e. match to an adverbial phrase or time referent).[9]

In the case of something like a tense marker, it is not clear what the pedagogical implications are for the computational complexity and L1 parser transfer positions are. In my model, the implications are this: learners must first learn the meanings of some adverbial expressions and then they must receive structured input in which tense markers are correctly processed. In this case, learners would be introduced to basic adverbials, some of which they may already know: 'right now', 'tomorrow', 'next week', 'yesterday', 'last week', 'two days ago', and so on. Then they would receive referential structured input activities in which the sentences they hear do not contain adverbs and contain a random mix of present, past, and future events. They would be asked to match the sentence with an appropriate adverb. For example:

Listen to each sentence and then select the word or phrase that goes with the sentence.
(1) [learners hear: John dropped the plate]
    a. right now   b. last night   c. in two days
(2) [learners hear: Mary will eat in the cafeteria.]
    a. right now   b. last night   c. tomorrow
and so on.

Several of these referential activities would then be followed by affective activities as described previously. For example, a list of possible activities performed by the instructor the previous evening is displayed. Learners select which activities they believe the instructor did last night and subsequently put them in order. There would be no adverbials of time in the sentences.

Not Just Input

A common misunderstanding of processing instruction has been that it merely contextualises grammatical features in input-based activities (see, e.g. DeKeyser & Sokalski, 1996; Erlam, 2004; Salaberry, 1997; Toth, 2000). When this is the case, both researchers and practitioners have missed the point that unless the activities tackle a particular processing problem and force learners to process/parse sentences in ways they would not do otherwise, then there is no processing instruction. Or, if activities fail to consider intervening processing issues (e.g. lexical semantics, event probabilities), the impact of the activities could be diminished if not nullified. Thus, processing instruction goes beyond other approaches predicated on much simpler notions such as awareness. Here I am referring to text enhancement, input flood, recasts and others. Under these approaches, the idea is that if formal features are made more salient in the input, they will attract learner attention and if learner attention is directed to formal features, there is a greater likelihood they will be processed in some way (see, e.g. Gass, 1997; Schmidt, 1995, and elsewhere; Sharwood Smith, 1993). What makes these approaches simpler (and, as seen in the literature, less successful in the long run) is they ignore the problem of processing; just because something is made more salient or more frequent in the input does not mean that learners will process it correctly or even process it at all (see, e.g. the discussion in Wong, 2005 as well as Wong & VanPatten, 2003). To put this another way, how is it that these approaches ensure that learners actually make correct FORM-MEANING/FUNCTION MAPPINGS between formal features of language and the meanings and functions they express? A simple case in point with English dummy *do*: when learners hear questions such as *Do you wanna go? Do you think he's right?* How do we know they process the dummy verb as an auxiliary without meaning whose function is to carry person and tense as opposed to some kind of question marker as is used in, say, Japanese? Thus, learners may indeed 'notice' *do*, but they may process it incorrectly (which explains why we encounter learner utterances such as *Do you can do these?*).

Processing instruction, then, goes beyond the concept of merely noticing something in the input and aims at two things: (1) altering learners' processing procedures (in the long run) and (2) getting learners to make correct (better) form-meaning/function mappings (in the short and long-run). Processing instruction has not been without critics, to be sure. One major criticism appears in DeKeyser *et al.* (2002; see also Salaberry, 1998). This particular criticism is that processing instruction contains an inherent contradiction: it purports to promote acquisition and yet contains both explicit instruction (i.e. explanation) and negative evidence. Prior to structured input activities, learners generally receive some kind of explanation about what they are going to learn. During referential activities, learners are told whether their answers are correct or not; this may or may not be accompanied by any reference as to why they are wrong when they answer incorrectly. ACQUISITION, by definition, is not amenable to explicit instruction or negative evidence; only LEARNING is (in a Krashenian sense). In VanPatten and Oikennon (1996), Wong (2004b), Farley (2004), Sanz and Morgan-Short (2004) and Fernández (2005), it has been shown that explicit information/instruction is not a necessary component of processing instruction nor a causative factor; structured activities alone are sufficient,[10] albeit it seems that explicit information can help learners BOOTSTRAP themselves into processing quicker than if it is absent, at least for some structures but not for all (Fernández, 2005). That explicit information/instruction is sometimes beneficial but is not necessary is completely consistent with the definition of acquisition, that is, acquisition being a byproduct of comprehension. In processing instruction, what explicit information actually does is push accurate comprehension (parsing) along. If learners are told how to interpret a sentence and are given information about what parts of sentences mean, this promotes comprehension. Promoting comprehension in turn promotes acquisition.

As for negative evidence, there are two issues here. The first concerns what negative evidence is. Negative evidence that cannot work is explicit correction, telling learners not to say it one way but to say it another, and so on. This is called direct negative evidence. There is also INDIRECT NEGATIVE EVIDENCE; evidence about doing something wrong that comes in the way of a confirmation check, a recast, or some NEGOTIATED MEANING. It is generally accepted in all theories that such indirect evidence can indeed be useful to acquisition but that it cannot be necessary because it is inconsistently offered and is sometimes contradictory (see, e.g. Marcus, 1993, for L1 and Schwartz, 1993, for L2). So, indirect negative evidence in and of itself is not the problem; the issue deals with robustness of its provision. The second issue regarding negative evidence has to do with input and output. Negative evidence in the general literature refers to evidence triggered by learner output. In processing instruction, negative evidence is a response to learner processing of input. If learners select picture A to match with an utterance when only picture B illustrates what the utterance means, they are told that their selection is wrong. In this scenario, learners are not getting negative evidence about their output. They are getting information that their comprehension is wrong. Again, assisting comprehension is consonant with the processes involved in acquisition, that is, comprehension is a precursor to acquisition. The kind of negative evidence offered during structured input activities is precisely what learners would need in the natural world to correct processing problems and enhance comprehension. That is, they would need to be confronted with a mismatch between what they are observing and what they think they are hearing (Carroll's failure scenario). This type of mismatch forces the processors to readjust themselves and add or delete processing procedures. In processing instruction, rather than wait for this to happen accidentally as it would in the real world – or maybe never happen – the issue is simply forced early on. What is more, in structured input activities, the feedback is consistent and it is constant; it is not haphazard as it might be in the real world during communicative interactions during which learner miscomprehension may go unnoticed.

Processing instruction has enjoyed a rich and robust research agenda as evidenced in the many publications investigating it and the variables contained in the research design. The basic findings of the research are these:

- processing instruction is better than more traditional approaches to grammar in which drill and form-only activities either predominate or precede a focus on meaning (Cadierno, 1995; VanPatten & Cadierno, 1993) and is always as good as and sometimes better than approaches in which output activities are all meaning-based (Benati, 2005; Collentine, 1998; Farley, 2001; Silver, 2000);
- explicit information is not necessary for processing instruction; structured input activities alone are sufficient to induce changes in learners' mental representations of language (Benati, 2004; Farley, 2004; Sanz & Morgan-Short, 2004; VanPatten & Oikennon, 1996; Wong, 2004b) although learners may process some structures sooner than others when explicit information is provided prior to structured input activities (Fernández, 2005), assuming of course learners understand the explicit information;
- the beneficial outcomes of processing are reflected by a variety of assessment tasks, including INTERPRETATION TASKS and OUTPUT TASKS ranging from sentence level to video-narration (the above research plus Sanz & VanPatten, 1998);
- processing instruction appears to have durable effects, not just SHORT-TERM EFFECTS (VanPatten & Fernández, 2004).

Conclusion

As the field of SLA continues to explore the nature of input processing as a fundamental component of acquisition, explanations about why learners have difficulty with some structures as opposed to others will compete. In this chapter, we briefly examined three: O'Grady's, Carroll's and mine. To some degree they compete; in other ways they are complementary. But competing accounts of input processing do not necessarily mean that PI is somehow fundamentally flawed or that we cannot continue to explore the limits of its applicability in instructed SLA. As I have argued elsewhere (VanPatten, 2004b), the results of research on PI itself (leaving aside any model of input processing) are simply too suggestive not to think we are on the right path in terms of an overt pedagogical intervention – and this intervention is consonant with basic ideas of acquisition, such as, acquisition's dependence on input and a primary focus on meaning. As processing accounts evolve, PI may remain the same but instead have a different rationale for its benefits. In the end, my belief is we will converge in the classroom as we will in the theory and our conclusion will be this: processing matters.

Notes

1. NOM = nominative, ACC = accusative, RC. Prs. = relative clause, present tense. Thus, *lul* is the accusative marker in Korean, *nun* is the relative clause marker, and *ka* is the nominative marker.
2. This point was originally made by White (1987).
3. There are corollaries to these principles, but they are not necessary for the present discussion. See VanPatten (2004a, 2004b) for details.
4. This is a revised version of the original LPP and is based on discussions in Harrington (2004), Carroll (2004b) and VanPatten (2007).
5. An earlier version of the LPP suggested that the parser simply skipped over redundant markers, an account not as satisfactory as the current one.
6. A number of researchers have noticed the same thing in the output of learners, namely, that they rely on lexical forms (words) rather than grammatical markers to signal information. Thus, in the early output of learners, tense is signaled by adverbs and adverbial expressions rather than verb inflections (see, e.g. Bardovi-Harlig, 2000 and Klein, 1986).
7. DAT = dative.
8. The sentences translate as 'I admire her, I respect her, I hate her, I call her often, I see her when I can, I understand her well'. The sentences in that follow, regarding a male relative, translate as 'I admire him, I respect him', and so on.
9. It should be noted that early research on orders of acquisition revealed that learners of English as L2 mastered verb morphemes in the following order: *-ing*, past tense, 3rd person *-s*, which is predicted by the principle discussed here (see, e.g. Dulay & Burt, 1974a, as well as the discussion of the morpheme order studies in Lightbown & Spada, 2006). For a perspective that involves current linguistic theory, see Hawkins (2001, Chapter 2).
10. For those involved in L2 situations for which there is no common L1 that an instructor may rely on to explain something, the fact that structured input activities alone are sufficient to push acquisition along should help to overcome the language barrier.

Chapter 3

Input and Second Language Development from a Dynamic Perspective[1]

MARJOLIJN VERSPOOR, WANDER LOWIE and KEES DE BOT

Introduction

Can one acquire a second language effectively only through meaningful INPUT without being provided with opportunities for output, interaction, or explicit instruction? Verspoor and Winitz (1997) present data that suggest that it is possible for intermediate learners of ENGLISH AS A SECOND LANGUAGE to improve their receptive English vocabulary, grammar and reading skills just as much through a pure listening comprehension approach as through an approach that involves output and meaningful interaction in a classroom setting. What factors could play a role in making such an approach effective?

Linguists such as Krashen (1985, 1994) and Long (1996) maintain that meaningful input is one of the most important factors in language development in general and in SECOND LANGUAGE DEVELOPMENT[2] (SLD) in particular. Without continued input, there is no ACQUISITION and ultimately no retention of the skills in the second language. For a definition of 'input' and 'input processing', we will follow VanPatten and Cadierno (1993: 46). Input is language that encodes meaning to which the learner attends for its propositional content. However, the relationship between input and LEARNING may not be straightforward. For input to lead to acquisition or learning, it needs to be processed. Input PROCESSING involves using those strategies and mechanisms that help make connections between particular language forms and their meaning during comprehension. At the same time, comprehension is not limited to language processing, as one can comprehend a message by looking at a picture. In addition, subtle differences in the way input is processed may affect comprehension. For example, Anderson and Lynch (1988) point out that there are degrees in processing input, ranging from total non-comprehension due to an inability to segment a continuous stream of speech to full comprehension, enabling a listener to construct a coherent interpretation. In other words, the same input is not processed in the same way by all learners. Taking a dynamic perspective as a starting point, we claim that the same input is not processed in the same way by the same learner at different times because the learning process itself is constantly changing in a learning/ attrition continuum due to a complex, dynamic interaction between input and all other factors affecting language development.

In this chapter, we will look at the role of input in language development and SLD from a Dynamic Systems Theory (DST) perspective, which implies that development is non-linear, adaptive, interactive, resource dependent and self organising and results from both interaction with the environment and internal re-organisation (Thelen & Smith, 1994). In addition, language learning is an iterative process, which means that the present state of the learning system is the result of all previous steps or iterations (Van Geert, 1994). We will consider a number of specific learning mechanisms that have been proposed for language learning. In the end, we will come back to our initial question in more detail and explain how a DST perspective can account for the language acquisition that may take place under a comprehension approach.

The Basic Characteristics of Dynamic Systems

> If the world were formed by stable dynamical systems, it would be radically different from the one we observe around us. It would be a static, predictable world, but we would not be here to make the predictions. (Prigogine, 1996: 55)

We argue that just like the world, a language – a first or second one, in society or in an individual – is not a stable system and therefore it has not been possible to make exact predictions concerning a number of issues in the field of SLD. For example, despite years of rigorous research into the role of input in SLD, we still cannot predict exactly what and how a learner will acquire from it. However, before elaborating on the role of input in language development from a dynamic perspective, we will first explain what we mean by Dynamic Systems Theory (DST) and what some of its main characteristics are. The approach we present here is part of what has become known as 'nonlinear dynamics'. It results from findings in astro-physics, economics and population studies that state that linear models predicting changes on the basis of a set of the parameters cannot explain what actually happens (Nicolis & Prigogine, 1989). In linear dynamics, systems tend to reach a stable equilibrium, but many real-life processes such as health, real-life human relationships and language development appear never to reach such a state. One of the crucial assumptions of nonlinear systems is that such a stable END STATE may never be reached (Lewin, 1999).

In brief, DST is the science of the development of complex systems over time. Complex systems are sets of interacting variables. A striking example of a simple complex system is the double pendulum: while it has only two variables or degrees of freedom, the trajectory of the swing is very complex.[3] Like in many complex systems the outcome of the development over time (the exact trajectory of the swing) cannot be predicted because the dynamic interaction of the variables keeps changing over time and therefore leads to unpredictable outcomes. Another characteristic of dynamic systems is that they are nested. Every system is always part of another bigger system, with the same dynamic principles operating at all levels. Consequently, dynamic systems are characterised by what is called 'complete interconnectedness': when one variable changes, this change will affect all other variables that are part of the system.

As they develop over time, dynamic sub-systems have a habit of moving spontaneously towards specific states, which are preferred, though unpredictable: so-called 'attractor states'. An example of different attractor states is the change of the gait of a horse: with increasing speed, the gait will change from a trot to a gallop. However, this transition is not only determined by the change in speed, but comes about as an interaction of speed, the surface, the horse's motivation, the interaction with the jockey, and so on. States that are never preferred and settled in are so-called 'repeller states'.

Stable dynamic systems are those in which slight changes in the initial conditions produce correspondingly slight effects. But the development of a dynamic system may also be highly dependent on its initial state, where 'small perturbations in the initial conditions are amplified over the course of time' (Prigogine, 1996: 30) and minor differences at the beginning can have dramatic consequences in the long run. This is called 'the butterfly effect', a term proposed by the meteorologist Lorentz to account for the huge impact small local effects may have on global weather (Gleick, 1987). This observation is closely related to the notion of non-linearity. The size of an initial perturbation of a system and the effects it may have in the long run do not normally show a linear relation. Some minor changes may lead to major effects, while these major perturbations may be absorbed by the system. The system will ultimately tend to settle into an attractor state from a variety of initial states.

As systems are constantly changing in interaction with their environment (that is, with other systems), they will show variation, which makes them variably sensitive to specific types of input. And the same input may have different effects at different moments in time. In natural systems, development is dependent on resources: analogous to the double swing in a natural environment where friction is present, all natural systems will tend to come to a standstill when no additional resources are available to sustain them.

So far, we have described the main characteristics of DST and how they may apply to complex systems in general. In the following section, we will argue that a language system can also be seen as a complex system in which sub-systems interact continuously with each other and with their environment. Therefore, language development can be seen as a non-linear process in which complexity is an emergent rather than a fixed property. Another point is that at different stages in the development of language, the system may be affected differently by specific factors, depending on available resources and the development and ENTRENCHMENT of different attractor states.

Language Development as a Dynamic Process

As several authors have now argued (De Bot *et al.*, 2005, 2007; Larsen-Freeman, 1997; Van Geert, 1991; Verspoor *et al.*, 2004), language in general and an individual's language system in particular can be seen as a dynamic system in its own right as it includes the present knowledge of all the individual's varieties and languages which continually interacts with internal and external forces and therefore is never the same at any two points in time. Unlike the GENERATIVE LINGUISTIC view (e.g. Chomsky, 1986), which assumes that there are steady states in autonomous language systems, a DST view holds that within the larger system of a language used by a speech community, there are many interdependent sub-systems, among which are the unique language systems of individuals that continuously interact with each other. Similarly, the knowledge one individual has of different languages and varieties can be considered as a dynamic system in its own right, and it will change over time due to a complex interaction of a wide range of factors, such as the amount of exposure to and attention given to them.

Whereas some non-generative, older behaviourist-based learning models implicitly assumed that learning is a linear process, the DST stand on learning is that the process is non-linear and is therefore not reversible in that it cannot be 'undone'. In a reversible model of language learning, learning is the effect of an operation on a representation in the sense that representation Y becomes representation Y' through the application of a learning procedure Z. In such a line of thinking, the reverse of such a procedure (assuming it exists) would be $Y = Y' - Z$. In other words, the learning can be unraveled by knowing the state of the representation before learning and the learning procedure. Such a learning model is implicitly assumed, for example, in programmed language learning approaches such as proposed by Lado (1964), where steps of learning are defined narrowly and learning is taking a small step in the execution of a learning procedure like analogical reasoning or pattern learning. In its structured grammar drills, the learning is completely programmed and predictable, and failure to make the next step is interpreted as non-learning.

In a dynamic systems approach, in contrast, most developmental processes, including learning, are seen as irreversible in the sense that the application of procedures does not necessarily have the same effect in all conditions and in all states a system is in. An analogy is the different stages at which it is possible to separate egg white from egg yolk. In a fresh or boiled state, there is no problem separating them, but in a scrambled state, the egg can not be unscrambled. The 'irreversibility' of learning can be illustrated with the following example. Suppose a child has learned to associate the concept of dog with positive experiences until one day the child is bitten fiercely by a dog. Depending on the circumstances, the child may not be able to completely erase the negative experience and overcome the negative associations entirely.

Language development is also non-linear in the sense that the learning does not occur smoothly. When a young child is in the process of learning his or her first language, the changes are very rapid and noticeable. However, the system never stops changing and even an adult L1 changes over time as a person may adopt new vocabulary items and expressions or adapt his or her pronunciation or grammar. Changes in L1 may actually be most noticeable when an adult is exposed to an L2, as both his or her L1 and L2 will be affected (Kecskes & Papp, 2000). Interestingly, from a DST perspective, language acquisition and attrition are both forms of development. Another example of not only non-linearity but also interconnectedness in the learning process can be derived from the role of PRECURSORS. Van Geert (1991) and Robinson and Mervis (1998) show that syntactic and lexical development in children can best be modelled as a precursor model in which the development of syntactic aspects of language is dependent on lexical development. The grammatical system will only become more complex once a threshold in lexical development is reached. These findings support the idea of limited resources in the sense that lexical development seems to level off once syntactic development shows a spurt, suggesting that the available resources can only be spent once, and that lexical and syntactic developmental processes compete for resources.

Learning a language means discovering and storing meanings of words and patterns of combinations of words in different stages. In L1 acquisition the child first has to establish what Clark (2003) has called ontological categories. The most important categories are Objects, Actions, Events, Relations, States and Properties. The child has to find out how these categories are given form in his or her language. As Croft (1991) shows, there is a strong correlation between word class and ontological category: nouns typically denote objects, verbs denote actions and adjectives denote properties.

How children learn to link word types and categories is a matter of considerable debate in the L1 acquisition community. In the UNIVERSAL GRAMMAR/ UG tradition (Chomsky, 1986), it is assumed that children have inborn knowledge of syntactic categories and their abstract properties, so their task is basically to uncover the forms that go with those categories. In the Usage-Based tradition led by Tomasello (1999), no such inborn knowledge is assumed, and it is claimed that both the ontological categories and the word class distinctions can be learned with general learning mechanisms in interaction with the child's rich linguistic environment. Moreover, the usage-based tradition holds that grammatical categories do not exist a-priori, but are 'temporal, emergent, and disputed' (Hopper, 1998: 156).

In research on L1 development it has been proposed that learning the link between word classes and categories takes place through what has been called BOOTSTRAPPING.[4] The term refers to mechanisms through which a simple system activates a more complicated system. In language acquisition theory, three types of bootstrapping have been proposed: syntactic, semantic, and pragmatic. All three are based on simple mechanisms to arrive at more complex knowledge about form-function mappings.

Syntactic bootstrapping (Landau & Gleitman, 1985) refers to the hypothesis that syntactic information is used to arrive at the meaning of words. When new words are encountered in a sentence that can be parsed on the basis of available syntactic knowledge, this knowledge is used to infer meaning components of that word. Most L1 research has focused on verbs, and the idea is that the number of arguments a verb appears with and how these are arranged provide clues to the meaning of the verb (see Gleitman, 1990). Semantic bootstrapping refers to the hypothesis that children utilise conceptual knowledge to create grammatical categories when acquiring their first language. In accounting for the way in which children learn the formal vocabulary of the adult grammar, Pinker (1984) has proposed the Semantic Bootstrapping Hypothesis. This hypothesis states that children infer the identity of syntactic entities in input based on the presence of semantic entities. This is seen as evidence for how semantic categories tend to bootstrap syntactic categories, showing that innate syntactic knowledge has to be applied (see also Pinker, 2003). The assumption behind semantic bootstrapping is that children have inborn knowledge about syntactic categories, but they need to find instances of these categories in the input. Grimshaw (1981) has suggested that children are also endowed with what she calls 'semantic flags' to notice differences between ontological categories, like 'action' or 'concrete object'. They will use the combination of knowledge on syntactic categories and knowledge of ontological categories to map forms and functions in the input. In addition, the child will receive contextual and morphosyntactic information to determine category membership. She will notice when learning English that some words are preceded by words like 'the' or 'a' and that multiple instances are referred to with words ending in -s.

Semantic and syntactic bootstrapping have their origin in the UG tradition of L1 development. They are based on innateness assumptions for both word classes and ontological categories. The empirical support for both types of bootstrapping is limited and there does not seem to be an argument to prefer one over the other as an explanation for some of the basic mechanisms of language development. As Bowerman and Brown (2006: 39) conclude in the introduction to their book on cross-linguistic aspects of argument structure, 'both semantic and syntactic bootstrapping can provide the child with valuable information. But (that) these two procedures must often work together in a dialectic to arrive at a satisfactory outcome, rather than running off separately'.

One problem with both syntactic and semantic bootstrapping is that they are based on the assumption that children use and perceive words in terms of clear syntactic categories: for example, a word is used as a noun, verb, preposition or another word class. A study on the development of the use of prepositions in language development by Van Geert and Van Dijk (2003) suggests that such adult-like categories do not apply in the early stages of development, but as a DST perspective would predict, they emerge during the developmental process. Using inter-rater reliability data of transcribers of child language, they show that the dichotomies (e.g. it is a preposition or not) can be replaced by a fuzzy logic approach in which the 'degree of membership' is used to categorise elements of speech. Rather than classifying a word like 'in' as a preposition from the first time it appears in spontaneous speech, it may be preposition-ish in early stages, with a category degree of membership of 0.5 rather than 1.0 (a 'real' preposition) or 0 (not a preposition at all). Degree of membership of a category does not fit well with the idea that such categories are inborn, but is in line with arguments that both category membership and meaning gradually emerge on the basis of vast amounts of input. Interestingly, the data presented by Van Geert and Van Dijk show that with increasing age of the children observed, the agreement between observers increases as well; in other words, category membership for a particular language emerges over time, but not simply because time passes, rather, because more input is used to establish patterns of use. These findings are in line with Tomasello's remark that it is not at all clear that children operate with adult-like categories (Tomasello, 2000: 67).

Pragmatic bootstrapping (Oller, 2005; Snow, 1999), in contrast to semantic and syntactic bootstrapping, refers to the hypothesis that children produce utterances to achieve communicative goals, and that in first instance unanalysed chunks are used to achieve these goals and only later on syntactic and semantic analysis on the word level takes place. According to Snow (1999), pragmatic bootstrapping is a process in which the child's early non-linguistic pragmatic intentions and achievements (e.g. 'more' for requesting food) constitute the bootstraps that she uses as a source for developing a complex grammatical system of language. Pragmatic bootstrapping is not just another form of bootstrapping following the same line of logic as in semantic and syntactic bootstrapping. In fact, the use of the term 'bootstrapping' may be misleading, because it starts from a radically different position. The main difference between pragmatic bootstrapping on the one hand and semantic and syntactic bootstrapping on the other is that in the former no innate knowledge of language is assumed, though there are language-specific perceptual mechanisms that facilitate early language learning. Thus, while semantic and syntactic bootstrapping start from the primacy of words and syntactic categories at the sentence level, and with the child as a processor of input and extractor of information from that input, pragmatic bootstrapping gives a much more active role to the child within the language learning context. The child can make sense of words, phrases and CONSTRUCTIONS because of the available visual and contextual input. The approach is pragmatic in the sense that the child uses language to achieve a pragmatic goal. Utterances are not there for their own sake but to achieve something for the child, like food, attention or fun. For this goal, the child will use whatever communicative means she has at her disposal. The child will typically use what Smith *et al.* (2003) have called 'social iterations', that is, social learning events in other people that provide cues for effective communication. Basic notions like 'more' or 'no' are learned from the usage of language by peers and caretakers. Such notions are the core of utterances that are expanded over time.

One question that is not addressed in pragmatic bootstrapping is how learners discover and begin to use the patterns of the language system, traditionally called GRAMMAR. The generative view holds that children acquire a language because they have an inbuilt universal grammar, called the LANGUAGE ACQUISITION DEVICE (LAD), which gives them the 'COMPETENCE' to learn the language. Of course, children and people in general make ERRORS and mistakes when they use language, but within the generative view these slips are considered 'PERFORMANCE errors' and do not really reflect their real linguistic competence. The generative view also implies that language is a rather closed, fixed system, which is incompatible with a DST view. A theory much more in line with DST thinking in that categories emerge in development is the one developed by Bates and MacWhinney. They reject the Chomskyan notion of 'competence' and prefer to use the term 'performance grammar', which they define as 'A unified theory of pragmatic, semantic and perceptual strategies that adults and children use to comprehend and produce sentences, inside and outside of a discourse context' (Bates & MacWhinney, 1981: 174). Based on this definition of grammar, Bates and MacWhinney developed their Competition Model. In agreement with the notion of 'pragmatic bootstrapping' discussed above, this model is based on the assumption that there is a direct mapping between the functional level (i.e. the representation of the meanings and intentions to be expressed) and the formal level (i.e. the forms in the surface structure of a sentence that express those meanings and intentions). It is also assumed that language acquisition and later sentence interpretation takes place on the basis of a limited number of sets of information or 'cues'. Instances of such cues are word order patterns, subject/verb agreement, case markings and degrees of animacy. For example, in most English sentences, the subject occurs before the verb and subject/verb agreement is often not explicitly marked, so in English, a strong 'cue' would be the word order (the first nominal is usually the subject) and a much weaker cue would be subject/verb agreement. In other words, an English speaker is likely to interpret a sentence such as 'The cow lick the boys' as an event in which the cow is doing the licking, even though the verb actually agrees with 'the boys'. In Dutch, however, where verb/subject agreement is marked more often, the translation equivalent 'De koe likken de jongen<u>s</u>' would be more likely to be interpreted as an event in which the boys lick the cow because the verb has a plural marker. Each language system has its own assembly of different cues that interact in complex manners, but cues that are very frequent or very salient in the input are more robust than cues that are very infrequent or subtle, and learners only gradually develop a feeling for the role of such cues in the language to be learnt. Because it is impossible to give an exact set of rules to explain how this assembly of cues interact to express a meaning, the role of different cues in different languages is thought to take place mainly implicitly and not every learner will acquire the language in exactly the same manner. In other words, the learner has to be exposed to the language to pick up on all the different cues and discover how they interact.

To summarise this section, we have argued that language development is dynamic and that a child's grammar emerges, not because the grammatical categories exist a priori, but because the child uses language in meaningful interaction within a real world social context where the child can pick up on cues for effective communication. And in line with DST, the way he or she learns the language cannot be predicted exactly. It will depend on a great many different factors such as the language to be learned, the amount of exposure, aptitude, motivation, context, amount of meaningful interaction, and so on. In the next section, we will focus in particular on the role of input within the interactional setting from a DST perspective.

A DST Perspective on the Role of Input in Language Development

Not surprisingly, the role of input has been one of the hot issues in language learning for a long time. In different theories, it figures in different shapes: as a trigger of associations (see Elman *et al.*, 1996), a trigger of combinations of innate parameter settings in syntax (see Chomsky, 1986) and as a building block of representations (McClelland & Rumelhart, 1985). What is new in a DST approach is that the interaction between a system or organism and its input is in itself dynamic and changing over time. As Van Gelder and Port (1995) argue in the introduction to *Mind as Motion*, the main issue is change over time:

> The cognitive system is not a discrete sequential manipulator of static representational structures: rather, it is a structure of mutually and simultaneously influencing change. Its processes do not take place in the arbitrary, discrete time of computer steps: rather, they unfold in the real time of ongoing change in the environment, the body, and the nervous system. The cognitive system does not interact with other aspects of the world by passing messages and commands: rather, it continuously coevolves with them. (McClelland & Rumelhart, 1995: 3)

While co-evolving with its environment over time, a dynamic system continually depends on resources, and it continually adapts, interacts and self-organises. Moreover, first or second language development is an iterative process, which means that the present state of the learning system is the result of all previous steps or iterations. In the following sub-sections, we will address each of these aspects of dynamic systems with regard to the role of input in language development.

Input as resource

Input consists of sounds or words in print in sentences and texts, and as mentioned above, it should be seen as one of the resources that enables learning or growth (Krashen, 1985). But input is also needed to keep the system going (Van Geert, 1991); like any other natural system, language has a natural tendency to decline when not used and people may even forget their first language if it is not used. Under some models, including DST, the most commonly used metaphor is that of a connectionist network in which connections between nodes are strengthened by co-occurrence of bits of information (Rumelhart & McClelland, 1986). Non-use leads to decline of connections and accordingly to a weakening of the network as a whole. Therefore, input is needed as a resource for both maintenance and growth.

In L1 research there is a now a strong tradition of measuring the relation between a child's input and development. Data from Tomasello (2000), and Diessel and Tomasello (2000) show that there is a rather close relation between the two, in particular in early L1 acquisition. For example, Diessel and Tomasello (2000) show that there are several interacting factors that can explain the acquisition order of relative clauses by English children, but one of the main factors is the ambient language. Detailed studies that focus on the relation between L2 development and the frequency and type of input are rare, but for example, Larsen-Freeman's (1976) account of the morpheme order studies in terms of their frequency of occurrence and a whole issue in *Studies in Second Language Learning* (2002: 24 (2)) on frequency effects in language processing shows that many aspects of a second language can be accounted for in terms of their relation to frequency of occurrence. In that same issue, Ellis (2002) gives an extensive and convincing review of the literature concerning frequency effects in all components of language learning, from word segmentation and word recognition to formulaic utterances and syntax. However, it should be noted that in the studies mentioned, not only frequency but also salience and similarity are considered factors involved in acquisition.

Input and iteration

The development of dynamic systems is characterised by the occurrence of iteration, which is the repeated application of a procedure that leads to changes of the system. Although iterations may affect the whole system because of the interconnectedness of systems and subsystems, the bits of information the system deals with are specific (Van Geert, 1991). Applied to the development of language, the extraction of new information relating to a word's meaning or the learner's repeated attempts to pronounce a foreign sound can be seen as specific bits of information that constitute a sequence of iterations. Even though the learners' attentional resources are used to focus on certain aspects of the input, this does not mean that only those aspects focused on have an impact on iterative learning.

Input and adaptivity

For language development the crucial issue is that because the system is constantly changing, the input co-evolves with it. As discussed above, this means that the same piece of information will have a different impact at different moments in time because the conditions under which the interaction with the environment takes place have changed. Input becomes particularly relevant when it creates what Piaget (1970) has called 'cognitive conflict': a mismatch between the internal state of the system and the new information. Therefore, what becomes INTAKE depends on the state of a system. As Van Dijk and Van Geert (2005) argue, a system that is moving from one attractor state to the next may be more open to change than a system that has reached an attractor state. For example, once a child has developed an adequate lexicon to express what her or she wants to say, the lexicon may reach a temporary attractor state. At that time the child may focus more on forming longer utterances, and while doing so will show a great deal of variation at first, some days reverting back to one-word utterances, another day using many six-word utterances and the next day mainly three-word utterances. After a while, the range of sentence patterns the child uses will stabilise again and show less variation and another sub-system, including the lexicon, may be developing more. What is being processed, therefore, will depend on the particular developmental stage of the learner. An incipient learner of a language may miss most of what is being said or provided as input, so only some of the sounds of the words in the input may be SALIENT enough to be noticed or recognised. With increasing proficiency more can be noticed and processed. The changes in what can become intake reflect the adaptivity of the system.

Input and interaction

In classical behaviourism, there is a simple line of development of less complex to more complex and the requirement for the over learning of basic elements to enable the processing of more complex elements (Skinner, 1957). In this view, sounds (that is, PHONES) need to be perceived and recognised first before syllables can be detected, which are necessary in turn to perceive words, which are needed in turn to perceive longer sequences, and so on. In language as a complex system such a linear progression from simple to complex no longer holds. In effect, as was argued above, there are different co-evolving layers of information that interact with each other and the environment. Studies investigating aural word recognition suggest that word segmentation (according to both TRACE and SHORTLIST MODELS[5]) is strongly dependent on subtle phonemic distinctions (for an overview, see McQueen & Cutler, 2001). However, at the same time, skills in word perception also enhance the development of skills in recognising PHONEME distinctions and relations at the sentence and text level. We do not know what the elements of processing and learning are, but it is quite likely that the size and types of these chunks are not fixed over time and that they are variable across individual learners.

The gradual unravelling of meaning from the input may be seen as dynamically dependent on the learner's own developmental characteristics on a variety of levels. A term that may also be used in connection with this is Vygotsky's (1978) ZONE OF PROXIMAL DEVELOPMENT (ZPD), which relates to general cognitive development. In relation to what a child can generally learn from input and instruction, the ZPD is defined as the distance between a child's real mental age and his or her ideal mental age after a period of learning. If that distance is too small or too large, no learning will take place. Optimal learning will only take place if the input or instruction is given within the child's ZPD. However, no linear relation can be assumed between the instruction and the child's cognitive development, which has its own dynamics. This is convincingly shown by Van Geert

(1994), who developed a dynamic growth model for Vygotsky's mechanism of ZPD. Through simulating general cognitive development, Van
Geert shows that 'the dynamic relationship between the actual and the
potential development level explains not only the change in the actual
level, but also in the potential level or ZPD' (Van Geert, 1998: 638). The
idea of ZPD is reminiscent of '$i+1$' in Krashen's (1985) Monitor Model, but
the difference is that ZPD does not assume fixed stages, but rather development that takes place in dynamic interaction with all other factors, itera-
tively, including the development itself. The relative effect of input in
language development will thus be most effective when it is within the
individual learner's ZPD at that moment in time.

Provided input is within the learner's ZPD, the learner can use semantic or syntactic bootstrapping to unravel the meanings of unknown words
or to figure out syntactic patterns (Oxford, 1990). However, we believe
that especially pragmatic bootstrapping, in which the meaning of linguistic input is unraveled with the help of visual cues, as discussed above, is
the most effective type of bootstrapping at beginning stages when the linguistic input itself is not yet meaningful. The learner's strategies are basic
and therefore not really different for L1 or L2 learners or for children or
adults. The main difference is that learning strategies are sometimes used
consciously by older L2 learners in instructed settings, while in early L1
development these strategies are mostly used unconsciously (though children sometimes do engage in metalinguistic reflection when playing with
words and constructions).

Input and self-organisation: Interaction with environment and internal reorganisation

Similar to the differential effect of input at different moments in time,
the same type, whether aural or written, and amount of input is likely to
have significantly different effects for different learners, not only because
those learners have different initial conditions when taking on the task of
learning a language, but also because the way in which the different
resources will interact over time will be variable. Considering this view, it
may be better to replace the concept of 'input' with that of 'processing'
and see 'processing' as 'acquiring' or 'learning'. In the past, we tended to
think about input in language development in terms of a one-way stream
of information from the outside to the inside of a system that is in itself
stable and not influenced by the fact that is in interaction with another
cognitive and social system. But following VanPatten, it is likely that the
input a student receives, while interacting with the environment, may be
processed differently at different times, going from more meaningful-to-
form relations to less meaningful-to-form relations:

> ... learners process input for meaning, before anything else, the impli-
> cation being that given the limitations on working memory and the

nature of the learner's developing linguistic system, learners may process input in ways that are less than optimal (for acquisition that is). (VanPatten, 2002a: 241)

After the learner has processed some input for meaning and has been able to make form-meaning connections for the content words he or she will have more resources available to process the same input (or very similar input) for less meaningful forms. This clearly points to the dynamically changing nature of input processing.

Effectiveness of an Input-Only Approach

So far we have argued that a learner's receiving of input is a dynamic process in which the degree of processing depends on the developing system of the learner. The question we now turn to is whether a teaching approach consisting of input only (a comprehension-based programme) can be as effective as one that combines input with interaction and output. Comprehension-based programmes for SECOND LANGUAGE LEARNERS were originally created by Winitz and Reeds (1973), Asher (1977), and Postovsky (1977, 1981). In this section we will report on three studies to show that an input-only approach may be equally effective for teaching general language knowledge; however, as one study points out, there are limits to a 'Do it Yourself' approach, and in the very long run interaction, output and feedback may be needed for accuracy in the output (see Chapter 5 by de Jong).

The Verspoor and Winitz (1997) study referred to in the introduction is based on the premise that input should be just beyond the learner's level of language knowledge, but the authors reject Krashen's (1981) proposal that language input can be designed as a set of increasingly complex and discrete levels of comprehensibility in terms of morphosyntactic complexity. Instead, they define COMPREHENSIBLE INPUT globally and in reference to the lexicon. The approach was designed to teach components of different LEXICAL FIELDS through implicit instruction, focusing on a particular lexical field such as 'walking', 'school' or 'telephone'. Each audio tape was accompanied by a booklet that contained the text in written mode and cartoon-like pictures that made the message clear. Students determined themselves how often they listened to a particular tape, so the language course was entirely self-paced and self-regulated. Even though this approach contained neither explicit nor implicit focus on form or forms, nor any predetermined sequence of grammatical constructions, the method of only providing input turned out to be effective. There was no significant difference found on the Michigan Test of English Language Proficiency (consisting of a grammar, vocabulary and reading comprehension sub-test and a listening comprehension sub-test) between a group that participated only in the pure listening comprehension approach and a group that had course work focusing on writing, reading and speaking.

In the Verspoor and Winitz study only receptive skills were tested, but there is also evidence that an input-only approach has a positive effect on output. Lightbown (1992) and Lightbown *et al.* (2002) report on a longitudinal study in French-speaking Canada involving 800 young students beginning in Grade 3 (age eight) from four different school districts. Before they began their English classes, at the end of the first year, and at the beginning and end of two subsequent years, a variety of tests, tasks and questionnaires were administered to all students. The control group received a regular ESL programme consisting of a variety of listening and speaking activities. The experimental group engaged in a comprehension-based programme. Students read stories and other English material and listened to accompanying tape recordings, independently, without lessons, tests or feedback from their teachers. The texts were read clearly and slowly by a NATIVE SPEAKER. The readers were not graded but students were encouraged to first read a number of books from Menu 1 before proceeding to Menu 2, and so on. The first menus included some very simple material in which pictures provided very good support for understanding. Lightbown *et al.* summarise the findings of the first study as follows:

> It was found that students in the experimental programme performed at least as well as students in the regular programme on measures of listening and reading comprehension and vocabulary recognition. More surprisingly, perhaps, they also performed as well on measures of the ability to produce spoken English on a picture description task and an oral elicited imitation task. (Lightbown *et al.* 2002: 432)

Based on these findings, the authors suggested that the comprehension-based programme provided students with a special kind of 'quality input' not generally available in either AUDIO-LINGUAL or 'communicative' second language classrooms.

In a follow-up study, the same students were tested again after six years of learning English in either the experimental or the regular programme. Data were gathered from more than 225 students, but several school programmes had meanwhile switched from regular approaches to comprehension-based approaches, so only four smaller groups remained: two experimental groups of 30 (EX1) and 43 (EX2) students respectively and two regular groups of 27 (RG1) and 14 (RG2) students respectively. The students of the first three groups had participated in the original programme, but the second regular group (RG2) had not, and no ESL data was available prior to Grade 6 (age 11). Students kept on being instructed in their respective teaching approaches.

Test batteries were administered after Grade 6, 7 and 8 (ages 11, 12 and 13). No significant differences between the groups occurred in Grade 6 (at the end of elementary school), no significant differences in Grade 7, but at the end of Grade 8 differences between the groups became apparent. At that time the test battery also included a written text, which was analysed for accuracy, among other things. One surprising finding was that students from the experimental group were very poor spellers and seemed to have less access to the L2 words. However, the overall pattern in the language measures taken was that students from the experimental group performed as well as students from the regular groups. However, even though there was not a significant difference, the first regular group (RG1) showed a tendency to perform better. Lightbown *et al.* conclude in their findings of the first study that the experimental students seemed to have had a very good start in learning their second language, but eventually after six years of comprehension-only, the students had gotten bored with the approach and also performed less than their peers on written output:

> The follow-up study reported here shows that by the time they reached secondary school, students who had remained in essentially comprehension-based instruction had maintained a level of comprehension that was comparable to that of students in the regular programme. However, students in the regular programme, who were receiving more guided instruction, were able to do things with English that the students in the unguided learning situation could not. (Lightbown *et al.*, 2002: 452)

The findings of these three studies suggest that an input-only approach, provided it contains input that the learners can comprehend with the help of clear articulation and pictures or visual aids, is as effective at beginning and intermediate levels as a COMMUNICATIVE APPROACH with interaction and output. In our conclusion, we will try to account for these findings from a DST perspective.

Conclusion

We have argued that an individual's language system is a dynamic system, in which sub-systems are completely interconnected so that when one variable changes, all other variables are affected. We have focused in particular on the role of input as one factor within the language system and argued that it is one of the main resources in language development. However, the language system does not simply 'take in' input, but it interacts with it, adapts it, and reorganises itself in the process. Having established this, we need to find an explanation from a DST perspective for the findings that a comprehension approach with neither output nor interaction in the usual sense of the words and without explicit or implicit FOCUS ON FORM or forms, nor any predetermined sequence of grammatical constructions can be so effective.

As we argued above, input is a major resource and iterations are needed for learning to take place. A comprehension approach can give the second language learner an enormous amount of one-on-one input and plenty of iterations in a clear and consistent manner. The tape, CD or DVD will happily and tirelessly repeat the same words and phrases as often as the learner wants; moreover, the approach is controlled to such an extent that earlier words and phrases are repeated over and over again in new contexts, allowing for both plenty of repetition and of opportunity to make sense of new words and phrases in other contexts (for more detailed description of such a program, see Chapter 6 by Stephenson).

Every time the learner has processed a particular phrase in the programme, the language system *adapts*, *interacts* and *reorganizes*. The learning process is dynamic in that everything the learner has processed before will be available for subsequent processing of new material. Assuming the learner is motivated to learn from the input, he or she is not just a passive container that receives some input, but a very active problem solver who anticipates, predicts, and thereby interacts with the input continuously and builds on what he or she already picked up previously.

In line with DST thinking, Winitz (1981c) points out that so much must be learned simultaneously that a learner can acquire only parts of sentences and words initially; in other words, there is selective sensitivity. At first, with pragmatic bootstrapping, the learner will attempt to distil the meanings of the most salient words through the visual aids. When the learner has achieved some degree of automaticity in attaching some sense of a meaning to some of the words, he or she has enough resources left to pay attention to less salient parts such as pronunciation of some particular sounds or discovery of some grammatical regularities and semantic or syntactic bootstrapping may take place. At some points in the program, the learner may have noticed that a particular construction re-occurs quite frequently. On the one hand, the learner may then very consciously try to deduce an explicit rule; on the other hand, by merely mentally rehearsing or by repeating words and constructions, he or she will also implicitly INTERNALISE other aspects of morphology and syntax.

And what is more, the learner can do so without tiring his or her teacher and without having to be embarrassed about his or her inability to form grammatically complete utterances and he or she can do so completely at his or her own pace, letting the programme adapt to his or her own needs. We therefore feel that programs revolving around comprehension could be a viable addition or alternative in language teaching programs, especially at beginning levels to acquire a threshold level of vocabulary, in situations where the teacher may not be able to teach communicatively, for example in situations where class sizes are too large for a great deal of individual work.

Because the proof of the pudding is in the eating, we decided to learn an entirely unknown language to us, Indonesian, using a commercially available self-instructed aural comprehension method, and to conclude on a light note we will report briefly on one particular example to illustrate that the same 'input' may have different effects at different times.

In the program simple sentences that are different on one or two aspects are presented in spoken and written form and the task is to find the picture that matches the sentence heard. In the program no grammar rules are given, so all grammar learning is implicit as far as the program is concerned. We found that, as VanPatten would predict, we first focused on discovering the meanings of the content words. We easily discovered that *wanita* was a woman and a *mobil* a car, but the meaning of the word *tua* was more difficult to discover. After a while, it became clear that it means 'old'. Even though we had heard constructions such as *seorang wanita tua* or *sebuah mobil tua* from the very beginning, it was not until we were familiar with the more meaningful elements that we began to even 'notice' *seorang* and began to wonder what its function was. Is it a demonstrative, an adjective or even a verb? We began to detect and focus on the variation in similar constructions. *Sebuah mobil tua* refers to an old car but the word *sebuah* probably has the same function as *seorang* in the previous sentence, and it was not until much later we discovered that *seorang* usually refers to humans and *sebuah* to things.

One of the most surprising findings to us was how many repetitions we actually needed before we could even remember new words and phrases. We found that doing the exercises, listening to the sentences over and over again and trying to understand their meanings did not have an effect only on the aspects focused on, but also on other aspects for which almost unconsciously hypotheses were formed and tested in the background. In other words, as a DST perspective would predict, each time a particular construction occurred it was processed differently, very much depending on how much we had already 'acquired' before the time we heard it again.

Notes

1. We would hereby like to thank three anonymous reviewers for their thoughtful and helpful comments. We also would like to thank Sybrine Bultena for copy editing the manuscript.
2. We prefer to use the term Second Language Development over Second Language Acquisition because it takes account of the multitude of dynamically interrelated processes in the bilingual mind, involving both gain (acquisition) and loss (attrition).
3. See http://www.maths.tcd.ie/~plynch/SwingingSpring/doublependulum.html for an illuminating illustration.
4. This term alludes to a legend about Baron von Münchhausen, who was able to lift himself out of a swamp by pulling himself up by his own hair. In later

versions he was using his own boot straps to pull himself out of the sea which gave rise to the term bootstrapping.

5.   The TRACE model and its successor the Shortlist model describe in detail how humans are able to perceive meaningful units from a continuous stream of speech sounds. Their main idea is that we start off with a wide range of possible competing lexical candidates and that we gradually reduce the number of candidates using linguistic and acoustic cues until one 'word' is left.

Chapter 4

The Comprehension Hypothesis Extended

STEPHEN KRASHEN

Introduction

In this chapter I review the evidence for the COMPREHENSION HYPO-THESIS in oral language and literacy, and discuss the possibility that the Comprehension Hypothesis provides a plausible explanation for non-human language acquisition. The clearest data comes from several areas of research in animal language but we will also briefly consider what some of the possibilities are for other non-human species.

The Comprehension Hypothesis

The Comprehension Hypothesis states that we acquire language and develop literacy when we understand messages, that is, when we understand what we hear and what we read, when we receive 'COMPREHENSIBLE INPUT' (Krashen, 2003). Language ACQUISITION is a subconscious process; while it is happening we are not aware that it is happening, and the competence developed this way is stored in the brain subconsciously.

Studies have shown that several affective variables are related to success in language acquisition – anxiety (low anxiety is correlated with more success in language acquisition), self-esteem (more self-esteem is related to success in language acquisition) and motivation, with 'integrative motivation' (a desire to belong to a certain group), related to long-term success in language acquisition (until membership is achieved), and 'instrumental motivation' (to accomplish a task) related to shorter term success (until the task is done).

To relate affective variables to the Comprehension Hypothesis, it has been hypothesized that for input to enter the 'LANGUAGE ACQUISITION DEVICE' the acquirer must be 'open' to the input: the 'AFFECTIVE FILTER' must be low, or down. This view considers affective barriers to be outside the 'language acquisition device', a hypothesis that predicts that affective factors will not influence the nature of acquisition or the order of acquisition of the parts of language (Krashen, 1982a, 2003).

Smith (1988) hypothesises that for language acquisition to take place, the acquirer must consider himself or herself to be a potential 'member of the club' of those who speak the language. It is easy to translate this idea into the affective filter framework: When integrative motivation (Gardner & Lambert, 1972) is high and anxiety is low, the affective filter is lowered, and those late-acquired aspects of language that mark club membership are acquired.

Club membership explains why we do not always acquire all varieties of language we are exposed to, why, for example, older children prefer the language of peers over the language of their parents.

The Comprehension Hypothesis has had several inventors and has been known by several different names. I have referred to it as the INPUT HYPOTHESIS in previous publications. Well before my work began, Frank Smith and Kenneth Goodman have hypothesised that 'we learn to read by reading', by understanding what is on the page (e.g. Goodman & Goodman, 1979; Smith, 2004). Asher (2000) and Winitz (1981c) among others, also hypothesized that comprehension is the mechanism underlying language acquisition in publications that predate mine.

Output Hypotheses

The chief rivals of the Comprehension Hypothesis are two kinds of 'output plus feedback' hypotheses. The SKILL-BUILDING HYPOTHESIS maintains that we acquire language when we consciously learn rules of grammar and vocabulary, and we learn to read by first consciously learning the rules of phonics. Output helps us by making our knowledge more 'automatic' through practice and by providing a domain for ERROR correction, which helps us arrive at a better version of our rule. This approach is also known as 'direct teaching' or formal instruction.

The COMPREHENSIBLE OUTPUT HYPOTHESIS maintains that language acquisition occurs when we say something and our conversational partner does not understand, forcing us to notice a gap in our competence. We then try again until we arrive at the correct version of the rule.

The evidence reviewed here and elsewhere (references to follow) strongly supports the Comprehension Hypothesis for both literacy and language development, and the evidence for both is similar.

Direct Confrontations

We first examine direct confrontations, studies in which comprehension-based methods are compared with methods based on rival hypotheses.

Experimental studies

For SECOND LANGUAGE ACQUISITION at beginning stages, comprehensible-input based methods such as TOTAL PHYSICAL RESPONSE and NATURAL APPROACH have been shown to be more effective than skill-building based methods (for reviews, see Krashen, 1982a, 1994, 2003). For beginning literacy development in the first language, students in classes in which more real reading is done outperform those in classes in which less reading is done (Krashen, 2002a).

The results at the intermediate level are similar. In SECOND LANGUAGE DEVELOPMENT, comprehensible subject matter teaching in the second language, known as 'sheltered' subject matter teaching, has been shown to be as or more effective than traditional intermediate instruction for literate, intermediate level foreign language students (research reviewed in Krashen, 1991).

In both first and second language development, students who participate in classes that include in-school self-selected reading programmes (known as sustained silent reading) typically outperform comparison students, especially when the duration of treatment is longer than an academic year (reviews include Krashen, 2003, 2004, 2005).

Correlational studies

Crucial correlational studies are those that compare the Comprehension Hypothesis with competing hypotheses, using multivariate methods.

Using multiple regression, Gradman and Hanania (1991) reported that 'extracurricular reading' was a strong and significant predictor of performance on the TOEFL examination for international students taking the test abroad. Extremely problematic for OUTPUT HYPOTHESES was the result that the amount of 'extracurricular writing' and 'extracurricular speaking' reported were negatively related to TOEFL performance.

Lee (2005) examined predictors of writing performance of university students studying English as a foreign language in Taiwan. The results of a structural equation model analysis revealed that the amount of free reading students reported doing was a significant predictor of writing performance, but the amount of free writing done was not. Also, students with a stronger belief in the efficacy of reading and writing instruction did not do better on the writing test.

The Effect of Applications of Rival Hypotheses

Increasing comprehensible input clearly results in more language acquisition and more literacy development; we consistently see positive correlations between the amount of reading done and progress in reading, as well as the amount of aural comprehensible input received and language development (Krashen, 1982a, 1988a, 2003). But adding more direct instruction or output either does not result in more development or results in only very modest improvement. When improvement occurs, it occurs just where the MONITOR HYPOTHESIS predicts it will.

Direct instruction: Grammar

Studies done over the last century have failed to find a significant effect for the teaching of grammar on the reading and writing of NATIVE SPEAKERS of English (for reviews, see Hillocks, 1986; Krashen, 1984).

In the field of second language acquisition, a parade of studies done in the last decade has attempted to demonstrate that grammar instruction is beneficial. Truscott (1998) and Krashen (2003) have reviewed many of these studies and conclude that they only demonstrate that grammar study has a very limited effect: The subjects used in these studies are students who are familiar with grammar study and who generally accept the claim that grammar study is useful. Yet, after a considerable amount of study, gains are typically very modest, are demonstrated only on tests in which there is a clear FOCUS ON FORM, and typically fade with time.

These results are consistent with the Monitor Hypothesis: Consciously learned grammar is only available as a Monitor or an editor, and the constraints on Monitor use are severe: The user has to know the rule (see the COMPLEXITY ARGUMENT below), have time to apply the rule, and be thinking about correctness (Krashen, 1982a, 2003).

Direct instruction: Vocabulary

A few studies of direct instruction of vocabulary seem to have produced what appear to be remarkable results (Nation, 2001: 298). But the 'advantage' of these methods is only apparent. As argued in Krashen (1989), vocabulary teaching methods that appear to be very efficient do not provide a deep knowledge of words, with their full semantic and syntactic properties, generally providing only synonyms or short definitions.

Direct instruction: Spelling

There is good evidence that direct instruction in spelling has limited effects (Krashen, 1989). Here are some samples of this research. Over 100 years ago, Rice (1897) reported no relationship between the amount of time devoted to spelling and spelling achievement, when measured on tests involving words in sentences and compositions.

Cook (1912) tested high school and college students who had just completed a semester of intensive study of spelling rules. There was no difference in spelling accuracy among those who said they knew the rules and used them, those who said they knew the rules and did not use them, and those who said they did not know the rules. As we will see later, Cook also reported that few students really knew the rules.

More recent confirmation comes from Wilde (1990), who estimated that each spelling word learned through direct instruction takes about 20 minutes of instructional time. Given the huge number of words we learn to spell, this result strongly suggests that instruction cannot do the job.

Direct instruction: Phonics

The claim has been made that methods including more phonics instruction ('intensive systematic phonics') are more effective than those that include less (NICHD, 2000). Garan (2002), however, has demonstrated that students in classes in which more phonics is taught are superior only on tests in which students are asked to pronounce lists of words in isolation. They do not do significantly better on tests of reading comprehension given after grade one.

Correction

As noted above, the skill-building hypothesis claims that language acquisition and literacy development depends on output plus error correction; when we are corrected, we change our idea of what our conscious generalization is, and come to a better version of the rule. Correction thus is thought to impact consciously learned knowledge.

The research on correction parallels the research on grammar. The results of a number of studies (Krashen, 1994, 2002b; Truscott, 1996) indicate that correction, whether in class or in the 'informal' environment, has no impact; that is, students who were corrected showed no gains, or were similar to comparisons who were not corrected or were corrected less. When error correction has been shown to have an effect, the impact is modest, and the effect occurs just where language acquisition theory predicts it should have an effect, that is, when the conditions for the use of conscious learning are met, when the acquirer knows the rule, has time to apply the rule, and is focused on form. In all studies in which error correction had an effect, the measure used emphasized form, and the subjects had done a great deal of conscious learning.

Output

As noted earlier, output fails as a predictor of second language competence when compared to reading; more speaking or writing does not result in more language or literacy development, but more reading does (see Gradman & Hanania, 1991, for speaking and writing; Lee, 2005, for writing; for other studies, see Krashen, 1994).

In addition, adding writing to reading-based methods has not been shown to have a consistently positive effect on language development (Mason, 2004; Smith, 2006).

One of the few studies to even examine whether increasing the amount of comprehensible output increases language proficiency is Nobuyoshi and Ellis (1993). Of the three subjects, only two showed improvement after interacting with a teacher who requested clarification each time they did not produce the past tense correctly. In both cases, the number of instances produced was very small and in one case the gain was modest. Also, all three subjects had studied the past tense rule, and had been clearly focused on it in the session. The improvement may have simply been the result of their being reminded to use a consciously learned rule that they had all certainly studied in school.

Izumi _et al._ (1999) and Izumi and Bigelow (2000) induced comprehensible output in several ways. In one condition, for example, they asked adult second language acquirers to write essays requiring the use of a target structure, then provided written input containing this structure, focusing subjects on the structure by asking them to underline forms in the input they felt were necessary to help them rewrite their essay. Subjects were asked to 'reformulate' or reconstruct the text they had read containing the target form. Subjects improved either not at all or very little in this condition and in similar tasks in both studies.[1]

Mason (2004) is relevant both to this section as well as the previous one. Students of English as a foreign language in Japan who participated in an in-class free reading program volunteered for one of three supplementary activities: writing short summaries of what they read in their first language (Japanese), writing short summaries in English or writing summaries in English and having their errors corrected. There were no differences in gains in reading and vocabulary among the groups. The extra output (writing) in English and getting corrected did not result in more English language acquisition.

The Complexity Argument

The complexity argument presents a serious problem for any rival hypothesis that insists on the necessity of consciously learning rules of language or writing.

As has been documented elsewhere, there are too many vocabulary items to be learned one at a time; estimates of adult vocabulary size in the first language range from about 40,000 to over 150,000 words (Krashen, 2004; Smith, 1988). Also, word meanings are often subtle and complex, for example, the difference between 'vagrant' and 'homeless' (Finegan, 1999), and word knowledge often requires knowledge of grammatical properties (e.g. whether a verb is transitive or intransitive).

A number of papers have confirmed the enormous complexity of many rules of phonics (see Smith, 2004). In Krashen (2002c) I argue that attempts to provide simpler versions of complex phonics rules result only in more complex versions.

Spelling rules are also varied and complex (Smith, 1994). Cook (1912) demonstrated that even 'simple' rules that teachers think are obvious and teachable (e.g. the famous 'i before e' rule) are often not. In his study, high school and university students took a spelling test on words that exemplified spelling rules the students had studied the previous semester. When asked to state the rules, many could not recall them at all. Those who did often recalled a version that was much simpler than the one they had just studied.

Similar arguments have been made for grammar (Krashen, 1982a), and writing style (Krashen, 1982a; Smith, 1994).

The Scarcity Argument

> I thought the answer (to how we learn to write) must be that we learn to write by writing until I reflected on how little anyone writes in school, even the eager students, and how little feedback is provided … no one writes enough to learn more than a small part of what writers need to know. (Smith, 1988: 19)

In Krashen (1994) I reviewed the research on the frequency of oral output, writing, and correction. The results in all cases confirm Smith's conclusion, and eliminate any strong view of the role of output and correction as a cause of language acquisition.

The data on the frequency of comprehensible output is similar (Krashen, 1988b, 2003). Acquirers do not talk all that much, compared to how much they hear, and when they do talk, they do not often make the kind of adjustments the Comprehensible Output Hypothesis claims are useful in acquiring new forms.

In some studies, language acquirers produced as little as one instance of comprehensible output per hour of interaction (Lyster & Ranta, 1997; Pica, 1988).

Shehadeh (2002) claims that his subjects (Shehadeh, 2001) and Iwashita's (2001) subjects did much better, producing two instances of comprehensible output per minute of interaction. According to my reading of Iwashita's paper, it was one instance per minute. More relevant, however, is the fact that in both studies, the situation was set up to explicitly induce comprehensible output, interactions in which partners had to work together to accomplish a task. Iwashita also notes that subjects made more syntactic than lexical modifications, but does not provide data. Comprehensible output is of limited value if it is only produced in contrived situations.

Acquisition Without Instruction/Output

Studies showing acquisition without instruction and acquisition without output also present serious problems for strong versions of skill-building and any output-based hypothesis.

The professional literature in reading contains many cases of children who learned to read on their own, with no, or very little, instruction on sound-spelling correspondences (e.g. Goodman & Goodman, 1982).

Very high levels of development of second language competence even for adults without formal instruction has been reported several times in the professional literature (Ioup *et al.*, 1994; Krashen, 2000).

High levels of vocabulary development without instruction appears to be the norm. Very few of those with large vocabularies report that they worked through vocabulary-building books (Smith & Supanich, 1984). In addition, 'read and test' studies confirm that readers can improve their vocabulary (and spelling) from reading alone. In these studies, readers read passages containing unfamiliar words, and are given a (surprise) test afterwards. Researchers concluded that when an unfamiliar word was seen in print, 'a small but reliable increase of word knowledge' typically occurred (Nagy & Herman, 1987: 26).

Case histories of great writers confirm that reading alone is enough to develop a very high level of competence in writing. Richard Wright, for example, tells us that in an attempt to become a writer, he 'bought English grammars and found them dull. I felt I was getting a better sense of the language from novels than from grammars' (Wright, 1966: 275).

Spelling development without instruction has been confirmed for school children as well as second language acquirers. Cornman (1902) showed that dropping formal spelling instruction had no effect on spelling accuracy for school children, whether measured in isolation or in compositions (see Krashen & White, 1991, for a confirmation of Cornman's results using modern statistics). Hammill *et al.* (1977) reported that children who had spelling instruction spelled better than uninstructed students in Grades 3 and 4, but the differences disappeared by Grades 4 and 5. This suggests that spelling instruction, when it works, only succeeds in helping children learn to spell words that they would have learned to spell on their own anyway. Haggan (1991) showed that fourth year Arabic-speaking English majors at the University of Kuwait made fewer spelling errors in their writing than first-year students, even though little emphasis was put on explicit teaching of spelling in the curriculum. Spelling competence can also grow without output, or writing: similar to results reported for vocabulary acquisition, a number of studies have confirmed that each time readers read a passage containing words they cannot spell, they make some progress in acquiring the correct spelling (e.g. Nisbet, 1941). Readers also show deterioration in their spelling ability when they read misspelled versions of words they know (Jacoby & Hollingshead, 1990).

Preparing for TOEFL by Reading

Mason (2006) provides an example of acquisition without the presence of rival approaches that has enormous practical implications. Five adult second language acquirers in Japan who had studied English as a foreign language in classes that included free voluntary reading of graded readers agreed to engage in a recreational reading program to prepare for the TOEFL. Each of the five chose somewhat different reading material, according to their own interests, with favorite authors including Sidney Sheldon, Paulo Coelho, Judy Blume and Bertice Berry. In addition, several continued to read graded readers.

Subjects read for between one to four months, and took alternate forms of the TOEFL test before and after doing the reading. The average gain was 3.5 points per week on the overall test, and improvement was seen on all three components, listening (2.2 points), grammar (3.6 points) and reading (4.6 points). This gain is about the same as one sees with a full time TOEFL preparation class given in the United States and is consistent with Gradman and Hanania's (1991) results, presented earlier, showing that reading is an excellent predictor of TOEFL performance.

In addition to the evidence presented just above, in-school free reading studies confirm the acquisition of reading ability, vocabulary, spelling and grammar without instruction.

Combination Hypotheses

Two weak forms of the Comprehension Hypothesis have been discussed, or assumed:

(1) Weak version 1: Comprehension is necessary but not sufficient. Without formal teaching and/or comprehensible output, the acquirer will not reach the highest levels of competence.

I think the evidence is consistent with this version, but only in the sense that supplements can add competence of a different kind, consciously learned knowledge of language. As argued above and in previous publications, there are limits on how much language can be consciously learned and limits on its application. Nevertheless, consciously learned language can have value. Consciously learned rules of grammar can be used to edit output when the conditions for Monitor use are met, which occurs during the editing stage of the composing process. Conscious knowledge of a few basic rules of phonics can, at times, help make texts more comprehensible for beginning readers. Occasional explanation of an unknown vocabulary word or grammatical rule can occasionally serve to make input more comprehensible, whether or not it contributes to the acquisition of the item.

(2) Weak version 2: Acquisition is slow. Conscious learning and/or output can speed up the acquisition process.

There is no evidence for this view. Direct comparisons of acquisition-based methods and methods based on rivals consistently show acquisition-based methods to be better, that is, faster. Of course, it is possible that some optimal mix of acquisition and learning will prove to be best, but so far this has not been the case. Adding output and correction, in fact, has been shown to make progress less efficient, not more (Mason, 2004).

Animal Language

Research in animal language has examined the acquisition of communication systems that animals develop in interaction with others of their own species (but not always their own subspecies), as well as cases of animals acquiring human language (sign).

Vervet monkeys

During the first two to three years of their lives, young vervet monkeys acquire alarm calls that alert others to the presence of a predator. The calls are predator-specific. Hearing a specific alarm call from one monkey results in the others taking appropriate action, for example, climbing a tree in one case, hiding in a bush in another.

The appropriate calls are gradually acquired. Very young monkeys (up to two to three years old) make 'mistakes', not distinguishing between predators and non-predators, and confusing types of predators.

When young monkeys get the call right, the call is often repeated by an adult, and this 'reinforcement' is more likely to result in a correct alarm call by the young monkey the next time. This has been interpreted as evidence for a feedback model of acquisition (Cato & Hauser, 1992; Hauser, 1996). Also in support of an output plus feedback hypothesis is the finding that young monkeys have been seen to be punished for inaccurate alarms. Hauser (1987, reported in Cato & Hauser, 1992) observed five cases in which a young monkey gave an inappropriate alarm call and was punished (bit or slapped) by the mother. In three out of four cases, the young monkey's next attempt to give the same alarm call was correct, suggesting (but not demonstrating) that correction worked. Cheney and Seyfarth (1990: 135), however, 'found no indication that mothers pay particular attention to infants who have behaved inappropriately'.

There is also evidence for the Comprehension Hypothesis. Cheney and Seyfarth (1990) report that young monkeys look at adults before responding to alarm calls, and that looking at adults increased the likelihood of a correct reaction to the alarm call, suggesting that the adults' behavior is the context that makes the alarm calls comprehensible. In addition, comprehension appears to precede PRODUCTION of alarm calls: Cheney and Seyfarth (1990: 137) report that six- to seven-month-old monkeys

consistently respond appropriately to alarm class, but the ability to produce an adult-like alarm call takes another 18 months to develop.

Birdsong

A major breakthrough in research on the acquisition of birdsong was
Marler's (1970) discovery that the white-crowned sparrow will only acquire
the song typical of its species if the song is presented during a critical
period, 10–50 days after birth. Marler demonstrated that birds that were
raised in isolation and presented with tape-recordings of their species'
song acquired 'abnormal' versions of the song if they heard it before they
were 10 days old or after they were 50 days old.

The birds acquired the songs from input alone: There was no interaction with other birds (songs were presented on tape), no communicative
use of the song, no feedback on success, no comprehensible output.

Subsequent research has increased the parallel between acquisition of
birdsong and human language by demonstrating the importance of social
context, what we have called a low affective filter and the impact of 'club
membership' (Smith, 1988). Baptista and Petrinovich (1984) reported that
white-crowned sparrows can acquire songs beyond the 50-day limit (up to
100 days) if they hear the song from a live bird, not a tape recording. In
fact, if the first song has been solidly acquired, a second song can be
acquired up to 200 days later, even if both are not the regular song of the
bird's species (Petrinovich & Baptista, 1987).

What is particularly interesting and supportive of the club membership
concept is the finding that birds prefer the live song of a different species
to the recorded song of their own species. For birds, apparently, a close
friend is better than a distant relative.

Not all species can fully succeed in song acquisition from tape-recorded
input alone. Starlings can acquire some features of song from tape, but do
much better with a 'live tutor'. Chaiken et al. (1993) reported that both
'tape-tutored' and 'live-tutored' starlings 'developed songs displaying the
basic features of species-specific song formation' (Chaiken et al., 1993:
1079), but the tape-tutored starlings' songs had 'syntactic and phonological abnormalities' (Chaiken et al., 1993). Nevertheless, the tape-tutored
starlings did much better than starlings raised in isolation, and 'were able
to abstract general rules of song organization from the training tapes ...'
(Chaiken et al., 1993).

The interesting question for the Comprehension Hypothesis is which
aspects of the live input are essential for full acquisition of birdsong. The
advantage could be context and/or affective factors (club membership).
And of course, some version of the comprehensible output or output
plus correction hypothesis may be at work, with the live bird providing
feedback on appropriateness (comprehensible output) or form (output

plus correction). From the description in Chaiken _et al._ (1993) it appears that starlings who were live-tutored were very focused on the input: 'The young birds appeared attentive to their tutors' singing. They perched near the tutor, oriented towards him, and ceased other activities' (Chaiken _et al._, 1993: 1089); West _et al._ (2004) also note that starlings, like other species, have a 'listening posture', a position in which they are quiet and cock their head to and fro while listening. When a starling hears a new sound, they 'stop vocalizing to digest the vocal bite' (West _et al._, 2004: 384).

Is output/singing necessary to acquire song?

Songbirds typically go through several stages in acquiring song (Marler, 2004: 19), a subsong stage ('reminiscent of infant babbling'), a 'plastic song' stage in which the bird sings a variety of songs heard previously (60 days duration), and a crystalization stage in which the bird chooses among the plastic songs. Anesthetising parts of the vocal control mechanism during the subsong and plastic song stages does not result in any deficit in subsequent song production in the zebra finch (Pytte & Suthers, 2000), supporting the hypothesis that actual production is not necessary for the development of song.

Disruption of the speech mechanism in later stages, however, did impair song development.[2]

Analogous studies with humans, the result of injury, have shown that language acquisition can proceed normally without babbling (Lenneberg, 1962) and that aural comprehension and written competence can develop without the ability to speak (Fourcin, 1975).

Chimpanzees acquiring human language (sign)

Fouts' descriptions of the acquisition of sign by one chimp, Washoe, contain a great deal of evidence for the Comprehension Hypothesis (Fouts, 1997).

Attempts to teach Washoe sign using direct instruction and conditioning failed, but 'Washoe was picking up signs left and right by seeing us use them' (Fouts, 1997: 78); by the time she was five, she had acquired 132 signs and a rudimentary syntax similar to that developed in early human language acquisition (Fouts, 1997: 101–103). Fouts' conclusions are consistent with the Comprehension Hypothesis:

> Nobody was teaching, much less conditioning, Washoe. She was learning. There is a very big difference. Despite the misguided attempts in the first year to treat Washoe like a Skinnerian rat, she was forcing us to accept a truism of chimpanzee and human biology: The child, not the parent, drives the learning process. If you try to impose a rigid discipline while teaching a child or a chimp you are working against the boundless curiosity and need for relaxed play that make learning

possible in the first place. As the Gardners finally conceded: 'Young chimpanzees and young children have a limited tolerance for school.' Washoe was learning language not because of our attempts to school her but despite them. (Fouts, 1997: 83)

Loulis, Washoe's adopted son, was the first non-human to acquire human language from another nonhuman. Loulis began acquiring sign right away, 'by watching his mother' (Fouts, 1997: 244), eventually acquiring 24 signs in 18 months. In a striking example of the effect of club membership, Loulis only acquired the signs he saw used by other chimps, not those used by humans.

There is, however, also evidence that direct teaching works in helping chimps acquire sign. In several instances, Washoe attempted to teach Loulis signs directly, using 'molding', taking Loulis' hand and shaping it into the appropriate sign. In one instance,

> with Loulis watching, Washoe signed FOOD over and over when one of the volunteers brought her a bowl of oatmeal. Then Washoe molded Loulis' hand into the sign for FOOD and touched it to his mouth several times ... This maternal hands-on guidance seemed to work because Loulis promptly learned the FOOD sign. (Fouts, 1997: 244)

Aliens

It is possible that alien language will be completely different from human languages. McKenna (1991) has suggested that aliens are already here and are already communicating with (some of) us: the aliens are psilocybin mushrooms and communication happens when we eat them.

Science-fiction writers often assume that at least some aliens will use ordinary human-type language, or languages that are easily translated into human language by translating devices.

The universal translator of Star Trek has little trouble doing this, acquiring and translating at the same time. Its occasional problems and hesitations reveal that it operates on the principle of comprehensible input: the translator does not try to produce and then adjust its system when the communication fails (comprehensible output) nor does it get corrected. Rather, it listens and understands, and gradually acquires the system (see e.g. *Star Trek Deep Space Nine*, Episode 30: 'Sanctuary').[3]

A great deal of communication with aliens has been reported in accounts of UFO alien abductions. In the vast majority of cases, communication from alien to human is telepathic (e.g. Fuller, 1966; Jacobs, 1998). It is not clear whether the aliens understand spoken language; Jacobs argues that human–alien communication is also telepathic (http://www.ufoabduction.com/telepathy5.htm). Clearly, research in this area has only begun.

Conclusion

It can be argued that making a reasonable case for the Comprehension Hypothesis in these domains does not add support for the hypothesis. According to the rules of science developed by Karl Popper, we only progress when we falsify a hypothesis. Finding additional evidence for a hypothesis or showing that the hypothesis applies to cases beyond those for which it was originally designed, does not add to its believability. Nevertheless, it is impressive when this happens.

Notes

1. McDonough (2005) reported a positive relationship between progress on the acquisition of question formation and the amount of modified input produced ($r = 0.67$) for Thai students of English as a foreign language. During the three treatment sessions, each lasting ten minutes, all subjects who received clarification requests produced a total of only 32 instances of modified output related to questions. As 30 students were in this group, this averages to about one instance of modified output per subject. This sheds some doubt on the relationship between amount of modified output produced and acquisition and confirms that comprehensible output is scarce (see text).
2. The changes were, however, not species atypical, but were 'within the range of variation present in songs of ... adult zebra finches' (Marler, 2004: 184).
3. In general, Star Trek gets a mixed report card on language acquisition theory. In the first episode of the series *Star Trek Enterprise*, Ensign Sato was observed using a version of the AUDIO-LINGUAL METHOD in teaching an alien language at Starfleet Academy (*Star Trek Enterprise*, Episode 1: Broken Bow). But in a subsequent episode, Sato presented a perfect portrayal of a Monitor over-user (Krashen, 1981), hesitant to speak without a firm conscious knowledge of the grammatical system of an alien language. Captain Archer persuaded her that the survival of the Enterprise was more important than the subtleties of the future tense.

Chapter 5

Second Language Learning of Grammar: Output Matters Too

NEL DE JONG

Introduction

Beginning learners of a second language often report that listening comprehension seems easier than PRODUCTION of grammatically correct structures. For example, a learner of Spanish may easily recognize gender agreement in *el coche rojo* 'the red car' when listening to a Spanish-speaking friend, yet experience difficulty in selecting the correct form of *rojo* 'red' when telling this friend about a coveted new car. In general, learners may feel that it is easier to apply their knowledge of grammar during listening than during speaking.

This ANECDOTAL EVIDENCE leads to several important questions about the nature of second language learning: if there is indeed a difference in ease of PROCESSING during listening versus production, what is the source of this difference, and what does it imply about the nature of grammar acquisition, and language learning in general? This chapter starts out with a short review of different types of knowledge involved in language learning and teaching. Then, a study is discussed that investigates the relationship between comprehension and production in learning second language grammar.

Grammatical knowledge, and knowledge in general, can exist in several forms. First, psychologists as well as linguists have made a distinction between 'explicit' and 'implicit' knowledge (e.g. DeKeyser, 2003; Ellis, 1994; Krashen, 1994; Schmidt, 1994a, 1994b; Sharwood Smith, 1994b; Williams, 1999). For example, language learners may be aware of the grammatical rules they are learning, and may even be able to articulate these rules, whether with linguistic terminology or in everyday language. Such knowledge is often referred to as EXPLICIT KNOWLEDGE. However, learners may also be able to produce grammatically correct language without being aware of the grammatical rules. Evidence to this effect can be taken to suggest that they have IMPLICIT KNOWLEDGE.

It is often nontrivial to determine whether learners have implicit or explicit knowledge of a particular grammatical rule. If learners are able to verbalize their knowledge, this may be taken as an indication of explicit knowledge. In this process, however, the learners may have verbalised a rule that they had not been aware of before, by thinking of examples they have previously heard or constructed themselves using their implicit knowledge. Likewise, implicit knowledge is difficult to assess for the very reason that the learners are not aware of their knowledge. It may only be attested in PERFORMANCE, which may also involve explicit knowledge, because learners may possess and use both types of knowledge simultaneously. It can therefore be difficult to tease apart the contributions of implicit and explicit knowledge in any given task. Implicit and explicit knowledge are not mutually exclusive. Indeed, as a rule, both types of knowledge may coexist in natural language processing.

The distinction between implicit and explicit knowledge is related to the distinction between 'automatic' and 'controlled' processing. Implicit knowledge is often considered to be automatic. AUTOMATIC PROCESSING is often characterized as performance that is typically fast and accurate. In addition, automatic processes can be executed in parallel with other processes (DeKeyser, 2001; Segalowitz, 2003; Segalowitz & Hulstijn, 2005). Whereas implicit knowledge involves automatic processing, explicit knowledge is considered to involve CONTROLLED PROCESSING, which requires attentional resources, and may be slower and more error-prone (Ellis, 2005). One way to test whether knowledge is automatic is to use a technique that is called the 'DUAL-TASK' PARADIGM (DeKeyser, 1997; Gilhooly *et al.*, 1999; Tyler, 2001). Because automatic processing can proceed in parallel with other processes, in the dual-task paradigm participants are asked to perform two tasks simultaneously. If in one task processing is automatic, there will be little interference with another, simultaneous task. This paradigm is widely used in COGNITIVE PSYCHOLOGY research, but less so in second language research. One exception is a study by DeKeyser (1997), in which students performed mental arithmetic while doing a language task. Performance on the language tasks was not affected by the arithmetic task, perhaps because that task was too easy. Performance of the arithmetic task itself was not reported. Another study (Tyler, 2001) required participants to judge the correctness of single-digit equations (e.g. $2 + 4 = 6$) while listening to a text. The difference in the number of correctly judged equations in single- and dual-task condition yielded index scores, where higher scores indicate higher processing demands of the listening task. It was found that the index was higher for non-native speakers of English who had not been given the topic of the text than for those who did know the topic and for NATIVE SPEAKERS of English (who either had or had not been given the topic). Tyler concluded that non-native speakers rely more on topic knowledge (i.e. pragmatic, or world, knowledge) in language comprehension, as compared with native speakers.

Researchers have also distinguished between 'declarative' and 'procedural' knowledge (Anderson, 1993, 2005; Anderson & Fincham, 1994; Anderson *et al.*, 1997, 1999). DECLARATIVE KNOWLEDGE includes knowledge of facts (e.g. 'Paris is the capital of France', 'In Spanish, adjectives usually come after nouns'). PROCEDURAL KNOWLEDGE, on the other hand, is knowledge of how to perform a certain task – for instance, how to drive a car or how to use the correct word order when speaking Spanish. In several studies (Anderson, 1983, 1993; Anderson & Fincham, 1994; DeKeyser, 1997) it has been found that procedural knowledge is skill-specific. This means that a skill improves most in the type of task that has been practiced (e.g. reading computer code, writing Spanish sentences), and much less – or not at all – in an opposite task (e.g. writing computer code, reading Spanish sentences). Declarative knowledge is thought to be more flexible, that is, task-independent.

A third distinction has been made between language comprehension (listening and reading) and production (speaking and writing). In particular, some evidence suggests an asymmetry between these two skills. For instance, Izumi (2003) found a difference between receptive and productive processing of relative clauses in L2 English, arguing that different types of relative clauses put different demands on processing because of word order and center-embedding. During comprehension, word order problems may be resolved more easily than center-embedding, because the former can be resolved more locally. During production, on the other hand, word order and center-embedding may place equally high demands on processing. Consistent with this idea, DeKeyser (1997) has shown that learners of an artificial language improved mostly in the skill they had been trained in, that is, in either comprehension or production. He concluded that comprehension and production rely on different knowledge systems and processing mechanisms, and therefore require separate practice.

At the same time, comprehension and production are not entirely independent. For example, some studies have shown that speakers tend to repeat syntactic structures that they have recently either produced or comprehended. This phenomenon is called SYNTACTIC PRIMING. Speakers who have just heard a sentence like 'The mother read a story to her son', are more likely to describe a picture as 'The boy gave the girl a book' than as 'The boy gave a book to the girl', although both formulations are grammatically correct. Pickering *et al.* (2000) reviewed a number of syntactic priming studies, and concluded that what is shared between comprehension and production consists of morphosyntactic and lexical information, such as gender and lexical category (noun, verb, adjective). According to this view, grammatical procedures cannot be shared, because the directions of comprehension and production are opposite.

Some researchers (see e.g. Chapter 6) have argued that a second language can be learned initially through reading and listening (comprehension) and can then be used in writing and speaking (production) as well. In the 1980s, for instance, a number of researchers argued that production should be postponed until after an initial SILENT PERIOD (e.g. Asher, 1982; Davies, 1980; Krashen & Terrell, 1983; Nord, 1980, 1981; Winitz, 1981a, 1981b). In support of this view, Krashen (1985) articulated the INPUT HYPOTHESIS, which states that SECOND LANGUAGE ACQUISITION is driven by COMPREHENSIBLE INPUT that is at a level just above the current level of the language learner ($i + 1$).[1]

VanPatten and associates have conducted several studies examining effects of a particular type of instruction on second language learning (e.g. VanPatten & Cadierno, 1993; VanPatten & Oikkenon, 1996; VanPatten & Sanz, 1995). They claim that training should be designed to change the way INPUT is processed so that students learn the relation between the form and the function of words. Since, according to their view, the same knowledge is used for speaking and writing, accuracy in production will increase as well. This instructional approach is called 'Processing Instruction' (PI). PI aims to increase the communicative value of the structure to be learned, so that form-meaning connections are formed. PI is typically contrasted with instruction that consists of rule explanations and a series of mechanical, meaningful, and communicative output activities. Evidence and counterevidence for the effectiveness of PI is reviewed by VanPatten (2002b). Not all grammar rules easily lend themselves to form-meaning connections, however, so PI may not be appropriate for all types of grammar instruction. For instance, gender agreement in languages such as Spanish is often independent of lexical meaning: many words that are marked for grammatical gender refer to concepts that lack obvious masculine or feminine properties.

Further, some evidence suggests that comprehension practice alone may not be sufficient to increase accuracy in production; production practice might be necessary as well. De Bot (1996), for instance, argued that production practice only serves to reinforce knowledge that has already been acquired through comprehension. In other words, comprehension practice may form the basis for LEARNING, and production practice may provide fine-tuning. However, if learners start producing too early, before they have acquired knowledge about a grammar rule, they may have to fall back on other knowledge, such as default forms (e.g. a regular past tense instead of an irregular form), or their first language. English learners of Spanish, for instance, may put Spanish adjectives in front of the noun – as in English – instead of after the noun – as in Spanish. These strategies often lead to grammatical errors.

The evidence on second language acquisition reviewed above led to the following research questions.

Research question 1: Does accuracy in producing a grammatical CON-STRUCTION improve after listening to many instances of that construction even in the absence of forming form-meaning connections?

Research question 2: Does an early start with using a grammar rule in speaking lead to persistent grammatical errors in speaking?

The present study focuses on learning to use grammar rules in spoken production. The goal of training was to increase implicit knowledge of grammatical patterns; explicit knowledge of grammatical rules was not targeted. Therefore, the two experimental groups were not explicitly informed of the rules. Rather, their training consisted of listening to, or speaking, a large number of grammatical constructions that represented applications of the target rules. Rich and extended practice was predicted to facilitate acquisition of implicit knowledge. The control group did not receive these examples, but instead read through an explanation of the rules. In the post-tests, the control group had to rely on their explicit knowledge. While this design was intended to contrast implicit and explicit instruction, it is important to note that the experimental groups may have discovered the rules, or formulated their own rules to account for observed patterns in the training data. To investigate this possibility, a questionnaire was administered in which participants were asked whether they had discovered a grammar rule, and if so, they were asked to describe it.

Method

Participants

The participants in this study were 59 students enrolled in non-language-related programs at a university or other institution of higher education in Amsterdam, and they were paid for their participation. Participants were informed that the goal of the study was to examine how people speak and comprehend other languages. All participants were native speakers of Dutch, and had learned English, German and French in secondary school for a period of three to six years. It is therefore expected that all participants were familiar with the concept of grammatical gender and gender agreement. Participants had little or no knowledge of any Romance language other than French. Data from four participants were eliminated from the analysis for reasons related to illness, insufficient vocabulary knowledge, technical problems, or early termination of the experiment. Fifty-one complete data sets were available for analysis.

Materials

The language to be learned was a simplified version of Spanish. There were 20 nouns, eight adjectives, two prepositional phrases, four verbs and two proper names (see Appendix). The rule to be learned was gender agreement between the adjective and noun, as shown in (1) to (4). In Spanish, the form of a great number of adjectives depends on the gender of the noun they modify. This means that if the noun is masculine, many adjectives take the suffix -o, as in *rojo* in (1a) and (3a). On the other hand, if the noun is feminine, many adjectives take the suffix -a, as in *roja* 'in (1b) and (3b). In the present study, four adjectives were of this kind, taking -o for masculine and -a for feminine. Some adjectives, however, such as *azul* in (2) and (4), do not take a suffix, and therefore have the same form for masculine and feminine. Four adjectives of this kind were included in this study. The adjectives whose form changes according to gender are referred to here as *overtly agreeing adjectives*; the adjectives that do not change form are referred to as *invariable adjectives*.

(1a) En   el   círculo aparece el   coche   roj-o   dice   José
      In   the   circle appears the   car   red-MASC   says   José
      'In the circle appears the red car, says José.'

(1b) En   el   círculo aparece la   fuente roj-a   dice   José
      In   the   circle appears the   fountain red-MASC says   José
      'In the circle appears the red fountain, says José.'

(2a) En   el   círculo aparece el   coche   azul   dice   José
      In   the   circle appears the   car   blue-[MASC] says José
      'In the circle appears the blue car, says José.'

(2b) En   el   círculo aparece la   fuente azul   dice   José
      In   the   circle appears the   fountain blue-[MASC] says José
      'In the circle appears the blue fountain, says José.'

(3a) El   coche   en   el   círculo se   vuelve   roj-o   dice José
      The   car   in   the   circle REFL   turns   red-MASC   says José
      'The car in the circle turns red, says José.'

(3b) La   fuente   en   el   círculo se   vuelve   roj-a   dice José
      The   fountain in   the   circle REFL   turns   red-FEM   says José
      'The fountain in the circle turns red, says José.'

(4a) El   coche   en   el   círculo se   vuelve   azul   dice José
      The   car   in   the   circle REFL   turns   blue-[MASC] says José
      'The car in the circle turns blue, says José.'

(4b) La   fuente   en   el   círculo se   vuelve   azul   dice José
      The   fountain in   the   circle REFL   turns   blue-[FEM] says José
      'The fountain in the circle turns blue, says José.'

Two types of sentences were used throughout the experiment. In one type the adjective was next to the noun, in attributive position (see Examples 1 and 2). In the other type of sentence, the adjective was in predicative position, and a number of words appeared between the noun and the adjective (see Examples 3 and 4). The recordings of the stimulus sentences were spoken by a native speaker of Spanish. The participants listened to these sentences on headsets, which had a microphone to record their responses in the production tasks. No translations of the words or sentences were given, but instead, line drawings clarified the meanings of the words.

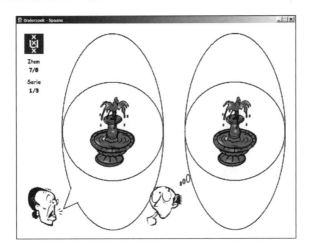

Figure 5.1 Screenshot of a trial in the sentence–picture matching task. The aural stimulus was 'En el círculo aparece la fuente roja, dice José' (*In the circle appears the red fountain, says José*)

These drawings were made specifically for this study by a professional graphics designer. The meanings of the verbs *to appear* and *to turn* were simulated by the pictures being built-up in small blocks very quickly, and by changing from white to a different color (see Figures 5.1 and 5.2). (We also refer the reader here to two other chapters: Verspoor *et al.* (Chapter 3) and Stephenson (Chapter 6), who discuss such an approach with regard to Winitz' Learnables.) The user interface for this experiment was developed by the author with Authorware 6 (McGraw *et al.*, 2000; Schmidt, 2001), and it was run on Gateway Premium II personal computers.

Procedures

The participants were assigned to one of three groups. One group of 17 participants received a training that consisted solely of comprehension tasks. A second group (18 participants) received training with production as well as comprehension tasks. The control group comprised 17 subjects. They did not receive training on gender agreement: they performed tasks identical to those of the second group but with adjectives that did not show agreement (i.e. invariable adjectives), like *azul* 'blue' in (2) and (4). This group, unlike the first two groups, received an explanation of the gender agreement rule right before the posttests. Henceforth, the three groups are referred to as ComprOnly (comprehension training only), Compr+Prod (comprehension and production training) and RuleExpl (rule explanation), respectively.

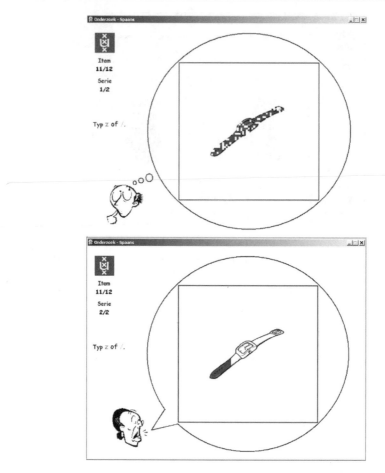

Figure 5.2 Two screenshots of trials in the self-paced listening test with attributive adjectives (top) and predicative adjectives (bottom) during the visualisation of appearing and changing color. The aural stimuli were (top) 'En el cuadro aparece el reloj rojo, cree Javier' (*In the square appears the red watch, thinks Javier*), and (bottom) 'El reloj en el cuadro se vuelve rojo, dice José' (*The watch in the square turns red, says José*)

All tasks involved either listening or speaking; there were no reading or writing tasks. The training and test tasks were performed in a computer laboratory during four 90-minute sessions over a period of two weeks. On average, the sessions were four days apart. The breakdown of training and testing into four sessions was as follows.

Session 1: vocabulary training
Session 2: sentence training

Session 3: gender agreement training
Session 4: gender agreement training and posttests

None of the participants had learned Spanish before the experiment, so the first session consisted of vocabulary training. First, words were presented together with a picture to clarify their meaning; no translations were given. Then, each word was presented and students chose which of two pictures corresponded to the word (e.g. for the word *el coche*, 'the car', student chose between a picture of a car and picture of a fountain). Productive knowledge was trained in a task in which students named a picture. The correct answer was played and students judged whether they had named the picture correctly. Adjectives were presented in the masculine form only, which may have affected comprehension and production during the training and testing of gender agreement (see Results section).

Vocabulary tests were administered at the end of the first session, at the beginning of sessions 2 and 3, and before the posttests in session 4. Participants were required to reach target proficiency levels on each task before they could proceed to the rest of the training. The criterion for comprehension accuracy was 100%; mean response times were required to be shorter than 1.0 second (for nouns and adjectives) or shorter than 1.2 seconds (for other words). The criterion for production accuracy was 75%, and response times were required to be shorter than 4.0 seconds for all word categories. Vocabulary tests were identical for all three participant groups.

The second session consisted of training tasks in which the participants familiarised themselves with the procedures and the sentences to be used in training. This session was also identical for all three groups. All sentences contained invariable adjectives, as in (2) and (4), so that the agreement rule was not yet apparent. This session consisted of two sequences of comprehension tasks and one sequence of production tasks. Each sequence consisted of four parts: (1) a training task with attributive adjectives, (2) a test with attributive adjectives, (3) a training task with predicate adjectives, and (4) a test with predicative adjectives.

In the third session the participants in group ComprOnly and Compr+Prod performed the training tasks with the overtly agreeing adjectives, such as *rojo/roja* 'red', and *negro/negra* 'black'. This means that the participants in group ComprOnly heard sentences in which the agreement rule was applied, and the participants in group Compr+Prod also spoke sentences to which they applied the rule. Group RuleExpl heard and spoke only sentences with invariable adjectives, such as *azul* 'blue', so that they did not use the agreement rule. This session consisted of three sequences. For group ComprOnly all sequences involved comprehension. For groups Compr+Prod and RuleExpl the first sequence involved comprehension, and the next two involved production.

The fourth session consisted of two parts. In the first part, training was continued: two sequences of comprehension tasks for group ComprOnly, and for group Compr+Prod and RuleExpl one sequence for comprehension and one for production. Again, group RuleExpl heard and spoke only invariable adjectives. The second part of this session was identical for all three groups and consisted of the posttests for comprehension and production.

Training tasks

The goal of this study was to assess the effect of listening on learning, not the effect of inferring a rule from examples. Therefore, the tasks were developed in such a way that they could be performed on the basis of meaning alone: participants did not have to attend to form in order to give the correct answer. They received feedback about accuracy in the comprehension tasks by way of a green check mark/tick or a red cross.

Comprehension training task

The training task for comprehension was sentence-picture matching. The participants saw two pictures and indicated which picture matched the sentence they heard by pressing a key. Only one word was crucial for the decision: the noun; the noun in the prepositional phrase; the adjective; or the verb in the main clause. The latter was the crucial word in half of the items because it appeared near the end of the sentence and it immediately followed the adjective ending. Thus, participants were required to listen attentively to as much of the sentence as possible, including both the noun and the adjective that were relevant for gender agreement. All sentences were grammatically correct. There were 24 items in the first comprehension sequence in sessions 3 and 4, and 48 items in all other sequences.

Production training task

The training task for production required the Compr+Prod participants to orally describe a picture (picture description) within eight seconds. Then, a pre-recorded model response was played, and the participants indicated whether they thought their response was correct. All responses were recorded.

Test tasks

While the instructions during training encouraged only accuracy, the instructions for the test tasks encouraged both accuracy and speed. Reaction times were shown after individual trials and after blocks of 24 or 48 trials. Feedback about comprehension accuracy was provided by a green check mark/tick or a red cross.

Self-paced listening test

This technique involves the presentation of sentences in a word-by-word or phrase-by-phrase manner, typically with written stimuli (i.e. self-paced *reading*). Participants read the word or phrase and press a button to call up the next one. The time between button presses is an indication of the time required to read the word or phrase. These 'reading times' are expected to increase when processing difficulties arise, often as a result of ambiguity or ungrammaticality. Increases in reading times usually occur on the problematic word or phrase itself, but they might also spill over to the following word or phrase. This task has been used to provide a measure of the processing load of a number of different phenomena, including subject–verb agreement, verb–argument structure, relative clauses, and noun phrase arguments and adjuncts (Caplan & Waters, 2003; Deevy, 2000; Ferreira *et al.*, 1996; Juffs, 1998; Kennison, 2002; Konieczny, 2000; Pearlmutter *et al.*, 1999; Thornton & MacDonald, 2003; Weyerts *et al.*, 2002).

In the present study, this task was performed in the oral modality, and listening times were measured. The sentences were divided into five phrases, as illustrated in (5) and (6). Each phrase was spoken with an intonation as if it were part of a sentence. Participants were asked to listen to each sentence as quickly as possible, and to indicate at the end of the sentence whether it matched the picture by pressing a key. In each sentence, one word was crucial for the decision, as in the comprehension training task. This test consisted of 24 trials, half of which required a *match* response. Only responses to these trials were analyzed. All sentences were grammatically correct.

(5) En el círculo   – aparece   –   el coche   –   rojo   –   dice José
       PP V_1 NP   Adj V_2 + name
      In the circle   –   appears   –   the car   –   red   –   says José
           'In the circle appears the red car, says José.'

(6) El coche   – en el círculo   –   se vuelve   –   rojo   –   dice José
       NP   PP V_1 Adj V_2 + name
      The car   –   in the circle   –   turns   –   red   –   says José
           'The car in the circle turns red, says José.'

Longer listening times were expected for the adjectives, since they could show gender agreement with the nouns. Differences were expected between invariable and overtly agreeing adjectives, and between masculine and feminine adjective endings.

The presentation of the stimuli was rather unnatural because the sentences were presented as separate words and phrases, despite phrases being spoken with natural intonation. Therefore, another test was introduced as a more natural measure of processing during listening. Its content and procedures were similar to those of the self-paced listening task, except for the presentation of the aural stimuli, which were presented as uninterrupted sentences. Results of this test have been published in De Jong (2005a) and will not be reported here.[2] It should be noted, however, that the results converged with those of the self-paced listening test presented here.

Production tests

The production test was similar to the production training task, but did not include the pre-recorded model response and self-assessment. The tests each contained 24 trials, half of which contained nouns that had not appeared in the training of gender agreement, in order to test generalizability. The nouns had been trained and tested in the vocabulary tasks.

The production test was repeated in a dual-task condition. In this condition, before the drawings appeared, the participants tapped along with six clicks at 600-ms intervals. They continued tapping while they started speaking until the end of the recording. Dual-task paradigms such as these have been used, for instance, to test the influence of different types of working memory on reasoning, or to test the automatisation of language skills (DeKeyser, 1997; Gilhooly *et al.*, 1999). In the present study the paradigm was used to assess the use of explicit knowledge of the agreement rule, which requires attention and controlled processing. It was expected that consciously applying this rule would compete for attention with the tapping task, resulting in lower accuracy in the production of gender agreement, and/or in lower consistency in tapping.

Results

Vocabulary tests before and during the training sessions showed that vocabulary knowledge was good, and similar for all groups. A post-experimental questionnaire showed that all groups had explicit knowledge of gender agreement, although slightly fewer participants in group ComprOnly correctly described the rule than in group Compr+Prod and RuleExpl.[3]

Self-paced listening test

The self-paced listening test was administered after the first comprehension sequence in session three, and as a posttest. Accuracy was high (96%, 97% and 96% for the three tests, respectively) and similar for all groups, because the decisions of whether the sentence matched the pictures was reasonably easy since the vocabulary and the sentences had been trained. The response times for the first four phrases (see Examples 5 and 6) were analysed with an ANALYSIS OF VARIANCE with repeated measures. Only response times of correct responses were included.

The analysis of variance revealed that there was no main effect for Group, but there was a significant interaction of all five other factors: Adjective

Position (attributive, predicative), Phrase (prepositional phrase, verb, article+noun, adjective, main clause), Test (pretest, posttest invariable adjectives, posttest overtly agreeing adjectives), Gender (masculine, feminine) and Group (ComprOnly, Compr+Prod, RuleExpl), $F(12, 312) = 1.784$, $p = 0.050$. The mean listening times are presented in Figure 5.3. Because the five-way interaction is difficult to interpret, only significant lower-level interactions are discussed here, with a focus on the listening times of the adjectives. The lowest-level effects and interactions are not discussed.

The interaction Test × Group ($F(4, 104) = 4.791$, $p = 0.001$) shows that listening times decreased for all groups, but more so for groups ComprOnly and Compr+Prod than for group RuleExpl. More specifically, group RuleExpl's listening times were similar for both posttests, that is, the tests with invariable adjectives, and with overtly agreeing adjectives. This can be seen in Figure 5.3, where the bullets are below the triangles for groups ComprOnly and Compr+Prod, but at similar heights for group RuleExpl. This result indicates that group RuleExpl processed overtly agreeing adjectives relatively slowly. It should be noted that this was the first time they heard these adjectives in sentences.

The interaction of Phrase × Gender × Group ($F(6,156) = 2.975, p = 0.009$) reveals that listening times for feminine adjectives were somewhat longer than for masculine adjectives. A *post-hoc* analysis of variance was performed that contrasted the performance of the two groups that had heard and spoken sentences with gender agreement (the 'trained' groups, ComprOnly and Compr+Prod) with the group that had not yet heard or spoken such sentences (the 'untrained' group, RuleExpl). It showed that only the trained groups listened longer to feminine adjectives; for group RuleExpl there was no significant difference between the masculine and feminine adjectives. In addition, the Phrase × Test × Gender interaction ($F(6, 312) = 3.879, p = 0.001$) shows that for adjectives the effect of gender showed up only with overtly agreeing adjectives. Therefore, it seems that it was feminine agreement that was processed relatively slowly by groups ComprOnly and Compr+Prod.

The interaction between Phrase, Test and AdjectivePosition ($F(6, 213) = 21.084, p = 0.000$) reflects that in the posttests all phrases were listened to more quickly in sentences with overtly agreeing adjectives than with invariable adjectives (probably due to a retest effect), except for prepositional phrases, nouns in the predicative condition, and – crucially – feminine adjectives in predicative position. Taken together, these results suggest that feminine adjectives were processed relatively slowly, and primarily so for overtly agreeing adjectives in predicative position.

In contrast, processing of the other phrases seemed to be slowed down by masculine nouns, which is suggested by the interaction between AdjectivePosition and Gender ($F(1, 52) = 4.634$, $p = 0.036$), in combination with the above mentioned interactions. Masculine nouns were processed

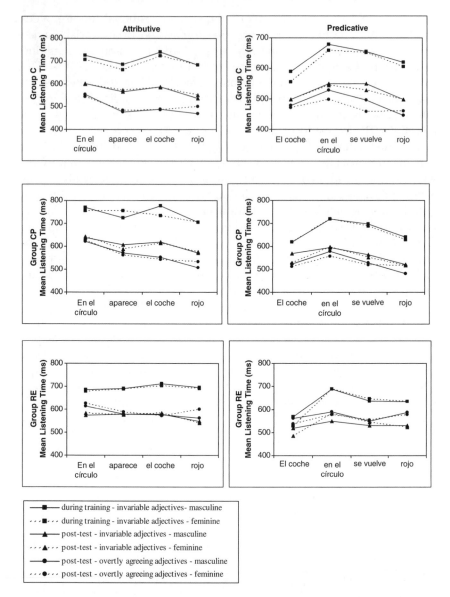

Figure 5.3 Listening times (in ms) in the self-paced listening tests. C = ComprOnly, CP = Compr+Prod, RE = RuleExpl

slowly, and caused spill-over effects on subsequent phrases in the predicative condition. This can be seen in Figure 5.3, where solid lines are often above the dotted lines. This difference disappeared in the posttest with overtly agreeing adjectives, probably because feminine adjectives were processed relatively slowly.

In summary, processing speed generally increased during training, and was higher for the trained groups than for the control group. The trained groups were slowed down by feminine adjectives in predicative position, while the control group was slowed down by both overtly agreeing adjectives in general.

Production tests: Accuracy

The oral responses from the production tasks were recorded and listened to twice by the experimenter to assess accuracy. Pronunciation errors were ignored when words were recognizable. Some responses that were difficult to understand were listened to by a second person. When both judgments were different, the responses were discarded (32 out of 64 unclear responses). Of all other responses, accuracy of the adjective ending was analyzed with an analysis of variance with repeated measures. Data from the posttest were discarded from one participant from group ComprOnly, one from group Compr+Prod and two from group RuleExpl because more than 35% of their responses were unanalyzable, because they contained one or more incorrect words. Of the remaining data, overall 88% of the sentences were analyzable.

Table 5.1 presents the accuracy scores of all groups at the production posttests. The analysis of variance revealed that there were main effects for Group ($F(2, 48) = 6.568$, $p = 0.003$), and Gender ($F(1, 48) = 34.927$, $p = 0.000$), and significant interactions for Gender × Group ($F(2, 48) = 4.820$, $p = 0.012$), and Gender × AdjectivePosition ($F(1, 48) = 4.029$, $p = 0.050$).

The interaction between Gender and Group is important because it shows that there were differences between the groups, although only with respect to feminine forms. *Post-hoc* analyses of variance were performed that contrasted group ComprOnly and Compr+Prod on the one hand with group RuleExpl on the other hand. They showed that the two trained groups produced fewer correct feminine forms than control group RuleExpl ($F(2, 49) = 6.327$, $p = 0.015$). Another *post-hoc* analysis of variance, contrasting the two trained groups, revealed that group ComprOnly produced fewer correct feminine forms than group Compr+Prod ($F(2, 33) = 4.760$, $p = 0.036$). In other words, the receptive training did not result in high accuracy in production in comparison to the control condition (i.e. group RuleExpl); instead, it resulted in lower accuracy. Further, the early introduction of production did not result in low accuracy in production in comparison to the comprehension training; indeed, it resulted in relatively high accuracy.

Gender clearly influenced performance, since accuracy was much higher for masculine forms than for feminine. In addition, more correct feminine adjectives were produced in attributive position than in predicative position, which was reflected by the interaction between Gender and Adjective Position, $F(1, 48) = 4.668$, $p = 0.036$. There were no significant differences

Table 5.1. Accuracy score means (in proportions) of the production post-tests. Standard deviations are enclosed in parentheses

Group	Single-task		Dual-task	
	Masculine	*Feminine*	*Masculine*	*Feminine*
Compr	*Attributive*			
(*n* = 17)	0.93 (0.13)	0.45 (0.37)	0.93 (0.09)	0.53 (0.40)
Compr+Prod (*n* = 18)	0.92 (0.17)	0.77 (0.31)	0.93 (0.11)	0.78 (0.30)
RuleExpl (*n* = 16)	0.94 (0.12)	0.91 (0.18)	0.97 (0.06)	0.86 (0.25)
	Predicative			
Compr (*n* = 17)	0.92 (0.15)	0.51 (0.41)	0.94 (0.14)	0.48 (0.46)
Compr+Prod (*n* = 18)	0.97 (0.06)	0.69 (0.27)	0.92 (0.11)	0.74 (0.31)
RuleExpl (*n* = 16)	0.98 (0.05)	0.84 (0.27)	0.95 (0.09)	0.81 (0.33)

in accuracy between the single- and dual-task conditions. However, performance on the secondary task was affected, as described below. Taken together, the accuracy on the production posttest was highest for group RuleExpl and lower for group ComprOnly. Group ComprOnly's advantage in the comprehension tests did not seem to transfer to performance in the production test. Interestingly, accuracy did not appear to be the result of memorised combinations of nouns and adjectives. An analysis reported in De Jong (2005b) showed that accuracy of agreement was not higher for nouns that had occurred during training ('trained nouns') than for nouns that had not occurred during training ('untrained nouns'). The learners were clearly able to generalise their knowledge of gender agreement to untrained nouns.

Production tests: Tapping consistency

The secondary task in the dual-task production tests was finger tapping. This task was also performed as a single-task (finger tapping only) in order to establish a baseline measure. The mean distance to the target latency of 600 ms between two taps was measured for each trial, for example, latencies of 630 and 570 ms were both considered as a distance of 30 ms. The mean distances for the three tasks were: (1) 39.13 ms for single-task tapping, (2) 76.84 ms for dual-task production with invariable adjectives, and (3) 79.23 ms for dual-task production with overtly agreeing adjectives.

Table 5.2. Consistency of tapping: means and *SDs* (in parentheses) of the standard deviations on the tapping tasks. Low standard deviations indicate high consistency, and high standard deviations low consistency.

		Dual-task	
Group	*Single-task*	*Invariable*	*Overtly agreeing*
ComprOnly ($n = 17$)	29.30 (6.61)	88.81 (14.03)	95.19 (13.04)
Compr+Prod ($n = 18$)	27.98 (4.99)	93.49 (16.51)	93.68 (13.20)
RuleExpl ($n = 16$)	28.80 (4.69)	100.95 (13.78)	105.39 (14.48)

An analysis of variance revealed no differences between the groups, but there was a main effect of task.

The standard deviations of the tapping latencies in each individual trial were calculated to provide a measure of the consistency of tapping (see Table 5.2). Low standard deviations indicate high consistency, and high standard deviations indicate low consistency. An analysis of variance with repeated measures showed that there was a significant main effect for Task ($F(2, 96) = 911.711$, $p = 0.000$), and a significant interaction between Task and Group ($F(4, 96) = 2.890$, $p = 0.026$). The standard deviations were much higher in the dual-task conditions than in the single-task tapping condition. In addition, they were higher when overtly agreeing adjectives were produced than when invariable adjectives were produced. It seems, therefore, that consistency of tapping was most affected when the learners were producing sentences with overtly agreeing adjectives.

A *post-hoc* analysis of variance contrasted the trained groups (ComprOnly and Compr+Prod) with the untrained control group (RuleExpl), and revealed significant effects of Task ($F(2, 98) = 823.127$, $p = 0.000$), and Group ($F(1, 49) = 6.142$, $p = 0.017$), as well as a significant interaction Task × Group ($F(2, 98) = 4.481$, $p = 0.014$). The interaction showed that the standard deviations of the trained groups together were somewhat lower (i.e. consistency was higher) than those of group RuleExpl, but only in the two dual-task conditions. Another *post-hoc* analysis of variance compared the two trained groups and did not reveal a significant difference between groups ComprOnly and Compr+Prod. Combined, these post-hoc analyses suggest that the control group, RuleExpl, was less consistent in tapping because they needed more attention for the primary production task than the two trained groups, ComprOnly and Compr+Prod.

Discussion

The tests show that processing speed in comprehension increased during training. In the posttests, group ComprOnly was fastest and was largely unaffected by gender and the presence of overtly agreeing adjectives.

Groups Compr+Prod and RuleExpl, however, were slower and were affected by these adjectives. It thus seems that the comprehension training led to fast processing of overtly agreeing adjectives, but this effect did not generalise to the production tasks, for which group ComprOnly showed the lowest accuracy, and group RuleExpl the highest. However, group RuleExpl seemed to require more attention in completing the production task, as indicated by their relatively lower consistency on the concurrent finger tapping task. It is important to note that the differences between the groups were found almost exclusively on the overtly agreeing adjectives, and these differences were related to gender. This suggests that it was indeed gender agreement that affected processing speed.

The first research question asked whether comprehension practice can improve accuracy in production. The learners who had had comprehension training responded fastest in the comprehension tests, and they reached a modest accuracy in the production tasks. Therefore, it seems that they had acquired some knowledge. However, this group made more errors in the production tasks than the two other groups so it seems that types of training other than mere comprehension may increase accuracy more. The second research question was whether premature production hinders acquisition. This question can be answered negatively. The learners who started early with production training reached a higher level of accuracy than the learners who had comprehension training. In addition, an analysis that was not reported here showed that accuracy increased during training, suggesting that not all errors persisted throughout the training (De Jong, 2005b). It can be concluded that comprehension skills did not generalize completely to production skills, and production practice improved production skills.

This seems contrary to what VanPatten and associates have observed; in their studies accuracy in production increased after the comprehension practice of Processing Instruction, or PI (e.g. VanPatten & Cadierno, 1993; VanPatten & Oikkenon, 1996; VanPatten & Sanz, 1995). The difference in results may be due differences in comprehension training. Whereas PI involves FORM-FUNCTION MAPPING and activities in which the target grammatical structures are linked to meaning, in the present study the grammatical structure to be learned was not meaningful: the meaning-based decisions in the training tasks could be made regardless of the adjective endings. The conclusions from this study therefore should be interpreted as a result of this particular type of training, involving only exposure and no form-function mapping.

This type of training also did not involve rule explanations, although students in the Compr and Compr+Prod conditions may have deduced rules from the examples. The post-experimental questionnaire indicated that this may have been the case. If so, this would mean that all three groups had access to declarative knowledge, which, as explained before, is more flexible than procedural knowledge in that it can be used in the execution of different skills (i.e. in both production and comprehension, regardless of training). Only the two trained groups, however, had task-related exposure that should have led to increased procedural knowledge. On the other hand, some studies have shown that procedural knowledge that was acquired for one skill cannot be used for another skill (Anderson, 1983, 1993; Anderson & Fincham, 1994; DeKeyser, 1997). Thus this explanation, the participants in group ComprOnly may have relied on procedural knowledge for the comprehension tasks, but should not have been able to apply procedural knowledge in the production tasks. Indeed, their relatively poor performance on the production posttest suggests this was the case. Group Compr+Prod, on the other hand, likely had developed procedural knowledge for both the comprehension and the production tasks, and group RuleExpl had access to flexible declarative knowledge by virtue of their acquaintance with explicit rules prior to testing.

Another explanation for the lack of generalizability in group ComprOnly may be the difference between the processes involved in comprehension and production of gender agreement, as argued in De Jong (2005b). When listeners hear a noun and an adjective in Spanish, both of these words will give information about their gender (e.g. *el coche* 'the car' is masculine, and *rojo* 'red' is masculine as well). Speakers, on the other hand, first have to choose the noun and adjective stem (e.g. *coche*, and *roj*-), then the article and the adjective ending (*el* and-*o*). Thus, listeners have information about gender presented to them, and they check whether the noun and adjective agree in gender. Speakers, on the other hand, have to select the gender of the article and adjective. Comprehension and production are thus clearly different processes. They do, however, make use of the same forms, such as articles and adjective endings. Therefore, there may also be some transfer from comprehension skills to production skills, and vice versa.

Conclusion

In conclusion, these results appear to suggest that it would be most beneficial to give language learners only explicit instruction about grammar rules, because explicit knowledge can be used for both comprehension and production skills and appears to result in accurate production. It is important to keep in mind, however, that the dual-task production test showed that the RuleExpl group needed to allocate more attention to the production tasks than the ComprOnly and Compr+Prod groups. In addition, this study focused on only one grammar rule, while in real language situations, many rules need to be applied simultaneously. It will be very difficult, if not impossible, for learners to attend to all grammar rules at once when they are speaking. And if they have to think about *how* to say something, they have less time to think about *what* to say.

It should be noted that the training tasks in this study are not proposed as good classroom practice; they are merely used to show the effect of processing for comprehension and production on grammar learning. Real classroom tasks need to be less repetitive and to be designed with attention to the needs and goals of the learner. In addition, future research will need to investigate further what the relation is between comprehension and production skills, and what types of training can improve these skills.

In sum, it seems that performance does not always readily generalize from comprehension training to production tasks, and therefore production skills seem to require separate practice. In short, input matters, but output matters too.

Notes

1. This has been a controversial issue for several decades. Jordan (2004: 180), for instance, argues that the Input Hypothesis is not testable and does not give an explanation for how comprehensible input results in acquisition.
2. Part of the results of the self-paced listening test were also published in De Jong (2005a), but those only included listening times for the adjectives.
3. See De Jong (2005b) for a more detailed analysis.

Appendix

The vocabulary used in the training and test tasks. Words indicated with * were withheld from the training tasks. Words indicated with [x] were used in the production posttests, in order to test generalizability from trained to untrained items.

Nouns		Adjectives		
Masculine	*Feminine*	*Overtly agreeing*	*Invariable*	*Other*
el guante[x]	la fuente[x]	rojo/a	azul	Aparece
'the glove'	'the fountain'	'red'	'blue'	'appears'
el peine	la torre	negro/a	verde	se vuelve
'the comb'	'the tower'	'black'	'green'	'turns'
el coche	la nave	rosado/a	gris	en el círculo
'the car'	'the boat'	'pink'	'grey'	'in the circle'
el cheque*	la llave*[x]	morado/a	marron	en el cuadro
'the cheque'	'the key'	'purple'	'brown'	'in the square'
el diente*[x]	la nube*			dice José
'the tooth'	'the cloud'			'says José'
el collar[x]	la nariz			cree Javier
'the necklace'	'the nose'			'thinks Javier'
el jersey	la sartén[x]			
'the sweater'	'the frying pan'			
el reloj	la prisión			
'the watch'	'the prison'			
el farol*[x]	la postal*			
'the streetlamp'	'the postcard'			
el papel*	la pared*[x]			
'the paper'	'the wall'			

Chapter 6

Learner Attitudes Towards Comprehension-based Language Learning[1]

JOHN STEPHENSON

Introduction

This chapter comprises an overview of ATTITUDES towards comprehension-based language learning (the 'COMPREHENSION APPROACH', henceforth 'CPA'), gathered via learner diaries made during a self-study programme. Although experiences of second language (L2) learning through just listening to and understanding a foreign language have been researched in the past (e.g. Benson & Hjelt, 1978; Gary & Gary, 1981; Lightbown *et al.*, 2002; McCandless & Winitz, 1986), research has tended to focus on comparing the CPA to 'traditional' methodologies involving an emphasis on grammar awareness. Using diarists whose previous experience has been of the teaching approach currently predominant in the UK and widely used elsewhere – 'communicative language teaching' (CLT), also known as the 'COMMUNICATIVE APPROACH' (e.g. Sato & Kleinsasser, 1999; Savignon, 1997; Savignon & Wang, 2003) – may lead to comparisons that are relevant both to SECOND LANGUAGE ACQUISITION (SLA) researchers and teachers contemplating comprehension-orientated classroom activities. Furthermore, the study of learner attitudes (e.g. Wenden, 1999) is perhaps more fruitful when self-study factors out the influence of the classroom teacher and peers.

To address the issue of attitudes towards the CPA, undergraduates familiar with CLT followed 10 introductory self-study lessons in Japanese or Spanish. These lessons, named *The Learnables*, involved understanding pictures through listening to the language, and did not include reading, speaking or grammar explanations. Each student was required by the SLA course they were taking to record progress in a diary as they followed each lesson (*cf.* Goh, 2000; Halbach, 2000; Huang, 2005); these consisted of a large number of candid entries. Results are reported below through a selective review of comments.

These diary entries raise the practical issue of whether an early emphasis on learning through speaking restricts opportunities to do what language users do much of the time: interact with messages through comprehension rather than PRODUCTION. Learners' comments point to the conclusion that adults can benefit from and develop a positive attitude towards comprehension-based approaches if they are prepared to commit to an initial period of uncertainty. The diaries also show that previous experiences exert a crucial and often negative effect on new ways of learning, which in addition may not suit learners' individual styles or culture-based expectations. To further complicate matters, the diaries reveal that in the absence of speaking or writing, learners develop their own strategies to recall oral language. When they imagine how the new words may be written, ORTHOGRAPHY can enforce erroneous representations that persist into production (see Bassetti, this volume). Familiarity with SLA research also appeared to affect attitudes, though the diarists were able to direct their comments to relevant research areas.

Before turning to the diaries, the next three sections of the chapter set out: the similarities and differences between the CPA and CLT in terms of their broad principles; description and critical discussion of *The Learnables*; and the study's methodology. Section four consists of a detailed analysis of the diaries, relating writers' comments to previous studies. Discussion focuses on the effects of prior learning, attitudes towards learning without speaking or reading, perception of progress, and the influence of cultural background on learner attitudes. Finally, a conclusion summarises the main points drawn from the students' experiences.

The Comprehension Approach and Communicative Language Teaching

Simplifying the definitions of the CPA and CLT, in the early stages, the former emphasises understanding an L2, and the latter use, with an emphasis on production (speaking and writing). The CPA may delay oral production to avoid ERRORS, based on the assumption that production-orientated activities could bring these on, for example, because learners would have had little time to identify new sound patterns (McCandless & Winitz, 1986; Winitz & Yanes, 2002). Neither approach is an alternative to the other, because for both the goal is 'communication'; they can be complementary components of a full language programme, employed for learners at different proficiency levels and in different classroom activities. Compare the more common versions of the CPA with 'strong' and 'weak' CLT:

- CPA: emphasises comprehension, minimising learner stress as prerequisites for production/communication (e.g. Krashen &

Terrell's (1983) classroom-based 'NATURAL APPROACH'), and/or learning non-verbally, via understanding and performing actions [Asher's (1969) 'TOTAL PHYSICAL RESPONSE']; suitable for self-study, for example, *The Learnables* (Winitz, 2002). Can be aligned with 'GENERATIVE LINGUISTICS' (see Young-Scholten & Piske, this volume), though methods originated not from linguistic theory, but from applied linguistics and teaching research.

- 'Weak' CLT: production-based classroom activities such as pair conversations supplemented by other techniques, for example, grammar exercises. Particularly popular in Western classrooms, and the subject of many mainstream methodology textbooks (e.g. Richards, 2006), teaching manuals (e.g. Scrivener, 2005), in response to educators' identification of lack of oral fluency as major problem (Tsui, 1996).

- 'Strong' CLT: for example, TASK-BASED LEARNING (e.g. speaking to complete a classroom project relevant to real life), where knowledge of language use emerges from conversational interaction and (mainly oral) production. Less widespread and less suitable for beginners (Scrivener, 2005).

Similarities between the approaches

The CPA and CLT share a number of similarities such as an emphasis on 'communication' (where this includes understanding as well as production), minimal error correction and avoidance of the first language (L1). Both aim to enable the learner to communicate (Krashen & Terrell, 1983), and both involve 'conveyance of meaning for a purpose' (VanPatten, 1998: 928–929). Both value 'learning by doing', but differ as to what constitutes the 'doing'. Neither emphasises learning *about* grammar (memorising rules, as in the grammar-translation method) or activities abstracted away from a meaningful context (as in e.g. the AUDIO-LINGUAL method).[2] Error correction is avoided, except where it interferes with meaning. Errors are a natural part of the learning process; however, while 'weak' CLT may involve grammar-focused exercises to promote self-correction of errors, the CPA tries to eliminate one of their sources: the imposition of stressful speaking activities. Any speaking must therefore occur in as relaxed an environment as possible (Krashen & Terrell, 1983). Neither ignores the observation that progress proceeds in stages (Lee & VanPatten, 2003: 19–21). For example, Dulay and Burt (1974a) found that the English suffix *-ing* is produced first by all learners, with, for example, third person singular *-s* much later. Instruction cannot alter this order (Krashen, 2003: 1–2), but can delay emergence of forms (VanPatten, 1987). However, this does not mean exposing the beginning learner to manipulated, unnatural INPUT which is stripped of 'difficult' forms (Krashen, 2003: 2). Finally, both approaches discourage use of the L1: while communicative classrooms may confine this to shortcutting to understanding when communication breaks down (Scrivener, 2005), in the CPA, teachers do not speak in the L1 at all, but may acknowledge – in the L2 – queries conveyed in the L1. Both may avoid direct translation with beginning to pre-intermediate learners on the understanding that words are not learned easily through rote memorisation (Sagarra & Alba, 2006), and such techniques encourage the learner to perceive learning as largely a matter of replacing L1 words with exactly equivalent L2 versions (Lee & VanPatten, 2003; Winitz, 2002, 2003).[3]

Differences between the approaches

The main differences between the two approaches are highlighted in Table 6.1; there is a considerable overlap, and drawing a strong distinction between the approaches is probably misleading since most teachers will draw on elements of both.

The materials used in this study broadly follow the principles in the second column above; however, there are several other features involved, which the next section will discuss.

Table 6.1 Comparison of CLT and the CPA

Communicative language teaching	*The comprehension approach*
Assumptions about the nature of language and learning	
(1) Based on *model* of education: learning language is about *how* to communicate fluently, appropriately ('COMMUNICATIVE COMPETENCE' Canale & Swain, 1980; Hymes, 1972); L2 emerges *through* communication. Classroom activities prioritise productive 'fluency' over grammatical 'accuracy' (Scrivener, 2005).	Based on *theories* of language, acquisition (e.g. Ortega, 2007; White, 2003), and Krashen's (1982a) *Monitor Model* (VanPatten & Williams, 2007), about *why* it's possible to learn[4] –' comprehension precedes production'; 'COMPREHENSIBLE INPUT' a communicative prerequisite (Krashen & Terrell, 1983: 58; Lee & VanPatten, 2003).
(2) Activities promoting acquisition and conscious awareness of grammar, meaning, use of language ('metalinguistic knowledge') help learning (Schmidt, 1990; Sprang, 2006).[5]	'ACQUISITION' and 'LEARNING' fundamentally differ; conscious focus on grammar rules only temporarily beneficial, in limited contexts, for example, writing, speeches, grammar tests (Doughty, 2003; Krashen, 1982a, 2003), possibly misleading (Barcroft, 2003), or fails to affect *linguistic competence* (Schwartz, 1993; Young-Scholten, 1995).

(Continued)

Table 6.1 *(Continued)*

(3)	Focus on managing conversation in society (Hymes, 1972): learner as communicator developing *sociolinguistic competence* (knowing what to say when), conversation strategies, e.g. requesting clarification (*strategic competence*), and spoken, written coherence (*discourse competence*). Each as or more important than knowledge of language itself (Canale, 1983; Canale & Swain, 1980).	Norms of interaction may be noticed, but productive use delayed. Early CPA speaking activities do not push learner beyond current stage; for example, at childlike *one-word stage* (Bloom, 1973) simple replies to syntactically complex questions accepted (Krashen & Terrell, 1983). Classroom extends production when it emerges naturally (Krashen & Terrell, 1983).
	Procedures and implementation	
(4)	Intended for all levels (Savignon, 2003), but requires (usually classroom) conversation partner; self-study also encouraged, for example, listening (Lee & VanPatten, 2003).	Especially suitable for beginners and self-study; classroom-based CPA may be teacher-centric due to no focus on production-orientated group work (Krashen, 2003).
(5)	Use of range of materials to encourage production (Scrivener, 2005), alongside teacher input: pictures, written word, worksheets, realia, 'authentic' materials, for example, news reports (Nunan, 1998). 'Teacher talking time' minimised to allow more learner talking (Nunan, 1998).	Teacher provides extensive spoken input, e.g. instructions to follow, pictures and realia to encourage non-verbal responses, promote understanding. Production occurs when learners ready (Krashen & Terrell, 1983).
(6)	Learning proceeds through focusing on meaningful language production (Savignon, 2003), e.g. making up dialogues in groups, with a supporting role for listening (Scrivener, 2005). 'Drilling' (repeated production of structures) may be used (Scrivener, 2005), preferably to meaningfully convey information (Lee & VanPatten, 2003). Learners may also communicate non-verbally (Asher, 1969), and though they are encouraged to speak in L2 (Scrivener, 2005), the L1 can be useful resource (Scrivener, 2005).	Emphasis on listening encourages linguistic development (Krashen, 1996; McCandless & Winitz, 1986); 'routines and patterns' (drilling), early speaking shunned due to low creative use of language (Krashen & Terrell, 1983), anxiety promotion (Krashen, 2003), exposure to other learners' errors (McCandless & Winitz, 1986). Learners communicate non-verbally, speak in the L1 (Asher, 1969; Krashen, 2003; McCandless & Winitz, 1986).

The Learnables: Comprehension-based Learning Materials

This study adopted as teaching materials the first 10-lesson course in Harris Winitz's self-study multi-language series *The Learnables* (Winitz, 2002), consisting of a picture book with accompanying audio recordings. *The Learnables* has been the subject of research, typically involving comparison studies, but not learner attitudes; see for example McCandless and Winitz (1986); Verspoor *et al.* (this volume).

Assumptions underpinning *The Learnables*

The Learnables is firmly orientated in comprehension as a prerequisite to subsequent stages of development where learners may choose to speak, read and write the language. As well as Krashen's (1982a) MONITOR Theory, the materials are strongly inspired by research on naturalistic L2 acquisition in pre-adolescent children, who typically develop very high levels of competence in a second language without much grammar instruction, enforced production or consistent use of writing (e.g. Snow & Hoefnagel-Höhle, 1978).

Of course, the view that comprehension is the fundamental basis of learning is richly debated (see e.g. Ellis, 2005, for an example of research focused on the role of explicit instruction in language learning). In addition to the main points of the CPA outlined in Table 6.1 above, *The Learnables* involves several (controversial) methodological points (Winitz, 2002).

First, the idea is that language emerges indirectly through understanding successively more complex structures, from single words to full sentences; in the materials, these are often only tenuously related in meaning. This avoids 'semantic fields' (Comrie, 2000) of related words (e.g. *knife, fork, spoon*) which, when introduced together, can easily be confused and hinder vocabulary development. Items in *The Learnables* are repeated, based on the premise that frequency promotes development. However, numerous studies suggest that more than frequency is involved (e.g. Lightbown, 2004). Batstone (2002) is among those who also argue that the learner may only understand through context, so fail to convert input to 'INTAKE' (linguistic information, e.g. tense, that becomes intuitive linguistic knowledge), and on this basis argues for explicit instruction. Furthermore, De Jong (2005a, see also this volume) concludes that a listening-based environment can promote acquisition, but this is will not minimise grammatical errors in production.

Second, *The Learnables* avoids everyday 'real world' communication and 'authenticity' of materials as being too complex, and instead focuses on building up recognition of common vocabulary and structures, which can be usefully employed later. The materials are designed for any learner of any background, learning any language. The onus is on the learner to reinterpret these to accord with their own culture, as they may also have to do in the communicative classroom (Bax, 2003; Harmer, 2003). *The Learnables* materials involve NATIVE SPEAKERS based on the premise that learners will otherwise pick up non-native speakers' errors which are likely to resist later correction; 'FOSSILISATION' will occur (e.g. Han, 2004; but see also Jenkins (2000), who de-emphasises the importance of a NATIVE-LIKE model in L2 phonology).

The method strongly recommends that learners do not attempt to mimic what they hear orally (the instructions in Winitz (2002) read 'DO NOT REPEAT THE WORDS OUT LOUD' [*sic.*].[6] The idea is that this encourages 'foreign accent' – TRANSFER (or 'interference') of L1 pronunciations (Krashen & Terrell, 1983; Weinberger, 2006). This view is based in part on the observation that pre-adolescent L2 learners usually become more native-like than adults in terms of accent and eventual fluency (e.g. Winitz *et al.*, 1995). In their 'NATURALISTIC' learning environment, speaking is less likely to be required from the outset, so some children evidence an initial 'SILENT PERIOD' in which oral production is delayed, perhaps allowing them time to INTERNALISE more native-like linguistic structures (McCandless & Winitz, 1986).[7] Post-puberty learners without extensive speaking may similarly benefit from a delay in L2 speaking.

No reading or writing is involved at the beginner level. The method considers that these can mislead learners into mispronouncing words because – for instance – written English is not a faithful phonetic record of speech (Meyer, 2002; Teschner & Whitney, 2004), and L2 sound-letter correspondences are unknown to beginners (Young-Scholten, 2002; *cf.* Dickerson, 1991, for orthography as an aid to pronunciation; Bassetti, this volume, on the role of orthography in L2 phonology). For example, Japanese *onna no hito* ('woman', *Learnables* lesson one) is typically pronounced with a sound more like *sh* for *h*, but as this goes unwritten in both ROOMAJI and the native KANA WRITING SYSTEMS, orthography cannot be directly used to support pronunciation. The solution is to ensure that the learner has considerable experience of hearing this form to establish it before the otherwise misleading written form is introduced. Another orthographic effect applies to memory: Barcroft (2006) has supplied evidence that writing words down to remember them distracts beginning learners. However, unlike *The Learnables*, some forms of the CPA *do* encourage reading and writing, as this opens up more input to the learner (Krashen & Terrell, 1983).

Finally, it should be noted that *The Learnables* materials may serve as a supplementary activity for learners of all backgrounds (e.g. class homework; home-schooling), rather than as the exclusive source of L2 activity. Learners may still seek out extra materials, meaningful production activities, dictionary definitions, grammar explanations, conversation partners, and so on. *The Learnables* lacks such support, but also purports to circumvent learner errors attributed to inadequate or misleading textbook explanations (Blyth, 1997).

This chapter now turns to a small-scale case study of the reflections of a group of university L2 learners who experienced a comprehension-based approach for the first time, using *The Learnables*.

The study

The Learnables: Procedures

Each of the 10 lessons in *The Learnables: Book 1* (Winitz, 2002) consists of repeated but increasingly complex black-and-white pictures which illustrate accompanying native-speaker audio recordings in one of a selection of languages. These are designed to incrementally build up vocabulary and structure to achieve an overall familiarity with the language. Winitz (2002) claims that the user will 'learn 1500 words in the first 20 hours of lessons'. These materials are easy to use and are accompanied by clear instructions before the lessons; for the procedure and example illustrations, refer to the Appendix.

Methodology

Diaries

Students involved in the study recorded their experiences as they followed *The Learnables: Book 1*. Use of diaries rather than, for example, questionnaires requires some explanation. Diaries can record how impressions of learning change over time; they are less restrictive than a questionnaire where learners only respond to what the researcher specifically asks, and in most cases only record a limited range of comments (Sakui & Gaies, 1999). It is difficult to investigate learners' internal feelings unless given the opportunity for free introspection (Granger, 2004).

No specific diary format was imposed to increase the chances that students would record more of their own impressions (see Halbach, 2000, for this approach). In addition, no constraints were placed on how the students submitted their diaries.

Participants

A review of previous diary studies has not returned a precedent for the selection of the participants in the present study, namely undergraduate students of linguistics following an SLA course for which learning an L2 was required. The completed diaries did not count towards final grades, so course credit was not a motivating factor.

Fifteen students handed in diaries with permission to use the information they contained; since many comments were judged similar, representative extracts from 10 appear here. Six of these students were native speakers of British English, who were at least average achievers, since none subsequently failed the SLA course. Of the remaining four, two were native speakers of Japanese, one of Arabic and one of Luxembourgish; a group of mixed linguistic and cultural backgrounds allows consideration of how such variables affect attitudes. The average age was 19, and all but one, an English speaker, were female. All had experience of foreign or second language learning, mainly from school, and since the students from the UK and Luxembourg had encountered CLT, they were predicted to be able to make relevant observations contrasting this with the CPA. The Japanese speakers had more limited CLT experience, and were familiar with grammar-translation-orientated activities from their schooling.

For several reasons, most students followed the lessons in Japanese. Its selection served to expand linguistics students' awareness of non-European languages, and the lack of a widely-used alphabetic writing system meant students were deprived of written input in compliance with the ground rules of the method. It was hoped that this restriction would be acceptable to students if they knew that *roomaji* would be of limited use. Students were not prohibited from seeking extra materials, or from attempting to converse with native speakers. The Japanese and the Arabic-speaking students followed the (Latin American) Spanish lessons. All participants' prior knowledge of their 'TARGET LANGUAGE' was very minimal.

Results

The author reviewed all diaries for comments on attitudes to the features of *The Learnables* that students were unlikely to have previously experienced, for example, absence of speaking. Three specific diary styles emerged, with some overlap: daily comments; entries divided into sections, for example, one for each lesson; and final reports in which the experience as a whole was reflected upon. Some students wrote an introduction and/or conclusion covering the reasons for studying the language and their initial expectations. All entries were written in English, with occasional transliterations or attempted 'phonetic' renderings of L2 items. Only four were handwritten rather than word-processed, having been recorded at the time of learning. In all other cases, students had clearly retained earlier notes which presumably they later edited to varying degrees.

The next section first defines terms relevant to the diarists' experiences, followed by a detailed analysis of comments. This includes: effects of prior experience, including beliefs; perceived usefulness of materials; absence of speaking, reading and writing and learning strategies developed. Codes indicate the individual student with the first letter and their L1 with the second: (E)nglish, (J)apanese, (L)uxembourgish, (A)rabic; for example, 'B/E' is learner B, L1 English. Substantial comments are numbered for ease of reference, and preserve the diarists' original spelling, punctuation and use of emphasis.

Definitions

An *attitude* involves two main ideas: the learner's own *concepts* of what is to be learned are separate from their *beliefs* - what they think is 'true' about those concepts (Benson & Lor, 1999). Wenden (1999) observes that beliefs are susceptible to change through experience; the diarists' exposure to a new method of language learning provides evidence. Another point touched upon below is how learners who might have low 'tolerance' of potentially ambiguous language (presented without supporting translation/explanation) may be less successful in adapting to *The Learnables*. The diaries reveal an interesting perspective on *tolerance of ambiguity* (White, 1999).

Effects of prior experience

Learners make several references to how they have been taught, mainly through formal education. A/E refers to previous learning as 'production based teaching', showing that for her the main difference is the emphasis on understanding. K/E comments that it is difficult to 'break free' from previous experiences of language learning, perhaps implying metaphorically that these are seen as restrictive. Other students are more positive about previous classroom learning:

(1) I definitely preferred the communicative style of language teaching I received at school. I found the words and phrases we learnt more useful for everyday life, and I liked the fact I understood what I was learning. I also felt more in control of my learning, and I felt more motivated by having others around me. (B/E)

B/E's preference is to be part of a group in order to learn and to speak in it, as evidenced respectively by the comments about the apparently higher motivation from learning with others and the apparent usefulness of what was taught. The reference to understanding what was being learned points to a low tolerance of ambiguity. Such a learner likes to be shown how L2 forms are used. Although there are 'right answers' in the *Learnables* multiple-choice tests, it does not convey language unambiguously:

(2) [I was] [...] unsure of the structure of the utterances [...] although I found I was able to understand what was happening using the nouns I already knew. I also found it quite hard to work out exactly what was going on in the pictures [...] I found it quite frustrating not knowing what all the words in an utterance mean [...] I am finding that I am definitely picking up more features with repeated listening. (B/E)

Here, tolerance of ambiguity emerges as the student learns more; she starts to become more comfortable with new structures heard even if the meaning is not obvious.

Perceived usefulness of _The Learnables_

Comment (1) illustrates a recurring theme in the diaries: while _The Learnables_ may be enjoyable for some, few believe it teaches anything 'useful'. Within communicative language teaching, 'authentic' material for listening activities is valued (Rost, 1990), so it is not surprising that the pictures used in _The Learnables_ are not seen as relevant to the 'real world':[8]

(3)   What is the reward in knowing the chunks 'big house' or 'the pencil is in the cup' and a range of random single words? (D/L)

(4)   I got eight out of ten [...] I thought it was a good way to test it, but all it really shows is that I can remember the sounds of some random Japanese words and connect them to equally odd collections of pictures! (E/E)

The Learnables' approach rests on the principle that input gives a specific word or a CONSTRUCTION such as coordination (e.g. _and_), which can later be extended to other contexts. For one learner, this allows the rewarding experience of correctly predicting sentences as yet unheard:

(5)   If I look ahead to pictures that I have not heard the accompanying sentence for, it is easy to anticipate the structure [...] I was able to understand some of the structure of Japanese, which was being spoken around me, even when the content was at a level too advanced for me to understand. I could pick out a verb even if I didn't have any idea what it was [...]. (C/E)

C/E seems able to draw on his experience to identify parts of the utterance as spoken by native speakers (in the dormitory where he lived), indicating emergence of phonological and syntactic awareness.

This section suggests that, although they were students of SLA, these learners' beliefs about their own second language acquisition are not based on academic knowledge, but on their language learning experiences (MacDonald _et al._, 2001). A possible consequence of attitudes based on prior learning could be that explaining an unfamiliar methodology, as Krashen & Terrell (1983) recommend, will have little effect.

Absence of speaking

The Learnables requires that learners do not attempt to immediately repeat what they hear; students initially found this frustrating, with an even division between those who get used to it and those who continue to reject the imposition of a childlike 'silent period' (see above):

(6)   I find it quite frustrating that I am not allowed to speak. It is only natural for me to want to pronounce the words and structures I learn. The learnables replicate an artificial silent period which I feel I do not want to go through. (D/L, 1st lesson)

D/L is aware of the silent period, but sees this as natural only for children. This is perhaps an example of how high metalinguistic awareness as a result of the study of linguistics might affect one's approach to language learning. For D/L and others, speaking also helps marshal their thoughts, and lack of speaking is equated with lack of thinking about language:

(7) Am I allowed to *think* about the words, sentences and structures I have heard? Am I allowed to try and figure out the underlying structure[?] (D/L, pre-learning comments)

(8) Found listening to The Learnables for the first time rather confusing; not sure how looking at the pictures and listening to the words that they are is going to work in terms of learning another language. (A/E)

(9) [...] being told not to speak doesn't stop me from making assumptions based on my English. (K/E, 2nd play of numbers practice)

The conclusion that *The Learnables*'s methodology involves absence of thinking can perhaps be traced to the instructions. In simplifying SLA issues, the materials risk confusion in the way its methodology is explained. Winitz (2002) includes the following:

> There is no vocabulary to memorize. You will learn in the same way you learned your first language. By listening and absorbing the language, you will soon think in the foreign language.[9] (Winitz, 2002: 4)

Above, while K/E decides that silence does not equal a ban on personal reflection, it is not so surprising that D/L worries about the relationship between thinking and learning, as the instructions imply that acquisition will proceed by osmosis (passively 'absorbing' language). *The Learnables* does not support osmosis, however, as the materials are designed to highlight and gradually contextualise new structures, enabling learners to break down what they hear (Winitz & Yanes, 2002). The use of 'learn' may also mislead, as another diarist notices:

(10) If by 'learn', Winitz means 'be able to recognise', then I think it is possible that his claim is true. (B/E)

K/E also provides a comment regarding an early attempt at speaking that some research frameworks (e.g. Dickerson, 1991) would offer as evidence that learners should be given extensive written support for memorisation and pronunciation, even at a potential cost (see Young-Scholten, 2002; Barcroft, 2006):

(11) I tried to pronounce some of the words I remembered – they [Japanese native speakers] couldn't recognise them at all! (K/E)

Alternatively, this example shows the consequences of early speaking within the silent period; minimally, it indicates learners are capable of moving from comprehension to production themselves, but that early attempts at talking with native speakers may come to grief. In any case, these materials do not rule out a learner-driven move to production once their listening experience has helped them to establish some linguistic competence.

The main points from this discussion are: learners generally consider speaking helpful and it is preferable to listening for some; learners resist the idea of 'absorbing' language, since they want to engage with the materials through speaking; speaking is still possible, though difficult. The next section explores how early speaking leads to a possibly false sense of achievement.

Association of achievement with recall

Lack of immediate recall

Students seem overwhelmingly to associate 'achievement' with 'production'; though *The Learnables'* instructions warn that it is necessary to hear a word many times before successfully producing it, students identify lack of productive recall as a problem:

(12)   I want to see whether I can say the words exactly as the speaker says it. I guess I like to feel that I have achieved something. (I/A)

(13)   … I feel like I forget a lot of the words straight away, and definitely wouldn't be able to reproduce them. I'm finding this quite frustrating, because I'm used to learning vocabulary for exams, and hence being able to reproduce all the LEXIS I have learnt. I almost feel like I'm wasting my time learning the language, if I can't reproduce it. (B/E)

(14)   […] I feel I cannot apply what I should supposedly know of the language in other situations, such as in my [Japanese] evening course. (D/L)

Granger (2004) pursues the idea that Western-style mainstream language teaching and learning often leads learners to the view that speaking should be prioritised over comprehension and non-verbal communication. In contrast to the above comments, C/E finds that, while his command of Japanese is not productively high, what had been learned is satisfactorily available, as compared to his experience of learning German and British Sign Language (BSL):

(15)   The basic syntactic structures in The Learnables seem very well ingrained in my mind […] The equivalents in German and BSL seem more vague, and I constantly find myself having to check sentences.

The little Japanese I know seems very internalised [...] I do not find it necessary to translate my thoughts into English. This is not so with numbers in German or BSL. (C/E)

C/E illustrates how some learners bypass 'thinking in English'. D/L prefers a more formal approach involving thinking about words and phrases with plentiful opportunities to speak, so does not enjoy the experience of comprehension-based learning – see comments (3), (6), (7) and (14). A problem for *The Learnables* is that those who prefer production may, on encountering a difficulty, resort to a strategy such as imitation, which involves precisely those activities whose controversial use the course warns against.

Mnemonics: A learner recall strategy

Some students evidence individual learning strategies such as *mnemonics* (Thompson, 1987) to improve recall. Here, this involves associating the sound of the L2 word to be learned with the sound of an L1 item:

(16)   [...] the Japanese 'big aeroplane' [*ooki hikooki*] seems to be very similar to the English 'hokey-cokey'![10] (A/E)

(17)   I was finding a way of associating the word with the picture, for example 'gruma' [*kuruma*] meaning car, is similar to the noise of a car engine, 'ggrrrrr', thus I was also learning via association. Also if I could find no English word that sounded similar and simply began to re-associate that word with that picture, for example 'ecogi' [*hikooki*] meaning plane, is difficult to spell or associate, thus whenever the picture of a plane appeared I thought about corgi's [*sic*], as in the dogs ... (L/E)

Use of mnemonics may well have the effect of establishing erroneous phonological representations. Japanese has no consonant clusters such as /gr/, but vowels may be voiceless and thus difficult for learners to initially perceive. Associating *kuruma* with 'ggrrrrr' thus concretely specifies a non-existent consonant cluster. So, strategies such as mnemonics can promote recall, but may also establish early non-target representations.

Absence of reading and writing

The Learnables deprives the beginning learner of written input, based on the view that orthography encourages misperception and mispronunciation. Although *roomaji* is not widely employed for written Japanese, students feel that written support is necessary:

(18)   Am I not bound to mishear words if I never see them written down? (D/L)

Initially, learners are indeed likely to form an incomplete picture of L2 pronunciation (e.g. Piske *et al.*, 2001). However, this comment confuses spoken with written language (see above). Attitudes towards writing may be culture-dependent, since one of the Japanese learners of Spanish saw some aspects of writing as potentially problematic:

(19)   At least I don't need to worry about spelling and all sorts with 'The Learnables'. (F/J)

Extensive and early written text can lead to other consequences, where reading becomes central. Research also indicates, for example, that orthography can affect (and alter) spoken word recognition (e.g. Muneaux & Ziegler, 2004). That orthographic form is involved in early L2 acquisition is indicated by another entry from L/E:

(20)   I was aware that my mind was subconsciously producing an orthographic representation of the words that I was hearing while associating it with the pictures. In a novel way it was like I was reading the words […] Furthermore by visualising the spellout of the word the pictures did not simply represent a sound on tape but an (English) spelt word. (L/E, 1st lesson)

Even without written text exposure, literacy has a strategy-building effect that could influence later pronunciation. With this strategy to retain what she has heard, L/E is clearly aware that knowledge of written English appears to be biasing her listening, even when no foreign language spellings are involved, and that this may lead to an incorrect representation. Alphabetic literacy itself, then, may be sufficient for the learner to create the 'deviant' L2 forms to which Young-Scholten (1998) refers.

Perception of progress

While I/A reveals that 'it is rewarding in that I find myself understanding a lot of vocabulary in a short time', most students seem frustrated by a perceived lack of progress:

(21)   I found this method of learning quite frustrating, because I spent a long time listening to the tapes, and feel that I hadn't achieved anything, although judging by my test results, this can't have been the case. (B/E)

However, students who exhibit a good deal of scepticism about the effectiveness of *The Learnables* nevertheless report success on the multiple-choice tests that follow every second lesson. Some reconcile this with existing beliefs by attributing it to guessing or 'common sense':

(22)   Test 100% but sometimes only by a process of elimination – understanding half of phrase/recognising noun and using common sense – not actually 'acquired'. (K/E)

Students observe, as per the instructions in Winitz (2002), that the process requires repeated listening:

(23)   I don't understand what the [*sic*] some of the pictures depict. I come to associate what is said with pictures <u>but</u> without knowing their actual meaning. Only realise meaning after many repetitions or advancing further in lesson. (K/E)

K/E shows how learning coincides with students' emerging understanding that progress is possible when structures are heard many times. She also observes that progress involves the development of one's own strategies:

(24)   I formulate hypotheses and see if they are proven or not by the data. These pictures and sentences used seem to encourage hypothesis testing. (K/E)

As the range of structures increases, students are aware that they understand more of the language after initial uncertainty:

(25)   When I listened and looked at the book, I recognised most of the words, and felt as though I was getting to know them. However, I found that as soon as the tape stopped playing, I could only remember a handful of the words [...] Later on in the evening, I listened to the tape while doing a bit of work [...] I did find that I recognised some words and phrases, and that the pronunciation of the words seemed to be clearer than it had been previously. (B/E)

The implications of learners' awareness and HYPOTHESIS testing without classroom support are unclear; are they drawing specifically on prior learning experiences or is this emerging naturally?

Attitudes of the Japanese learners of Spanish

Some responses to achievement may be partly dependent on cultural background. The Japanese native speakers learning Spanish seem to be more accepting of comprehension-based learning:

(26)   Till now I've always tried to figure out what words mean exactly what they mean in English each time, and also tried to figure out how all the agreements work and etc., but now I notice that I am more relaxed and not thinking too much about grammar. I can understand it, so that is all right. (F/J)

(27)   I did not think about grammar much since it is complicated. I tried to understand the meanings from pictures and words. (G/J)

This attitude towards a non-traditional method is surprising, since despite a public commitment to CLT, Japanese state school language teaching remains largely 'traditional' (Sakui, 2004); oral comprehension and communicative ability is often de-emphasised, with grammar knowledge seen as a prerequisite to speaking (Gray & Leather, 1999; Sakui & Gaies, 1999: 487). Similar to Horwitz's (1999) speculation for Korean learners of English, these Japanese students may simply be exhausted by the difficulty of learning under traditional methods and are relieved to find an alternative.[11] Supporting this, Sakui & Gaies (1999) found that Japanese learners of English were dissatisfied with their language learning experiences, and prioritised enjoyable learning and listening to native speakers.

An alternative explanation appeals to the popular view that Japanese culture emphasises both ambiguity in relationships and silence in communication (Davies & Ikeno, 2002). Furthermore, while other students make no mention of the different way that politeness is encoded in the L2, for the Japanese this is of some importance:

(28)   When a customer asks a menu to a waiter [*sic*], the way to ask sounds impolite for me because it sounds too direct, strong as if he commands. (G/J)

The Learnables uses the same book for a range of languages, which could limit its ability to convey cultural nuances. Where learners' background culture organises the language of respect or politeness very differently, they also have the additional task of learning to see interactions in a novel perspective, so that their use of language becomes more appropriate to the context. A classroom can provide support here (Harmer, 2003; *cf.* Bax, 2003), and/or materials that are specifically tailored to learners from particular backgrounds (e.g. Gray & Leather (1999) recommend activities for Japanese learners of English).

Students' final comments on the CPA

So far, discussion suggests that *The Learnables* often engenders negative attitudes, particularly in those students used to more communicative approaches. However, diarists did make a series of positive comments, particularly during later lessons. The following is a representative comment:

(29)   ... I was rather sceptical at first as to whether I would actually 'learn' anything, but I know that I have. Still not convinced it is the best way to learn a new language if you actually want to use it in the near future ... I would like to continue my learning of Japanese using The Learnables, as I have enjoyed it and found it fascinating. (A/E)

Even though the material is not viewed as 'useful', A/E finds the material enjoyable and interesting; previous expectations are being re-evaluated in the light of new experience. One should not conclude that this equals an overall move to support for comprehension-based approaches, however; this new attitude stands alongside prior experience, rather than replaces it (White, 1999).

Conclusion

This review of learners' attitudes as recorded in the diaries of a group of university students reveals several points about comprehension-based learning. Firstly, absence of speaking is a major hurdle to progress for some, where the ability to recall words and constructions was prioritised. Cultural background appears to exert a strong but non-obvious influence. Although the sample is small, both Japanese learners accepted the methodology more readily than the other students, who saw comprehension and non-verbal activities as less useful in promoting recall; they rejected the idea that extensive listening leads to higher spoken fluency in the long run. This was apparently due to prior CLT experience rather than knowledge about SLA research. Even if the materials seemed to work, existing attitudes were not replaced; rather, beliefs were often adapted. This was particularly evident in students' reconciling their attitudes with positive test progress. A possible conclusion is that attitudes are resistant to change unless students feel they can extensively measure their learning. Perhaps due to experience of CLT, the most obvious way for them is via speaking. Alternatives such as hypothesis testing were strategies that only a minority employed. All this points to a strong need for reassurance from the materials or teacher regarding future opportunities for production, to promote tolerance of ambiguity in the beginning stages of learning. Given that anxiety decreased as students progressed and understood more, this is recommended.

In addition to hypothesis testing, strategies such as visualising written words were used for retention of L2 items. The data does not measure actual progress to reveal whether those learners were also more successful than those who preferred CLT. Neither do they clarify whether strategies had been developed elsewhere and then transferred to *The Learnables*, or if they were devised independently. It is also unclear to what extent all learners would develop their own strategies, or how much an absence of writing and speaking contributed to this effect. An issue for future research is whether and how learners without classroom, teacher and written text support rely on previously learned strategies, or create new ones. Furthermore, perhaps classroom learner strategies could be cultivated via an awareness of how and which strategies emerge under comprehension-orientated conditions.

Finally, as a validation of diary studies, it is unlikely that many of these points – and others, such as how recruitment of English orthography seemed to exert a strong effect on perception and production – would have emerged had students not been given the opportunity for free introspection. Future research will no doubt continue to use diary studies to gain insights into how learners perceive their acquisition of a new anguage.

Notes

1. Thanks to the students who allowed their diaries to be used as the basis for this research; two anonymous reviewers for their extensive commentaries; and Martha Young-Scholten for recommending this topic.
2. See Krashen and Terrell (1983: 7–16) and Scrivener (2005: 38–40) for reviews of other approaches.
3. For example, a learner of French who is allowed to conclude that '*fenêtre* means *window*' may overgeneralise this explanation, assuming that a (counter or teller) window (*guichet*), and a (shop) window display (*vitrine*) employ the same word in French.
4. A *model* is a description of *how* rather than *why*, a *theory* an explanation of *why* rather than *how* (VanPatten & Williams, 2007: 2–5) – in these cases, how it is possible to learn versus why learning is possible.
5. But (*cf.* Truscott, 1998), at least for vocabulary (VanPatten, 1989) and initial perception of new structures (Lee & VanPatten, 2003; VanPatten, 2004; this volume).
6. In Winitz (2003), the 6th edition of the workbook, this requirement is narrowed to not attempting mimicry while taking the lesson; it may be allowed at other times.
7. See Gibbons (1985) for criticism of the 'silent period' research and the alternative view that lack of speaking in child learners is a consequence of L2 incomprehension.
8. But note that attitudes towards real-world relevance do not reflect reality. Other than (UK English) *aeroplane*, all nouns and verbs of lessons one and two appear in the top 10% of a list of 86,800 commonest words in the British National Corpus's 100-million-item samples of written and spoken English (http://www.natcorp.ox.ac.uk); see http://www.wordcount.org, accessed 24th September 2007).
9. Other than suggesting that learners will be able to 'think' in the foreign language, these claims are absent from the later edition of *The Learnables: Book 1* (Winitz, 2003), which the students in the present study did not use.
10. US 'hokey pokey': a traditional group dance.
11. Similarly, American learners have been shown to develop a positive attitude to *The Learnables*, following prior learning experiences that were largely grammar-based (Winitz & Yanes, 2002).

Appendix

Instructions for users of *The Learnables*

Familiarise yourself with the numbers 1–10 using the recording preceding the first lesson.

Each lesson's 100 test items are divided into sequences numbered from 1 to 10. The word, phrase or sentence is heard twice, e.g. '*one ... car ... car ... two ...*

Take each lesson two to four times, sometimes without the book and perhaps while doing other activities.

Listen to the lesson all the way through; do not pause or return to earlier points.

Do not repeat the words out loud.

In each test following every second lesson, choose one answer from three possibilities for each of 10 items. Proceed if 80% are correct; otherwise, the lesson should be repeated.

(Winitz, 2002)

To exemplify this procedure, readers unfamiliar with Japanese are invited to guess the meanings of the pictures in Figure 6.1 below, taken from lessons one and five, the latter conveying the story of a man in a restaurant. What is heard is printed in *roomaji* below the pictures, but this is not seen by learners (answers immediately following):

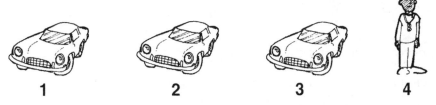

Figure 6.1 Example lessons with audio transcripts (from Winitz, H. 2002, *The Learnables, Book 1* (5th edn). Copright © [2002] International Linguistics Corporation. Reproduced with permission).

Lesson 1
Ichi. Kuruma. Kuruma.
Ni. Kuruma. Kuruma.
San. Kuruma. Kuruma.
Yon. Isa. Isa.

Lesson 5
Nana. Ueeta-ga mizu-o motte kimasu. Ueetaa-ga mizu-o motte kimasu.
Hachi. 'Sumimasen, moo sukoshi aisukuriimu-o kudasai.' Sumimasen, moo sukoshi aisukurilmu-o kudasai.'
Kyuu. Minna-ga waratte imasu. [*laughing sound*]. Minna-ga waratte imasu. [*laughing sound*].
Juu. 'Sumimasen, aisukuriimu-o kudasai.' 'Sumimasen, aisukuriimu-o kudasai.'

Answers (minus repeated items)
Lesson 1
One. Car.
Two. Car.
Three. Car.
Four. Doctor.
Lesson 5
Seven. The waiter is bringing a glass of water.
Eight. 'Excuse me, I'll have a little more ice-cream, please.'
Nine. Everyone is laughing.
Ten. 'Excuse me, I'll have some ice-cream, please.

Chapter 7

The Hidden Paradox of Foreign Language Instruction Or: Which are the Real Foreign Language Learning Processes?

WERNER BLEYHL

> *The enemies of truth are not lies, but convictions.*
> Friedrich Nietzsche

> *'Now, what I want is, Facts.'*
> Mr Gradgrind in: Charles Dickens. Hard Times

Introduction: The setting for Input, Intake and Learning

Input – Intake – Learning (in a generic sense) are three terms which are intrinsically related. If INPUT is the mass of stimuli offered to the sensory system of the learner, INTAKE is that part which the learner selects according to her or his sensory and cognitive means, possibilities, and interests. LEARNING then is that what the learner makes of Intake and preserves over a certain amount of time for appropriate use in his or her cognitive apparatus.[1]

If one reflects on the relationship of these three concepts a moment longer, one realises that they merge into a dynamic spiral. The physically describable, objective **Input** comes alive only when the individual's mind starts to process at least parts of it, elevating sections of the **Input** to a mental level and turning it into **Intake**. The linguistic form thereby performs its function as a vessel for ideas and concepts. **Learning** may then occur on a more conscious level involving meaning. On the one hand, new concepts may emerge to grapple with the complexity of the world around one, while on the other hand, new language forms (including their various patterns of linguistic behaviour) may become INTERNALISED as helpful tools for handling those concepts mentally and communicatively. As we know from empirical observation (e.g. Largo, 2001) the learner's concepts are always prior to the active use of the linguistic forms. In other words there is no language growth without a foundation of activated mental concepts.

In brief, we have the dynamism of a hermeneutic circle: an ever widening circle of acquired knowledge when experience and expectation are critically compared, concepts adjusted and/or new insights inserted in existing mental structures which are then ready and open for new experience and so forth. The *crucial point* is that the decisive processes are vastly beyond the realm of human consciousness. According to the neuroscientist Singer (2001), our sensory organs select only a few signals out of the broad spectrum of signals that are in principle available to us in our surroundings. Our primary perception, however, makes us believe that what we have taken in is all that there is. We bridge gaps with our own constructions.

Kandel (2006) maintains that every sensory system analyses the incoming information, dissects it and then reconstructs it according to the sensory systems' connections and rules. Our sensory systems are but generators of hypotheses.

So modern neurosciences do nothing but confirm Immanuel Kant's epistemological shift which philosophically did away with naive realism – yet, naive realism is still rampant in present foreign language teaching (FLT). Kant pointed out that it is not the objects in this world which our mental activity circles around but it is just the other way round: it is our capacity of perception that determines the objects around us.[2]

It remains the merit of Harris Winitz to have drawn – and anticipated – in his COMPREHENSION APPROACH (Winitz, 1981c, 1996) the methodological consequences of that insight. He maintains (a) that language ACQUISITION can only be a nonlinear process and (b) that the door opener to language is LEXIS since grammar is lexicon driven, a consensus now common in modern linguistics (Carter & McCarthy, 2006; Lewis, 1993; Tracy, 2000). Listening to Winitz's *Learnables* (Winitz, 1981d), a series of 'talking pictures' about everyday situations that lead the learner into the world of the foreign language in ever widening concentric circles, the mental categories of the various domains (intonational, phonological, lexical, syntactic, etc.) develop in the attentive learners. Their motivation is kept up when they realise that – not being overcharged with immediate PRODUCTION – they can quickly and successfully understand a relatively high quantity of meaningful lexis. Concepts and rules that regulate the behaviour of those lexical items develop subconsciously.

The selection of **Intake** is vastly beyond human consciousness. Neurosciences (Greenfield, 2000; Kandel, 2006; Roth, 2001; Spitzer, 2002) and foreign language acquisition research (Diehl *et al.*, 2000; Pienemann, 1998) have taught us that **Learning** a language (as well as human memory) is far beyond human consciousness. This means that the presentation of **Input** – the teacher's task – has only a chance of becoming effective if that **Input** is – at least partly – admitted to the sub- and unconscious perception and evaluation systems of the learner. In other words, if the teacher does not want to waste her time and energy (and that of her students), she has to be aware of the individual learner's selection and learning processes in order to gear and offer Input accordingly.

If the conditions of language learning are not respected – and a number of traditional teaching conceptions stand in the way – the best of didactic intentions may become counterproductive leading eventually to the paradox of **FLT** by making **FLT** less and less effective. This short chapter concentrates on those highly complex processes of learning and touches upon a few observations pertaining to these processes.

Look into a Classroom: A Scene at School

The following video transcription (Schwab, 2002) is of a scene in an English language class of beginners age six in Germany. It could, however, have been taken in any beginners' class of any age group in any country (see Table 7.1).

Table 7.1 Scene 'What's your name?'

Line	Person	Transcription	Commentary/video
1	T	My name is [ɪz] (,) Mrs (,) A.	Pupils are sitting in a circle
2			
3	T	what's your name (?)	
4	P1	my name **is** [ɪs] B. (.)	
5	PB	B.	T. turns to individual pupils.
6	T	well done (,) now listen (-) my name *is* [ɪz] Mrs A. (,)	
7		what's your name (?)	
8	PD	(softly, insecurely) my name is [ɪs] (D.?) (.) ..	
9	T	my name *i s* [ɪz] Mrs A. (,) what's your name (?)	
10	PF	(very softly) my name's F. (.)	
11	T	my name *i s* [ɪz] Mrs A. (,) what's your name (?)	'Is' very much lengthened
12	PG	my (,) name (,) **is** [ɪs] (,) G. (.)	

(Continued)

Table 7.1 (*Continued*)

13	T	do you remember (,) the bee (') my name *i s* [ɪz] (-)	
14		try it .. like a bee zzzzzzzz	
15	Ps	zzzzzzz	No visible reaction
16	T	stop (.) and now (,) my name (,) *i s s* [ɪzz]	
17	Ps	zzzzzzz	
18	PF	my name **is** [ɪs]	
19	T	what's your name (?)	
20	PS	my (,) name (,) **isch*** S. (-)	
21	T	what's your name?	
22	PH	my name **is** [ɪs] **H**. (.)	
23	T	her name *i s* [ɪz] **H**. (,) what's your name (?)	
24	P2	H.	
25	P3	My name **is** (..) (.)	The teacher gives up!
26	P	well done (.) oh Kooky what about you (?)	
27			

*In the local dialect German *ist* [ɪst] (English 'is' is never a problem of semantics for the learner) has been assimilated to *isch* [ɪʃ], a form considered as non-standard that should be avoided at school.

It does not seem to be an over-interpretation if we deduce certain theories behind the teacher's methodology:

(1) Learning is understood as imitation.
(2) Learning is understood as an input-output event, that is, it is tacitly assumed that somehow there is a 1:1 relationship between teaching and learning. This naive position assumes that (a) there is no difference between input and intake and (b) learning has occurred once input can satisfactorily be reproduced. The only reason for such an assumption – to put it more directly – is that the human brain is taken as a slate of wax which only needs imprinting.
(3) Learning is understood as a step-by-step linear process.
(4) Language teaching therefore 'must' follow a 'grammatical progression'.

(5) 'CONSCIOUSNESS RAISING'/the cognitive approach by instilling declarative (abstract) knowledge into the learner is understood as a guarantee against forthcoming problems.
(6) The teacher sees herself as the captain, the steersman and the organiser of the learner's mental activities and mental processes.
(7) The methodological strategy adopted is that a linguistic goal (here: *is* with the pronunciation of [z], where /z/ is a PHONEME absent in the local dialect) is wrapped into a pseudo-communicative setting. (In our case: the names of the pupils are known to everyone; no new information – meaningful to the learners - is being imparted.)

As the learners demonstrate by their behaviour, none of these age-old didactic ideas functions as hoped. The honest conclusion is: The traditional concept PPP (PRESENT–PRACTISE–PRODUCE) simply does not work. The question is: Why not? Why do learners have problems with such easy input, such a seemingly easy task, deliberately and carefully simplified by the teacher?

The answer is: Traditional FLT is based on a number of misconceptions, including those on input. In its obsession with language form, traditional FLT, in its intellectual narrowness, does not take into account fundamental claims in modern anthropology such as:

(1) The brain's primary concern is with meaning (*cf.* Roth, 2001).
(2) Most of the brain's activities – also in dealing with language – occur subconsciously. Consciousness has a very limited power in the field of language (Bleyhl, 2001; Diehl *et al.*, 2000).[3]
(3) Our brain is a social organ since it develops its capacities – including its linguistic ones – during social interactions. In other words, man is the outcome of her/his enculturation. The process of the brain's perpetual self-organisation – in all acceptance of the great importance of childhood – means that 'you never use the same brain twice', a neurological discovery not so far from Heraclitus's conviction that 'You can't step twice into the same river.'

Language, provided the appropriate conditions are given, will emerge in a process of self-organisation (e.g. Bleyhl, 1993; Lightbown, 1985, 1992; MacWhinney, 2002).

The Task of Foreign Language Teaching (FLT)

A short look at the scene 'What's your name?', set out in Table 7.1 above, reveals that language learning is not a trivial process. Rather, it requires the development of the various linguistic subsystems in the learner; the linguistic subsystems must be constructed by the learner her- or himself for later creative use. It is the teacher's task to provide the respective conditions, the respective input. This is exemplified in the field of phonology, lexis, and syntax.

Establishment of the new phonemic system

Foreign language teachers are often unaware of how skilfully evolution prepares man for language, how carefully the phonemic system of the child's linguistic community is installed. If natural principles are respected in FLT, the teacher will avoid a great deal of personal frustration and spare the students, too.

The establishment of the phonemic system in the infant

Human beings are held to be born with a genetic disposition for language (Dehaene-Lambertz & Dehaene, 1994; Eimas *et al.*, 1971). At birth babies can discriminate *all* of no less than one hundred PHONES of natural human languages. There is a slight preference for those of the mother tongue, indicating that language acquisition starts pre-natally (Gopnik *et al.*, 1999). During the first six months, that is, prior to the time infants begin to master higher levels of language learning, the infants' perceptual-cognitive and perceptual-motor systems are constantly being altered by linguistic experience (Kuhl *et al.*, 1992; Kuhl, 1998). During this period, in all cultures, mothers – with a seemingly inborn didactic faculty – often 'hyperarticulate' phones subconsciously in order to help the infants. The language heard 'remodels the map' of perception (see Figure 7.1). The mental map of phonetic 'prototypes', that is, speech sounds that are identified by adult speakers as ideal representations of a phonetic category, is then established. Thus the child's experience of contrasts with neighbouring phones is essential. These prototypes will later develop a magnet effect (the NATIVE LANGUAGE MAGNET MODEL, which means that sounds falling into those areas will be perceived as representations of the respective phoneme. They will determine CATEGORICAL PHONEMIC PERCEPTION, the influence of which was seen in Table 7.1.

There is dual support of evolution for phonemic perception apart from the general gift of hearing:

(1)   There is that inborn pre-disposition for phonemes to be activated and specified through listening experience (e.g. Kuhl *et al.*, 1992; Wode, 1994b) as a 'co-operation' between Nature and Nurture.
(2)   In addition there is a physiological change in the infant that guarantees a relatively stable system of language tradition over the generations. By the age of six months the larynx, that is, the voice box with the vocal cords, of a baby whose larynx hitherto is similar to that of the primates, moves further down. Only then is speech production physiologically possible. This marks the onset of the babbling phase. The development of the motor programme for language production can now start. (This will take time, for example, the most difficult sounds

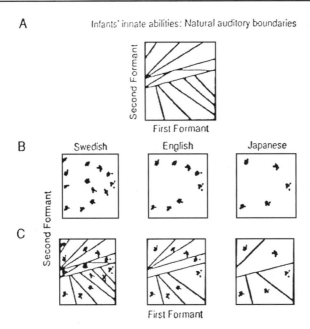

A   Infants' innate abilities: Natural auditory boundaries

Figure 7.1   The Native Language Magnet (NLM) model (from Kuhl, P. 1998, The development of speech and language. In T.J. Carew, R. Menzel and C.J. Shatz (eds) *Mechanistic Relationships between Development and Learning* (p. 61). Copyright © [1998] John Wiley & Sons Limited. Reproduced with permission).

in the /s/-group may not be mastered till the age of 10 or later.) The child will now set out to develop non-trivial, highly sophisticated motor programmes to produce speech. One must keep in mind that for the articulation of one syllable about one hundred different muscles from the tip of the tongue down to the diaphragm are involved. This means that evolution prevents wild production attempts. In other words, the message is: Nature does not want us to speak before the phonological system is mentally established (see Bleyhl, 2003b).

The infant's mapping at the phonological level is a prerequisite for coping with words. It is worth noting Kuhl's observation that this occurs 'in the absence of any formal instruction or reinforcement of the infant's behavior. In this sense, the "learning" that transpires is outside the realm of the historical versions of learning described by psychologists' (Kuhl, 1998: 60).

The establishment of the phonemic system in the second language learner

Learners of a second or a foreign language start with the language perception developed for their mother tongue. The magnet effect of that system will categorise the phonemes of the other language accordingly (*cf.* the scene in Table 7.1). Since perception determines production we cannot expect adequate production without adequate perception.

To give an example: Notorious are the problems of Japanese learners of English trying to distinguish /r/ from /l/. Since there is no /l/ in their language they cannot perceive the difference (see Figure 7.2). The naive language amateur finds it is hard to believe that a SECOND LANGUAGE LEARNER is not automatically able to perceive the actual physical reality, the actual physical differences between certain sounds.

Yet the human brain is capable of learning, despite all the age-dependent restrictions discussed in the literature (e.g. Bleyhl, 2003a; Long, 1990) and despite the window of development narrowing by the age of nine for speech sounds (Peltzer-Karpf & Zangl, 1998: 15). Special listening training programmes with carefully enunciated and lengthened problematic speech sounds, where learners – action-oriented – discover the differences themselves, can be successful, also with adults, in a few weeks (see also Piske *et al.*, 2001).

The idea that a reliable system of speech perception should be established before speech production is required is also valid for foreign language learning in the classroom. Empirical research has shown that those foreign language classes where listening comprehension is the main focus at the beginning and where speaking is not insisted on straight away later show much better pronunciation and – persistent – higher self-confidence when communicating (Bleyhl, 1996; McCandless & Winitz, 1986). Krashen's (1982a) 'silent period' is more than simply to be tolerated.

It is the faculty for perceiving the respective phonemes that is a prerequisite for the acquisition of lexis and thus for listening comprehension. And listening comprehension is the prerequisite of learning to read and write. This holds not only in first language acquisition but also in SECOND

A

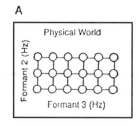

B

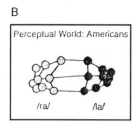

C

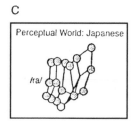

Figure 7.2 Physical (acoustic) versus perceptual distance (from Kuhl, P. 1998, The development of speech and language. In T.J. Carew, R. Menzel and C.J. Shatz (eds) *Mechanistic Relationships between Development and Learning* (p. 59). Copyright © [1998] John Wiley & Sons Limited. Reproduced with permission).

LANGUAGE ACQUISITION as studies of young L2 learners with immigrant backgrounds reveal (Marx & Jungmann, 2000).

Again we have an example of circular causation that is, of the mutual cooperation of Nature and Nurture. As the studies of the development of phonemic perception clearly reveal, 'comprehended input' and experience are essential for the growth of our categories of perception (Kuhl *et al.*, 1992). The precondition for production is that there is an appropriate perceptive apparatus which in turn is the precondition for successful imitation. This appropriate perceptive apparatus is much more subtle than the often advocated 'language awareness'. Imitation is not a primary but a secondary skill.[4]

Establishment of the appropriate new concepts, that is, the lexicon

Let us for a moment assume that language is 'matter'. And in a second step let the reader be reminded of Plato's attitude towards matter: He maintained that matter as such has no reality; it is wakened into reality only if ideas, concepts are present in such matter. Also for Wittgenstein (1963: 28) it is crystal clear: A symbol without meaning is irrelevant. Largo (2001) attempts to pinpoint exactly how a concept, a word, develops. Figure 7.3 shows Largo's findings on the relatedness between mental development,

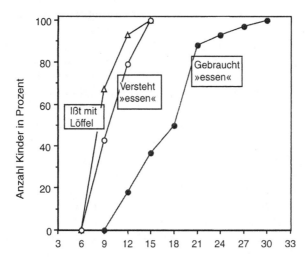

Figure 7.3 Relatedness between mental development, physical activities, linguistic input, understanding, and speaking (from Largo, R.H. 2001, *Babyjahre. Die frühkindliche Entwicklung aus biologischer Sicht* (p. 318). Copyright © [2000] Piper Verlag GmbH, München. Reproduced with permission).

physical activities, linguistic input, understanding and speaking. The lines indicate (1) the percentage of children ('Anzahl Kinder in Prozent') that eat with a spoon ('Ißt mit Löffel'), (2) understand the word *essen* 'eat' ('Versteht »essen«') and (3) use the word themselves ('Gebraucht »essen«'). It also shows the range of INDIVIDUAL VARIATION along the age scale.

The same applies to the foreign language learner: Form has no relevance without meaning, without function. Yet, form and the various features of language have to be recognised and classified as well. This means that on all those interdependent levels of language, a respective process of categorisation is necessary. Input is 'objective'. Meaning is not. When an innocent looking sentence such as 'I saw a man on the hill with a telescope' (an example sentence given to students to make them aware of the ambiguity of everyday language) is analysed, it becomes obvious that not only does a word need context and well-formed clauses, but the understanding of a particular situation is necessary (see Figure 7.4).

So linguistic reference at any given moment must be recognised as a social act. And we also have to recognise the empirical fact that a linguistic referent (be it a word or a whole sentence such as 'I saw a man ...') can only be understood in the context of social interaction, that is when speaker and hearer are aware of the perspective of the respective other. The implications of this insight go far. Focusing primarily on linguistic form, on grammar, and so on, is not justifiable, it does not do justice to the function of language. A scene where a linguistic utterance is made (such as the example above) and where at least two persons pay attention to the same situation is (a) not restricted to mere perception, nor is it (b) a purely linguistic event. Such a scene of commonly shared reality contains many more features which correspond to the world and to the social situation.[5] What is decisive for mutual understanding is joint attention, awareness of the perspective of communication partners, awareness that interlocutors carve out the same section of the infinite world. Language comes to life in social interactions, and language is learned in social interaction and not when the learner is confronted with bits and pieces of input, nor when language is reduced to one dimension. Our perception and understanding of language is the product of simultaneous interactions between all language levels, sensory and non-sensory, whereby language can only make sense with the help of our simultaneously activated knowledge of the world. Language relies on memory, and 'every memory exists in a nested group of other memories, which, in turn, rely on the integrated operations within the whole body' (Greenfield, 2000: 197).

Meaning is thus not inherent in the signs, in the language symbols, but in the mind of the perceiver. When we turn to written language and look at Figure 7.5, we see only the horizontal threesome of signs. The central

"I saw the man on the hill with a telescope."
Ich sah den Mann auf dem Hügel mit einem Fernrohr.

1. I saw₁ (the man on the hill) (with a telescope₁).

2. I saw₁ (the man (on the hill)(with a telescope₁)).

3. I saw₁ (the man on (the hill with a telescope₂)).

4. I saw₂ the man (on the hill) (with a telescope₁).

5. I saw₂ the man on (the hill with a telescope₂).

6. I saw₂ the man (on the hill with a telescope₁).

Figure 7.4   The multiple meanings of a sentence (from Bleyhl, W. (ed.) 2000, *Fremdsprachen in der Grundschule. Grundlagen und Praxisbeispiele* (p. 13). Copyright © [2000] Bildungshaus Schulbuchverlage Westermann Schroedel Diesterweg Schöningh Winklers GmbH. Reproduced with permission).

one is undoubtedly the letter B. However, when we only see the vertical threesome we have the number 13. In other words, it is our brain that does the work of interpreting and of generating meaning.

This act of interpretation – as perception psychology and GESTALT PSYCHOLOGY have maintained for a long time – is not a linear, but a non-linear process, as a glance at Figure 7.6 (What word is…?) reveals. In order to decide whether the first letter is an R, one has to know what the two other letters are, and so on. The various stimuli are simultaneously taken

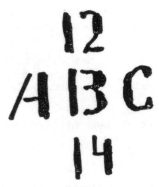

Figure 7.5 The mind creates the meaning – A-B-C or 12-13-14

Figure 7.6 What word here is partly obliterated by ink-blots? (from LINDSAY, *Human Information Processing*, 2E. © 1977 Wadsworth, a part of Cengage Learning, Inc. Reproduced by permission. www.cengage.com/ permissions).

in, processed and then the interpretation that makes the most sense is filtered out. A linearly working computer will never be able to 'read' this figure. Here neurobiology can give us an explanation because we now know about the modular organisation of the brain and about the continuous cooperation of those modules, that is, their continuous interchange of 'information'.

The question arises: What enables the brain to construct meaning to any primarily arbitrary input? The answer is that it is the sum of the previously experienced social interaction that empowers it. The decisive point is that during social 'joint attention' situations it is the interpersonal timing that guarantees the joining of the attention and of the mental activities. Here language and other sensual experiences are bound together. Thereby it is the immediacy of the social coordination that is crucial. Striano (cited in Wilkens, 2006) has presented clear evidence that if during mother-infant interaction cycles the mother's reaction is retarded longer than one second, the infant smiles more seldom. It shows signs of uncertainty in that it shows means of self-appeasement more frequently (namely touching itself). If more than three seconds pass before the mother's response is transmitted, then the infant will not recognise that the mother's words were an answer to its earlier questioning behaviour. So if parents do not react immediately to the impulses of their babies, the latter do not recognise that they were the initiators of an interaction and they fall into a pit of helplessness. The development of social competence and self-reliance is impaired. (This corresponds precisely to the neurolinguistic and neuro-physiological findings of neural synchronisation according to Hebb's principle of 'Neurons that fire together wire together'. See, e.g. Damasio, 1994; Kandel, 2006; Singer, 1990; Spitzer, 2000, 2002.)

In foreign language teaching, it is the creation and maintenance of such situations of joint attention where teachers provide the learners with the most linguistic input. The teacher's methodological means are techniques like TOTAL PHYSICAL RESPONSE (Asher, 1977), and that of storytelling (e.g. Bleyhl, 2002): techniques that are all the more effective the more sensitive the teachers are to the behavioural – for example, the body language – feedback of the students. In storytelling it is just the 'magical' narrator who succeeds in involving and maintaining the attention the longest and thus provides the learners with a high quantity of input. Such a magical narrator uses a wide range of paralingual and non-verbal means of communication such as mimicking and body language. Good stories can add respective emotional and intellectual involvement and thus heighten the quality of input.

Establishment of the new grammar

Although highly illustrative examples of the wide field of grammar cannot be demonstrated here, one such example can be mentioned: the problematic choice between the simple present and present progressive, which opens up a complex world proving that consciousness can never master at the moment of application (see Maule, 1991). Bland (1988: 65) sums up her studies in the field as follows: 'Not only does the progressive have different effects on different types of verbs, but it has also different effects on different speech acts.' In brief, also summarising Brindley (1987), grammatical aspect is not teachable. It is subconscious sensitivity to grammar that the learner requires, and as a prerequisite, the sensitivity for situations, for people and their sensitivities. This is all the more so since grammar is meaning-driven. It is merely a product of the viewpoint (Buckmaster, 2003: 11, 7). What is needed is a mental grasp of the entire, specific situation. This sensitivity is acquired while experiencing language input in meaningful interaction. Thereby the brain as our pattern-seeking device extracts the rule itself (see Christison, 1999; Spitzer, 2002). We do not stick solely to the examples experienced; we can be creative with language.

The traditional assumption in foreign language teaching (that teachers have to teach rules and have the learners practise them one by one) is not justified and is refuted by considerable neurolinguistic and other empirical research. The learner's brain needs a range of examples to enable the brain to construct the rules. The learner's grammatical knowledge is implicit knowledge, knowledge that is not directly accessible to consciousness (Schwartz, 1999; Schwarz, 1996: 49). Consciousness raising, focusing on form, may help an individual learner after he or she has accumulated a critical mass of respective experience. The learner needs a mass of (interesting) input, and once a critical mass of about 400 to 500 lexical items has been internalised (Marchman & Bates, 1994), syntax emerges. It can also be argued that this holds in foreign language classes with three to five lessons a week.

This means that the curriculum, the input arrangement in the widest sense, has complete freedom and need not respect a grammatical curriculum, provided learners understand the message. The curriculum has to provide a whole range of varying phenomena for it is only by experiencing the contrasts that the peculiar qualities of each linguistic phenomenon can be discovered.

Grammatical and morphological acquisition sequences in English

Morphology and grammatical structures are acquired not at random but in a sequence, pointed out earlier by Dulay *et al.* (1982). And, contrary to traditional beliefs of language teaching, this sequence cannot be altered through teaching or specially arranged input (*cf.* Diehl *et al.*, 2000; Ellis, 1992; Wode, 1981). Pienemann's (1998) list runs as shown in Table 7.2.

The message to the foreign language teacher is (1) that this sequence cannot be altered through instruction, (2) it is also independent of the learner's age and intelligence. (3) Furthermore, the influence of the learner's first language is negligible, it is at the most marginal (also see Hawkins, 2001). The interior logic of the development of the highly interrelated hierarchy of the language-specific processing resources is described and explained in Pienemann (1998). It is noteworthy that the principles of acquisition are similar in L1 and in L2 acquisition. One note of warning should be added here: Insistence on the production of language structures far beyond the immediate level of development will delay, if not jeopardise, the further language development of the individual learner (Diehl *et al.*, 2000: 375; Pienemann, 2006: 47).

The Paradox of FLT

Philosophically speaking it is the heritage of Cartesian rationalism that in foreign language teaching so many still believe in the basically reductionist input–output model of language learning.[6] Input revolving

Table 7.2 Acquisition sequence in English according to Pienemann's Processability Theory (rearranged, from Lenzing, A. 2004 Analyse von Lehrwerken für den Englischunterricht in der Grundschule (p. 37). Copyright © [2004] FMF Landesverband Schleswig-Holstein. Reproduced with permission.)

Stages	Phenomena	Examples
1	Words	Hello, Five Dock, Central
	Formulae	How are you? Where is X? What's your name?
2	S neg V(O)	Me *no* live here./I *don't* live here.
	SVO	Me live here.
	SVO-Question	You live here?
	-ed	John play*ed*.
	-ing	Jane go*ing*.
	Plural -s (Noun)	I like cat*s*.
	Poss -s (Noun)	Pat*'s* cat is fat
3	Do-SV(O)-?	*Do* he live here?
	Aux SV(O)-?	*Can* I go home?
	Wh-SV(O)-?	*Where* she went? *What* you want?
	Adverb-First	*Today* he stay here.
	Poss (Pronoun)	I show you *my* garden.
	Object (Pronoun)	Mary called *him*.
4	Copula S (x)	*Is* she at home?
	Wh-copula S (x)	*Where* is she?
	V-particle	Turn it *off*!
5	Neg/Aux-2nd-?	Why *didn't* you tell me? Why *can't* she come?
	Aux 2nd-?	Why *did* she eat that? What *will* you do?
	3sg-s	Peter lik*es* bananas.
6	Cancel Aux-2nd	I wonder *what he wants*.

around a particular – usually formal – language feature is presented to the learner, who then has to reproduce and practise carefully didactised language. In fact, it is a misguided attempt to linearise learning as much as possible. The result is the tragic irony of FLT. The weaker the teachers feel themselves to be while handling the foreign language, the more they rely on teaching grammar and on letting the learners write to produce a solid basis for evaluation, that is, for marking their grammatical errors. What is thought to be a good thing, namely grammarising [be it in the form of organising the course according to an (always arbitrary) grammatical progression or be it by instilling declarative, metalinguistic knowledge in learners who are never all ready for it] achieves the opposite of what is intended. Since success is not quickly achieved, learners repeat the same errors and more parcelling of language and more grammarising takes place.

Finally we come to *the ultimate paradox in FLT*: The more instruction focuses on linguistic form, the more instruction is organised in a regulatory way, the more it advances in small steps, the poorer the results are. The more the evolutionary given language acquisition capacity is suffocated by well-meaning, overprotective didactic intentions, the more the outcome is frustration. In contrast one can experience that the more instruction is based on the presentation of interesting content, the more language is authentic and embedded in relevant contexts, the more students are stimulated to roam the world of the new language according to their interests (the more the evolutionary given capacity is trusted and room is allowed for hypothesis testing), the faster, the more sustained that particular foreign language is learned and the better the results are. To note a few reasons:

(1) Since consciousness can focus only on one idea at a time (the consensus in the neurosciences) focusing on form invariably takes place at the expense of focusing on meaning.

(2) It is the interplay of the many linguistic and paralinguistic dimensions that facilitates the non-linear processes of language learning.

(3) Comments from students who were informally questioned after FLT sessions of grammarizing language regularly go as follows: 'The more the teacher explains the less we understand.'[7]

(4) Foreign language learning in traditional classes is felt by learners to be 'a painful experience ... [a] task requiring considerable intellectual activity on their part' (Ellis, 2002: 177). In other words, FLT becomes an intellectual endeavour, turning off the majority of learners, who are then left with a notorious fear of failure. The detrimental effect of fear on learning, however, is widely known and can also be explained by neuroscience (Roth, 2001; Spitzer, 2004). One set of findings relates to the well-known avoidance strategy and the self-consolation of the learner who convinces himself that he is 'not gifted in languages'.

(5) On the other hand, such traditional grammarising is not convincingly successful even with intelligent students at elite universities [see the birth history of Asher's Total Physical Response (Asher, 1977)].

(6)   One of the most comprehensive studies made, the DESI *(Deutsch-Englisch-Schülerleistungen-International)* Study (Klieme *et al.*, 2006; Schröder *et al.*, 2006) evaluating the English language competence of 14-year-old students after four years of English language instruction in schools in Germany reveals that those schools which achieve the poorest results have curricula and textbooks with the slowest linguistic progression and regulate the course most intensively.

One interesting finding to emerge from the DESI study is that those students who had had bilingual subject matter teaching (some only in one school subject) were two years of language development ahead of their traditionally taught fellow students. Another surprising result was that excellent and poor language performers hardly differed in their grammaticality judgements, that is, in 'language awareness'. In other studies where the *Learnables* (Winitz, 1981b) were used, there was evidence that implicit language learning outperformed courses stressing explicit language learning (Bleyhl, 2001; Winitz & Verspoor, 1991).

Conclusion

This chapter is not ready to call for a complete ban on focusing on form in FLT; awareness of form is naturally part of first and natural language learning. However, decades of teaching experience and classroom observation point to the conclusion that what is generally seen as a remedy, namely the consciousness raising that is quite often intimidating to learners, turns out to be counterproductive. This chapter has tried to make the reader aware of the compelling findings in developmental psychology that claim metacognitive and metalinguistic insight are secondary (Stern, 2002). For consciousness raising (and traditional teaching) to have a positive effect on language learning a prior critical mass of experience in the respective domain is required. That is, the learner must have adequately processed a necessary amount of input, and this is best achieved when the learner has had the opportunity to listen to and comprehend meaningful language. The teacher's task thus consists of not only presenting language input which the learner finds worth dealing with, but also in devising tasks that challenge the learner emotionally and intellectually and that give her/him immediate feedback on whether what is deduced is tenable. A trivial, yet practical example for the teaching objective of the /s/ vs. /z/ distinction in the scene 'What's your name?' (Table 7.1) could be to present an appropriate picture and then ask the learners 'Show us the *ice* the polar bear is sitting on', 'Show us the *eyes* of the polar bear' where perceptual differences become connected to their function. Since we can safely say that language processing is grounded on 'the direct processing of embodied perspectives of the type that were also important during the period of mimetic communication' (MacWhinney, 2002: 36; see also Bateson, 1981) the involvement of images leads to more sustained learning.

So it comes as no surprise that types of language learning scenarios such as immersion teaching (Petit, 2002; Wode, 1995, 2004), bilingual subject matter teaching, CONTENT AND LANGUAGE INTEGRATED LEARNING (CLIL) (Klieme *et al.*, 2006) or TASK-BASED LANGUAGE LEARNING and teaching (Ellis, 2003) are considerably more successful than traditional FORM-FOCUSED LANGUAGE LEARNING. What these arrangements have in common is that the learner is not squeezed into a language structure, but may respond to an intellectual challenge according to her or his respective competence. Such scenarios leave space for language hypothesis testing and non-sanctioned language production since in these settings the focus truly is primarily on meaning.[8]

Notes

1. The reader is challengingly invited to fill in by means of her/his imagination the metaphor of comparing foreign language learning to the processes of selecting (a) food, (b) eating and (c) digestion (including all the processes of metabolism necessary for growth and maintenance). There, too, most of the decisive processes occur beyond the control of consciousness, a fact which so far has not been too detrimental to the human race.
2. Concepts like 'consciousness raising' run the danger of becoming chimeras with people educated in theoretical linguistics, an education that had coined their categories of perception. Such categories cannot be superimposed onto a linguistically non-educated normal foreign language learner. The learner, like any linguist, can develop such categories only secondarily after having experienced and acquired sufficient language (Stern, 2002).
3. Neuroscience sees the brain as a dynamic self-organising system with simultaneously cooperating networks. It is the synchronic simultaneous activity (oscillation in the same rhythm) of neurons out of assemblies in various areas that characterises this cooperation and creates temporally new temporal assemblies according to the respective functional task, even across areas that process the incoming information of a particular sense. Since all languages have the same temporal structure of speech (of about three seconds), it can not be assumed that language is determined by rules of syntax but can safely be seen as dependent on the basic temporal structure of the brain's working rhythm (Pöppel, 1985: 71).
4. This does not contradict the fact that certain imitative capacities are inborn, such as sticking out one's tongue. A new born baby is capable of doing this when it sees it being done. And even if those 'mirror neurons' (which mentally train motor programmes for actions that a spectator sees others perform) do play an important role for imitating actions and even for understanding the emotions of others (Bauer, 2006), in language imitation, children obviously need some preliminary training.
5. Schulz von Thun (2005), a communicational psychologist, in the wake of Karl Bühler and Paul Watzlawick, points out that levels for a given utterance are at least fourfold: (1) a content level, (2) an appellative level, (3) an expressive

level and (4) information with regard to the social relationship between the communicators.

6. The basic inadequacies of Cartesian thinking for language teaching are the fundamental separation of mind and body, the isolation of phenomena, and the assumption that cognitive activity is all conscious (see also Damasio, 1994).

7. Investigations on how grammatical explanations intended as a help are understood and misinterpreted even by good students (Zimmermann, 1992) turn out to be almost 'horror studies'.

8. At the neuorological level, these scenarios are opportunities for triggering the activity of dopamine decisive for neural growth and connection building.

Part 2

Input Matters in Phonology

Chapter 8

Input as a Critical Means to an End: Quantity and Quality of Experience in L2 Phonological Attainment

ALENE MOYER

Introduction

This chapter explores new understandings of the significance of INPUT for long-term attainment in a second language (L2) with an emphasis on the phonological realm, where much of the relevant research is emerging. While the short-term impact of input has been given much attention recently (see Moyer, 2006 for a brief review of listening comprehension research), it is only over the long-term that we can see what lasting benefits input may have. I first contextualise the issue, outlining how input has been defined in the research traditionally, in order to contrast those early measures with new methodological developments. AGE OF ONSET and LENGTH OF RESIDENCE are briefly discussed, followed by more recent measures such as language contact and language use as indicators of authentic TARGET LANGUAGE input.

Two main assumptions guide the discussion and conclusions: first, that *long-term attainment in L2 is a reflection of both quantity and quality of input,* and second, that *the learner's orientation to the target language is the main force behind how s/he utilizes L2 input.* This focus on *input as experience* assumes a learner who is actively engaged in the acquisition process, not a passive bystander for whom exposure alone is sufficient – that is clearly not the case for most late learners, and even for many who begin early. The collective research points to the need for a greater focus on how and why input matters, vis-à-vis these indicators: (1) *sources of input,* namely, domains that serve personal and informal communicative functions; (2) *intention toward L2,* exemplified by the shift toward L2 as the primary language.

Traditional Measures of Input in L2 Phonology

Age of onset

Over the last three decades, SECOND LANGUAGE ACQUISITION (SLA) research has provided strong evidence for the negative impact of a late start in L2 (beyond early childhood), typically measured as AGE OF ARRIVAL to the target language (TL) country (for immigrants). Here, I will use the term age of onset, or AO, since it applies equally well to classroom and non-classroom learners (both in and beyond the TL environment). Brought to the forefront of SLA research by Johnson and Newport (1989) and Long (1990), the linear relationship between AO and attainment in morphology, syntax and phonology in L2 has been firmly established (Birdsong, 1992; Bongaerts *et al.*, 1997; Coppieters, 1987; Fathman, 1975; Flege *et al.*, 1995a, 1995b, 1999; Jia *et al.*, 2002; Johnson & Newport, 1989; Moyer, 1999, 2004a, 2005, 2006, 2008; Munro & Mann, 2005; Patkowski, 1980; Purcell & Suter, 1980; Thompson, 1991; see Hyltenstam & Abrahamsson, 2003 for a comprehensive review). At the same time, some SLA scholars dispute whether the CRITICAL PERIOD for language learning is truly 'critical', or unyielding, based on evidence for NATIVE-LIKE performance among small subsets of late learners (Birdsong, 1992; Birdsong & Molis, 2001; Ioup *et al.*, 1994; Olson & Samuels, 1982; Van Boxtel *et al.*, 2003; White & Genesee, 1996). The possibility of 'separate' critical periods for phonology versus other aspects of language seems strong, given that 'exceptional' learners are more prevalent when tasks are focused on grammar, as in grammaticality judgments (Birdsong, 1992; Birdsong & Molis, 2001; see Long, 2005 for a recent critical discussion), but appear far less often for phonology.

It is important to point out that evidence for and against a critical period in language learning has been problematic for a number of reasons. First and foremost, learners across studies are rarely matched in terms of experience with L2 (especially instruction) and motivation to sound native, meaning that the input received is not comparable, nor is learner orientation to the target language. For phonology, comparability has been particularly problematic because some pronunciation tasks are 'seeded' with difficult sounds (Moyer, 1999, 2004a, 2007; Thompson, 1991) while other studies avoid this in order to more readily fool the raters, thus offering a limited view of what constitutes phonological abilities (see Long, 2005 for discussion; also Moyer, 2007). Conclusions from one study therefore do not necessarily (in)validate those of another, and scattered evidence for so-called 'exceptional' learners is too inconsistent to be generalizable.

The second, and perhaps most compelling, problem is that AO is inherently connected to other input concerns such as length of residence and instruction in the target language. This means that much of the purported evidence for a critical period has been over-interpreted, except where factors other than AO are taken into account.[1] A third problem is that, despite a long history of evidence suggesting the importance of socio-psychological orientation factors (e.g. motivation, ATTITUDES toward the target language, etc.), some scholars are dubious about the role they play, in part because an early start in L2 presents a kind of conundrum; it is typically associated with more positive affiliations and attitudes toward the target language, deeper connections culturally and socially, and so on. In other words, we cannot be sure which is the more direct or predominant force – age or AFFECT – for L2 learners; the observed significance of affective factors could be an ARTEFACT of their relationship to AO (see Oyama, 1976).[2] As a counterpoint, recent studies on learners across an AO range demonstrate the relative (statistical) power of affective and experiential factors for phonological fluency (Moyer, 2004a, 2008).[3] At this stage, however, the directness of any given factor is unclear, and the potential conflation of age with its concomitant factors presents an ongoing methodological challenge.

These points of debate notwithstanding, statistical modeling should not be the predominant force guiding SLA research and theory. The gap in our understanding can be stated simply as this: While a late start could indicate (largely unobservable) neuro-cognitive constraints on one's ability to acquire language to a native level – and especially for accent – AO is essentially a reflection of exposure; it does not tell us anything about the structure or utilization of the input received, for example, whether we can discern any patterns in the availability of authentic input for very young learners as opposed to older ones, or why some learners seek out more opportunities to use L2 than others. These considerations are important given that AO is highly correlated to instruction and education in the target language, contact with NATIVE SPEAKERS (NS), intention to reside in-country, desire to sound native, comfort with cultural and linguistic assimilation, and so forth (see Jia *et al.*, 2002; Moyer, 2004a, 2008). In short, because of its close association with numerous aspects of experience, input, and orientation, AO leaves much to be desired as an explanation for what is a very complex endeavor – one that is, by its nature, grounded in a social framework.

It is a truism that first language acquisition takes care of itself, meaning that all children become native-level speakers (assuming normal social, cognitive and psychological conditions), but this is clearly not so for those acquiring a language later in life.[4] Here, authentic input and the opportunity to develop linguistic fluency in a supportive environment are no longer guaranteed, yet their importance does not diminish. These are fundamentally QUALITATIVE issues that have been treated only preliminarily in the research on age effects thus far. Keeping with the traditional focus on QUANTITATIVE measures of L2 experience then, we turn to length of residence, the second most common yardstick for measuring L2 input.

Length of residence

As a simple, continuous measure, length of residence (LOR) has long been studied as a factor in ultimate attainment in L2 phonology (Asher & Garcia, 1969; Flege *et al.*, 1995b; Moyer, 1999, 2004a, 2008; Oyama, 1976; Thompson, 1991; see also Flege, this volume). As with AO, its impact has been over-simplified (or under-explained) because, as a discrete measure only, it reveals nothing about the quality of TL experience. In addition, it is highly correlated to AO and thus its independent effect is unclear. It has been a mainstay in age effects research for at least two reasons, however: (1) it lends itself to quantification, and is therefore easily tested for statistical significance (but see Note 1); (2) in-country residence presumably measures the learner's exposure to authentic input, and thus, meaningful use of the target language. Anecdotally, however, we all know of immigrants with many years' residence in their adopted countries who never come close to native-like proficiency in accent (or morphosyntax). Perhaps because this second assumption is *not* universally valid (i.e. in-country residence does not guarantee quality input or interaction), statistical tests of its significance have been inconsistent (see Piske *et al.*, 2001 for discussion). Flege and Liu (2001) put this issue to the test by comparing 60 students and non-students (all Chinese immigrants to the United States) on phonemic recognition, listening comprehension and grammaticality judgments. The statistical analyses indicate that LOR is not significant for the non-students, meaning that extra years in-country do not matter. For the students, LOR is highly significant even when effects from other (possibly conflated) variables are partialled out. The authors speculate that the kind of input students received from native speakers, as well as teachers, made the difference, and this is why LOR was significant. In other words, just living in-country does not necessarily lead to greater attainment; input and practice play a pivotal role.

Like AO, LOR is not a terribly descriptive measure of L2 experience, and it is an unreliable predictor of L2 phonological attainment. Despite several decades of inquiry, there is little discussion of what underlies these statistical contradictions. One obvious conclusion is that mere exposure is not enough; LATE LEARNERS must engage in the L2 environment in certain ways, taking advantage of the surrounding input to further their fluency. Circumstances favorable to such endeavors naturally vary across learners, depending on age as well as ethnic, social, educational and professional background. It is no real surprise, then, that different populations in different settings produce variable results.

A recent example illustrates the complexity underlying the LOR construct. In a study of immigrants to Germany with extensive experience in the language, Moyer (2004a) was able to correlate performance on a number of tasks (read-aloud and extemporaneous, guided speaking) with specific L2 input factors such as contact with native speakers, instruction in the target language, and many others. Measurements of these factors included quantitative survey data on the numbers of hours per week, as well as qualitative survey and interview data on the consistency of contact with native speakers over time, contexts for L2 use, sense of self and identity in the second language, and so on. An analysis of introspective, guided interviews for these learners (AO mean 12 years; LOR mean six years) supported the conclusions from the quantitative analysis. Together, this integrated approach to the experience issue confirms the following psychological, social, and cognitive implications of LOR:

(1) *Psychological:* LOR correlates to a sense of satisfaction with attainment, personal motivation toward L2, and sense of overall fluency.
(2) *Social:* LOR correlates to frequency of spoken contact with NS, and intention to reside permanently in-country.
(3) *Cognitive:* LOR correlates to overall years of L2 instruction as well as L2 educational experience (other subjects taught in L2), instructional emphasis on interactive and communicative use of L2 (not just formal translation-type activities), amount of classroom feedback on pronunciation, and types of phonological training (Moyer, 2004a: 143).

In sum, a longer LOR indicates optimal instruction and targeted feedback, as well as greater contact with native speakers, and implies numerous other social and psychological benefits. Importantly, similar relationships are found for AO among this group, with one additional noteworthy set of correlations: Older learners report greater reluctance to initiate social contact with Germans, and do not typically ask for feedback on their German, that is, they do not seek to improve their fluency in the same ways as younger learners do. Taking all of this into consideration, we can conclude that learner orientation and input work together as they decisively impact attainment; those with more instruction and more personal contacts are judged significantly closer-to-native in accent, and they express greater sense of confidence and identity in L2 (see Moyer, 1999, 2008 for similar findings).

Not surprisingly, AO and LOR typically demonstrate overlapping connections to these kinds of experiential and socio-psychological factors (see Jia *et al.*, 2002; Moyer, 2008; Purcell & Suter, 1980). Yet because such connections are seldom acknowledged as relevant to the critical period/maturation issue per se, we find ourselves at a sort of methodological standstill. Many facets of L2 experience and orientation underlie traditional exposure-type measures like AO and LOR. Only by examining how these concomitant influences are interwoven can we come to a deeper understanding of their observed impact.

Recent Research: Input as Language Contact and Use

With the prominence of LOR and AO firmly established in the research, several detailed aspects of L2 input have recently come to light, especially for the phonological realm. This section examines how language use and contact reflect not just exposure, but the actual utilization of input to positive ends.

One way to measure input beyond years of total exposure is to look at language contact, or opportunities for language use. This is not so straightforward, however, and has rarely been approached empirically for that reason. Language contact, in general, can imply any number of things, including formal instruction, structured or unstructured activities beyond the classroom, personal communications, daily business transactions, academic or work-related endeavors, and so on. This implies a range of INPUT QUALITY, authenticity, formality, interactivity, and so on, and thus, specific criteria are needed to narrow down some points of focus. This section briefly considers both the quantification and the qualification of L2 contact and use, based on a few specific criteria recently shown to be significant for L2 phonology.

Time on task

Perhaps the most common measure of language contact among instructed learners is the number of semesters or years spent studying the language. It is highly significant for long-term outcomes in L2 phonology according to a number of studies (Diaz-Campos, 2004; Elliott, 1997; Flege & Liu, 2001; Flege *et al.*, 1999; Moyer, 1999, 2004a; Purcell & Suter, 1980), but not consistently so (*cf.* Flege *et al.*, 1995b; Thompson, 1991; see Piske *et al.*, 2001 for review), perhaps due to the fact that it is not as straightforward a measure as it appears. There are inevitable differences in the quality of instruction, both because of the teacher's own linguistic skills, and the inherent circumstantial differences of setting, curriculum, pedagogical approach, class size, and so on. This makes comparisons across studies somewhat tenuous.

As for what kinds of instruction are most effective for developing a more authentic accent, COMMUNICATIVE APPROACHES appear to be preferable to grammar-translation (Moyer, 2004a), likely because they focus on meaning and interaction, and thus assist in the possible restructuring of L2 hypotheses and learner 'uptake' of new target forms (Lyster & Ranta, 1997; Swain, 1995; Swain & Lapkin, 1995; see Pica, 1994 for review). Overt instruction on suprasegmentals like stress, pitch and intonation patterns also appears to be significant, though too few studies have looked at this factor, so these are preliminary conclusions only (see Derwing & Rossiter, 2003; Elliott, 1997; Missaglia, 1999; Moyer, 1999, 2004a). At this point, we can (cautiously) conclude that instruction does represent input and practice, at the very least, and that exposure to it is beneficial for accent, especially when activities are targeted to segmental and suprasegmental accuracy and authenticity.

Another way to test language contact is to measure the number of hours spent using L2 beyond the classroom. With regards to hours on task, two criteria have recently demonstrated significance for phonological attainment: (1) weekly or daily hours spent on L2-oriented activities; (2) use of L2 relative to L1. Simply looking at hours on task, one of the most interesting sets of findings comes from an early study by Purcell and Suter (1980) which shows that contact with native speakers in formal (work and school) domains is significant for accent, but not nearly as significant as informal contact, such as living with a native speaker (measured as total contact months) (see also Flege & Fletcher, 1992; Tahta *et al.*, 1981). More recently, segmental accuracy has been shown to improve based on amount (days per week) of L2 use beyond the classroom (Diaz-Campos, 2004). (Syntactic performance has similarly been shown to benefit – see Moyer, 2005 for supporting evidence.) As for L2 use relative to L1, Flege and his colleagues have established strong support for this criterion (Flege & MacKay, 2004; Flege *et al.*, 1995b, 1999, 2002; *cf.* Flege & Liu, 2001; Thompson, 1991). To succinctly characterize this relationship: the more L2 use, the better, for both production and perception of non-native PHONES and PHONEMES.

To summarize, time on task does have benefits for second language accent, understanding that such impact varies across individuals, but the evidence is not terribly consistent. Any conclusions about how much is 'enough' would thus be premature at this point. Having examined *how often* or *how much* input makes a difference, we turn to the underlying – and more vexing – question: *must input be directed, or used, in certain ways?*

Contexts for L2 use

Once we move beyond easily quantifiable measures, the boundaries become fuzzier and the evidence far more scarce for *qualifying* L2 use.[5] Although sociolinguistics has long confirmed contextual patterns of language variation (see Giglioli, 1972) there is noticeable resistance to a context-bound paradigm within the cognitively-oriented mainstream of SLA research. The past several decades have seen a growing division between cognitively-oriented SLA scholars, and those who support a more integrated, externally-focused framework (see Collentine & Freed, 2004 for discussion). For our purposes here – examining the critical importance of input – straddling these paradigms is unavoidable; input is essential to any cognitive processing model because input fuels knowledge restructuring. It also underlies any sociologically – or psychologically – constructed model because receiving input implies communication within a learning environment, and this naturally calls to question all sorts of social and psychological issues that impact input processing. Bringing these points to bear on the language use discussion here, two specific criteria have recently come to the fore as significant: (1) the use of L2 in informal, personal domains; (2) the multiplicity of L2 contact domains, discussed below.

Using the target language informally, especially to build personal, social connections beyond a formal instructional setting, is clearly significant for long-term syntactic (Moyer, 2004b, 2005), phonological (Flege *et al.*, 1995b; Moyer, 2004a; Purcell & Suter, 1980), and even listening comprehension abilities (Moyer, 2006). This can be determined by surveying both frequency and consistency of contact, measured as hours of contact with native speakers per week (Moyer, 1999, 2004a, 2005, 2006, 2008). In addition, participants may describe their primary target language interlocutors as native speakers, other non-natives, or a combination. In Moyer's studies on accent, accent is consistently correlated to primary contact with native speakers while in-country. In addition, interactive, conversational kinds of contact and language use, as opposed to passive or receptive activities that involve mostly listening or writing, are far more likely to correlate to native-like performance (Moyer, 2004, 2006, 2008). As for access to multiple contact domains, the combination of instructional (formal) *and* informal contexts is a far more powerful predictor of attainment than is either type by itself, for several aspects of L2 ability (Moyer, 2004, 2005, 2006, 2008).

While the exact nature of these connections is unclear, it is fair to conclude that the interactive, personal nature of the input in these contexts is key. Several findings support this conclusion. First, greater informal contact with native speakers is highly significant for accent (Moyer, 2004a, 2008; see also Flege *et al.*, 1995b). Second, living with a host family is apparently more beneficial to attainment than is a dormitory-type experience for several types of language fluency (Moyer, 2005), possibly because a family setting ensures a consistent, intimate setting for interactive language contact (also, a dormitory setting does not guarantee contact to native speakers). Simply put, a home environment is a sure bet for optimal input and practice. Moreover, living with a family likely enhances one's perceived need (and desire) for greater fluency because meaningful communication is a necessary precondition for comfort in that environment.

To summarize, recent work shows that L2 use positively impacts several levels of language fluency, including phonology, when it is characterized by a variety of contact domains. The extent of native speaker (NS) contact is not just about hours of use; it represents meaningful opportunities to take in (and generate) authentic input. This makes sense from a cognitive processing point of view because multiple and complex opportunities for L2 use ensure rich input and meaningful communication (which is undoubtedly circular if more contact leads to more language use). From a socio-psychological point of view, multiple contact domains (formal and informal, interactive and receptive) indicate that various communicative and social functions are being served (for supporting evidence, see Moyer, 2008). Here we are reminded that language fluency develops in conjunction with language affiliation and identity: Multiple opportunities for language use indicate a deep investment in L2, all of which leads to growing confidence and ability (also circular).[6] For phonology specifically, several researchers have examined the significance of identity, investment, and sense of self or place in the socio-cultural context, that is, against the backdrop of the target language community (Major, 1993; Moyer, 2004a; Piller, 2002).

While these orientation factors are associated with cognitive and social strategies for improving fluency (e.g. consciously imitating native speakers' production of difficult phonemic contrasts, joining organizations to enhance NS contact, avoiding L1 speakers in favor of L2 use, as shown in Moyer, 2004a), it is not easy to understand the role these factors play through discrete measures alone. Qualitative data can help point to fuller and more appropriate interpretations of quantitative data (such as that provided by scalar and categorical questionnaire responses). Moyer's (2004a) integrated analysis of quantitative and qualitative data for immigrants to Germany shows that greater confidence in L2 and contact with native speakers are closely tied to strong affiliation with the target language, both linguistically and culturally. The combined analyses clearly point to identity as it relates to assimilation as well as attainment. Furthermore, a closer analysis of several participants' interviews shows how complex, and even contradictory, the identity issue can be. Some learners speak openly about their conflicting senses of affiliation between L1 and L2 (culturally as well as linguistically), and several also separate investment in the language from a cultural affiliation when political, cultural, and social orientations of the host country present a moral or cultural dilemma, or result in negative experiences (such as discrimination).

Because these socio-psychological issues are so complex, and because they shift in response to changing circumstances, it is not possible to confidently pinpoint their impact on attainment. It is likely, however, that these factors lead to specific behaviors, which can be directly identified and measured with some degree of accuracy and predictability.

Connecting Input and Attainment in the Big Picture: Quantity and Quality Concerns

The discussion above supports the idea that input should be more directly viewed as a reflection of language contact and use, especially in reference to learner orientation, since this determines how the learner actually *utilizes* the input available. Simply put, successful attainment in a second language – in the first language as well – relies on optimal levels of input, quantitatively and qualitatively.

As discussed above, quantity of input has been operationalized as length of residence, years of instruction, and more recently as time on task and proportion of L2 to L1 use. All appear to play a role in attainment, and the evidence cited here generally supports the significance of overall amount of input. Still, time on task does not tell the whole story. For one thing, amount of input is not (universally) sufficient to push the learner toward native-levels of ability, as evidenced by late learners who have lived years – even decades – in-country, yet maintain a distinctly non-native accent. Quantity may therefore be a better predictor of attainment if examined in terms of actual L2 use. To truly capture how this makes a difference, we must find out *why* learners use the target language as they do, that is, for what functions and to what social and psychological effects. This leads us to the importance of input *quality*, which concerns the context-bound conditions for L2 use. The evidence cited above clearly shows how fundamental input is to attainment in a second language accent, pointing to the following conclusions:

(1) Contexts for L2 use correlate significantly to accent (and morphosyntax) when they include both personal/informal domains – not just formal/professional ones – and when they are available from a number of sources.

(2) Consistent contact with native speakers – beyond brief business-like transactions such as standing in line at the grocery, ordering food, and so on – is significant for transcending predicted age constraints on phonological acquisition.

Another way of stating this is that rich opportunities for language use underscore what is essential for native-like attainment in phonology: authenticity and breadth of meaningful practice. Using L2 across multiple domains inherently means that many communicative functions are covered, including: expressive, emotional and social ones, as well as referential, or concrete ones, like exchanging basic information (the kind of function that language instruction is typically limited to). Attainment is clearly best served by rich and varied language use opportunities.

One additional conclusion – more preliminary, perhaps – is that the structuring of language use opportunities is a purposeful endeavor, and learners are more likely to pursue them when they feel no threat, either socially or psychologically. Recent qualitative methods have opened up the research along these lines so that can we explore the essence of how learners and input connect.

Acknowledging that SLA is effortful and complex – not something that takes place in a laboratory setting, or by default when one resides in-country – the evidence cited here underscores the necessity, and consequences, of learner engagement. For phonology in particular, recent work indicates that experience and orientation constitute a kind of circularity: Those with greater opportunities for L2 use also express more positive orientations toward the target language and culture. They tend to develop social strategies to increase contact to native speakers, and cognitive strategies to reflect on their own linguistic precision (Moyer, 2004a, 2004b). Such conscious strategies result in increased meaningful input and practice. To illustrate the consequences of this circularity, I refer again to the German context. Many immigrant communities in Germany face poor living conditions and relative social and geographical isolation (see Fennell, 1997; Moyer, 2005 for a review of early studies on immigrants to Germany, including the ZISA[7] database; *cf.* Schumann, 1978 for his well-known study on 'Alberto', a Spanish speaker acquiring English in the United States). To what extent can L2 German users develop real linguistic fluency under such conditions, especially with limited (or no) access to formal instruction, few possibilities for establishing personal contacts with Germans, and no intention of residing permanently? With this in mind, the quality/quantity issue can be boiled down to one simple and obvious maxim: *The opportunity to use language meaningfully across various contexts, and serving multiple communicative and social functions, is fundamental to native-like attainment, whether in L1, L2 or beyond.*

Conclusions: Moving the Research Forward

Throughout this chapter, I have emphasized the importance of social and psychological orientations, particularly for phonology, where age constraints appear most prevalent, and where identity can constitute a place of resistance. In the interest of maintaining an established identity, some late learners are reluctant to pursue a native-like accent in L2 (Moyer, 1999), even when they do not live in the target language environment. Where SLA takes place as a byproduct of immigration, identity concerns can be more acute, especially when the extant social and political tenor determine the L2 user's potential to assimilate and/or integrate. If quality and quantity of input are limited, and expectations (or potential) for assimilation are low, attainment predictably suffers. Looking at it from the individual's point of view, if the target language is not deemed to be critical, neither to survival nor to self-image, there is little incentive to pursue advanced fluency.

Along with the individual's own set of motivations and orientations, SLA is subject to broader realities, like family attitudes and support for L2, access to formal instruction and/or education in L2, and so forth. These conditions should be acknowledged as 'gatekeepers' to input, and therefore as powerful influences on attainment. Understanding the individual's circumstances within these broader frameworks requires us to expand our methods to incorporate multiple types of data, especially qualitative data to augment quantitative analysis.

Coming back to the overarching framework of this chapter, if AO is in fact the most reliable indicator of attainment – especially for accent – can we explain its impact in terms of L2 input and use? The statistical link between age and outcome has long since been established. What is needed now is a greater understanding of what maturation implies in terms of the process of acquisition, in other words, what age means for *need*, *desire* and *opportunity to become native-like*.

Based on evidence from many studies, I have reiterated here (and elsewhere) an obvious generalization for SLA, namely, that an early start predicts a greater variety of input sources, ranging from formal to informal, and covering a wide array of contact domains. The resulting opportunities to use L2 lead to greater confidence and to greater fluency. To illustrate these inherent interconnections between learner and input schematically, Figure 8.1 brings together age of onset with its primary co-varying influences, shown here as 'clusters' of factors (i.e. multiple, related influences):

(1) the cognitive processing cluster (instruction and feedback received, learner strategies, and so on);
(2) the social processing cluster (contact with NS, language use domains, and so on);
(3) the psychological processing cluster (reasons for learning L2, attitudes, and so forth), as they relate to the learner's access to, and utilisation of, authentic input in the target language.

The primary realms of L2 processing are highlighted in bold, with the fundamental connections between them in the smaller (italicised) boxes (e.g. access and opportunity, styles and strategies, and so on).

As illustrated, input takes its place in the center, as each of these processing clusters – along with AO – directly affect how the individual learner utilizes input. The term 'strategic use of input' here emphasizes the fact that learners make choices, taking advantage of available input for language restructuring purposes in accordance with their own cognitive styles; setting specific intentions, goals and outward behaviors to suit their psychological perspectives; constrained (or perhaps encouraged!) by various avenues of access to the target language.

The objective of such a schematic is not to oversimplify the conundrum that is SLA; it is to underscore the integration of these multiple realms of influence and to highlight the idiosyncratic nature of what connects them. It must be noted that these four main influences – AO along with social, psychological, and cognitive factors – are presented here as universally

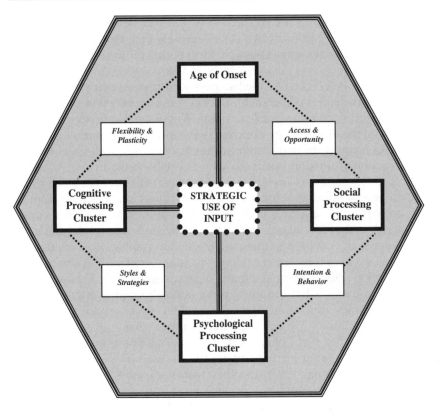

Figure 8.1 An integrated view of critical influences in SLA (adapted from Moyer, 2004a)

relevant, in fact critical to the processes and outcomes of SLA. At the same time, the balance of their contribution varies according to the individual learning situation.

To really push the research forward, we are at the stage where greater exploration is needed, not just confirmation of the same tried-and-true relationships. Recognizing the circularity between many influential relationships affecting SLA, can we ever know which factor, if any, takes precedence in the process? Maybe not, but we can reframe our focus to explore what kinds of input are typically available to learners of specific ages, and how these language contact sources contribute differentially to attainment. Such a focus on input as a critical means to an end would shift the prevalent emphasis away from 'failure' among late learners, and instead appreciate the cognitive and social flexibility required under potentially difficult circumstances.

Finally, considering the research over the past several decades as an evolving whole, I put forth two considerations that, to my mind, merit a great deal more attention as possible focal points for the study of input:

(1) The first area could be called sources, or domains, of input, and refers to the inclusion of personal, informal communication within one's repertoire of language use domains. By personal spheres of contact, I do not mean simply greeting one's favorite shopkeeper once a week, but engaging in real communication where some deeper social or emotional function is served, such as establishing a new friendship. To the best of my knowledge, it is not possible to attain native-like fluency – at least not for phonology – without crossing over from the formal to the informal and personal mode, and only then if consistency in that sphere is maintained. Those late learners who make personal connections, and maintain these important sources of linguistic practice over time, are most likely to attain a native-like command of L2 phonology, and other aspects of language as well. This is possibly due to the fact that communicative interaction inherently involves a 'negotiation of meaning' (see Long, 1996), which could benefit long-term attainment by aiding learner comprehension of new linguistic features (Pica *et al.*, 1986; Swain & Lapkin, 1995), possibly leading to 'uptake', or what learners attempt to do with the feedback received (Lyster & Ranta, 1997). In other words, meaningful negotiation is likely far more significant for language acquisition than are so-called 'passive' exposure activities (see also Gass & Selinker, 2001; see Moyer, 2008 evidence regarding phonological attainment).

(2) The second consideration I have called *intention toward L2* for lack of a more precise term (Moyer, 2004a). In the context of this focus on input, one aspect seems particularly revelatory: the shift in language dominance toward L2. Thompson (1991) has suggested that those who lose their mother tongue stand a significantly higher chance of sounding native in L2 than those who maintain it (sad to say). Singleton (2001) makes a similar point. He argues that an AO of 10 years or earlier is indicative of a shift to L2, such that we are no longer really looking at 'L2' anymore if the target language has supplanted the mother tongue. This chapter has noted several interesting findings that support the veracity of these observations. The L2 user's access to multiple contact domains, a long residence [at least six years, according to Moyer's (2004a) data, and as many as 13 or more, according to Moyer (2008)], and the intention to reside long-term, are all significant to attainment – and all overlap with one another (and not coincidentally, with AO as well). This combination suggests a learner profile of sorts in that this trio of experiential and orientation factors predicts a fundamental shift in language affiliation. Such an assertion

holds up in light of the (inconclusive) results for traditional measures such as LOR: Where LOR results are robust, we are seeing evidence for learners who have made this fundamental linguistic shift. Since many learners never do, variable results for LOR are prominent. In other words, where participants across a broad range of LOR are studied, we find great variability because we capture those 'in-between' learners who are in the process of either shifting their language affiliation or holding firmly on to L1. When a clear dichotomy among study participants exists (e.g. Group 1 has 10+ years' LOR compared with Group 2 at 2 years or less, as in some of the research by Flege and colleagues), the outcomes are far more powerful for LOR. In the rare instance that LOR is further analysed for contact with NS and L2 use, its effects appear to be (statistically) independent from AO (such as in Flege *et al.*, 1999). This is a critical piece of evidence for my assertion here, because once that transition in language affiliation is made, the relationship between accent and LOR becomes clear and predictable. To my knowledge, this particular angle on the language dominance issue has only recently been addressed for morphosyntax (see Jia & Aaronson, 1999, 2003), but has not been investigated as directly for phonology.

For purposes of validation, we first need more exploration of L2 experience and input through qualitative data to develop a reliable set of measures that can be replicated. A solid beginning could be established through introspective reports and interviews – in conjunction with linguistic measures, of course – preferably on a longitudinal basis in order to capture how these language affiliations respond to external circumstance and socio-psychological orientation – neither of which is a static source of influence.

A gradual, yet substantial, shift is evident in the research in SLA, with L2 phonology front and center in this new emphasis on input and language use. Importantly, L2 learners are no longer viewed as 'deterministic input-output machines' (Jia & Aaronson, 2003: 133), as they once were. They are active participants in the process, even helping to construct the input, seeking out ways to make the best of whatever limits they perceive, both externally and internally imposed. Revising traditional models of inquiry to account for these complexities will help move the research forward to greater understandings of why input is so important.

Notes

1. ANOVA can verify the independence of certain factors, and multiple regression analyses can check for the predictive power of confounded factors against one another, for example, AO versus instruction or LOR (see Piske *et al.*, 2001 for discussion; see Flege & Liu, 2001; Moyer 1999, 2004a, 2008 for this kind of analysis).

2. Moyer (2004b) points out that some studies supporting the significance of sociocultural and sociopsychological factors lack actual linguistic data for the purposes of correlation. Some do include self-ratings of L2 abilities, but these are less reliable than measures like achievement tests, native speaker ratings, and so on. A balance of linguistic and non-linguistic factors is essential if we hope to capture the relative contribution of input factors in SLA (Moyer, 2004b: 52).

3. The combination of a survey and introspective interview data in Moyer (2004a), allowed for a deeper analysis of the acculturation process, the role of L1 and L2 for the individual's sense of place in the target language community, and the importance of linguistic and cultural resources for maintaining ties to the heritage language and culture (as well as acquiring greater skill in the second language). For specifics of the instrument and the analyses, see individual studies cited.

4. An early start may be optimal, but it does not ensure native-like attainment (see Flege *et al.*, 1995b; Moyer, 2008; Thompson, 1991). In the context of SLA research, native-like is typically determined to be performance that matches the performance of native speakers within the same study, serving as a 'baseline' for the production of target sounds. Native speakers are generally understood to be users of a language with exposure to that language since birth or very early childhood, having used it consistently throughout their lives. As noted here, some research shows that a very early start is not sufficient to assure such a 'target' match (cited above), thus, concepts like language dominance may be a more appropriate consideration (depending on the individual's circumstances). In short, the construct of 'nativeness' is not as black and white as it may seem. In fact, it has been criticized somewhat rigorously in recent scholarship for upholding an ideal that is both (unrealistically) monolingual and narrow in scope (see Cook, 1999, for example).

5. See Flege and MacKay (2004) and Flege *et al.* (1999) for the impact of language use in terms of *L1* usage domains. The relevance here is that frequency of L1 use – specifically, maintaining L1 across multiple and personal contact domains – is detrimental to the ability to produce and perceive L2 phonemic contrasts accurately. The authors maintain that this is due to the continued development of the L1 phonetic system, which has an impact on the perception (and development) of L2 phonetic categories.

6. See MacIntyre *et al.* (1998, 2003) for the 'willingness to communicate' (WTC) model as it relates to these notions. See Gardner and Lambert (1972) for early work on motivation in SLA.

7. ZISA is the acronym for the database, *Zweitspracherwerb Italienischer und Spanischer Arbeiter*, which resulted in numerous publications by H. Clahsen, J. Meisel, M. Pienemann, P. Muysken, and N. Dittmar, among others, from the 1970s through the 1980s. It has inspired a great deal of interest in uninstructed learners, with data generally supporting the idea of a 'universal' order of acquisition for certain syntactic and morphological features in German [but see Moyer (2005) for critical review; see also scholars such as Pfaff (1992) and Vainikka & Young-Scholten (1996, 1998) for more functional and input-based accounts of acquisitional phenomena in L2 German].

Chapter 9
Give Input a Chance![1]

JAMES E. FLEGE

Introduction

Many people, especially adults, retain a foreign accent in their second language (L2) after speaking it for many years. This and related findings have inspired great interest in the so-called effect of 'age' on L2 learning. Some believe that the learner's state of neurological and/or cognitive development when L2 learning begins (indexed by chronological age) is a much better predictor of the ultimate success in mastering the L2 sound system than any other factor, including the kind and/or amount of L2 input that has been received. For example, DeKeyser and Larson-Hall (2005) acknowledged that individuals who begin learning their L2 as children (often called 'EARLY' LEARNERS) are apt to receive more, and perhaps better, L2 INPUT than individuals who begin learning the L2 later in life. However, these authors suggested (DeKeyser & Larson-Hall, 2005: 88) that 'INPUT plays a very limited role' in predicting the outcome of L2 learning once variation in the age of L2 learning has been controlled using post-hoc statistical methods (see below). Earlier, DeKeyser (2000: 519) claimed that variation in L2 input cannot explain age effects because 'it is precisely in the linguistic domains where input varies least – phonology – that the age effects are most readily apparent'.

Researchers have seldom been clear about what they mean by L2 'input'. My own definition of L2 speech input is 'all L2 vocal utterances the learner has heard and comprehended, including his own, regardless of whether these utterances have been produced correctly by L2 NATIVE SPEAKERS, or incorrectly by other non-native speakers of the L2'. (Reading seems to have a negligible effect on L2 speech learning, apart from the occasional 'spelling' pronunciation of certain words that have been read but never heard (but see Bassetti, this volume: Chapter 10). The purpose of this chapter is to evaluate DeKeyser's (2000) view regarding the scant importance of L2 speech input through a review of existing literature.

Background

Input clearly matters for native language (L1) speech acquisition. By school age, most children can be understood when they speak as the result of having learned to perceive and produce distinctions between L1 PHONEMES (e.g. /f/ and /s/ in words like 'fat' and 'sat'). As children learn L1 phonemes, they become perceptually 'attuned' to how those phonemes are phonetically implemented (e.g. Jusczyk, 1993), developing long-term memory representations for each contrastive unit which then guide development of the language-specific articulatory motor routines needed to implement phonemes in specific contexts (e.g. to produce /t/ in word-initial as opposed to word-final position). For example, children acquiring Spanish and English learn to produce a different kind of contrast between /t/ and /d/. The L1-Spanish child learns to produce an unaspirated [t] (having short-lag VOICE ONSET TIME values in word-initial position) whereas the L1-English child learns to produce an aspirated [tʰ] (e.g. Flege & Eefting, 1987, 1988). As a result of this kind of phonetic learning, children can soon be identified as belonging to a specific speech community.

Both phonemic and phonetic learning in the L1 affects subsequent L2 speech learning, which is akin to putting 'new wine in old bottles'. In early stages of learning, L2 words are mistakenly heard as consisting of the most similar L1 phonemes, even when the constituent L2 phonemes do not exist in the L1 or are produced in a phonetically different way. Not surprisingly, L2 words are then produced using the articulatory motor routines acquired earlier in life for producing L1 words. For example, L1 Spanish speakers tend to produce the word 'taco' in English using vowels and consonants ('sounds', for short) that are found in Spanish ([t], [a], [k], [o]) rather than using the correct English sounds (i.e. [tʰ], [ɑ], [kʰ] and [oʊ]). Phonetic errors in the production of all four phonemes in English 'taco' can be detected auditorily by native speakers of English, and so contribute to the perception of a Spanish accent (Flege & Munro, 1994). To take another example, L1 Spanish learners of English tend to use Spanish /i/ when producing English words like 'beat' (containing /i/) and 'bit' (/ɪ/) because Spanish has just one phoneme in the portion of vowel space occupied by English /i/ and /ɪ/ (Flege *et al.*, 1997).

DeKeyser's claim (see above) implies that early and LATE LEARNERS receive equally adequate L2 input but differ in their use of the input received. Two broad explanations have been offered in the literature to explain why this might be so. First, the ability to learn speech might be reduced at puberty (or even earlier, according to some) following a 'CRITICAL PERIOD' triggered by neural maturation (e.g. Scovel, 1988, 2000). As discussed by Moyer (1999), it is widely believed that learning which occurs after the critical period is subject to 'neurological or motor skill constraints' not present when the L1 was learned. Such constraints are thought likely to render native-like production of an L2 'highly unlikely or impossible' (Moyer, 1999: 82). The critical period hypothesis implies that the sensory-motor capacities needed to establish the L1 sound system are unavailable, or are of diminished efficacy, in the post-critical period L2 learner.

Second, establishment of the L1 sound system might itself inhibit L2 speech learning, independent of the effect of neural or cognitive development. By school age, most children have developed perceptual representations for L1 sounds that have become attuned to L1 phonetic details. Although these 'language specific' representations continue to be further refined through childhood (e.g. Hazan & Barrett, 1999), they are already sufficiently robust by the age of five to six years to interfere with the development of new perceptual representations for L2 sounds. Such interference might take the form of a perceptual 'filter' that removes the language-specific phonetic details that define L2 sounds before they can influence existing perceptual representations (Iverson *et al.*, 2003). If the sensory information associated with language-specific phonetic details can not be detected and stored in long-term memory representations, they will not be available to guide the development of correct, language-specific patterns of articulation. Alternatively, prior L1 speech learning might inhibit the development of representations for new phonemes (Bosch *et al.*, 2000: 193) or the modification of existing ones (Sebastián-Gallés & Soto-Faraco, 1999).

Both the 'critical period' and 'interference' accounts imply that L2 input will be used less effectively after a certain age. A core claim of the Speech Learning Model, or SLM (e.g. Flege, 1995, 2003), on the other hand, is that L2 learners of all ages can auditorily detect cross-language phonetic differences, and that they retain all of the original capacities used during L1 speech learning, including the ability to establish new representations and to convert the sensory-based information stored in perceptual representations into articulation.

In my opinion, L2 input is generally less adequate than the input received during L1 learning, especially for late learners of an L2. The young child's primary L1 model is usually the speech of the primary caretaker (in some communities, the mother) and a small circle of close friends and family members. These individuals typically speak the same dialect of the L1, exaggerate certain phonetic contrasts for the child's benefit, and tend to say simple things repeatedly. L2 input is usually more variable, however. Often, the first L2 input that (eventual) emigrants receive is the speech of a foreign-accented teacher in their country of origin, prior to emigration. After arrival in a predominantly L2-speaking country, immigrants hear the L2 spoken by native speakers from diverse dialect backgrounds. They also hear other non-natives, some who speak a different L1 and some who are compatriots. The L1-inspired foreign accents of the compatriots tend to match the immigrants' own foreign accents, and thus tend to reinforce them.

Length of Residence (LOR)

A variable that has been examined frequently in L2 research is immigrants' LENGTH OF RESIDENCE (LOR) in an L2-speaking country. LOR is thought to index how much, overall, the L2 has been used for communication. It seems reasonable to think that if the *amount* of L2 input matters, then measures of L2 speech should be correlated with LOR (e.g. the longer the residence, the milder the foreign accent). However, as observed by DeKeyser and Larson Hall (2005), LOR effects reported in the existing literature have tended to be small or non-significant. For example, Flege *et al.* (2006) tested Korean children who had arrived in the United States (US) at an average age of nine years old. The Korean children differed according to LOR, with three vs. five years of residence. Sentences produced by the Korean children and age-matched native English children were recorded at two times separated by 1.2 years (T1, T2). The sentences were later rated for degree of foreign accent by a panel of native English-speaking listeners. The Korean children's sentences received lower ratings than the native English children's did, indicating the presence of foreign accent (both in by-talker and by-listener analyses). Neither the difference between the three-year and five-year LOR groups, nor the difference between T1 and T2 (a 1.2-year LOR difference) reached significance.

The findings just reported might be interpreted to mean that L2 speech is influenced strongly by interference from the L1, even in children, but not by amount of L2 input. However, the results of a longitudinal case study by Winitz *et al.* (1995) challenge both conclusions. These authors recorded a Polish boy, 'AO', over a seven-year period beginning soon after his arrival in the US at age seven. English sentences produced on five occasions by AO, and a single time by groups of native English boys and non-native boys aged 9–10 and 12–18 years, were rated by native English-speaking listeners. AO's ratings increased rapidly over his first year in the United States, becoming indistinguishable from ratings of the native speakers' sentences (Figure 9.1). As in the study by Flege *et al.* (2006), sentences produced by the other non-native boys received lower ratings, indicating a foreign accent.

Why did AO show a strong effect of LOR whereas the Korean children tested by Flege *et al.* (2006) did not? Winitz *et al.* (1995) attributed AO's success to his having listened to English for an extended period before attempting to speak it. (By hypothesis, this prevented AO's self-heard errors from being reinforced.) Another possible explanation is that AO showed a strong LOR effect because he received far more native-speaker input than is typical for young immigrants. AO was the only son of non-English speaking Polish immigrants who had settled in a small, rural town in Missouri. He attended a school that did not offer ENGLISH AS A SECOND LANGUAGE (ESL) classes because there were so few other non-English

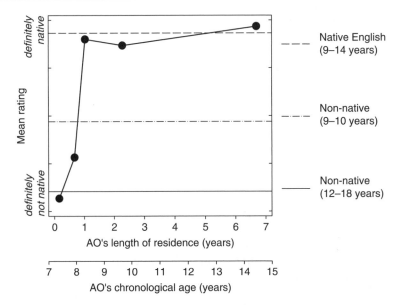

Figure 9.1 Mean ratings obtained in a longitudinal case study by Winitz *et al.* (1995) for a Polish boy who immigrated to the United States as well as three reference groups (see text)

speaking families in the town. The other immigrant boys in the study, on the other hand, were enrolled in ESL classes in schools located in a large city, where contact with other immigrants was common.

When taken together, the two studies just reviewed suggest that large LOR effects will be obtained only for immigrants who receive a substantial amount of *native-speaker* input. Indirect support for this inference comes from a case study by Ioup *et al.* (1994). These authors demonstrated an excellent pronunciation of Arabic by a native English adult who had learned Arabic through IMMERSION while living in Egypt.

A study examining Chinese immigrants to the United States also suggested the importance of native-speaker input. Flege and Liu (2001) tested Chinese adults who had arrived in the United States at an average age of 27 years. Half of the participants had a relatively short LOR (mean 2.7 years, range 0.5–3.8 years), and half had a relatively long LOR (mean 6.6 years, range 3.9–15.5 years; see Table 9.1). The two LOR-defined groups (*n* = 30 each) were subdivided according to occupational status. The 'students' had been enrolled in an American university during most or all of their stay in the United States. The 'non-students' had received little or no education in the United States, and held full-time jobs that required little use of English (e.g. biomedical research assistant, housewife). The students, both those with a short and long LOR, needed to speak English

Table 9.1 Characteristics of the four groups of Chinese participants ($n = 15$ each) examined by Flege and Liu (2001)

	Short LOR		Long LOR	
	Non-students	*Students*	*Non-students*	*Students*
LOR (years)	1.7	2.5	6.6	7.3
Age (years)	30.7	29.5	34.9	32.5
AOA (years)	29.1	27.0	28.2	25.1
% Use	45	47	47	54

Note: Age, chronological age; AOA, AGE OF ARRIVAL in the United States; LOR, length of residence in the United States; % use, self-reported percentage use of English.

often in order to interact with their professors and fellow students, whereas the non-students did not.

Flege and Liu (2001) administered three tests via headphones: a listening comprehension test; a test of grammatical sensitivity; and a test assessing the identification of word-final English stops. Had Flege and Liu (2001) not considered occupational status, the 30 participants with an average LOR of 7.0 years would not have differed significantly on any test from the 30 participants having an average LOR of 2.1 years. However, the significant LOR × Occupational Status interactions obtained in ANOVAs for all three tests indicated that the effect of LOR depended on occupational status (Figure 9.2). Simple-effects tests revealed that the long-LOR students obtained higher scores than the short-LOR students on all three tests ($p < 0.05$), whereas differences between the short- and long-LOR non-students never reached significance.

It is important to note that Flege and Liu (2001) did not directly measure their participants' L2 input. On a questionnaire, the students and non-students provided similar self-estimates of percentage English use. The long-LOR students reported using English only slightly more than the short-LOR students did (mean difference = 7%). Much the same held true for the short- versus long-LOR non-students (mean difference = 2%), suggesting that the differing effect of LOR for students and non-students was not related to how frequently English was used. The results suggest, therefore, that L2 speech performance may improve measurably only for immigrants – such as the students – who receive a substantial amount of native-speaker input.

Why did percentage English use not differentiate the students and non-students? Perhaps the participants' percentage estimates were inaccurate (see, e.g. Bernard *et al.*, 1984). Or, perhaps quality of L2 input is more important than quantity. This would make sense if, for example, the

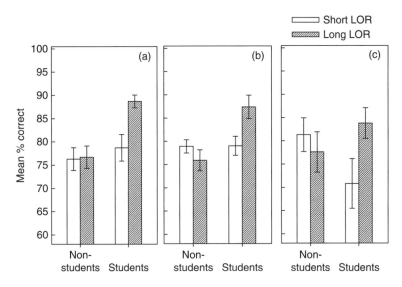

Figure 9.2   Results obtained by Flege and Liu (2001) for Chinese adults differing in occupational status (student vs. non-student) and LOR on tests of language comprehension (a), grammatical sensitivity (b) and identification of word-final stop consonants (c). The error bars bracket ±1 SE

students tested by Flege and Liu (2001) had received less foreign-accented English input than the non-students did because they attended school with native English speakers. The students' consonant identification scores showed a significant positive correlation with LOR (the longer the residence, the greater the accuracy, $r = 0.42$, $p = 0.02$) whereas the non-students' scores showed a negative correlation ($r = -0.34$, $p = 0.06$). This could be explained if the students' main model for English was native English speakers' correct productions of word-final stops whereas the non-students' main model was Chinese-accented English, in which final stops are often omitted (e.g. Flege & Davidian, 1984).

AOA and Language Use

As noted by DeKeyser and Larson-Hall (2005), partial correlation analyses have suggested that the effect of LOR on L2 speech learning is relatively unimportant. Consider, for example, the findings of Flege *et al.* (1995b). The 240 native Italian participants tested by these authors, who differed according to age of arrival (AOA) in Canada, used a seven-point scale to estimate their frequency of use of Italian (at home, in social settings, and overall in the preceding five years). Frequency of English use was estimated on a separate portion of the same questionnaire. Degree of foreign accent was significantly correlated with both the L1 and L2 language use estimates. The more the Italians reported using English, the milder their foreign accents in English tended to be ($r = 0.57$). (An inverse correlation was observed between frequency of Italian use and foreign accent in English; $r = -0.37$.) However, an even stronger correlation was obtained between AOA and foreign accent ($r = 0.85$). The correlation between English use and foreign accent remained statistically significant when the effect of AOA was partialled out ($r = 0.31$), but this partial correlation was much smaller in size than was the correlation between AOA and foreign accent after the effect of frequency of English use was partialled out ($r = -0.78$).

Statistical results like these do not prove that the frequency of L2 use (and, by extension, input) is unimportant. However, they do suggest that L2 frequency is a less important predictor of L2 speech learning than AOA is. More precise estimates of the predictive power of AOA and language use can be drawn from the six analyses summarized in Table 9.2. Each analysis is based on an examination of some aspect of L2 speech learning by four groups of immigrants ($n = 18$ each). The participants in analyses 1–4 were Italians who differed in AOA to Canada (means = 8 vs.

Table 9.2 Self-reported use of the L1 in studies in which four groups of participants ($n = 18$ each) differed orthogonally in AOA (early vs. late) and self-reported L1 use (high vs. low)

		Early		*Late*	
Analysis	*Variable*	*Low*	*High*	*Low*	*High*
(1) Piske *et al.* (2001)	Foreign accent in sentences	7%	43%	10%	53%
(2) Flege & MacKay (2004)	Discrimination of /ɑ/-/ʌ/, /ɛ/-/æ/, /i/-/ɪ/	"	"	"	"
(3) Flege *et al.* (2003)	Ratings of /ɑ ʌ ɛ æi ɪ/ in isolated words.	"	"	"	"
(4) MacKay *et al.* (2001a)	Identification of /p t k/ and /b d g/ in noise	"	"	"	"
(5) Flege *et al.* (1995b)[a]	Foreign accent in sentences	8%	47%	8%	47%
(6) Flege *et al.* (1999)[a]	Foreign accent in sentences	2.9[b]	3.9[b]	3.0[b]	4.1[b]

[a]Reanalysis for this chapter; [b]rating scale ranging from 'very seldom' (1) to 'very often' (5).

20 years) and self-reported percentage Italian (L1) use (means = 8% vs. 48%). Analyses 5 and 6 examined similar groups of Italians and Koreans (*n* = 18 each; drawn from studies originally testing 240 participants each). In all six analyses, significantly higher scores in L2 were obtained for early than late learners, and for individuals who reported using their L1 infrequently than frequently (*p* < 0.01 in ANOVAs). The lack of significant AOA × percentage L1 use interactions suggested that the frequency of L1 use had an effect on L2 performance that was independent of the effect of AOA.

The predictive power of AOA and percentage L1 use can be estimated by computing η_p^2 (partial eta-squared). As summarized in Table 9.3, AOA accounted for much more variance than percentage L1 use did in each analysis (average: 57.4% vs. 8.4%). This might be interpreted to mean that the percentage of L1 use (and its inverse in bilinguals, the percentage of L2 use) has relatively little effect on L2 speech learning. However, in my view such a conclusion is unwarranted because the language use estimates were based on self-reports, not measured directly. Nor can we be certain that the between-group differences in AOA and percentage L1 use were functionally equivalent. Different results might have been obtained had the groups differed more in terms of L1 use (say 8% vs. 78%) or less in terms of AOA.

Perhaps the most important reason for not drawing firm conclusions at this time regarding the relative importance of AOA and L2 input (indexed by self-reported frequency of use) is that few if any researchers believe that AOA is itself responsible for variation in L2 learning. The effect of AOA is often assessed because it is easy to measure and is related to a

Table 9.3 Percentage of variance accounted for (η_p^2) by age of arrival and percentage use of L1 (either Italian or Korean) in the analyses defined in Table 9.2

Analysis	Dependent variable	AOA	L1 use
(1) Piske *et al.* (2001)	Foreign accent in sentences	53.4	7.1
(2) Flege & MacKay (2004)	Discrimination of vowels	32.4	10.5
(3) Flege *et al.* (2003)	Vowel production accuracy	51.0	9.7
(4) MacKay *et al.* (2001b)	Identification of stop consonants	16.1	6.9
(5) Flege *et al.* (1995b)	Foreign accent in L2 sentences	65.7	7.1
(6) Flege *et al.* (1999)	Foreign accent in L2 sentences	53.1	10.9
	Mean	57.4	8.4

wide range of variables that have been hypothesised to affect L2 learning directly, including:

(1) state of neurological development when L2 learning begins;
(2) state of cognitive development when L2 learning begins (including aspects of memory that affect the size of processing units and the ability to recode variable sensory information into long-term memory representations);
(3) state of development of L1 phonetic category representations when L2 learning begins;
(4) L1 proficiency;
(5) language dominance;
(6) frequency of L2 (or L1) use;
(7) kind of L2 input (e.g. native speaker vs. foreign-accented).

AOA is not a 'simple' variable like percentage L1 use. It must be regarded as a 'macrovariable' because it is associated with the percentage L1 use, and also, to varying degrees, with the six variables just listed. It could hardly be the case, then, that percentage L1 use would account for as much variance as the macrovariable AOA. That being the case, it would be imprudent to conclude that the 8% of variance accounted for by percentage L1 use in Table 9.3 is small or unimportant.

Principle Components Analyses

One way to assess the influence of multiple predictor variables on the outcome measure in a behavioral study (e.g. degree of foreign accent) is to examine the effect of the multiple variables in a multiple regression analysis. Unfortunately, this cannot be done when the multiple variables are correlated with one another. One solution to the problem of 'multicollinearity' among predictor variables is to first submit the multiple predictor variables to a principle components analysis (PCA). The PCA derives a smaller set of 'underlying' factors that, being uncorrelated, can be evaluated as predictors of the outcome measure in a multiple regression analysis.

PCA analyses were applied to the questionnaire data obtained from 240 Italian immigrants to Canada (Flege *et al.*, 1995b), and 240 Korean immigrants to the United States (Flege *et al.*, 1999). In both studies, the participants' AOA ranged from two to 23 years, and degree of foreign accent in sentences was rated by native English-speaking listeners. Given that somewhat different questionnaires were used, only items common to both studies were examined in the analyses to be reported here. The first three were AOA, LOR and chronological age at the time of test. The fourth, which we will call 'frequency of L2 use', was the average self-rating of English use in three contexts (the home, social settings and overall in the five years preceding the study). 'L1 proficiency' was the average of four items: ability to communicate in Italian via telephone, to tell jokes in Italian, to pronounce Italian, and to remember how Italian words are pronounced. Finally, a derived variable called 'Motivation' was based on two questionnaire items (one asking participants how important they considered a good pronunciation of English to be, the other asking how much attention the participants paid to their own pronunciation of English).

As shown in Table 9.4, all six of the questionnaire variables except Motivation were correlated with degree of foreign accent in English. The strongest correlation was with AOA ($r = 0.85$ for both Italians and Koreans). That is, a good pronunciation of English was associated with an early age of arrival in North America, a young age at test, a lengthy residence in North America, a frequent use of English, and poor proficiency in the L1 (Italian or Korean). Importantly, these five questionnaire

Table 9.4 Correlations between language background questionnaire variables obtained from immigrants to Canada from Italy (Flege *et al.*, 1995b) and immigrants to the United States from Korea (Flege *et al.*, 1999)

	Italians (n = 240)					
	AOA	*Age*	*LOR*	*L2 use*	*L1 prof*	*Motive*
FA	−0.85*	−0.53*	0.28*	0.60*	−0.54*	−0.02
AOA	—	0.52*	−0.44*	−0.54*	0.56*	0.01
AGE	—	—	0.54*	−0.26*	0.20*	0.06
LOR	—	—	—	0.25*	−0.34*	0.05
L2 USE	—	—	—	—	−0.44*	−0.05
L1 PROF	—	—	—	—	—	0.04
	Koreans (n = 240)					
	AOA	*Age*	*LOR*	*L2 use*	*L1 prof*	*Motive*
FA	−0.85*	−0.56*	0.38*	0.61*	−0.64*	−0.12
AOA	—	0.68*	−0.42*	−0.58*	0.72*	0.16
AGE	—	—	0.38*	−0.30*	0.30*	0.14
LOR	—	—	—	0.35*	−0.53*	−0.04
L2 USE	—	—	—	—	−0.56*	0.07
L1 PROF	—	—	—	—	—	0.09

Note: FA, overall degree of perceived foreign accent; AOA, age of arrival; Age, chronological age; LOR, length of residence; L2 use, self-rated L2 use; L1 prof, self-rated proficiency in L1; Motive, self-rated motivation to pronounce English well; *$p = 0.01$.

variables were correlated with one another. For example, frequent use of English was associated with relatively poor proficiency in the L1 which, in turn, was associated with a lengthy residence in North America and infrequent use of the L1.

Table 9.5 summarises the underlying factors derived by PCA analyses from the six questionnaire variables. Two PCA factors were identified for the Italians, three for the Koreans. (The derived factors accounted for 100% of the variance in the six questionnaire variables in both analyses.) The first PCA factor for both groups, designated 'F1', had high loadings on (i.e. was defined by) the questionnaire variables AOA, L1 proficiency and L2 use. These three variables were so closely interrelated, in effect, as to be statistically inseparable. The second PCA factor, designated F2, had high loadings on chronological age and LOR. A third factor, F3, was identified only for the Koreans; it had high loadings on Motivation.

Scores based on the derived PCA factors were examined as predictors of foreign accent in a step-wise multiple regression analysis. As summarised in Table 9.6, both analyses accounted for 72% of the variance in foreign accent. More variance was accounted for by F1 (the composite of AOA, L1 proficiency, L2 use) than F2 (chronological age and LOR) for both the Italians (65% vs. 7%) and Koreans (67% vs. 4%). F3 (Motivation) accounted for just 1% of variance in the Koreans' foreign accent.

What do these results say about input? Given evidence that age at test does not affect degree of foreign accent (MacKay *et al.*, 2006), it seems reasonable to interpret F2 as an index of LOR which, in turn, indexes years of L2 use and, as discussed earlier, may be related to amount of *native-speaker* input. From this we might conclude that years of L2 use,

Table 9.5 Loadings on factors derived by principle components analyses of responses to language background questionnaires by Italian immigrants to Canada (Flege *et al.*, 1995b) and Korean immigrants to the United States (Flege *et al.*, 1999)

	Italians			*Koreans*		
Variable	*F1*	*F2*	*F3*	*F1*	*F2*	*F3*
AOA	0.892	—	—	0.902	—	—
L1 proficiency	0.783	—	—	0.874	—	—
L2 use	−0.753	—	—	−0.795	—	—
LOR	−0.548	0.799	—	−0.579	0.772	—
Age	—	0.927	—	—	0.876	—
Motivation	—	—	—	—	—	0.979

Note: F, factor; only loadings greater than 0.500 are shown.

Table 9.6 Step-wise multiple regression analyses examining the effect of derived factors (Table 9.5) on foreign accent in English sentences spoken by Italian (Flege *et al.*, 1995b) and Korean (Flege *et al.*, 1999) immigrants to North America

Study	Factor	R-square (adj)	R-square change	F	p
Flege *et al.* (1995b)	F1: AOA, L1 proficiency, L2 use	0.652	0.652	547.7	0.000
	F2: Age, LOR	0.718	0.066	55.8	0.000
Flege *et al.* (1999)	F1: AOA, L1 proficiency, L2 use	0.668	0.668	557.0	0.000
	F2: Age/LOR	0.704	0.036	29.8	0.000
	F3: Motivation	0.717	0.013	10.6	0.001

amount of native-speaker input, or some combination of both, influence degree of foreign accent.

It is not possible to disentangle the influence of the three variables (AOA, L1 proficiency, L2 use) that defined the F1 factor. That being the case, we can not be sure how much of the 66% of variance accounted for by F1 can be attributed to AOA and how much to input factors. However, given that AOA is a macrovariable with no real predictive power in itself, removing AOA from the PCA analyses might provide a preliminary indication of the combined effect of L1 proficiency and L2 use on foreign accent. Two additional PCA analyses were therefore carried out; they examined five questionnaire variables, AOA excluded.

The new PCA analysis of the Italians' data identified two underlying factors. F1 was defined by L1 proficiency and L2 use (loadings: −0.845, 0.816), and F2 was defined by age and LOR (0.920, 0.791). For the Koreans, F1 was defined by L1 proficiency and L2 use (−0.893, 0.842), F2 by age and LOR (0.902, 0.726), and F3 by Motivation (0.986). In multiple regression analyses, these new derived factors accounted for only slightly less variance in foreign accent than the original analyses did. F1 and F2 accounted for 50.2% and 7.4% of the variance, respectively, for the Italians; and 56.5% and 6.7% of the variance for the Koreans.

In sum, an F1 factor defined by self-reported L1 proficiency and L2 use accounted for an average of 53% of the variance in foreign accent. It is of course impossible to determine how much of this variance can be attributed to frequency of L2 use or to the quality of the L2 input received. It may be that as L2 proficiency improves with additional L2 input (and practice), the L1 attrites, thereby interfering less with the L2. It is also possible that other variables that co-vary with L1 proficiency and L2 use contributed to the potency of these variables.

Summary and Future Research

The research reviewed here confirmed that self-reported frequency of L2 use accounts for relatively little variance in L2 speech learning (about 5–10%), once variation in immigrants' AOA has been controlled statistically. It suggested that years of residence in an L2-speaking country (LOR) is likely to influence L2 speech learning only for immigrants who regularly receive a substantial amount of native-speaker input. It would be imprudent, however, to conclude from the existing research that L2 input is unimportant. Indeed, there are two reasons to think that previous research has underestimated the predictive power of L2 input.

First, L2 input is often confounded with other factors that may influence success in L2 speech learning. For example, frequency of L2 use typically shows an inverse correlation with AOA (the later the arrival, the less frequently the L2 is used). The potential predictive power of L2 use often goes unnoticed because it is correlated with AOA which, in turn, is associated with a wide range of variables hypothesized to affect L2 learning (e.g. state of neurological maturation, state of L1 phonetic system development, and so on; see Flege *et al.*, 2006).

Second, L2 input was not actually measured in the research reviewed here (or in any published study the author is aware of). It was estimated using participants' self reports of frequency of L2 or L1 use via items on a questionnaire (either rating scales or percentage estimates), and was thus subject to error.

Why has previous research shown such a serious methodological limitation? I suspect that, in many cases, researchers have not attempted to measure L2 input because they assumed that doing so is impossible. Indeed, practical and ethical limitations would prevent researchers from videotaping, and then subjecting to quantitative analysis, the input received over years of a person's daily life.

Although it may indeed be impossible to directly measure L2 input, it should be possible to obtain more accurate estimates. One technique that might be used for this purpose is the Experience Sampling Method or ESM. The ESM provides a reliable and ecologically valid method for quantifying everyday activities (e.g. Csikzentmihalyi & Larson, 1987; Moneta, 1996) because it overcomes limits (e.g. Bernard *et al.*, 1984) on people's ability to provide accurate retrospective information on their daily behaviour. The ESM technique is based on the observation that people are better able to accurately report an aspect of their current activity or state than to report on that activity/state over a long interval of time (e.g. 'the past 5 years').

As an example, the ESM could be used to quantitatively assess the English-language input received by native Spanish immigrants to the United States. Participants who had given informed consent would each be provided with a cell phone equipped with a special response template. They would be called at five randomly specified times during their waking hours on each of 30 consecutive days. In response to each call, participants respond to up to four simple questions:

(1) Have you been speaking to anyone in the past 5 minutes? [Y/N; If N, terminate]
(2) How many people were native speakers of English? [1 2 3 4 5 6 more]
(3) How many people were native speakers of Spanish? [1 2 3 4 5 6 more]
(4) How many were native speakers of some other language? [1 2 3 4 5 6 more]

Brief (<3 min) daily participation would generate up to 150 responses to questions 2–4, which could then be used to estimate percentage of L2 use, the percentage of L2 input from native English speakers, the percentage of L2 input likely to be foreign-accented, and the percentage of L2 input likely to be Spanish-accented. Response validity could be ascertained by assuring that some calls occurred in contexts in which participants could be observed directly. Quality of input might be assessed quantitatively by occasional recordings, obtained via the cell phone, of simple sentences produced by the participants' interlocutors.

If a substantial number of participants were tested, the MATCHED SUB-GROUP TECHNIQUE (e.g. Flege *et al.*, 1999) could be used to control for expected confounds between L2 use and other variables. For example, child immigrants usually have less schooling in the home country than adult immigrants do, and may have less fully developed L1 phonetic systems when they begin learning an L2. This, taken together with their less frequent L1 use, ensures greater L1 attrition by child than adults immigrants (Köpke, 2004). However, individual differences exist in terms of how well the L1 is maintained and how often the L2 is used. This pattern makes it theoretically possible to identify, within a larger sample, subgroups of participants who have been matched for L1 proficiency and AOA but differ in L2 use, or subgroups matched for L2 use and AOA who differ in L1 proficiency.

The procedures just outlined will, alas, require substantial resources. This brings us to another factor that may be indirectly responsible for an underestimation of the importance of L2 input. As first discussed by Flege (1987), theoretical commitment to the view that most variation in L2 speech learning can be explained by the Critical Period hypothesis seems to have impeded the search for other potential sources of variation in L2 learning. Researchers who are dogmatically committed to the Critical Period hypothesis might be unwilling to commit the resources needed to properly evaluate the role of L2 input. The same would hold true for researchers who are strongly committed to other hypothesised predictors of L2 learning such as the state of development of L1 phonetic categories (e.g. Flege, 2003) or age-related changes in the cognitive processes that are relied on in L2 learning (e.g. DeKeyser, 2000).

In sum, more and better research will be needed to determine if, as some claim, input is relatively unimportant in L2 learning. To adequately assess the role of L2 input, the input that learners of an L2 actually receive must be assessed more accurately. Measuring L2 input may be impossible, but better estimates of L2 input can and must be obtained. Doing this will require the expenditure of substantial resources (time, money, creativity). For this to happen, researchers must first decide to *give L2 input a chance* to explain variation in L2 learning.

Note

1. This chapter was supported by the National Institutes of Health. The author thanks Cristina Burani and three reviewers for comments on a previous version.

Chapter 10

Orthographic Input and Second Language Phonology

BENEDETTA BASSETTI

Introduction

For many instructed SECOND LANGUAGE LEARNERS, much second language input is not spoken, but written INPUT. Unlike children acquiring their first language (L1), second language (L2) learners are often exposed to L2 written input from the early stages of the learning process, and written input can constitute a large part of their overall L2 input. SECOND LANGUAGE ACQUISITION (SLA) researchers have mostly shown little interest in the differences between spoken and written input. While spoken and written language differ in terms of structures and vocabulary (see Halliday, 1990), more interestingly for this chapter, written representations provide a visual analysis of language. For instance, the English WRITING SYSTEM represents PHONEMES as individual letters and words as strings of letters separated by spaces, although neither phonemes nor words are isolated units in the spoken language. Different writing systems represent different units of language: while alphabetic writing systems (such as Italian) represent phonemes, consonantal writing systems (such as Arabic) represent consonants, syllabic writing systems (such as Japanese KANA) represent syllables, and morphemic writing systems (such as Chinese) represent morphemes. Writing systems also vary along a continuum of PHONOLOGICAL TRANSPARENCY, with some writing systems showing a highly regular correspondence between the written symbols and the sounds of the language, and other writing systems having much less regular correspondences between ORTHOGRAPHY and phonology. For instance, the Italian writing system is much more phonologically transparent than the English one, because in Italian each letter or letter cluster corresponds to one phoneme; among morphemic writing systems, Chinese hanzi (Chinese characters) are more phonologically transparent than Japanese kanji (Japanese characters), because most

191

Chinese hanzi have only one reading whereas most Japanese kanji have different readings depending on the context. In general, no writing system represents the spoken language with a complete one-to-one correspondence between symbols and sounds as is found in phonetic transcriptions (Cook & Bassetti, 2005). Even highly transparent writing systems such as Italian are not fully transparent, often because they represent the morphology as well as the phonology of the language. For instance, Italian represents the syllable /a/ as <a> when it means 'at' and as <ha> when it means 'has' (the symbols '<' and '>' denote orthographic forms), and Japanese kana has two different symbols for the sound /o/, one used when it is an object marker and one used in all other instances. Writing systems were not created to provide an analysis of language. Orthographic representations of the spoken language are not neutral, and could therefore interact with the spoken language input.

This chapter will focus on the effects of the orthographic representation of the second language on learners' L2 phonology. Many language teachers are aware of the effects of L2 orthography on L2 pronunciation. However, what exactly these effects consist of has not been studied much. This chapter argues that the L2 ORTHOGRAPHIC INPUT interacts with the AUDITORY (L2) INPUT, thus affecting L2 learners' mental representations of L2 phonology. Learners' NON-TARGETLIKE phonological representations in turn result in non-targetlike realisations of phonemes, syllables and words. Such orthography-induced pronunciations do not exist in the native speakers' speech which L2 learners are exposed to, and cannot be attributed to the influence of learners' L1 phonology or to universals of phonological acquisition. L1 phonology and orthography interact with L2 auditory and orthographic input, to affect L2 learners' phonological representations, which are then reflected in L2 production (pronunciation and spelling) and in PHONOLOGICAL AWARENESS tasks. In order to underscore the importance of the orthographic representation of spoken language, this chapter will avoid the generic terms 'written input' and 'spoken input', and will instead talk about 'ORTHOGRAPHIC INPUT' (see Young-Scholten, 2002) and 'auditory input'. The following section will review findings about the effects of L2 orthographic input on L2 pronunciation.

Evidence of Effects of L2 Orthographic Input on L2 Pronunciation

Positive effects of L2 orthographic input

There is evidence that the orthographic representation of the second language helps L2 learners perceive and realise target phonemes, syllables and words. For instance, it is well-known that Japanese learners and users of ENGLISH as a SECOND LANGUAGE (ESL) generally cannot perceive the difference between English /l/ and /r/, because these two L2 phonemes are phonetic realisations of the same L1 Japanese phoneme. Unless specifically trained (Flege *et al.*, 1996), Japanese ESL learners cannot distinguish for instance 'lip' from 'rip', or 'clown' from 'crown'. Still, it has been argued that if Japanese ESL learners are able to articulate [l] and [r], they just need to know whether an L2 word is spelled with an <l> or an <r> and they will be able to pronounce it (Brown, 1998; Eckman, 2004). The positive effects of L2 orthographic input can be seen in a study which found that Chinese-speaking beginner learners of French are more accurate in realising a uvular fricative /ʁ/ in a consonant cluster (e.g. *traîneau*) when they hear the target French word while seeing its written form, compared to when they only hear the word (Steele, 2005). Steele claims that, in the absence of orthographic information, Chinese learners of French perceive (and therefore pronounce) the cluster as a consonant followed by aspiration, for instance perceiving and pronouncing the target /tχ/ as the L1 PHONE [tʰ]. Instead, the orthographic representation shows that the spoken word contains two consonants, which L2 learners therefore pronounce in their output. Another study (Erdener & Burnham, 2005) looked at monolingual adult speakers' ability to perceive and repeat words in an unknown language. English and Turkish speakers listened to and repeated a series of words in Irish and Spanish. Under some conditions, participants only heard the L2 words, under other conditions they heard the words while seeing their written form. Results showed that participants were more accurate in repeating L2 words they had seen written, compared with words they had only heard.

The studies reported above show that orthographic input may facilitate L2 production in certain respects, and that this may happen at various stages of L2 acquisition, from first exposure to beginner and higher levels of proficiency. Orthographic input therefore might be seen to lead to a qualitative difference between preliterate children's phonological acquisition and literate adults' L2 phonological acquisition. Preliterate children acquiring an L1 or L2 phonology must be able to make a phonemic contrast before they can produce it. For literate L2 learners, the orthographic input provides a visual and permanent analysis of the auditory input, which may complement a defective perception and thus enable learners to produce phonemes they have difficulty perceiving.

Negative effects of L2 orthographic input

While orthographic input can help L2 learners produce target L2 pronunciations, it can also lead to some non-targetlike pronunciations which would probably never occur if learners were only exposed to auditory input. Some of the various non-targetlike pronunciations L2 learners produce, including some phone additions, omissions and substitutions, may be caused by the orthographic representation of L2 phonology.

L2 learners sometimes realise phonemes for which there is no evidence in the auditory input they are exposed to (*phone additions*). For instance, Spanish learners of English can add a vowel before 'Spain', pronouncing it as *'Espain'; this is due to their L1 syllable structure, which does not allow the sequence /sp/ in word-initial position (asterisks denote non-targetlike pronunciations). However, there are cases of additions that can only be explained by orthographic input, as L2 learners realise phonemes that do not exist in native speakers' speech, but correspond to 'silent letters' in the orthographic input. These *spelling pronunciations*, whereby learners pronounce silent letters (for instance pronouncing a /b/ in 'debt' or 'climb'), are probably the most obvious example of orthography-induced non-targetlike pronunciations. Indeed, the Longman Pronunciation Dictionary (Wells, 2000), which targets advanced and upper-intermediate learners of English, warns learners against such pronunciation errors. That learners do so is shown in a study of 13 Italian children (Browning, 2004), which found that all children pronounced the L2 English word <walk> with an /l/. Another example of orthography-induced phone addition is the use of EPENTHETIC vowels in adults who were learning a set of words in Polish (Young-Scholten, 1998; Young-Scholten *et al.*, 1999). The use of epenthesis, as the 'e' in 'espain' mentioned above, is a frequently studied aspect of L2 phonology acquisition, and it is often due to learners' L1 phonology. Young-Scholten (1998; Young-Scholten *et al.*, 1999) found that their test subjects added epenthetic vowels when faced with complex consonant clusters they found hard to pronounce. Research shows that in general children acquiring languages with complex consonant clusters tend to solve the problem by omitting consonants (Weinberger, 1987). Young-Scholten (1998) argued that adults prefer EPENTHESIS over OMISSION because they want to retain all the consonants they see in the orthographic input; rather than omitting consonants, learners then add vowels. This is in line with the predictions of Weinberger's 'recoverability', according to which L2 learners who cannot yet pronounce consonant clusters will add vowels rather than omit consonants, because adding vowels allows them to retain all consonants in their underlying representations. Interestingly, Young-Scholten also found that adults use epenthesis when they learn a word by both hearing it and seeing its orthographic form. When only auditory input is provided, L2 learners primarily simplify consonant clusters by omitting consonants, as native-speaking children do (Young-Scholten *et al.*, 1999). This again reinforces the possibility that this case of epenthetic vowel addition may be due to orthographic input.

Second language learners not only add phones, they also omit phones that are present in the L2 auditory input (*phone omissions*). For instance, L2 learners can omit one consonant from consonant clusters, pronouncing 'hold' as *'hol'. Omissions may be due to universal patterns of phonological acquisition, which also appear in the early phonologies of native speakers as well as in all L2 learners regardless of the characteristics of their L1 phonology (Tarone, 1978). However, there are omissions that are better explained as a consequence of orthographic input, as L2 learners omit phones that are not represented in the orthographic input. Bassetti (2007) looked at the pronunciation of specific Chinese diphthongs and triphthongs by Italian final-year (third-year) university students of Chinese. These students are exposed to much orthographic input written in PINYIN (i.e. Chinese written using the Roman alphabet). Pinyin represents the diphthongs and triphthongs under analysis in two ways: in syllables with no initial consonant it represents all vowels, but in syllables with an initial consonant it omits one vowel. For instance, /iou/ is spelled with the three letters <you> in syllables with no initial consonant, and with the two letters <iu> after a consonant (e.g. /liou/ is spelled <liu>). Bassetti compared L2 learners' pronunciations of the same diphthongs and triphthongs in syllables spelled with all vowels and syllables spelled without one vowel. Results showed that learners often omitted the vowel that was omitted in the orthographic representation. For instance, learners pronounced [iou] correctly in the syllable /iou/ (spelled as <you>), but pronounced it as *[iu] in /liou/ (spelled as <liu>). No omissions took place in diphthongs and triphthongs that are always spelled consistently, such as /iɑu/ (which is always spelled with three letters). Another possible case of omission due to orthographic input was found in a study of Korean ESL users (Lee, 2004). In Korean, the glide /w/ is sometimes omitted in speech. Lee found that Korean ESL learners reading an English text aloud sometimes omitted /w/ when preceded by a consonant and followed by a vowel. This omission only occurred when /w/ was spelled as <u>, but almost never when it was spelled as <w>; for instance, learners omitted /w/ in 45% of occurrences of 'quickly' but in only 5% of occurrences of 'twin', where learners instead added an epenthetic vowel in order to retain the /w/. Lee claims that this difference is due to orthography, as Korean ESL learners perceive /w/ as the consonantal ONSET of a syllable when it is spelled with <w> but not when it is spelled with <u> because of characteristics of the Korean romanisation system. It appears that at least some cases of phone omission may be due to L2 orthographic input.

Second language learners can also replace a phone with another one (*phone substitutions*). For instance, Italian learners of English can pronounce 'thin' as 'tin', because the phoneme /θ/ does not exist in Italian phonology and is therefore realised as the phone [t]. There is anecdotal evidence that some substitutions are caused by the L2 orthographic representation, because learners incorrectly assimilate an L2 phoneme with an L1 phoneme when they are represented by the same GRAPHEME (i.e. letter or letter combination). For instance, Italian ESL learners can pronounce 'special' (/speʃəl/) as *[spetʃəl], substituting [tʃ] to /ʃ/, because in their L1 orthography the grapheme <ci> represents the phoneme /tʃ/ (D'Eugenio, 1985; Kenworthy, 1987), although /ʃ/ exists in their L1 phonology; while in the opposite direction French learners of Italian can substitute [s] to /tʃ/ and pronounce the L2 word *centro* ([tʃentro]) as *[sɛntro] (Costamagna, 2000) because of the French pronunciation of the grapheme <c> (as in <celle>, pronounced [sɛl]). Similarly, Spanish learners of English sometimes realise /j/ as an affricate similar to /dʒ/ in words spelled with word-initial <y> (e.g. <you> pronounced as *[dʒuː]), presumably because in L1 Spanish a word-initial letter <y> represents a voiced affricate (Speck, 2001), although the target /j/ exists in their L1 phonology.

The possibility that orthography leads L2 learners to equate L2 and L1 sounds was suggested by Pennington (1996) who noted that misleading associations of L1 and L2 sounds could be caused by the written language. Some systematic evidence comes from a study by Zampini (1994). In this study English learners of Spanish pronounced various Spanish words with a [v] instead of a /b/, even though the Spanish language does not have the phoneme /v/. While the phoneme /v/ was not present in the auditory input, or indeed in the phonological repertoire of the target language, the letter <v> was present in the orthographic input (where it is pronounced [b]). Interestingly, these substitutions occurred not only in reading, but also in conversation (albeit less frequently). Furthemore, these substitutions were more frequent in students who had four semesters of L2 learning, compared with students who had two semesters. While this did not support Zampini's expectation that more proficient learners should be less affected by orthography, she pointed out that the more advanced students had been exposed to more orthographic input. Another example of orthography-induced phone substitution can be found in a paper by Piske and colleagues (Piske *et al.*, 2002), who found effects of orthographic representations on the pronunciation of English vowels in Italian-English bilinguals. A group of Italians who had moved to an English-speaking country in childhood pronounced a series of English words which they heard and saw as a written list, followed by a series of pseudowords. Words and pseudowords contained target vowels which were later rated by native speakers for accuracy of pronunciation. Results showed that those Italian-English bilinguals who were frequent users of L1 Italian pronounced non-targetlike English vowels in pseudowords, because they pronounced these English vowels according to the Italian pronunciation of their vowel letter. For example, when bilinguals were asked to produce a nonword containing the same vowel as <red>, <dead> and <bed>, they pronounced [e] instead of [ɛ], because all these words are spelled with <e>, which in Italian is generally pronounced [e].

More evidence of orthography-induced phone substitution can be found in learners of Chinese. In Chinese there is no contrast between voiced and voiceless plosive consonants: these are always voiceless, and the contrast is between aspirated (where the closure is followed by a burst of air, as the /p/ in English 'pot') and unaspirated (as the /p/ in English 'spot'). In some Chinese romanisation systems, this contrast is represented by adding a superscript <ʰ>, as in <pa> and <pʰa>. However, almost all L2 learners are taught using *pinyin*, a romanisation system that represents the voiceless unaspirated plosives /p/, /t/ and /k/ with the letters <b>, <d> and <g>. This causes difficulty to those learners of Chinese whose L1 writing system uses the letters <b>, <d> and <g> to represent voiced consonants. One study found that Italian learners of Chinese often identify L2 Chinese /p/ with L1 Italian /b/, rather than Italian /p/, and pronounce it as a voiced consonant (Bassetti, 2006b). In this study, 11 intermediate-level Italian learners of Chinese pronounced a series of L2 syllables containing a voiceless unaspirated plosive (/p/, /t/ or /k/) followed by the same vowel. Participants pronounced the same list of syllables twice, first by reading a series of hanzi (i.e. without an alphabetic representation of phonemes), then by reading pinyin transcriptions (i.e. an alphabetic representation). Results showed that nine out of 11 learners produced at least one voiceless plosive as voiced. Out of 12 target consonants, learners produced on average three voiced consonants when reading hanzi and four when reading pinyin. Although learners produced more voiced consonants when they read the pinyin transcription than when they pronounced hanzi, the difference approached but did not reach statistical significance. A previous study of early beginners (Meng, 1998) had found stronger effects of orthography during pinyin reading than hanzi reading. The fact that learners are more affected by orthography while they are reading an alphabetic representation than when no alphabetic representation is provided again supports the possibility that these non-targetlike pronunciations are due to orthographic input.

L2 orthographic input can also lead learners to produce contrasts that do not exist in the L2 auditory input. In German, word-final obstruents are always devoiced. Although L2 auditory input contains no voiced obstruents in word-final position, English learners of German pronounce some word-final obstruents as voiced, presumably because they are spelled as voiced obstruents, for instance pronouncing [d] instead of [t] in <Bund> (Young-Scholten, 2002). Another example can be found in consonant length. In some languages consonant length is contrastive; for instance, in Italian /kɔpia/ and /kɔpːia/ mean 'copy' and 'couple' respectively (the symbol <ː> means that the preceding phoneme is GEMINATE or long); in Japanese /kite/ and /kitːe/ have different meanings ('coming' and 'stamp' respectively). In the Italian orthography, these geminates are represented by double consonant letters, e.g. <p> vs. <pp> in <copia> and <coppia>. In English phonology there is no contrast between short and long consonants, but English orthographic words can contain double consonant letters. There is evidence that Italian ESL learners pronounce long consonants in English words that are spelled with double consonant letters. For instance, all the Italian children in Browning's study (Browning, 2004) pronounced the [p] in 'apple' with a closure that was 50% longer than the average closure in /p/. In an ongoing study, the present author is looking at the effects of orthography on the pronunciation of English consonants in Italian ESL learners. Italian learners produced a series of English words pairs, in which both words contained the same plosive consonant in the same intervocalic context, but one word was spelled with one consonant letter and the other word with two, for example, 'happily' and 'rapidly', which both contain the consonant /p/ between /æ/ and /ɪ/. Participants heard an English sentence which contained one of these words, then heard the same sentence without the target word and produced the missing word in a carrier phrase. Preliminary results show that some Italian ESL learners pronounce longer consonants in English words spelled with double consonant letters, in line with Browning's findings with children (Browning, 2004).

Finally, the effects of orthographic representations are evident not only in speech production, but also in orthographic production (i.e. spelling). For instance, Japanese learners of English use the L1 romanisation system ROOMAJI to represent L2 English. While only very few English words are spelled with final <u>, romaji spellings of English words represent word-final consonants as syllables ending in <u> or <o>, for instance spelling England as <ingurando>. This leads to non-targetlike ESL spellings that are specific to Japanese learners, such as spelling <dress> as *<doresu> (Okada, 2005). While other factors cannot be ruled out, Okada claims that the main cause of these spellings is the influence of romaji on Japanese learners of English.

In conclusion, there seems to be evidence that L2 orthographic input affects L2 production (both spoken and written), and leads to some non-targetlike pronunciations that would not occur if learners were only exposed to auditory input.

Characteristics of Orthography-Induced Non-targetlike Pronunciations

All the studies reported in the previous section show that L2 orthographic input affects L2 pronunciation, leading to non-targetlike realisations of phonemes, syllables and words. These pronunciations can show one or more of the following properties (illustrated with examples from Bassetti, 2007):

(1) Pronunciations which do not exist in the L2 auditory input. For instance, Italian learners of Chinese never hear diphthongs such as

*/iu/ or */ui/ in Chinese speakers' speech, as these sequences are not permitted in Chinese. In fact, the vowels L2 learners omit have the greatest intensity and length in the syllable, and are therefore the most salient ones in the auditory input. Such vowels would be the least likely candidates for omission if learners were only exposed to auditory input.

(2) Pronunciations which cannot be attributed to the influence of L1 phonology. For instance, Italian learners of Chinese pronounce [uei] in syllables without an initial consonant, and only reduce it to *[ui] when it is preceded by a consonant. If this reduction was due to the influence of L1 phonology, it should occur consistently, in all contexts. Equally, since Italian has voiceless plosives, Italian learners of Chinese should have no problems assimilating Chinese /p/, /t/ and /k/ to their L1 voiceless plosives. L1 phonology cannot explain why Italians should pronounce these consonants as voiced, something which can easily be explained as a consequence of the pinyin orthographic representation of these consonants as <b>, <d> and <g>.

(3) Pronunciations which do not occur in the early phonologies of native-speaking children. For instance, although diphthong and triphthong reductions are attested in first language acquisition as well, Chinese children never omit the main vowel (Zhu, 2002); they can omit /u/ or /i/ from /uei/, but never /e/ as L2 learners do. Also, Chinese children's omissions occur in all contexts, whereas L2 learners only omit vowels in post-consonantal contexts. Chinese children and L2 learners reduce different RIMES: Chinese children reduce /iɑu/ the most, as it is the most difficult to articulate, whereas L2 learners never omit vowels from this triphthong, because it is always spelled with three letters. And finally, the order of acquisition is different: whereas Chinese children realise /iou/ correctly earlier than /iɑu/, intermediate L2 learners tend to realise /iɑu/ correctly and reduce /iou/ (all data about Chinese children is taken from Zhu, 2002).

(4) Pronunciations which are not traceable to universals of phonological acquisition. For instance, some features are MARKED, that is to say less common and less basic than others; such marked features are universally acquired later than UNMARKED ones (for a review of markedness, see Eckman, 2004). Since voiced consonants are more marked than voiceless ones, it is difficult to explain why Italian learners of Chinese should replace (less marked) voiceless consonants with (more marked) voiced ones, unless this is due to the influence of orthographic input.

(5) Pronunciations which reflect L1 GRAPHEME-PHONEME CONVERSION RULES (the rules that determine the pronunciation of graphemes). For instance, for Chinese speakers the spelling <ui> represents /uei/, but Italian learners reinterpret it as /ui/ because this is how it would

be pronounced in L1 Italian (e.g. <sui> represents /suei/ in Chinese and /sui/ in Italian). Similarly, for Chinese readers the letter <b> represents the phoneme /p/, but Italian L2 learners of Chinese recode this letter as /b/ following L1 grapheme-phoneme conversion rules. Such non-targetlike pronunciations would not occur if L2 learners were not already literate in their first language.

How L2 Orthographic Input Affects L2 Pronunciation

The literature shows that L2 orthography affects L2 phonology not only while L2 learners are being exposed to the L2 orthographic representation, but also in the absence of orthographic representations of phonology; orthography-induced non-targetlike pronunciations occur not only when learners are reading, but also when they are repeating spoken words in a task or reading hanzi (which do not contain phonological information). The orthographic input has somehow moved from the page to the mind of the learner.

It is possible that the link between orthographic input and L2 pronunciations may be non-targetlike mental representations of L2 phonology influenced by orthographic representations. Many researchers have noted the relationship between literacy and phonological awareness in native speaking children, and have argued that the onset of literacy seems to coincide with a quantitative or qualitative change in phonological awareness, or that preliterate children and illiterate adults cannot perform some metalinguistic tasks (for overviews, see Castro-Caldas & Reis, 2003; Cook & Bassetti, 2005; Tarone & Bigelow, 2005). When native speakers perform metalinguistic awareness tasks in their first language, their analyses of the spoken language can be affected by orthographic representations; for instance, after the onset of literacy children start counting more phonemes and more syllables in words spelled with more letters (<interesting> segmented as 'in-ter-es-ting' rather than 'in-tres-ting') (Ehri & Wilce, 1980). With regards to L2 phonological acquisition, Flege (1996) notes that the onset of literacy appears to be related to an increase in phonemic awareness, which could relate to an increase in L2 learners' tendency to equate L1 and L2 sounds around that age. According to Young-Scholten, it may not be a coincidence that for some researchers (e.g. Long, 1990) the critical period for phonological acquisition ends at age six, which is the age of literacy onset (Young-Scholten, 2002); literacy acquisition may be one of many factors affecting phonological development. Burnham also noted that the ability to distinguish contrasts in an unknown language is at its lowest at age six, when children start learning to read (Burnham, 2003). He claimed that when children learn to read they have to classify all phones as belonging to phonemic categories which are represented by different letters, and this is why on the one hand English children's ability to distinguish /b/ from /p/ peaks with the onset of literacy, while on the other hand children lose the ability to identify the phonological categories of another language. While the latter position is too extreme, as categorical perception is established well before the onset of literacy, it is indeed possible that literacy results in a reanalysis of the spoken language in terms of its orthographic representation.

The missing link between orthographic input and non-targetlike pronunciations could then be L2 phonological representations. There are indeed interesting parallels in the way orthography affects L2 learners' pronunciations on the one hand and native speakers' performance in phonological awareness tasks on the other hand. Some orthography-induced additions and omissions in L2 learners seem to parallel native speakers' performance in phoneme counting or segmentation tasks. For instance, literate English speakers count one more phoneme in words spelled with an extra letter, e.g. counting one more phoneme in 'pitch' than in 'rich' (Derwing, 1992); this is similar to L2 learners who pronounce <walk> as *[wɔlk] rather than /wɔɪk/. Indeed, second language learners' performance in phonological awareness tasks shows effects of L2 orthography in line with their non-targetlike pronunciations. Bassetti (2006a) tested the phonological awareness of English beginner learners of Chinese using a phoneme counting task. Participants counted the number of phonemes in a list of Chinese syllables (presented as hanzi) whose pinyin spelling represents all the vowels (e.g. /uei/ spelled as <wei>) and in syllables whose spelling omits one vowel (e.g. /tuei/ spelled as <dui>). In syllables whose pinyin spelling omits one vowel, most learners counted one vowel less. To confirm that the omitted vowel was indeed the one omitted in the orthographic representation, another small group of learners performed a phoneme segmentation task: they read aloud the same list of hanzi and pronounced all the phones in each syllable one by one. Results showed that learners omit in phoneme awareness tasks the same vowels they omit in speech production.

It appears that orthographic representations affect phonological representations in both L2 learners and native speakers. Still, there are two main differences:

(1) In native speakers orthography only affects phonological awareness tasks, whereas in L2 learners it may also affect pronunciation. This may happen because L2 learners do not master the target phonology before being exposed to orthographic input (although of course native speakers can also produce spelling pronunciations).

(2) Native speakers are only affected by orthography-internal factors, whereas L2 learners are affected by the interaction between their L1 orthography and their L2 orthography. For instance, L1 Grapheme-Phoneme Correspondence rules can affect the reading of

L2 graphemes, so that learners recode L2 Spanish <v> as /v/ (as in L1 English) rather than /b/ (as Spanish readers do), or recode Chinese <ui> as /ui/ (as in L1 Italian) rather than /uei/ (as Chinese readers do). Therefore, on the one hand orthography-internal factors can lead for instance to adding the phone [l] in 'walk', and this can happen both in native speakers' phonological awareness tasks and in L2 learners' phonological awareness tasks and actual pronunciations. On the other hand, a native speaker of Spanish could never substitute a [v] to a /b/; this is due to the presence of two writing systems in the mind of the L2 learner/user.

It is then possible that the L2 orthographic input, reinterpreted according to the L1 orthography-phonology conversion rules, interacts with the L2 auditory input, also reinterpreted according to L1 phonology, leading to non-targetlike phonological representations of L2 phonemes, syllables and words. Still, it should be noted that the interaction between orthographic input and auditory input could be more complex than it appears from the discussion above, first because orthography-induced non-targetlike pronunciations could be present in the L2 spoken input, and second because the L2 orthographic representation could affect the perception of L2 phonology. First of all, as Piske pointed out (Piske, personal communication, 21 August 2006), orthography-induced pronunciations may be part of the auditory input for instructed learners. When other learners produce non-targetlike pronunciations due to the L2 orthographic representation, these pronunciations become part of the auditory input learners are exposed to in the classroom. There is also a possibility that language teachers may produce spelling pronunciations when providing the citation form of words; the present author is aware that some Italian language teachers pronounce Italian phonemes /tʃ/ and /dʒ/ as [tʃi] and [dʒi] in the classroom, for instance pronouncing <ciao> as *[tʃiao] rather than [tʃao]. These orthography-induced pronunciations may be part of instructed learners' spoken input, reinforcing their own incorrect recoding of the orthographic input. Second, learners' mental representations of L2 phonology may affect their perception, leading them to perceive sounds that do not exist in the auditory input but are present in the orthographic representation. It is known that L1 phonology can lead L2 learners to perceive sounds that do not exist in the L2 auditory input, as in Japanese ESL learners who perceive non-existing vowels in English perception tasks due to the influence of their L1 phonology (Matthews & Brown, 2004). In the same way, if L2 learners' mental representations contain an extra phoneme, voicing, or consonant length as a consequence of orthographic input, learners could actually perceive in the L2 auditory input the extra phoneme, voicing or length represented in the orthographic input. The interaction between L2 orthographic input and L2 auditory input may be indeed rather complex.

Implications for Research and Language Teaching

The review above shows that orthographic input can be an important factor in the acquisition of second language phonology. One reason why this factor has received little attention could be the view, held by some theoretical and applied linguists, that spoken language is primary while written language is secondary (for a discussion, see Coulmas, 2003; Linell, 1982).

Although it is true that in the history of humanity spoken language precedes writing, the other arguments for the primacy of the spoken language do not necessarily apply to second language learners (see also the discussion in Cook, 2005). First, spoken language emerges earlier than written language in first language acquisition (i.e. children learn to speak before they learn to read), however in instructed L2 learners spoken and written language can emerge at the same time. Second, children learn to speak spontaneously but only learn to read with instruction, however L2 learners are often not instructed in how to read and write the second language, and develop L2 literacy naturally. Third, all normal children develop spoken language but not all develop written language, however L2 learners can develop the ability to read the L2 without the ability to understand the spoken language, or can develop the ability to write the L2 without the ability to speak it.

It appears that the spoken language is not primary in second language acquisition (at least in instructed contexts) as it is in first language acquisition. Researchers and language teachers should therefore take the role of written language into account more than it has hitherto been the case. Research on L2 phonology could in particular look at more examples of effects of L2 orthography. At the same time, it could also investigate which factors might modulate such effects. Such factors may include the characteristics of the L1 and L2 writing systems, including both the type of writing system and their level of phonological transparency. While all research reported in this chapter looked only at the effects of alphabetic writing systems, syllabic or consonantal writing systems could have different effects on L2 phonology. The degree of phonological transparency of both L1 and L2 writing systems could also play an important role. It is likely that native users of phonologically transparent writing systems rely on L2 orthographic input more than native users of phonologically opaque writing systems, and that learners of second languages that have phonologically transparent writing systems rely on L2 orthographic input more than learners of languages that have an opaque writing system. For instance, Erdener and Burnham (2005) found that, while all L2 learners were better able to repeat L2 words when they saw a written representation of the words, the effect was stronger or weaker depending on the level of phonological transparency of both L1 and L2 orthographies.

The Turkish and Spanish writing systems are phonologically transparent, whereas English and Irish are more opaque. Results show that, when repeating Spanish words, Turkish speakers were facilitated by the orthographic representation more than English speakers, probably because L2 learners whose L1 orthography is phonologically transparent can make better use of L2 orthographic input in processing L2 auditory input. On the other hand, when repeating Irish words, Turkish learners were negatively affected by the orthographic representation, while English learners were not, showing that native users of transparent L1 writing systems are more negatively affected by an L2 orthographic input that does not represent the L2 phonology transparently.

Apart from characteristics of writing systems, there are other factors that may modulate the influence of orthographic input. Learner-internal factors may also play a role. For instance, it would be interesting to test whether learners rely more on orthographic representations if they have lower phonemic coding ability (i.e. lower capacity to discriminate unfamiliar sounds and to retrieve them from memory). Level of proficiency and length of study could also be important factors, and although some researchers have looked at learners with different lengths of study or lengths of stay in a target-language environment, no longitudinal studies have been done to investigate the influence of orthographic input on the development of a second phonology. There could also be effects of learning context, as instructed learners may be more affected than uninstructed learners. Also, teaching methods that involve more use of written materials may lead to stronger effects of orthographic input. Another area of interest for researchers and teachers alike could be the difference between literate and non-literate adult L2 learners. Tarone and Bigelow (2005) discussed such differences and called for researchers to investigate the effects of illiteracy on SLA, and for teachers to adapt their teaching to the specific needs of non-literate L2 learners.

With regards to the practical aspects of everyday teaching in the classroom, several proposals have been put forward to reduce the potentially negative effects of orthography. One possibility is to avoid written input at least at the early stages of second language learning, as proposed for instance by the COMPREHENSION APPROACH (Winitz & Yanes, 2002). With specific reference to Chinese language teaching, Meng (1998) proposed that teachers should avoid using pinyin at the beginning. Others have proposed to provide modified orthographic input, that is, a 'foreigner-directed orthography'. For instance, there have been proposals for teaching Chinese using a modified version of pinyin, where either all vowels are represented (e.g. spelling /uei/ as <uei> rather than <ui>; Ye *et al.*, 1997), or the missing vowel is added in brackets (e.g. spelling /uei/ as <u(e)i>; Canepari, personal communication, March 2006). It has also been proposed to provide orthographic instruction, that is, a focus on orthographic forms, or to use pronunciation exercises or explicit pronunciation instruction that target the potential effects of the L2 orthographic input (Elliot, 1997; Zampini, 1994); one reviewer of this paper suggested that learners themselves could research aspects of their L1 and L2 writing systems to raise their own awareness. More research is needed to test whether these proposals are effective. For instance, in one study (Elliott, 1997) a group of English-speaking learners of Spanish learned that the Spanish grapheme <v> is pronounced [b] (rather than [v]) during a series of pronunciation instruction sessions. While pronunciation instruction significantly improved learners' realisations of various phonemes, the pronunciation of /b/ did not improve significantly. Both the experimental group and a control group who had not received pronunciation instruction made more pronunciation errors when [b] was spelled as <v> than when it was spelled as <b>. Furthermore, the experimental group mispronounced [b] when it was spelled as <v> more than when it was spelled as <b> both before and after pronunciation instruction, showing that perhaps instruction had not had a strong impact. Clearly more research is needed to evaluate the various proposals, but at least teachers should be aware of the potential effects of L2 orthographic input and make instructional decisions based on this knowledge.

Conclusion

Research on the role of input in second language acquisition has not seriously investigated the distinction between phonological and orthographic input. While children acquiring L1 phonology are only exposed to auditory input, L2 learners can be exposed to large amounts of orthographic input, from the very early stages of acquisition, after having learnt to read and write another language. This chapter argues that, in the same way that L2 auditory input is modulated by the presence of another phonological system in the learner's mind, L2 orthographic input is also modulated by the presence of another orthography. Orthographic input, sometimes reinterpreted according to L1 orthography-phonology correspondences, interacts with auditory input in shaping learners' L2 phonological representations; these in turn lead to non-targetlike pronunciations (as well as affecting spelling, phonological awareness tasks and possibly perception). The effects of orthography are evident when the L2 pronunciations are not attested in native children's early phonology, and cannot be explained in terms of effects of L1 phonology or universals of phonological acquisition. Rather, these can be attributed to the influence of a phonological form based on a non-targetlike recoding of L2 orthographic input. Researchers and teachers with an interest in L2 phonology would do well to bear in mind that input comes not only in a spoken but also in a written modality, and that orthographic input may have a significant impact on the L2 phonological system.

Acknowledgements

I would like to thank the editors and the anonymous reviewer for their insightful comments and help in improving my original draft.

Chapter 11

Second Language Speech Learning with Diverse Inputs[1]

OCKE-SCHWEN BOHN and RIKKE LOUISE
BUNDGAARD-NIELSEN

Introduction

Studies of cross-language speech perception and of second language speech have primarily been interested in examining the effects and interactions of three types of variables. These are *subject* variables, which characterize the non-native listener or learner [e.g. age of learning/acquisition (AOA), native language background and foreign language experience and usage], *stimulus* or *target* variables which characterize what the listener or learner is perceiving or learning (e.g. non-native consonants or vowels, or non-native place, manner or voicing distinctions, and the effect of phonetic context), and *task* variables which characterize data elicitation and experimental procedure (e.g. discrimination, identification or imitation tasks). The effects of these variables and their interactions have been extensively documented and reviewed by, among others, Strange (1992), Beddor and Gottfried (1995) and the contributors to Bohn and Munro (2007).

A central assumption of most cross-language and second language speech studies is that non-native subjects have been exposed (primarily) to just one variety of the TARGET LANGUAGE.[2] NATIVE SPEAKERS of this target variety typically provide baseline data, which are used as a benchmark to assess the non-native subjects' performance (e.g. Bohn & Flege, 1990, 1992). The assumption of a homogenous learning target is perhaps justified in a *second* language learning setting, in which learners live in the community whose language they are learning. However, we question the validity of this assumption for *foreign* language learning settings, in which the non-native language is not the primary medium of communication, nor necessarily taught by native speakers. Foreign language learners are typically exposed to a wider range of varieties of native and non-native uses of the target language than SECOND LANGUAGE LEARNERS.

We were reminded of this problem in a number of previous studies (e.g. Best & Bohn, 2002; Bohn & Steinlen, 2003; Gottfried & Bohn, 2002), in which native Danish speaking subjects were recruited on the basis of their responses to a questionnaire which elicited background information and, in particular, information regarding the subjects' English language experience. The questionnaire that we use in our laboratory elicits responses to questions relating to

- LENGTH OF RESIDENCE in an English-speaking country (LOR);
- length of English-language instruction in school (LEI);
- native language(s) of English-language teachers;
- target variety of English in school (e.g. Southern British, American, other);
- use of English (quantity; reading, writing, listening, speaking) (USE);
- proportion of exposure to different varieties of English; and
- target variety (i.e. which variety of English the speaker uses or aims for).

The questionnaire does not ask directly for the age at which L2 learning began. For those respondents who spent some time in a non-native language environment, this information is provided by the response to the LOR question (above). For respondents who never resided abroad, the onset of English instruction in school is known for each age cohort because it is the same for all grade school students in Denmark (i.e. fifth grade for the age group of our participants). Also, the questionnaire does not elicit information on the type of English instruction because it is much the same all over Denmark, with an initial exclusive emphasis on oral-aural communication, later additional emphasis on reading skills, and no detailed focus on the teaching of writing skills before Grade 9. The questionnaire responses usually allow us to compose subject groups which are homogeneous with respect to LOR, LEI, USE and teachers' L1. However, the diversity of target varieties of English to which potential subjects have been or are being exposed in school and in non-school settings, and the difficulty that potential subjects have when asked to indicate which variety of English serves as their model, suggest that the learning target is much less well defined than in second language settings.

The aim of the study discussed here was to explore whether foreign-accented speech could be meaningfully studied in the absence of a well-defined target. We examined the intelligibility of Danish-accented English vowels as produced by a group of native Danish speakers whose English language experience was typical of L1 Danes with no English experience beyond the obligatory foreign language teaching in grade, middle and high school. In general, the English language experience of L1 Danish speakers consists of foreign language classes in school (with a minimum of five years of instruction in English as a foreign language), of exposure to English through various media, and of uses of English in lingua franca settings. The pronunciation model for English in Danish schools is almost always Southern British English (as presented by teachers with L1 Danish; very few English language teachers are native English speakers). Media exposure to English takes place through subtitled movies (only children's movies are dubbed), TV features, shows and documentaries (mostly subtitled, rarely with voice-over, and never dubbed), and pop songs. Most of this media exposure is to American English accents, but a sizeable proportion of British English accents and Australian English can also be heard, as can – occasionally – other accents of English. Very little is known about the quantity and characteristics of English language use in lingua franca settings, but it is probably correct to assume that many native Danish speakers are exposed to a fair variety of native and non-native accents of English. This is true both at work because many Danish companies with foreign subsidiaries use English for company-internal communication, and it also true for travel because Danes, like many other Europeans, frequently spend their vacation abroad, where the lingua franca is most likely English.

In the present study, we selected participants with exposure characteristics to English as described above. We have reason to believe that, overall, the exposure to English of our subjects is typical of and similar to the exposure in many medium-sized European countries (like Denmark) in which English-language competence is relatively high, and English-language media consumption relatively great as compared to larger countries like Italy and Spain.

The heterogeneity of the speech learning target for native Danish learners of English as a foreign language makes any attempt to predict Danish-accented production of English speech sounds problematic. Current models of second language and cross-language speech perception base their predictions of perception, PRODUCTION and/or learning problems on the perceptual relationship of non-native to native speech sounds (Best, 1995; Best & Tyler, 2007; Flege, 1995). Any assessment of this relationship requires a fairly well defined non-native sound system such as can be found in NATURALISTIC, immersion based L2 acquisition (e.g. Bohn & Steinlen, 2003; Strange, 2007; Strange *et al.*, 2004). However, the responses that we received in preparation for earlier studies to our language background questionnaire clearly indicate that the non-native sound system in a foreign language setting can be quite ill-defined, and that the FL learners may be well aware of the ill-defined nature of their FL target.

As a first and necessarily impressionistic approximation to predicting some of the characteristics of Danish-accented English vowels, we compare how the acoustic vowel space is exploited in Danish and three accents of English (North American English, Southern British English and Australian English). The ACOUSTIC VOWEL SPACE is defined by the resonances of the vocal tract in vowel production. The first resonance (F1) corresponds fairly directly to the articulatory dimension of close-open, and the second resonance (F2), to the front-back dimension (for more detail, see Ladefoged, 2005). Because all languages make use of the same articulatory/acoustic vowel space, ACOUSTIC comparisons of how different languages or dialects arrange vowels in the vowel space can be instructive for all those interested in cross-language comparisons, including typologists and researchers in first, second or foreign language acquisition.

Figure 11.1 juxtaposes the location in the F1/F2 space of simple vowels or MONOPHTHONGS of Danish as spoken in the Aarhus region (East Jutland Danish, top left), Southern British English (top right), American English as spoken in Michigan (bottom left) and Australian English (bottom right).

Because it is not possible to assess the proportion in which various varieties of English contribute to the learning target for L1 Danish speakers of English, we cannot use models of L2 speech to generate precise predictions of the characteristics of Danish-accented English vowels. Apart from the problem that the mix of varieties to which L1 Danish learners are exposed cannot be quantified, there is the more general problem of

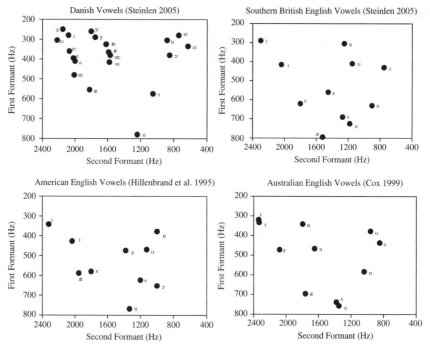

Figure 11.1   The monophthongs of Danish and three varieties of English in the F1/F2 space

predicting production and perception problems for vowels from acoustic cross-language comparison of vowels (Steinlen, 2005; Strange *et al.*, 2004, 2005). However, Figure 11.1 can be used to distil some general major differences between English vowel systems to which L1 speakers of Danish are exposed, and their L1 Danish vowel system.

A comparison of the panels in Figure 11.1 indicates that the Danish vowel system is characterized by a densely packed upper portion of the vowel space, whereas the lower portion of the acoustic vowel space is poorly exploited. That is, most Danish vowels are produced as close or half-close vowels; only three of the 20 Danish vowels shown in Figure 11.1 are half-open or open vowels. This distribution is very different from the one for the three accents of English considered here. In general, the vowels of Southern British, American and Australian English are more evenly distributed in the F1/F2 space. Another important general difference between Danish and English vowels is that the Danish vowel inventory is largely structured in terms of spectrally similar long-short vowel pairs, whereas temporal contrasts cover a range from quite irrelevant (American English) to somewhat relevant (British English) to highly relevant (Australian English) for the different accents of English. That is, all American English vowels differ clearly in quality (no overlap of vowel categories in Figure 11.1 for American English) so that temporal distinctions are unnecessary and, in fact, irrelevant in the perception of American English vowels by native listeners (Bohn & Flege, 1990). In Southern British English, the vowels in *hut* and *heart* are so similar in terms of quality that the temporal contrast is needed to differentiate these two vowel categories (Steinlen, 2005). In Australian English, vowel duration is an important means to keep the vowels in *heat* and *hit*, and in *hut* and *heart*, distinct (Cox, 1999, 2006).

The aim of the present study was to explore some of the learning problems that foreign language learners encounter when they attempt to produce English vowels without a well-defined pronunciation model, using Danish learners of English as an example. The characterization of Danish-accented English was done by assessing the intelligibility of Danish-accented English vowels as perceived by native speakers of Canadian English. We compared the intelligibility of the foreign-accented vowels to the intelligibility of the same vowels produced by native English speakers from three general dialect areas, namely, American English, Southern British English and Australian English. The vowel productions of the L1 English speakers were examined for intelligibility to obtain a basis for comparison for the intelligibility of the foreign-accented vowels. Native speakers of Canadian English were chosen to provide intelligibility data because it was assumed that Canadians would be familiar with a large variety of native and non-native English accents as Canada officially is a multicultural and multilingual nation. Large parts of the population are non-native speakers of English, and most Canadians are thus exposed to foreign accented English in their everyday lives.

We expected the listeners' error patterns, as well as error rates, to be specific for each speaker group, and this was indeed what we found. However, reduced intelligibility was observed for much the same vowels irrespective of speaker group. Our results suggest that one source of problems in learning the sounds of English is INPUT heterogeneity of English vowel systems in addition to native language interference.

Methods

Subjects

The non-native speaker group consisted of 10 male L1 Danish speakers (mean age: 26.5 years) from the Aarhus area in the eastern part of mainland Denmark (Jutland). All speakers had monolingual Danish speaking parents, and all spoke Danish with an East Jutland accent typical of educated middle class speakers from the Aarhus Region. The speakers had spent either no or only short periods of time in English speaking countries, and they had had five to eight years of English language instruction in school from teachers speaking Danish accented Southern British English. Two speakers stated that they aimed for a specific native variety of English (American and British English were each named once), but the remaining eight participants could not name a specific accent as their learning target.

The native speaker group consisted of five male speakers, two each of General American English and of Southern British English, and one of Australian English. The mean age of the L1 English speakers was 45.8 years. The five L1 English participants resided in Denmark when they were recorded, but they reported low proficiency in Danish.

Procedure (production data)

Each speaker read four randomised lists with the 11 monophthongs of English in a /bVt/ FRAME. The lists contained the words *beat, bit, bet, bat, burt, boot, but, bart, bot, bort* and *bUt*. Rhymes were provided for the non-words *bot* (rhyme word *bottle*) and *bUt* (rhyme words *foot, butcher*), but not for the unambiguous *bort*. The rhyme words were written in parentheses next to the target words on the reading list, and the participants were asked if they knew these words and how to pronounce them prior to the recording. The recordings were made in a sound-treated environment using a Sony electret condenser microphone (model EC-959a) and a Marantz audiocassette recorder (model CP 430). In preparation for the intelligibility test, the syllables were edited as follows: In those instances where the syllable initial /b/ was prevoiced, the prevoicing was edited out. Likewise, any release burst following closure for the final /t/ was edited out. We edited the syllables in this way so that the listeners would not be distracted from basing their responses on the vowel quality by irrelevant phonetic stimulus properties.

Procedure (intelligibility data)

The digitised /bVt/ syllables were PEAK-NORMALIZED (using a digital editing procedure to normalize the volume of each utterance so that perceived loudness differences would be minimal) and presented from a laptop PC over headphones (AKG model K240DF) to a panel of 10 L1 speakers of Canadian English. These judges were told that they would be listening to English syllables produced by non-native speakers and by native speakers from different dialect areas. Presentation was blocked by the speaker, and tokens were presented with an inter-stimulus-interval of 3.0 seconds. The judges responded by checking one of the 11 response alternatives listed in rows on a leaflet. The judges were familiarized to the task, first by reading out the response alternatives, and then by listening to the first of the four reading lists from each speaker. (Responses from the familiarization were not used for data analysis.)

Results

Overall intelligibility of the Danish-accented English vowels was somewhat lower than for the vowels produced by the native English speakers, but the mean percent correct identification for the 11 English vowels by the Canadian judges (75.9% for the L1 Danish speakers, 86.8% for the L1 English speakers) did not differ significantly for the two speaker groups ($t = 1.295$, $p = 0.210$). Tables 11.1, 11.2 and 11.3 present the results from the perception experiment in confusion matrices. The responses from 10 L1 Canadian English listeners for the native and non-native speakers' productions of English syllables (listed vertically) are given as percentages of response opportunities (listed horizontally). Table 11.1 presents the confusion matrix for the L1 Danish speakers, Table 11.2 presents the summary confusion matrix for the five L1 English speakers, and Tables 11.3a–c present the matrices for each of the three L1 English accents.

Table 11.1 shows that the 10 L1 Danish speakers' productions of five of the 11 English monophthongs were highly intelligible, with >90% correct identification for the vowels in *beat, bit, burt, boot* and *bart*. The L1 Danish speakers' productions of the remaining six English monophthongs ranged from fairly intelligible (88.0% correct identification for the vowel in *but*) to completely unintelligible (17.0% correct identification for the vowel in *bot*). (The correct identifications for *bot* were mainly due to just one of the Danish participants who had had more exposure to Southern British English than the other nine participants).

Table 11.2 presents the confusion matrix for the five L1 English speakers (two speakers each of North American English and of Southern British English, one speaker of Australian English). Only six of the L1 English speakers' productions of the 11 English monophthongs were highly intelligible, with >90% correct identification for the vowels in *beat, bit, bat, burt,*

Table 11.1 Confusion matrix for 10 L1 Danish speakers' production of English /bVt/ syllables as identified by 10 L1 Canadian English listeners. Each cell lists the percent responses (given horizontally) to the intended productions (listed vertically, three tokens/speaker)

L1 DK	beat	bit	bet	bat	burt	boot	but	bart	bot	bort	bUt
beat	95.0	2.7	2.3								
bit	1.3	94.7	4.0								
bet		44.0	54.3	1.3			0.3				
bat		32.7	65.0	1.3	0.7	0.3					
burt					99.3						0.7
boot						95.0	0.3		1.3		3.3
but				0.7	2.0		88.0	1.7	5.7	0.7	1.3
bart				0.3			1.7	96.7	1.3		
bot				0.3	1.7		75.0	3.7	17.0	0.3	2.0
bort								2.7	32.0	65.3	
bUt					0.7	24.7	8.0		2.0	0.3	64.3

Table 11.2 Confusion matrix for five L1 English speakers' production of English /bVt/ syllables as identified by 10 L1 Canadian English listeners. Each cell lists the percent responses (given horizontally) to the intended productions (listed vertically, three tokens/speaker)

L1 EN	beat	bit	bet	bat	burt	boot	but	bart	bot	bort	bUt
beat	94.0	6.0									
bit	6.7	92.7	0.7								
bet		0.7	80.0	19.3							
bat				94.7				5.7			
burt					100						
boot					2.7	93.3	0.7		0.7		2.7
but				4.7		0.7	73.3	20.0	1.3		
bart				2.0				97.3	0.7		
bot				0.7			12.0	20.0	63.3	3.3	0.7
bort								0.7	14.7	84.7	
bUt					0.7	10.0	5.3		1.3	1.3	81.3

boot and *bart*. The remaining vowels were clearly less intelligible, ranging in percent correct identification scores from 63.3% (for *bot*) to 84.7% (for *bort*). For both the native and the nonnative speaker group, it was largely the same set of vowels that the Canadian judges identified successfully. Likewise, there was considerable overlap across the two speaker groups in the vowels that were less intelligible. Surprisingly, the vowel in *but* was more intelligible when produced by non-native than by native speakers (88.0% vs. 73.3% correct identification).

Tables 11.3a–c present the results for each of the three L1 English speaker groups separately. These tables show that the three accent groups contributed in specific ways to the overall intelligibility of English vowels (as shown in Table 11.2). For example, the vowel in *but* was frequently misidentified by the Canadian listeners if produced by speakers of Southern British and Australian English, but it was almost always identified as intended if produced by speakers of American English. A one-way ANOVA revealed no significant difference for the identification accuracy for the American English (mean: 92.3% correct), the Southern British English (mean: 87.5% correct) and the Australian English speakers (mean: 74.6% correct, $F(2, 30) = 2.653, p = 0.087$).

Table 11.3a shows that the American English speakers produced the vowel in *bot* in a way that it was frequently misidentified by the Canadian listeners. We suspect that the very low intelligibility of the vowel in *bot* as produced by the American English speakers (mean: 56.7% correct) is

Table 11.3(a) Confusion matrix for 2 L1 speakers of American English

L1 AmE	beat	bit	bet	bat	burt	boot	but	bart	bot	bort	bUt
beat	95.0	5.0									
bit		100									
bet			85.0	15.0							
bat				100							
burt					100						
boot						96.7			1.7		1.7
but				1.7			95.0	3.3			
bart								100			
bot				1.7			23.3	18.3	56.7		
bort							1.7			98.3	
bUt					1.7	1.7	5.0		1.7	1.7	88.3

Table 11.3(b)   Confusion matrix for 2 L1 speakers of Southern British English

L1 SBE	beat	bit	bet	bat	burt	boot	but	bart	bot	bort	bUt
beat	**95**	5.0									
bit		**98.3**	1.7								
bet			**68.3**	31.7							
bat				**86.7**				13.3			
burt					**100**						
boot						**100**					
but				5.0			**66.7**	25.0	3.3		
bart				3.3				**95.0**	1.7		
bot									**95**	3.3	1.7
bort									25.0	**75.0**	
bUt						8.3	8.3		1.7		**81.7**

Table 11.3(c)   Confusion matrix for 1 L1 speaker of Australian English

L1 SBE	beat	bit	bet	bat	burt	boot	but	bart	bot	bort	bUt
beat	**90.0**	10.0									
bit	33.3	**66.7**									
bet		3.3	**93.3**	3.3							
bat				**100**							
burt					**100**						
boot					6.7	**73.3**	3.3				10.0
but				10.0		3.3	**43.3**	43.3			
bart				3.3				**96.7**			
bot							13.3	63.3	**13.3**	10.0	
bort									23.3	**76.7**	
bUt						30.0				3.3	**66.7**

primarily due to the merger of this vowel with the vowel in *bart* in many American English dialects. If this problematic vowel is excluded from the comparison of the three L1 English speaker groups, the differences in intelligibility between American English listeners (mean = 95.8% correct without the results for *bot*) reach significance in a one-way ANOVA ($F(2, 29) = 3.887$, $p = 0.032$). *Post-hoc* pairwise comparisons reveal that only the intelligibility scores for the American and the Australian English speakers differ significantly ($t = 2.757$, $p = 0.010$). The results for the Southern British English speakers did not differ significantly from American English speakers ($t = 1.089$, $p = 0.285$) or from the Australian English speaker ($t = 1.709$, $p = 0.098$).

Conclusions

The present study attempted to explore one aspect of foreign-accented speech, namely, the intelligibility of English vowels as produced by non-native speakers who learned English in a foreign language setting. A *foreign language* setting differs importantly from a *second language* setting in that foreign language learners are typically exposed to a variety of native and non-native accents of the target language, whereas second language learners can be assumed to encounter a more homogeneous learning target. At present, it seems that any prediction of speech learning problems of foreign language learners can only be based on fairly coarse-grained comparisons of the L1 sound system and general characteristics of the foreign language sound system. Acoustic comparisons and studies of the perceptual assimilation of foreign speech sounds to the L1 are unlikely to yield satisfactory predictions of speech learning problems because the precise weighting of varieties of the foreign language may present an insurmountable problem.

We addressed the problem presented by foreign (as opposed to second) language speech learning through an exploratory study that compared the intelligibility of Danish-accented English vowels, learned in a foreign language setting, to the intelligibility of English vowels produced by native speakers from three major dialect regions (North American English, Southern British English and Australian English).

As expected, the L1 Danish speakers produced English vowels that varied greatly in intelligibility. However, we were surprised to find that many of the vowels produced by the L1 English speakers were also lacking in intelligibility. Irrespective of whether non-native speakers or native speakers from different dialect areas had produced English vowels, approximately half of the inventory of the 11 English monophthongs was not highly intelligible for native English listeners. Furthermore, we found considerable overlap between the specific vowels lacking in intelligibility when these vowels were produced by native and non-native speakers.

- The vowels produced by the nonnative speakers in an intelligible manner were those in *beat, bit, burt, boot* and *bart*.
- The vowels produced in an intelligible manner by the native speakers were those in *beat, bit, bat, burt, boot* and *bart*.

One explanation for this overlap could be that intelligibility arises from the fact that these vowels are special: The vowel in *burt* is the only stressed central vowel, and the vowels in *beat, boot* and *bart* are CORNER VOWELS, that is, vowels that are produced close to the articulatory extremes with respect to tongue height and tongue position. This uniqueness may support intelligibility. However, we also found considerable overlap between speaker groups for vowels that were less well identified:

- The vowels produced less intelligibly by the L1 Danish speakers were those in *bet, bat, but, bot, bort* and *bUt*.
- The vowels produced less intelligibly by the native speakers were those in *bet, but, bot, bort* and *bUt*.

This overlap in reduced intelligibility across the native and the non-native speaker groups suggests that the reasons for non-native speakers' learning problems are not exclusively relational, that is, they do not only result from how the sound system of the foreign language maps on to the L1. Rather, the present study suggests that an additional source of learning problems for *non-native* speakers is inherent to a learning target that is highly variable. The least intelligible vowels in our study were also those that vary most across the varieties of English included here. The low intelligibility of certain native productions by *native* speakers may be relational and seen as arising from the different realizations of these particular vowels by the speakers and the listeners; the intelligibility of the vowels was greater for American and British English (the more familiar varieties of English to the Canadian listeners) than the intelligibility of (the less familiar) Australian English.

We conclude that some production problems in foreign language learning are due to settings in which the target is very heterogeneous. Further research should examine in more detail aspects of non-native speech when learners encounter a highly variable target. We suggest that future comparisons of native and non-native speech acknowledge the relative indeterminacy of learning target(s). The issue addressed in this study should be further explored in studies using broader designs (with a larger number of speakers from a mix of dialects that aims to be ecologically valid), including acoustic analyses to determine the basis of intelligibility.

Notes

1. Research supported by a grant form the Nordic Association for Canadian Studies. This chapter is based on a poster presented at the 147th meeting of the Acoustical Society of America, New York, 24–28 May 2004. Special thanks to John H. Esling for his generous support and hospitality.
2. A recent exception is Fox and McGory (2007), who examined the perception and production of vowels in Standard American English and Southern American English by two groups of L1 Japanese learners of English residing in Ohio and Alabama, respectively.

Chapter 12

Phonetic Input in Second Language Acquisition: Contrastive Analysis of Native and Non-native Sounds[1]

ANJA K. STEINLEN

Introduction

Many studies, when comparing vowels cross-linguistically or when predicting non-native vowel PRODUCTION, base their analysis on a comparison of PHONETIC SYMBOLS, at least as an initial 'tool'. In such an approach, phonetic symbols are compared which are used to transcribe the sounds of two languages. These comparisons usually provide the basis for predictions on how L2 learners would produce non-native sounds (e.g. Arnold & Hansen, 1982; Davidsen-Nielsen *et al.*, 1982; Dretzke, 1998; Eckert & Barry, 2002; Livbjerg & Mees, 2000; Mees & Collins, 1996; Scherer & Wollmann, 1986). The assumption is that non-native speakers transfer NATIVE LANGUAGE phonemes when attempting the TARGET LANGUAGE forms. According to Lado (1957), such an approach (i.e. the Contrastive Analysis Hypothesis, CAH) can be used to 'predict and describe the pattern that will cause difficulty in (L2) learning, and those that will not cause difficulty, by comparing systematically the language and culture to be learned with the native language and culture of the student' (Lado, 1957: vii). For the production of L2 sounds, Lado stresses 'the need for comparing native and foreign sound systems as a means of predicting and describing the pronunciation problems of the speakers of a given language learning another [language]'(Lado, 1957: 11). Cross-language comparisons and predictions for L2 sound production are based on PHONEMES, and those phonemes that are not part of the speaker's L1 are assumed to be difficult. More specifically, the assumption is that speakers TRANSFER native language phonemes when attempting the target language forms (Lado, 1957: 12), that is, similar sounds will not pose difficulty in learning, whereas different elements will be difficult to master.

For example, the vowels [ɪ, ɑː, ʊ] are transcribed with the same phonetic symbols in German and English. Therefore, one would not expect problems in the production of these vowels by German speakers of English (see e.g. Dretzke, 1998). It is this strong formulation of the CAH that motivated careful research, as such an approach is assumed to predict the degree of difficulty experienced by L2 learners with elements of the L2 sound system (i.e. targets not present in L1) as well as what types of substitutions the L2 speaker will produce (i.e. phonetically similar sounds from the L1).

In contrast to an ideal learning situation where the ambient language of an L2 learner of English is English foreign language learning usually takes place in a classroom context where students (and the teachers) are non-native speakers. Here, phonetic symbols in dictionaries and textbooks are often used as a tool to improve foreign language learners' pronunciation. German students, for example, are expected to handle these symbols confidently in Grade 10 (see e.g. 'Bildungsplan for Gymnasien in Baden-Württemberg, 2004'). However, this kind of textbook INPUT is far from satisfactory because the learners' pronunciation of English is often not target-like.

This paper will therefore argue that it is advisable to supplement the phonetic symbol method with ACOUSTIC data from native speakers (i.e. NATURALISTIC input). As an example (which can, of course, be generalized to any kind of L1/L2 contact situation), the pronunciation of Southern British English (SBE) vowels by native English speakers is examined, which, in most classroom contexts, still serves as the variant of English that most students in Denmark and Germany are exposed to. The non-native speakers of this acoustic study are Danish and German learners of English, who produced L1 Danish and German vowels, respectively as well as L2 English vowels.[2] English, Danish and German have been chosen because they are – as Germanic languages – typologically related but vary in terms of the size and properties of their respective vowel inventories (e.g. Steinlen, 2005). The method of ACOUSTIC ANALYSIS is used to examine in more detail how articulation differences within a phoneme (i.e. on a subsegmental level) may characterise an L1 and, in turn, contribute to a foreign accent in an L2. Therefore, this acoustic study critically evaluates the phonetic symbol method in the light of (1) the acoustic properties of vowels which are transcribed with the same phonetic symbols in two languages and non-native productions of these identically transcribed vowels, (2) DIPHTHONGISATION patterns in native and non-native vowel production and (3) effects of CONSONANTAL CONTEXT on the acoustic properties of native and non-native vowels.

Although it is well known that 'vowels transcribed with the same symbol do not necessarily have identical phonetic quality' (Disner, 1978: 21), such a contrastive approach is often used in pronunciation guides for Danish and German learners of English (e.g. Arnold & Hansen, 1982;

Davidsen-Nielsen *et al.*, 1982; Dretzke, 1998; Eckert & Barry, 2002; Livbjerg & Mees, 2000; Mees & Collins, 1996; Scherer & Wollmann, 1986). One purpose of this chapter is to contrast the results of acoustic analyses of identically transcribed vowels in English, Danish and German with findings on the same vowels as described in pronunciation guides for Danish and German learners and to determine how these English sounds are actually produced by Danes and Germans. The aim of such a comparison is to assess the reliability of the phonetic symbol method and to provide additional information on the acoustic properties of these identically transcribed vowels in L1 and L2 speech.

Second, many pronunciation guides observe that SBE [i:] and [u:] are typically pronounced with a glide (e.g. Arnold & Hansen, 1982; Eckert & Barry, 2002; Livbjerg & Mees, 2000; Mees & Collins, 1996; Scherer & Wollmann, 1986). However, such a diphthongisation pattern is neither noted for Danish nor for German vowels (Grønnum, 1998; Kohler, 1995). Without adequate native-speaker input, one may well imagine that Danish and German learners of English have difficulties to produce these vowels authentically. In textbooks, however, such pronunciation patterns are not visualized by phonetic symbols, although this information may be relevant for non-native speakers to help them to pronounce these L2 vowels target-like.

Third, it has been shown for many languages that the vowel target as produced in a citation and context-free form (i.e. in /hVt/ syllables) is usually not attained in COARTICULATED SPEECH, due to the influence of consonantal context (see e.g. the seminal studies by Lindblom, 1963 for Swedish; Stevens & House, 1963 for American English). Based on these observations, Flege (1988) wondered whether 'languages may differ according to the extent to which the articulation of a sound is permitted to influence the articulation of adjacent sounds ...' (see also Broad, 1976) and concluded: 'To the extent that coarticulatory patterns are learned in L1 acquisition, they are likely to be maintained in L2 production [...]' (Flege, 1988: 316). So far, pronunciation guides only refer to the fact that vowel length is determined by the presence or absence of voicing of the following consonants (e.g. Eckert & Barry, 2002; Mees & Collins, 1996). Second language speech research, however, needs to address the question as to how adjacent consonants affect vowel property, because such effects may also contribute to a foreign accent in L2 speech. In sum, the aim of this chapter is to show that phonetic descriptions of particular vowel sounds in pronunciation guidebooks are overly general and do not accurately match the actual production of sounds as measured by acoustic analysis.

Method

Subjects

Fifty male speakers participated in this study.[3] Ten native speakers of SBE (mean age 38.4 years, SD = 6.4) were selected because they spoke

British English with an RP accent or an accent very similar to RP.[4] The 10 native Danish speakers came from the Århus region (DA, mean age 26.8 years, SD = 3.6) and the ten native German speakers (GE, mean age 26.1 years, SD = 4.2) from Northern Germany (mostly from the Kiel region).

Additionally, native speakers of Danish and German produced English vowels, that is, Danish-accented English (DAE) and German-accented English (GAE) vowels: The 10 Danish speakers came from Jutland (DAE, mean age 23.6 years, SD = 3.2 years), the 10 German speakers came from Northern Germany (GAE, mean age 26.1 years, SD = 4.2). The subjects reported to have learnt English in school for nine years (starting in Grade 5) and had never spent any time in an English-speaking country.[5]

The Danish and English subjects were affiliated with the University of Århus, Denmark; the German subjects were students of the University of Kiel, Germany. The subjects served as unpaid volunteers and reported no hearing or speaking problems.

Speech materials

This study is concerned only with the SBE, DA and GE MONOPHTHONGS in stressed position. The native SBE speakers as well as the non-native DA and GE speakers produced the 11 monophthongs of SBE [iː, ɪ, ɛ, æ, ɑː, ʌ, ɒ, ɜː, ɔː, ʊ, uː]. The DA speakers produced 20 DA monophthongs [iː, i, eː, e, ɛː, ɛ, aː, a, ɑː, ɔː, ɔː, oː, uː, u, yː, y, øː, ø, œː, œ] and the GE group produced the 14 GE monophthongs [iː, ɪ, eː, ɛ, ɑː, a, ɔ, oː, uː, ʊ, yː, ʏ, øː, œ].[6] The vowels were recorded in three blocked contexts (/bVp/, /dVt, gVk/) in the sentences 'I say CVC again' (for the SBE, DAE and GAE speakers), 'Jeg siger CVC igen' (for the DA speakers), and 'Ich habe CVC gesagt' (for the GE speakers). Furthermore, all subjects produced the vowels in /hVt/ syllables in citation form. The total data corpus consists of 5400 CVC syllables: The SBE group, the DAE and the GAE group each produced 1320 SBE syllables (4 contexts × 30 speakers × 11 vowels × 3 renditions), the DA group 2400 DA syllables (4 contexts × 10 speakers × 20 vowels × 3 renditions) and the GE group 1680 NG syllables (4 contexts × 10 speakers × 14 vowels × 3 renditions).

Stimuli were recorded with high fidelity recording equipment (Marantz CP 430 tape recorder and Sony ECM-959A microphone) and digitised at a 11.02 kHz SAMPLING RATE with 16-BIT RESOLUTION after LOW-PASS FILTERING at 4.8 kHz and six dB/OCTAVE PRE-EMPHASIS. Further more specialized information on acoustic measurements is provided in Note 6.[7]

Results

The aim of this section is to assess the effectiveness of the phonetic symbol method and to provide more information as to how non-native speakers produce L2 vowels: The first focus (see next subsection) is on three vowels which are identically transcribed in SBE, DA and GE, namely [iː], [uː] and [ɑː]. The results of acoustic analyses of these vowels as produced by native and non-native speakers are contrasted with findings on the same vowels as described in pronunciation guides for Danish and German learners of English (e.g. Davidsen-Nielsen *et al.*, 1982; Livbjerg & Mees, 2000; Mees & Collins, 1996 for DAE; Arnold & Hansen, 1982; Dretzke, 1998; Eckert & Barry, 2002; Scherer & Wollmann, 1986 for GAE). Later, the degree of diphthongisation in the GE, DA and SBE vowels [iː] and [uː] is examined and compared to the production of these vowels by non-native speakers. Next, the focus is on acoustic data from native and non-native speakers which provide evidence as to the way in which consonantal contexts may affect foreign language vowel production because it is not well understood how these effects operate in L2 pronunciation. Such information is not provided when vowels are compared solely on the basis of phonetic symbols.

Phonetic symbols and acoustic analysis of identically transcribed vowels in /hVt/ syllables

To determine the usefulness of an analysis for native and non-native vowel production, based on a comparison of phonetic symbols, the acoustic properties of the identically transcribed SBE, DA and GE vowels [uː], [iː] and [ɑː] are examined as produced by native and non-native speakers in /hVt/ syllables. In this context, a given vowel is produced with minimal coarticulatory effects, that is, with essentially the same articulatory configuration as in isolation (e.g. Stevens & House, 1963).

For non-native vowel production, Davidsen-Nielsen *et al.* (1982) and Livbjerg and Mees (2000) note that DA speakers tend to substitute SBE tense [iː] with DA long [iː], and SBE TENSE [uː] with DA long [uː]. The supposed reason for this substitution pattern is that the auditory difference between DA and SBE [iː] and DA and SBE [uː] is apparently only slight and that, therefore, no production problems are predicted for Danish learners of English. For example, Davidsen-Nielsen *et al.* (1982: 18) state: 'Within the vowel system, substitution of the ... English sounds ([iː] and [uː]) by their nearest equivalents in Danish causes no difficulty in comprehension, nor does it give the impression of a foreign accent. Thus the monophthongs of SBE words like *feel, fool* ... can be replaced by the /iː, uː/ of DA words like *file, fugle* ...' (SBE *file, bird*). However, cross-linguistic acoustic analyses revealed significant differences between SBE [iː] and DA [iː]. A comparison of the production of [iː] by native and non-native speakers showed significant differences between SBE [iː] and DAE [iː] but not between DAE [iː] and DA [iː].[8] This suggests that DA speakers use their native [iː] to produce English [iː] (see Figure 12.1).

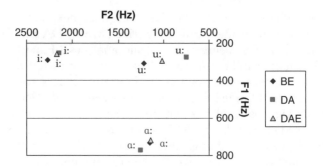

Figure 12.1   Location of SBE, DA and DAE [iː], [uː], [ɑː] in the F_1/F_2 space as produced in /hVt/ syllables

For the vowel [uː], Mees and Collins (1996: 127) state that '(l)earners generally replace English /uː/ by the Danish HULE vowel (SBE *hole*), Danish /uː/, which is closer and somewhat more back than English /uː/, but on the whole it's a good replacement for the English vowel'. An acoustic comparison showed that DA [uː] was produced considerably more back and higher than its SBE counterpart. Indeed, the DAE speakers did not render English [uː] NATIVE-LIKE: As Figure 12.1 shows, the DAE vowel [uː] was produced in between the native and the non-native vowel, that is, as a merged category. This result shows that instead of replacing the non-native vowel with the native vowel, the DAE speakers began to approximate English [uː].[9]

For Danish speakers, Mees and Collins (1996: 92) give the following advice for the pronunciation of SBE [ɑː]: 'The usual Danish replacement for the English ([ɑː]) vowel is the Danish vowel in *bare, mark*, but this vowel is too front … Make sure you say a vowel which is sufficiently back.' Indeed, as Figure 12.1 illustrates, SBE and DA [ɑː] differed in the location in the acoustic vowel space: DA [ɑː] was located more centrally in the ACOUSTIC VOWEL SPACE than SBE [ɑː]. In terms of acoustic vowel quality, SBE [ɑː] was pronounced native-like by the DA speakers, although SBE [ɑː] was significantly longer than DAE [ɑː].[10]

For SBE vs. GE, an acoustic analyses of [iː] and [uː] revealed significant acoustic differences, that is, GE [iː] and [uː] are located more front in the acoustic space than their SBE counterparts, despite the fact that these vowels are transcribed with the same phonetic symbols in the two languages. This confirms Eckert and Barry's (2002: 112) impression that SBE [iː] 'tends to be slightly lower' than its GE counterpart, whereas SBE [uː] is more open, less rounded and more front than GE [uː] (Arnold & Hansen, 1982; Eckert & Barry, 2002; Scherer & Wollmann, 1986). Acoustic analyses of non-native speakers' production of these vowels showed that the GE speakers did not produce native-like SBE vowels [iː] and [uː]: They

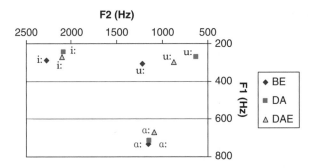

Figure 12.2 Location of GE, GAE, SBE [i:], [u:] and [ɑ:] in the F_1/F_2 space, produced in /hVt/ syllables

apparently rendered these vowels with values in between their GE and SBE counterparts, that is, as merged categories (see Figure 12.2).[11] For the production of SBE [ɑ:], Dretzke (1998: 39) predicts 'no major problems for German speakers', although Eckert and Barry (2002: 123) note that SBE [ɑ:] (as in SBE *hard*) is more retracted than its GE counterpart (as in GE *hart*, viz SBE: *hard*) (see also Arnold & Hansen, 1982; Scherer & Wollmann, 1986). An analysis did not reveal significant acoustic differences between these vowels. Surprisingly, the German speakers did not produce native-like SBE [ɑ:]: GAE [ɑ:] was located more back in the acoustic vowel space as compared to SBE [ɑ:], as Figure 12.2 shows.[12]

Acoustic analysis also revealed surprising results with respect to vowels that are not transcribed identically in two languages (see Figure 12.3). For example, there were no significant acoustic differences between SBE [ʌ] and GE [a], between SBE [ɪ] and DA [ɛ] and between SBE [ʊ] and DA [o], although these vowels are transcribed with different phonetic symbols (see also Davidsen-Nielsen *et al.*, 1982; Mees & Collins, 1996 on SBE [ʊ] and [ɪ] vs. DA [o] and [ɛ]; and Eckert & Barry, 2002; Scherer & Wollmann, 1986 on GE [a] vs. SBE [ʌ]). The non-native speakers produced these English vowels native-like as the acoustic differences between GAE and SBE [ʌ], between SBE and DAE [ɪ] and between SBE and DAE [ʊ] were not significant.[13]

Diphthongisation of vowels in /hVt/ syllables

A comparison of vowels across languages based on a comparison of phonetic symbols and subsequent predictions for L2 pronunciation may also not take into consideration that some monophthongal vowels in one language are produced with a degree of diphthongisation whereas their counterparts in another language are not diphthongised: For example, Wells (1962: 22) states that SBE '/i:/ and /u:/ are quite commonly

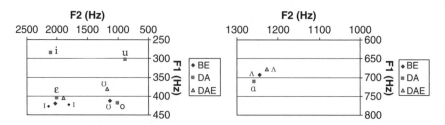

Figure 12.3 Location of SBE and DAE [ɪ], [ʊ] and DA [ɛ] and [o] (left panel) and of SBE, GAE [ʌ] and GE [a] (right panel) in the F₁/F₂ space as produced in /hVt/ syllables

diphthongs of the type [ɪi], [ʊu]'(see also e.g. Bauer, 1985; Henton, 1983; Wells, 1982). DA and GE monophthongs, on the other hand, are generally not considered to be diphthongised (e.g. Grønnum, 1998 for DA; Kohler, 1995 for GE). This diphthongisation pattern for the SBE high vowels has also been noted in many pronunciation guides for non-native speakers of English (e.g. Arnold & Hansen, 1982; Eckert & Barry, 2002; Livbjerg & Mees, 2000; Scherer & Wollmann, 1986). For example, Livbjerg and Mees (2000: 75) suggest that 'Danish speakers should try to copy the characteristic glide movement' of SBE [i:] and [u:]. However, a comparison of vowels solely based on a comparison of phonetic symbols does not provide such sub-segmental information which may be relevant for non-native speakers (e.g. Davidsen-Nielsen *et al.*, 1982; Dretzke, 1998; Mees & Collins, 1996).

In acoustic terms, diphthongisation is expressed as FORMANT FREQUENCY movement across the duration of the vowel. For example, the production of SBE [i:] and [u:] as [ɪi] and [ʊu], respectively, may be translated to a decrease in F_1 frequency. Therefore, formant movement which might be considered 'inherent' to the vowel was quantified by computing changes in F_1 from a point 25% through the vocalic duration to the 75% point in each /hVt/ syllable and transforming them into a percentage score. Following Nearey and Assmann (1986), 10% was used as the benchmark to characterise significant formant movement (also called 'vowel-inherent spectral change') in vowels.

The results showed that formant movement across the VOCALIC NUCLEUS exceeded 10% for F_1 for the SBE tense vowels [i:] and [u:]. In DA and in GE, however, formant movement throughout the /hVt/ syllables was slight, with no larger change than 10% for F_1 frequencies. That is, these DA and GE vowels were not produced with significant diphthongisation (see Figure 12.4). For the two non-native speaker groups, only DAE [u:] showed the same diphthongisation patterns as native SBE [u:] did. In this respect, Danish speakers produced the formant movement patterns of English [u:]

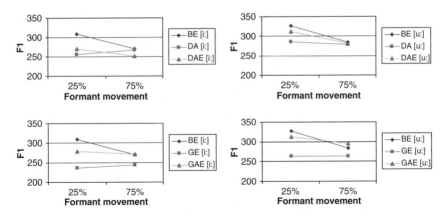

Figure 12.4 Percentage change in F1 for [u:] and [i:], from a point 25% through the vocalic duration to the 75% point in each /hVt/ syllable in SBE, DA and DAE (top panels) and in SBE, GE and GAE (bottom panels)

accurately and did not rely on their native Danish [u:], for which hardly any formant movement was found. DAE [i:], on the other hand, was not produced with formant movement that exceeded 10%, that is, the Danish speakers produced English [i:] with a pattern similar to their native DA [i:] which did not show any diphthongisation. Similarly, GAE [i:] and [u:] were produced just like their native GE counterparts, that is, with hardly any F_1 formant movement (see Figure 12.4).

Phonetic context effects in L1 and L2 vowel production

It is well-known that the acoustic properties of vowels are affected by consonantal context (e.g. Lindblom, 1963 for Swedish; Crystal & House, 1988; Ohde & Sharf, 1975; Schweyer, 1996; Stevens & House, 1963 for American English; Iivonen, 1995 for Finnish; Strange & Bohn, 1998 for GE). In acoustic terms, the phonetic reduction of the vowel is usually characterised by a decrease in the acoustic duration of the vowel and by formant undershoot (i.e. a change in formant frequencies from 'target' values reached in neutral contexts). Typically, bilabial, alveolar and velar plosive stop contexts have been chosen because they are easy to delimit from vowels in terms of WAVEFORMS and SPECTROGRAMS. However, such contextual effects are not mentioned in any pronunciation guides for foreign learners of English. This is probably due to the fact that consonantal context effects have rarely been studied in second-language speech. If it is true that languages differ as to the extent to which the articulation of one sound influences adjacent sounds, then one would expect these language-specific coarticulatory effects to be transferred from native to non-native

vowel production. The aim of this section is to acoustically analyse consonantal context effects on the vowels [iː], [uː] and [aː].

First, the effect of consonantal context /dVt/ on the vowel [aː] was
examined and compared to [aː] in /hVt/ context, which may be considered
a 'neutral context' (e.g. Stevens & House, 1963). Strong effects were noted
for SBE [aː] in the alveolar stop context. The alveolar context influenced the
vowels in such a manner that coarticulated [aː] was pulled towards [ʌ] in
the /hVt/ context. In turn, coarticulated [ʌ] was pulled towards the
position of [ɜː] in the /hVt/ context. Coarticulated [ɜː], then, became more
centralized. These ALLOPHONIC REALIZATIONS indicate that, in SBE, some
coarticulated vowels have their formant frequency values closer to the values of a different vowel category in the /hVt/ context (see Figure 12.5).[14]
Such effects were noted neither for DA [aː] nor for GE [aː]. Languages apparently differ in the extent with which consonantal context affects the acoustic
properties of vowels (Broad, 1976; Flege, 1988; Steinlen, 2005). Figure 12.5
also indicates that the Danish and German learners did not produce the
coarticulated English vowel [aː] in a native-like way: The acoustic values
of coarticulated [aː] differed significantly from [ʌ] in the /hVt/ context.[15]
In comparison to native SBE vowels, non-native vowel production does not
display such allophonic realizations due to consonantal context.

Second, the effect of the bilabial, alveolar and velar stop consonant
environment on the F_2 values of [iː] and [uː] in SBE vs. DA vs. DAE and in
SBE vs. GE vs. GAE was examined, replicating a method employed by
Ohde and Sharf (1975) and Schweyer (1996) for American English. Only
results for F_2 values are reported here because effects of consonantal place
of articulation are generally considerably larger on F_2 values than on F_1
values (e.g. Stevens & House, 1963). As Figure 12.6 shows, there is a
considerable increase in the values of F_2 for SBE [iː] as one moves from
the labial to the velar to the alveolar context. For SBE [iː], mean F_2 values
in the labial context were below those in the alveolar context, while the
mean values for the velar context did not differ from the values in the
/dVt/ context. For DA, on the other hand, the alveolar context did not
lead to an increase in the values of F_2 for [uː] and [iː] as compared to the
labial and the velar context. Thus, effects of consonantal contexts seemed
to be rather negligible in DA. The DAE speakers, finally, produced [uː] in
the /dVt/ context with higher F_2 values as compared to [uː] in /bVp/ or
/gVk/ syllables, just like native SBE speakers. No contextual effects,
however, were noted for DAE [iː] across the three consonantal contexts.
Thus, the DAE speakers parallel the contextual patterns found for SBE
[uː] and [iː].[16] This result suggests that it is possible for L2 speakers to
acquire the language-specific patterns of coarticulation associated with
the L2, which may differ from the L1.

For SBE vs. GE, the analysis on the effects of the bilabial, alveolar and
velar stop consonant environment on the F_2 values of [iː] and [uː] showed

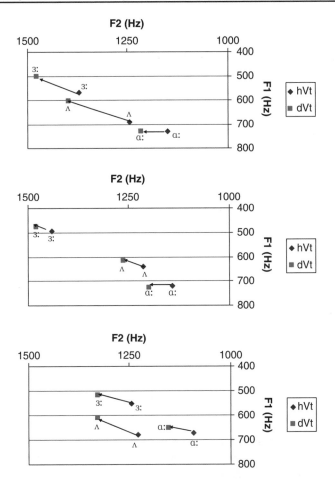

Figure 12.5 Location of [ɑː], [ʌ] and [ɜː] in SBE (top panel), DAE (middle panel) and GAE (bottom panel) in the F₁/F₂ space as produced in the /hVt/ and /dVt/ context. The arrows illustrate the change of location of these vowels in the two contexts

no coarticulatory effects on the F_2 values of GE [iː] and [uː]. Thus, the F_2 values of both GE and SBE [iː] did not differ across the consonantal contexts. However, the F_2 values of SBE [uː] were considerably higher in the alveolar than in the bilabial or velar context whereas the F_2 values of GE [uː] were the same across the three consonantal contexts. For the GAE vowels, the F_2 values of [iː] and [uː] were not affected by the bilabial, alveolar and velar contexts.[17] That is, the GAE group produced the same COARTICULATION PATTERNS in their L1 GE as in their L2 and this means

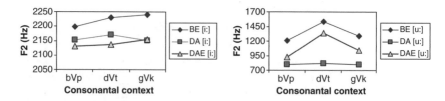

Figure 12.6   F$_2$ means for SBE, DA and DAE [i:] (left panel) and [u:] (right panel) in three consonantal contexts

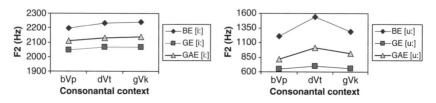

Figure 12.7   F$_2$ means for SBE, GE and GAE [i:] (left panel) and [u:] (right panel) in three consonantal contexts

that they deviated in their production of these coarticulated vowels from the native SBE speaker group (see Figure 12.7).

Discussion

In the present study, the L2 speakers did not pronounce all English vowels in a native-like way. Because certain characteristics of foreign-accented speech occur on a subsegmental (i.e. phonetic) level, they challenge predictions for non-native speaker production on the basis of solely comparing the phonetic symbols of two languages. For example, in DA, GE and SBE, three vowels are transcribed with the same phonetic symbols, namely [i:, ɑ:, u:]. However, these identically transcribed vowels were acoustically different from each other when produced in /hVt/ syllables. Moreover, differently transcribed vowels may have the same acoustic vowel quality: Even though SBE [ʌ] and GE [a], SBE [ɪ] and DA [ɛ], and SBE [ʊ] and DA [o] are transcribed with different phonetic symbols, the analysis did not reveal any significant acoustic differences between these cross-language vowel pairs (see also Disner, 1978). These results also have implications for predictions for non-native vowel production: One would normally not expect production problems for non-native speakers when the vowels of the L1 and the L2 are transcribed with the same phonetic symbols. In the present study, the DA speakers did not produce SBE [i:, u:, ɑ:] native-like nor did the GE speakers render SBE [i:, u:, ɑ:] authentically, although these vowels are transcribed with the same phonetic symbols in the L1 and the L2. On the other hand, some L2 vowels were produced native-like by the GE and DA learners of English although these vowels are transcribed with different phonetic symbols in the L1 and the L2: There were no acoustic differences between GAE and native SBE [ʌ] and [ɒ], between DAE and SBE [ɪ] and between DAE and SBE [ʊ]. The general applicability of phonetic symbols in cross-language comparison and subsequent predictions for L2 sound production has recently been criticized by Bohn (2002). He pointed out that the use of symbols is often arbitrary. For example, the vowel contrast in the German words *bieten* (to offer) and *bitten* (to ask) may be transcribed as /i:-i/ or /i-ɪ/, depending on whether the transcriber emphasizes the durational or the spectral contrast between these vowels (compare the different use of symbols for American/British English /i:/ and /ɪ/). The use of symbols may, therefore, also affect cross-language comparisons of speech sounds and consequently, predictions of possible production problems for L2 speakers. The choice of comparing either phonemes or ALLOPHONES across languages, as Bohn pointed out, already implies an answer to questions such as at which level similarity is perceived or at which level interlingual identification occurs. It seems therefore advisable not to rely on 'armchair methods' (Bohn, 2002) but to use acoustic data directly taken from the relevant speaker groups (see also Disner, 1978; Flege *et al.*, 1997; Højen, 2002; Kohler, 1981; Ladefoged, 1990; Rochet, 1995; Strange *et al.*, 2004).

This study also examined whether the non-native DAE and GAE speakers produced the English vowels [i:] and [u:] with diphthongisation pattern like the native SBE speakers. Non-native speech in this study was generally characterised by an absence of diphthongisation (except for DAE [u:]). These patterns are reflections of the L1 DA and GE, where [i:] and [u:] were not produced with diphthongisation. Languages seem to differ as to how they exploit diphthongisation in their vowel inventory. These results suggest that L2 learners have to learn not only the acoustic properties of non-native vowels, but also the language-specific patterns associated with diphthongised vowels. A comparison of vowels based on phonetic symbols only would not reveal such subsegmental cross-language differences. However, many pronunciation guides nowadays supplement their analysis with more finer-grained auditory–articulatory impressions and point out that diphthongisation patterns may be problematic for Danish and German learners of English (e.g. Livbjerg & Mees, 2000; Mees & Collins, 1996 for Danish; Arnold & Hansen, 1982; Dretzke, 1998; Eckert & Barry, 2002; Scherer & Wollmann, 1986 for German).

The results of acoustical analysis also showed that the effects of consonantal context on the vowels [i:], [u:] and [ɑ:] are apparently language-specific: In contrast to DA and GE, SBE coarticulated vowels were considerably more affected by consonantal context. This result confirmed

Broad's (1976: 420) suggestion that 'coarticulation effects may operate quite differently in different languages'. Furthermore, the language-specific extent of coarticulation on vowels is apparently transferred from the L1 to the L2. L2 learners, then, have to learn not only the acoustic properties of non-native vowels but also the language-specific patterns associated with coarticulated vowels. Some coarticulatory effects are apparently learnable: For example, DAE speakers produced coarticulated [u:] accordingly, that is, differently from the almost nonexistent coarticulatory effects in their L1 DA (see also Steinlen & Bohn, 2002). However, this was not the case for the GAE speakers who did not produce English [u:] with native-like coarticulation patterns. Furthermore, strong displacement patterns of coarticulated vowels (such as [ɑ:]) due to consonantal context were only found in SBE but not in DA and GE. Both non-native speaker groups transferred the pronunciation patterns from their L1 to the L2 and did not produce coarticulated [ɑ:] target-like. Similar results were obtained in a perceptual assimilation test where the identification of SBE by DA listeners varied as a function of the phonetic context in which vowels were presented (Bohn & Steinlen, 2003): The DA listeners either perceptually assimilated SBE vowels to different vowel categories depending on the context in which the vowels occurred, and/or the context affected the goodness of fit of the interlingual identifications (see also Strange *et al.*, 2005). These findings indicate that consonantal context effects play an important role in producing and perceiving native and non-native vowels.

Conclusion

In conclusion, this study demonstrated that native speaker data is an important tool in assessing and improving foreign-language pronunciation: In acoustic studies, native speakers are utilised as control groups in order to establish norms for target-like pronunciation of sounds by non-native speakers because non-native vowel production is not always well predicted on the basis of comparing phonetic symbols of the L1 and the L2. Even the narrowest phonetic transcription consists of static symbols with no inherent temporal specification – there is no simple way to transcribe the transition between two sounds. Thus, the phonetic symbol method does not take into account that the extent of coarticulatory effects may differ across languages and that vowel-inherent spectral change (i.e. diphthongisation) may be exploited in different ways. These language-specific expectations may be transferred from the L1 to the L2, and hence also contribute to a foreign accent in non-native vowel production.

In order to supplement written input (such as the phonetic symbol method), more recent pronunciation guides for learners of English often include tapes or CD-ROMs which contain listening exercises provided by native speakers, which are often used in classroom contexts (e.g. Eckert & Barry, 2002 for German learners; Livbjerg & Mees, 2000 for Danish learners of English; see Pfandl-Buchegger, 2005, for a review). In these tasks, non-native learners listen to native speakers' productions, which are either presented as minimal pairs, as cross-language near-homophones and/or embedded in stretches of speech such as poems, dialogues, limericks, and so on. The underlying assumption of this ear-training is that most pronunciation errors have a perceptual basis, thus, an improvement in perception might help to improve production (see e.g. Flege, 1995, 2003; Rochet, 1995). Specific training tasks have been designed to assess the progress of L2 performance in laboratory settings and showed promising results: For example, an identification training period of only six weeks had a positive effect on the production and perception of American English vowels by Japanese subjects (Lambacher *et al.*, 2005, see also Bradlow *et al.*, 1997 for similar results).

Such training techniques could also be used in a classroom context: For instance, to tackle the problem of coarticulated vowels and their target-like pronunciation in SBE by Danish and German learners, the L2 learners could listen to tokens in identification tasks, which contrast vowels embedded in neutral and consonantal context. Recall that coarticulated SBE [ɑː], for instance, changed its acoustic vowel quality in such a way that it resembled the neighboring vowel [ʌ] in the neutral /hVt/ context, but neither the Danish nor the German learners produced these coarticulated vowel target-like. Furthermore, identification tasks may also improve the pronunciation of the diphthongised SBE vowels [iː] and [uː], which (except DAE [uː]) were not produced target-like by the non-native speakers. For example, identification tasks using cross-language near-homophones (e.g. GE *Schuh* vs. SBE *shoe*, as recorded by native speakers in Eckert & Barry, 2002) could be created to tailor the needs of more advanced non-native speakers, who wish to improve their production beyond the segmental level.

Still, even after training L2 learners may not always know whether their production of non-native sounds is actually target-like. For the SBE vowels [iː] or [uː], for example, Mees and Collins (1996: 128) advised their Danish speakers 'not to extend this glide [...]. It's very slight and any exaggeration tends to sound like a Cockney accent'. How are L2 learners supposed to know whether their production of SBE [iː] or [uː] displays too much or too little diphthongisation, though? As large inter-learner variability is a commonplace in L2 speech performance (e.g. Barry, 1989; Bradlow *et al.*, 1997; Flege *et al.*, 1995b), non-native subjects may benefit from two approaches that focus more directly on the individual speaker: In a first step, non-native sound production may be rated for goodness by native listeners (e.g. Bradlow *et al.*, 1997; Lambacher *et al.*, 2005; Munro, 1993; Piske *et al.*, 2001, 2002; Trapp & Bohn, 2002). In such an approach, the non-native speakers of the present study could receive objective feedback from native SBE listeners with respect to their acceptability in pronunciation and would individually know how well they approximated diphthongisation in the SBE vowels [i:] and [u:]. In a second step, non-native speakers could receive articulatory training with explicit instructions and direct feedback. As Catford and Pisoni (1970: 477) note, articulatory training should ideally be provided by native language teachers who possess 'scientific knowledge of articulatory phonetics' to successfully lead L2 learners to the correct pronunciation and perception of non-native speech sounds. For example, SBE [u:] is not only produced with diphthongisation but also with a different acoustic quality when embedded in between consonants (especially in the alveolar context). SBE [u:] could be presented in minimal pairs (e.g. in the /hVt/ and in the /dVt/ context) which the learner then has to imitate. With appropriate articulatory feedback, non-native speakers could learn how to alter their tongue positions towards native speaker norms. One should keep in mind, though, that laboratory training cannot take the place of naturalistic exposure to a target language.

In sum, this chapter showed that, especially in a classroom context, it is imperative to supplement written input using the phonetic symbol method with naturalistic data taken from native speakers because the phonetic descriptions of vowel sounds in pronunciation guidebooks do not accurately match the actual production of sounds as measured by acoustic analysis.

Notes

1. This research was aided by the Danish Research Council. The author expresses her gratitude to Nina Rogotzki and three anonymous reviewers for their valuable comments.
2. The data reported in this chapter have been taken from Steinlen (2005).
3. The choice to only use data from male adult speakers was motivated by the fact that spectral analysis is more difficult to perform on female voices. Their harmonics are typically a good deal further apart than those of male voices, by virtue of the typically higher F_0, which makes it more difficult to discern the location of the formants in the spectrum (Disner, 1978). Ideally, studies should be based on large samples of speakers, both male and female.
4. The native British English speakers had come from southern England (or had lived there most of their lives). Resource limitations had made it unfeasible to test native British English speakers from a single, well-defined variety of British English. It was, however, taken care of that the subjects spoke a variety of English that can be regarded as 'neutral' British English in the sense that they did not speak with a noticeable regional accent. Subjects who did produce English vowels with a marked regional accent (e.g. /ʊ/ as the merger of /ʌ/ and /ʊ/) were excluded from the study.
5. In a language background questionaire, the non-native speakers of English were asked about the variant of English that they spoke. Subjects were

excluded if they spoke a variety of English that did not aim at 'neutral' British English (see above).

6. The phonetic transcription of the Danish vowels used in this study is based on Fischer-Jørgensen (1972) which is the seminal acoustic study on Danish vowels. Note, however, that slightly different notations may be found in other sources on Danish vowels (e.g. Grønnum, 1998; Livbjerg & Mees, 2000; Mees & Collins, 1996; Rischel, 1968). The phonetic transcription of the German vowels are based on Strange and Bohn (1998 and of the SBE vowels by Wells (1982).

7. Spectral analysis was performed using the LPC algorithms available in the Computerised Speech Research Environment 4.5 (CSRE) software. The frequencies of the first three formants were estimated by placing the centre of a 128 point Hamming window at three points in the vowel portion: A point 25% through the vocalic portion, the vowel centre at 50%, and a point at 75% of the vowel duration. The LPC order was computed manually from LPC spectra (15 coefficients), missing information due to merged formants or other obvious peak picking errors was supplied by successively increasing the LPC order by 2.

8. The speech production data of the three speaker groups (SBE, DA, DAE) were first analysed in separate Group (3 levels) × Vowel (4 levels) ANOVAS with formant frequencies (F_1 and F_2) in Hz as dependent variables. The ANOVAs revealed significant Group × Vowel interactions for the front-back (F_2) dimension ($F (3, 36) = 3.125$, $p < 0.05$), but not for the height (F_1) dimension ($F (3, 36) = 0.441$, $p > 0.05$). The Group × Vowel interactions were explored through one-way ANOVAs testing the effect of speaker group (SBE, DA, DAE) on the F_1 and F_2 values of individual vowels. The effect of group on the F_1 and F_2 values was significant for both vowels. The three groups differed significantly in their production of [i:] in F_1 ($F (2, 27) = 8.238$, $p < 0.05$) and in F_2 ($F (2, 27) = 3.591$, $p < 0.05$). Planned *post-hoc* tests revealed significant differences in F_1 and F_2 between SBE [i:] and DAE [i:] ($p < 0.05$) but not between DAE [i:] and DA [i:] ($p > 0.05$ for F_1 and F_2).

9. One-way ANOVAs explored the significant Group × Vowel interactions described in endnote 2. The three groups differed significantly in their production of [u:] in F_1 ($F (2, 27) = 4.698$, $p < 0.05$) and in F_2 ($F (2, 27) = 35.079$, $p < 0.05$). Planned post-hoc tests revealed significant differences in F_1 and F_2 between SBE and DAE [u:] ($p < 0.05$). However, significant differences in F_1 and F_2 ($p < 0.05$) were also found between DAE [u:] and DA [u:].

10. Separate one-way ANOVAs comparing native SBE, DAE and DA [ɑ:] revealed significant main effects for speaker group for F_2 ($F (2, 27) = 4.248$, $p < 0.05$) but not for F_1 ($F (2, 27) = 1.680$, $p > 0.05$). Planned *post-hoc* tests showed no significant differences in F_1 ($p > 0.05$) or in F_2 ($p > 0.05$) for native SBE vs. DAE [ɑ:], although SBE [ɑ:] was significantly longer than DAE [ɑ:] ($p < 0.05$). DA [ɑ:] and DAE [ɑ:] differed significantly in F_2 ($p < 0.05$) but not in F_1 ($p > 0.05$).

11. In order to determine whether the German group produced the English vowels differently from the native English speakers and from the native German speakers, planned *post-hoc* tests were carried out. The tests revealed significant differences in F_2 between SBE and GAE [i:] and [u:] ($p < 0.05$) and between native SBE and GAE [i:] and [u:] for F_1 ($p > 0.05$). Planned *post-hoc* tests revealed significant differences in F_1 and in F_2 or tense [i:] and [u:] in GE vs. GAE ($p < 0.05$).

12. The spectral and duration values of the vowel [ɑ:] were examined in separate one-way ANOVAs, which revealed significant main effects for language group

only for F_2 (F (2, 27) = 3.786, $p < 0.05$) but not for F_1 (F (2, 27) = 2.030, $p > 0.05$) or duration (F (2, 27) = 1.717, $p > 0.05$). Planned *post-hoc* tests did not indicate any significant temporal differences between native SBE [ɑː] and GAE [ɑː] ($p > 0.05$), although spectral differences were found for F_2 ($p < 0.05$). A comparison between native GE and GAE [ɑː] did not show any significant temporal or spectral differences ($p > 0.05$ for F_1, F_2 and duration).

13. Separate one-way ANOVAs were employed to determine the relationships between SBE and GAE [ʌ] and between GAE [ʌ] and GE [a]. No significant main effects were found for language group (F_1: (F (2, 27) = 0.434, $p > 0.05$; F_2: F (2, 27) = 0.514, $p > 0.05$; duration: F (2, 27) = 1.026, $p > 0.05$). Planned *post-hoc* tests did not indicate any significant temporal or spectral differences between SBE and GAE [ʌ] ($p > 0.05$ for F_1, F_2 and duration). No significant temporal and spectral differences were found for GAE [ʌ] vs. GE [a] ($p > 0.05$ for F_1, F_2 and duration). Analyses revealed significant differences between DA [ɪ] and SBE [ɪ] in F_1 and F_2 ($p < 0.05$ for F_1 and F_2). In addition, there were significant differences in F_2 between SBE [ɪ] and DAE [ɪ] ($p < 0.05$). No significant spectral differences were noted between DAE [ɪ] and DA [ɛ] ($p > 0.05$ for F_1 and F_2). No significant spectral differences were found between SBE [ʊ] and DAE [ʊ] ($p > 0.05$). However, DAE [ʊ] differed significantly in F_2 from DA [o] ($p < 0.05$), that is it is questionable whether Danish speakers actually used their native [o] to produce English [ʊ]. Furthermore, there were significant spectral differences between DAE [ʊ] and DA [u] for F_1 and F_2 ($p < 0.05$).

14. The results of separate one-way ANOVAs for F_1 and F_2 of [ɑː] and [ʌ] in the /dVt/ context vs. [ʌ] and [ɜː] in the /hVt/ context showed that coarticulated [ɑː] did not differ significantly in F_1 or F_2 from [ʌ] in the /hVt/ context (/dVt/ [ɑː] vs. /hVt/ [ʌ]: F (1, 18) = 0.996, $P > 0.05$) and that coarticulated [ʌ] did not differ significantly in F_1 or F_2 from [ɜː] in the /hVt/ context (/dVt/ [ʌ] vs. /hVt/ [ɜː]: F(1, 18) = 1.319, $p > 0.05$). Similar results were found for the velar context.

15. The results of separate one-way ANOVAs for F_1 and F_2 of DAE and GAE [ɑː] and [ʌ] in the /dVt/ context vs. [ʌ] and [ɜː] in the /hVt/ context showed that coarticulated [ɑː] differed significantly in F_1 or F_2 from [ʌ] in the /hVt/ context (for DAE: /dVt/ [ɑː] vs. /hVt/ [ʌ]: F(1, 18) = 6.554, $p < 0.05$, for GAE: /dVt/ [ɑː] vs. /hVt/ [ʌ]: F(1, 18) = 8.967, $p < 0.05$). Again, similar results were found for the velar context.

16. A 3 (context) × 2 (vowels) mixed design ANOVA for the F2 values of the SBE, DA and DAE vowels [iː] and [uː] in the /bVp/, /dVt/ and /gVk/ context for each speaker group was carried out and revealed significant main effects for Context and for the Vowel-by-Context interaction for English (Context: F (1, 27) = 12.559, $p = 0.000$; Vowel × Context interaction: F (2, 27) = 7.671, $p = 0.002$) but not for Danish (Context: F (1, 27) = 0.124, $p = 0.884$; Vowel × Context interaction: F (2, 27) = 0.004, $p = 0.996$. In order to explore the Vowel × Context interaction for the SBE speaker group, separate one-way ANOVAs were carried out, which revealed that the F2 values of SBE [uː] differed significantly across the bilabial, alveolar and velar contexts (F (2, 27) = 11.468, $p = 0.000$), whereas the F2 values of SBE [iː] did not (F (2, 27) = 1.080, $p = 0.354$). Planned *post-hoc* tests showed that the F2 values of SBE [uː] were significantly higher in the /dVt/ context than in the /bVp/ or /gVk/ contexts ($p < 0.05$ for all). In contrast, contextual effects for SBE [iː] were not significant ($p > 0.05$ for all). For the DA speaker group, one-way ANOVAs were not carried out because the interaction between Vowel × Context was not significant (F (2, 27) = 14.615, $p = 0.000$). The ANOVAs for the DAE

group revealed a significant main effect for Context ($F(1, 27) = 8.855, p = 0.001$) and for the Vowel × Context interaction ($F(2, 27) = 14.615, p = 0.000$). These effects were explored with separate one-way ANOVAs which revealed significant differences in F_2 for [u:] across the three contexts ($F(2, 27) = 16.796, p = 0.000$) but no significant differences in F_2 for [i:] ($F(2, 27) = 0.124, p = 0.884$). Planned *post-hoc* tests showed that, like in SBE, the F_2 values of DAE [u:] were higher in the /dVt/ than in the /bVp/ or /gVk/ context ($p < 0.05$ for all).

17. The repeated measures analysis for German did not reveal significant main effects for Context ($F(1, 27) = 0.731, p = 0.491$) and for the Vowel-by-Context interaction ($F(2, 27) = 0.132, p = 0.877$), therefore one-way ANOVAs were not carried out. Similar results were found for GAE (Context: $F(1, 27) = 2.911, p = 0.072$, Vowel × Context: $F(2, 27) = 1.418, p = 0.260$).

Chapter 13

Developing Non-native Pronunciation in Immersion Settings

HENNING WODE

Introduction

This paper is based on an ongoing long-term endeavor to characterize the development of the pronunciation of a non-native language in IMMERSION settings (IM) and to work out the implications for IM teaching. The starting point is the large number of parallels in terms of the phonological structures including the errors produced by L2 learners across the age range from age three to age 18 and older in such diverse learning situations as NATURALISTIC contexts vs. IM vs. traditional teacher-centered classroom instruction. From the theoretical point of view this gives rise to two issues. One is whether the abilities of human beings to acquire the pronunciation of a non-native language do, or do not, change as a function of age. If they do change it is important for teachers to be aware of the nature of these changes in order to be able to react to these developments in terms of instructional techniques. If, on the other hand, people retain their ability to learn additional languages, teachers should be aware of the fact that the development of the non-native pronunciation at the end of school is not necessarily the ultimate level people can attain.

The second issue is input. Given the obvious differences between the acquisitional situations and the nature of the INPUT resulting from them, what is the impact of input in view of the structural parallels and/or age? The age issue has traditionally been dicussed in terms of the notions of CRITICAL PERIOD(s) (e.g. Lenneberg, 1967; Long, 1990; Scovel, 1988). These notions imply restrictions on the extent to which the pronunciation of non-native languages can be learned and taught. Note that these restrictions are likely to differ depending on whether one assumes that people cannot, or that they choose not, to develop beyond a certain point. That is, if people cannot develop NATIVE-LIKE proficiency levels any more after a certain point in time, this point will constitute an insurmountable barrier to any kind of teaching of non-native pronunciation. However, no such barriers are implied, if it is assumed that for some reason learners fail to make progress although, in principle, they have the ability to do so. For many years I have taken the latter view (e.g. Wode, 1981, 2003). Of course, the issue is pertinent to any kind of foreign language teaching. But it is particularly relevant for IM, because such programs may start with children and older learners aged three to 16, thus encompassing the time span until after puberty. Recall the central role that the time of puberty has played in the debate on critical/sensitive periods.

The input issue is puzzling, because common sense would suggest that the outcomes will differ depending on the quality of the input, that is, whether the students are provided with native or native-like input, that is whether they are taught by teachers with a noticable L2 accent, and whether there is, in fact, remedial instruction as to the articulatory gestures required for the target language. The data reviewed below do not support such a simple claim. The data derive from English IM programs in Germany where learners range from age three to 18, that is, including, preschool/kindergarten, primary school and secondary school students. The data do not show any age-dependent differences in terms of the phonological structures. This implies that the phonological mechanisms, such as EQUIVALENCE CLASSIFICATION, PERCEPTUAL CONSTANCY, PERCEPTUO-MOTOR LINKS as the basis for the perceptual control of PRODUCTION, and TRANSFER are fully in place by age three at the latest. On the other hand, the data from older learners, such as those in the post-puberty age range, imply that these phonological mechanisms continue to be available after the age of compulsory schooling. Pathological cases aside, at the present time there is no empirical evidence suggesting that any of these mechanisms get eliminated or stop to be operative at any point in a given speaker's life span.

Subjects, Data, Methodology

IM has been surprisingly slow to catch on in Germany, in particular, for preschools and primary schools. The first IM programs were established towards the end of the 1960s. According to Canadian terminology,[1] they were EXTENDED CORE PROGRAMS involving only a low dose of late partial IM, and they were meant to serve schools at secondary age ranges. These programmes start in Grade 5 (age 10) as traditional LANGUAGE-AS-SUBJECT instruction (LAS). LAS is continued till the end of secondary school in Germany (age 18). But in Grade 7, an IM component is added in that two of the regular subjects, in general, geography and history, are taught entirely in the foreign language (for details, see Wode, 1995, 1998).

Preschool IM and IM at primary schools are just beginning to get established in answer to the three-language formula as the official language policy of the European Union, namely, that every child is to have the opportunity to learn at least three languages at a functionally appropriate level during his/her time in school (e.g. European Commission, 2004; Wode, 1995, 1998, 2001a, 2001b, 2001c). Although this paper focuses on IM at preschool, primary and secondary levels and thus spans the entire age range from three to 18, for reasons of space and the availability of empirical studies, the data from the late partial IM program can only be alluded to very briefly.

As for IM at preschool and primary school the data for this chapter come from a network of English IM programs modeled on early IM in Canada except that instead of one year of kindergarten at age five the German children start at age three in preschool via 100% IM, that is, throughout the entire day English is the only language used by the native-speaker teacher. Upon entry into primary school at age six they continue in such a way that all subjects except German are taught in English, resulting in approximately 70% of the teaching time carried in English and only 30% in German. In addition and also differing from Canadian IM, a small number of children without any knowledge of English are also admitted to such IM classes so that these students start IM at six. They are not given any special treatment; they are expected to catch up on their own – and they certainly do. By the end of Grade 4, at age nine or 10, in most cases even earlier, these children have become indistinguishable from the others on the basis of their English (Wode, 2004).

The early and the late IM programs relate to each other in such a way that the latter adds two options: Children who have not yet been introduced to English before, can use it to learn English as their first foreign language; those children who have attended English IM in primary school, can use it to continue with English and/or move on to their second foreign language. Note that with respect to the beginning of IM, this scheme allows for three entry points, namely, age three (beginning of preschool), age six (beginning of primary school for those children with no prior knowledge of English), and age 12 (the beginning of the IM component in the late partial IM programme after the children have had two years of LAS.[2]

The data for the late partial IM programme was elicited by asking triads of students to discuss how they would handle a difficult situation on a class trip to the Scottish Highlands (e.g. Wode, 1998). The primary school data come from picture narratives of the story *Frog, where are you?* (Mayer, 1969). This test is administered at the end of each grade level. The preschoolers are tested in a variety of ways through playing children's games, enacting specific roles in puppet shows, identifying objects on picture cards, etc. The data cited in this report derive from the latter task (for details, see Berger, 1999).

Phonological Development Across School Age

Since IM does not involve any explicit explanation or correction, learners only have perception to rely on as their major (only?) source of information as to the articulatory gestures involved. This means that perception controls production both with respect to ACQUISITION and use. The research on whether monolingual L1 children can discriminate non-native sound contrasts shows that there are already changes in the perceptual behavior of monolingual children by the end of their first year of life. By then, they have become particularly sensitive to the sound contrasts of their native language, and their perceptual categories are much the same as those of older children, adolescents or adults. As for non-native sound contrasts there are some that monolingual children fail to discriminate towards the end of their first year of life, whereas other non-native contrasts continue to be discriminated well into adulthood (e.g. Best *et al.*, 1988; Werker *et al.*, 1981; Werker & Tees, 1984. For reviews see, e.g. Bohn, 2002; Wode, 1999). It is these perceptual abilities that provide the basis for the development of production, including transfer (Wode, 1994a).

However, in what follows the concern will primarily be with L2 production. One reason is that the IM data presently available are production data. The second reason is that the arguments concerning age have, in the past, centered on the occurrence or nonoccurrence of transfer in production. And, third, the preschool material allows us to readdress the age issue and to make it more precise by asking what it is that is being affected by age, namely, whether there are any differences in the nature of the structures produced by L2 learners as a function of age, whether it is the level of proficiency attainable by L2-learners, or whether it is both. In Wode (1981) I suggested that there are no age differences with respect to phonological structures, but that there are age differences with respect to the proficiency levels that tend to be attained. Since then, the research on speech perception with infants has produced some of the most astonishing evidence to justify this distinction. As hinted at above and as argued in detail in Wode (1994a) the reason why there is transfer does not relate to any kind of development occuring at puberty, as may be argued based on Lenneberg (1967), nor at age six, as might be argued by Long (1990). As already stated above, before children learn to read and write the nature of phonological transfer is based on the perceptual developments occurring during the second half of the first year of life.

The beginnings

Since IM programs may start at any age, the beginning needs to be characterized in such a way that it applies to the entire age range. As for the range of four and older, research on non-IM data suggests that in terms of phonological structures and developmental sequences, there are no notable differences as a function of age except for one obvious reservation. The substitution patterns found with L2 learners reflect the state of development of their L1 phonological system. Of course, this is a peculiarity showing up only with very young children. This can be illustrated for a German child aged three years and 11 months. She is one of the four L1 German children whose L2 phonological development has been studied intensively at Kiel (e.g. Wode, 1981). At the time of first contact with English she did not yet distinguish between /s z (t)ʃ (d)ʒ/ in her L1 production; she replaced them by /θ ð/, as in [θøn] instead of [ʃøn] *schön (beautiful)*, [ʀaðə] instead of [gaʀaʒə] *Garage (garage)*, [vaɪθ] instead of [vaɪs] *weiß (white)*, [ðɒl] instead of [zɒl] *soll (shall, ought to)*. The dental nature of the fricatives was due to the fact that IG had a lisp. She transfered this pattern into her English resulting in, for example, *Johnny* [ðɒni] (0;4 (after zero months, four days), *Ginger* [ðɪnða] (0;9), *yes* [jɛθ] (0;18) *much* [matʰθ] (0;27), *fishing* [fɪθɪŋ] (0;30), *guys* [gaɪθ] (1;2). Such evidence suggests that after age four there is the kind of transfer familiar from older learners. Moreover, its structure and functioning appears to be the same across the entire age range after age four. The evidence below for the preschoolers will show that this state of affairs already applies at age three.

Preschoolers

There are two overriding issues with respect to the preschoolers. One is the achievement levels they are likely to reach in preschool and afterwards; the other one is the nature of the developmental process in terms of the structural properties of the evolving L2, in particular, whether the errors, individual variation, transfer, phonological processes, and so on, match, or do not match, those of older children and/or adults. The latter issue can be addressed by comparing the preschool data with the data from the four naturalistic child L2 learners of English of the Kiel corpus. Their age range was three years and 11 months to eight years and 11 months upon first contact with English in the United States.

The nature of the L2 substitutions

Table 13.1 lists those English phonemes that notoriously cause problems for German L2 learners/speakers. Although Table 13.1 summarises the data from the four Kiel children, it should be noted that it has already been shown that theirs parallels data from other age ranges and from other kinds of L2 acquisitional situations (Wode, 1981, 2003). The reason why the two older children HEI and BIR are included in Table 13.1 is to illustrate the parallelism across the age range.

The problems German speakers have with English, of course, derive from the fact that some of the distinctions of English do not exist in German. Amongst other things, German lacks /θ ð æ dʒ əʊ ɛɪ/; the German

Table 13.1 Segment substitutions for L2 English targets notoriously problematic for Germans during the initial stages of L2 acquisition.

L2 target	L2 substitution			
	HEI (8;11)	**BIR (7;11)**	**LA (5;11)**	**IG (3,11)**
Consonants				
/r/	w	ʀ	w	w
		w		
/θ-/	θ-	s-	θ-	θ-
	s-	θ-	s-	f-
/-θ-/	-θ-	-θ-	-θ-	
	-f-			
	-s-			
/ð-/	ð-	d-	ð-	d-
	d-	z-	t̬-	
	z-			
/-ð-/	-d-	-d-		
	-ð-			
/w/	w	w	w	w
	v	v	v	v
				f
/v-/	v-	w-	w-	w-
	w-		v-	v-
			ɹ-	
/-v-/	-v-	-v-	-v-	-v-
	-w-		-f-	
/l/	l	l	l	l
Vowels				
/æ/	ɛ	ɛ	ɛ	ɛ
/ɔʊ/	o	o	o	o
/ɛɪ/	e ~ ɛɪ	e ~ ɛɪ	e ~ ɛɪ	e ~ ɛɪ
/ɛʳ/	œə	œə	œə	œə
/ʋʳ/	ʋɐ ~ ʋə	ʋɐ ~ ʋə	ʋɐ ~ ʋə	ʋɐ ~ ʋə

Note: In these tables, a dash before a segment indicates that it is word-initial, a dash on either side that the segment is word-medial, and a dash before the segment that it is word-final. Segments without dashes do not specify pronunciation in terms of position in a word.
Source: Based on Wode (1981)

/r/ is uvular [R] or [ʁ]; there is no velar [ɫ]; there are no retroflex vowels; and no syllable-final voiced obstruents (see Moulton, 1962 for details).

Table 13.1 is focused on segment substitutions. It illustrates two kinds of substitutions, namely, those that result from transfer from the L1 and those that do not. The latter comprise the substitutions for /r/ except [ʁ]; the former all the others including the vowels and [ʁ] as a substitute for /r/. As explained in detail in previous publications (e.g. Wode, 1981), only [ʁ] substituting for English /r/ can be viewed as originating from transfer since it is very likely that BIR linked her German [ʁ] to the English /r/ because she was intrigued by the spelling of words like *orange*, which is spelled like its German cognate. In general, [w] is the predominating substitute for English /r/ in both L2 and L1 acquisition.[3] Note that, all in all, the data from the four children is not identical, but it is close enough across the respective age span of 4–9 to suggest that, basically, the children follow the same processes.

Transfer-based substitutions

Given the obvious differences in the learning situations between fully naturalistic situations vs. IM preschools it needs to be determined whether preschoolers procede differently or whether they conform to the pattern established in Table 13.1. Therefore, Tables 13.2 and 13.3 contrast the evidence for preschoolers vs. naturalistic learners. Table 13.2 has the evidence for five preschoolers for the transfer-based substitutions. The data for English /r/ is summarized in Tables 13.3 and 13.4.

Table 13.2 contrasts the data from five children of preschool age, two being non-preschool learners and three IM preschool learners. The latter three were chosen because they had been attending preschool for only half a year. Comparing the data in Table 13.2 will reinforce the conclusion derived from Table 13.1, namely, that the transfer-based developmental structures are much the same across the entire age range as well as across the various L2 learning situations.

Non-transfer based substitutions

The evidence on the acquisition of English /r/ is included here to indicate that the structural parallelism between the IM preschoolers and the four naturalistic learners also applies to those substitutions that are not due to transfer.

Previous research has shown that the retroflex /ɻ/ of American English and the frictionless continuant /ɹ/ of British English tend to be deleted or substituted by [w] (e.g. Wode, 1981). Table 13.3 presents the data from the three younger German children of the Kiel data base. The older child HEI is not included because as a fourth grader his literacy in German was too advanced so that he could well have made use of it, although,

Table 13.2 Segment substitutions as in Table 13.1 contrasting the two preschool children of Table 13.1 and the three youngest preschoolers. A 9 etc. = serial number for preschoolers; ( ) = number of tokens. LA and IG had a lisp.

L2 target	L2 substitution				
	LA (5;11)	IG (3;11)	A 17	A 9	A 19
Consonants					
/θ-/	θ-	θ-	s	s (7)	s (3)
	s-	f-	ts (2)	θ (1)	ts (1)
				ts (1)	
/-θ-/	-θ-		–	–	–
/ð-/	ð-	d-	–	–	–
	t̥-				
/w/	w	w	–	w (13)	w (3)
	v	v		v (1)	v (1)
		f			
/v-/	w-	w-	f (2)	f (6)	f (3)
	v-	v-		v (5)	v (1)
	ɹ-				
/-v-/	-v-	-v-	–	–	–
	-f-				
[ɬ]	l	l	l (2)	l	l (7)
Vowels					
/æ/	ε	ε	ε	ε (9)	ε (4)
				æ (1)	
/ɔʊ/	o	o	o (1)	o	o (1)
			a (1)		a (1)
/εɪ/	e ~ εɪ	e ~ εɪ		e	
/εʳ/	œᵊ	œᵊ	–	–	–
/ʋʳ/	ʋᵊ ~ ʋᵊ	ʋᵊ ~ ʋᵊ	–	–	ʋᵊ

Source: Wode (2003)

Table 13.3 Early L2 substitutions for English /r/ by three German children learning English as their L2 in a naturalistic setting. x = such substitutions are on record but not for that particular word

	L2 target	*BIR 7;11*	*LA 5;11*	*IG 3;11*
/r-/	Redding ready	x wɛdi	wɛdɪŋ x	wɛdɪŋ wɛdi
/CrV/	Craig Trinity Center Truck	kʰwɛk x tʰwak	kʰwɛːk tʰwɪnɪti θɛntɐ x	kʰwɛɪk x
/Vr/	hammer here	hɛmɐ hiɐ	hɛmɐ hiɐ	hɛmɐ hiɐ

Source: Wode (2003)

Table 13.4 Early L2 substitutions for English /r/ by German preschoolers. – = not attempted. Number in ( ) = number of tokens. A 17, A 9 etc. = serial number for preschoolers

	L2 target	*A17/3;10*	*A9/4;2*	*A19/4;10*	*A6/4;11*	*A8/4;11*
/r-/	robot red	– wɛɪ	– –	– ɹɛːt	wɒbat wɛt	– ɹɛt
/CrV/	green three	– –	gwin svi (3) tsvɪ	gɹin θɹi (2)	gwin svi (2)	gwin twi tɹi
/Vr/	car ears four	– – foɐª	– – fɒː fɑː fɒɐ	kaː øɐs foː	kaː (2) iəθ fɔ	kaʊ – fɔ
-/Vᵉ/	football player water	bɔl – –	fʊtbɔlɐ xʊtbɒlpleɐ wɔtɐ (2)	fʊtbalɐ – –	fʊtbɔl fʊtbɔlpleɐ wɔtɐ	fʊtbɔlpleɐ – –
/VrV/;	orange cherry	– –	– ʃɛʁi	ɒwɛnʃ ʃɛʁi	ɒwɪnʃ ʃɛvi	oːɪnʃ tʃɛvi

ªInstead of *two*.
Source: Wode (2003)

as a matter of fact, he did not do so. Table 13.4 shows the data from five preschoolers.

Table 13.4 contains two additional rows not included in Table 13.3. The evidence for /Vʳ/ of Table 13.4 is split into two subsets by listing those words that contain the final unstressed syllable – *er* in one row, and leaving the other cases of post-vocalic /r/ in another row. For both kinds of targets the preschoolers' input varied between /vᵉ/ and /vʳ/ depending on the variety spoken by the carepersons/teachers. In either case both the preschoolers and the non-preschoolers use their German /ɐ/ or /a/ as a substitute. In addition, the target environment /VrV/ is given a separate row in Table 13.4, because there were a few cases of [ʁ] and [v] substituting for the intersyllabic target /-r-/.

Individual variation

As one might expect, there is a wide range of inter- and intra-individual variation among the IM preschool children. Table 13.5 illustrates this on the basis of ten preschoolers (see Wode, 2003). The English targets are those that notoriously pose problems for German learners (recall Table 13.1). Table 13.5 is structured in such a way that the substitutions per child and word are ordered according to their frequency with the respective child.

The data here suggest that the range of inter- and intra-individual variation for the preschoolers is relatively large. Moreover, their productions tend to take quite some time before they stabilize into a pattern that is both stable for the individual speaker and homogeneous across the group. This is indicated by the fact that the variability is in evidence with all the children no matter how long they may have attended the IM preschool. That is, even after two and a half years of contact, as in the case of child A8, their productions still do not appear fully stabilized yet.

Primary school (ages 6;0–10;0)

The data for this section come from the same set of children that already provided the preschool data of Tables 13.2 and 13.4. However, recall that it is not only the IM preschoolers that are admitted to the IM programme. That is, while the majority of the children in the IM class attended the IM preschool, here referred to as the B-(bilingual) children, a smaller group of children are also admitted to the programme, although they did not have any knowledge of English at all at the start. They are termed the M-(monolingual) children. They are expected to catch up with the B-children – and they surely do.[4] By the end of Grade 4 at the latest, the M-children have become indistinguishable from the B-children with repect to their command of English, whatever the structural area.

As for L2 phonology, this mix of students allows us to pursue several issues. Since the M-students constitute an older age group than the preschoolers with respect to when they were introduced to English, both groups can be studied as to whether there are any differences between them and whether these correlate with the age of onset of L2 acquisition. The second issue is to determine how the students progress from grade level to grade level. And the third issue is to note how the M-children manage to catch up.

Table 13.5 Inter- and intraindividual variation for 10 preschoolers for those L2 English targets that are notoriously problematic for German learners. A5, A6 etc. = serial number for preschoolers ( ) = number of tokens

L2 target	A5	A6	A8	A9	A10	A11	A13	A14	A15	A22
Cons.										
/θ/	ts (2) s (1)	θ (4) s (3) t (2) tθ (1) ts (1)	θ (8) t (2) ʃ (1)	s (7) θ (1) ts (1)	θ (3) ts (3) d (1)	θ (4) s (2) z (1)	ts (5) θ (2) s (1) ʃ (1)	t (6) θ (1) s (1)	d (12) θ (2) s (2)	f (5) θ (3)
/w/	w (4)	w (9)	w (9)	w (13) v (1)	w (5) v (1)	w (4) v (1)	w (6) v (1)	w (7)	w (8) ɹ (1)	w (6)
/v/	f (3) v (2)	f (4) v (3)	f (4) v (3)	f (6) v (5)	f (4) v (1)	v (4) f (3)	f (3) v (3)	f (4) v (3) w (1)	f (5) v (5)	f (3ll) v (3)
[ɫ]	l (10)	l (11)	l (14)	l (11)	l (18)	l (10) ɫ (2)	l (6) ɫ (1)	l (9) ɫ (1)	l (18) ɫ (1)	l (12) ɫ (3)
/r/	w (10) v (3) ʀ (2)	w (9) v (8)	ɹ (8) w (4)	v (6) ʀ (5) w (2) ɹ (1)	w (5) ɹ (4) v (3) ʀ (2)	w (4) v (2) ɹ (2) r (2) ʀ (1)	v (6) w (2) ɹ (1) l (1)	v (5) w (5)	ɹ (11) w (10) ʀ (1) ʀ (1)	w (9) ɹ (8) ʀ (1)
Vowels										
/æ/	ɛ (4) a (2) ɛːɐ (1)	ɛ (5)	ɛ (5) æ (3)	ɛ (6) æ (1)	a (4) ɛ (1) æ (1)	ɛ (4) æ (1) i (1) ʌ (1) a (1)	ɛ (2) æ (1)	ɛ (2) a (2) ʊ (1)	ɛ (7) æ (1)	ɛ (5)
/oʊ/	oʊ (1) ɔʊ (1) o (1) ɔ (1)	ɔʊ (1) o (1) (1)	o (2)	o (1)	ʊ (2) ɔʊ (1) o (1)	ʊ (2) o (1)	ʊ (2) o (1)	ʊ (2) oʊ (1)	ʊ (2) ɔʊ (1) ɔ (1)	ʊ (3) ʊ (3) ɔ (1)
/ɛɪ/	ɛ (3) e (2) i (1) ɛɪ (1)	ɛɪ (3)	ɛɪ (5) ɛ (2) e (1) i (1)	ɛ (1)	ɛ (2) e (1)	ɛɪ (2) e (1) i (1)	ɛɪ (2)	ɛɪ (2) e (1)	ɛɪ (4) e (1)	ɛɪ (3)
/Vʳ/	Vᵉ V:		Vᵉ	Vᵉ (3)	Vᵉ (2) V:		Vᵉ	Vᵉ	Vᵉ	Vᵉ

Source: Wode (2003), Berger (1999)

Starting with the third issue, the figures in Table 13.6 (adapted from Sieg, 2004) clearly show that in terms of the percentages of target-like vs. non-target-like renditions the M-children trail the V- and the B-children by quite a margin in Grade 1. Note, however, that the gap continuously narrows as the children progress through Grades 1–4. In fact, by the end of Grade 4, there is little if anything to differentiate the three groups.

As for the second issue, namely, how the six-year-olds make their way into English phonology, there were no structural differences when

Table 13.6 Percentages of the group averages of the target-like renditions of the problematic sounds of Table 13.1 according to groups B, V, M in Grades 1–4. – = target does not occur; ( ) = very few instances

Group L2 target	B	V	M	Grade
/ð/	12.8	63.3	33.5	1.
	41.8	65	38.4	2.
	73.6	85.4	54.6	3.
	76.1	85.6	75.2	4.
/θ/	(87.5)	(100)	(0)	1.
	(75)	(71.4)	(100)	2.
	83.3	66.7	72.2	3.
	92.4	70.2	80	4.
/r/	67.7	95	63	1.
	90	92	86.1	2.
	74.3	87.1	80.7	3.
	82.9	84.3	81.1	4.
/w/	95.2	97.5	84.4	1.
	94	92.9	96.8	2.
	99.1	97.4	99.5	3.
	99.2	99.2	98.5	4.
[ɫ]	54.5	73.3	33.3	1.
	36.7	28.1	49.1	2.
	55	49.6	39.4	3.
	71.2	37	37	4.

(Continued)

Table 13.6   (*Continued*)

Group L2 target	B	V	M	Grade
/v-/	(50)	(100)	(0)	1.
	(50)	–	(0)	2.
	43.6	50	16.7	3.
	85.8	100	100	4.
/æ/	(9)	(17.9)	(0)	1.
	(16.7)	(37.9)	(34.7)	2.
	23.7	28	14.3	3.
	13.1	17.8	21.5	4.
/ɛɪ/	100	100	100	1.
	100	95.8	98	2.
	96.6	98.8	99	3.
	100	97.6	99.1	4.
/ɔʊ/	93.8	100	80	1.
	90.2	83.6	88.4	2.
	89.2	82.4	88.8	3.
	85.7	96	75.8	4.

Adapted from Sieg (2004)

compared with the IM preschoolers (Table 13.7). Both groups apply the same segment substitutions, the same transfer patterns, the same range of individual variation, and the same kind of German accent in their English. Moreover, Table 13.7 illustrates that the nature of the children's progress is such that the frequency of the non-targetlike renditions decreases from grade level to grade level.

As shown in Sieg (2004), by the end of primary school most of the problematic segments of Table 13.1 present hardly any problems to the children. The exceptions are /æ/ and a number of syllable structure processes where German and English differ so that transfer predominates, for example, devoicing of final voiced obstruents, nonvelarization of non-initial /-l(-)/, the excessive use of the glottal stop, insufficient vowel and/or consonant reductions. But note also that there seems to be a group effect in that no child reaches 100% correct on any of the problematic targets of Table 13.1 by the end of Grade 4. It appears unlikely that these residues are due to any lack of ability; it is more likely that this is a sociolinguistic

Table 13.7 Percentages of target-like (tl) and non-targetlike renditions of the problematic sounds of English of Table 13.1 according to grade levels. The substitutions are ordered according to frequency of occurance. Numbers are added in ( ) whenever there are only exceptionally few instances. – = deleted

Grade	1			2			3			4		
L2 target	tl	sub	%	tl.	sub	%	tl	sub	%	tl	sub	%
/ð/	29.5	[d] [z] [–]	59.1 7.6 3.8	45.2	[d] [z] [–]	33 19.7 2.1	71.9	[d] [z] [θ] [–] [tθ] [s]	17.7 8 1.5 0.5 0.3 0.1	79	[d] [z] [θ] [dð]	17.3 3.1 0.5 0.1
/θ/	69.2	[s]	30.8	80	[s] [t]	15 5	78.4	[s]	21.6	85.7	[s] [f]	13.3 1
/r/	72.3	[w] [ʁ] [ɹw] [r]	23.2 1.9 1.6 1.1	88.9	[ʁ] [w] [r] [–] [l]	4.6 4.3 1.4 0.5 0.2	73.5	[–] [w] [ʁ] [ɹw] [v]	12.7 8.7 3 1.9 0.2	84.2	[–] [w] [ɹw] [ʁ] [v]	11.4 2.1 1.1 1 0.2
/w/	93.3	[v]	6.7	94.5	[v] [ɹ]	4 1.4	98.9	[v] [ɹ] [–]	0.8 0.2 0.1	99.1	[v] [ɹ] [ɹw]	0.6 0.2 0.1

(Continued)

Table 13.7 (Continued)

Grade	1			2			3			4		
L2 target	tl	sub	%	tl.	sub	%	tl	sub	%	tl	sub	%
[ɪ]	57.1	[ɪ]	42.9	38.9	[ɪ]	61.1	49.6	[ɪ]	50.4	54.7	[ɪ]	45.3
/v-/	50	[w] [f]	30 20	33.3 (3)	[w]	66.7	44.2	[w]	55.8	94	[w]	6
/æ/	8.9	[ɛ] [a]	89.8 1.3	26.3	[ɛ] [a]	73.1 0.6	20.2	[ɛ] [a] [ɔ] [ɛɪ]	78.5 0.5 0.5 0.3	17	[ɛ]	83
/ɪə/	100	–	–	98.9	[e]	1.1	98.3	[ɛ]	1.7	99.1	[ɛ]	0.9
/ʊə/	93.2	[o]	6.8	88.4	[o] [ɔ] [oa]	10.2 1 0.3	88.7	[o] [ɔ] [aʊ]	10.8 0.3 0.2	84.2	[o] [ɔ] [aʊ]	14.9 0.6 0.3

Adapted from Sieg (2004)

group effect familiar from other countries and other IM programs, for example, French IM in Canada (e.g. Lyster, 1987) or German in France (e.g. Petit, 2002). The more the students talk English in class, the more they – automatically – turn into mutual models for each other. This is particulary noticeable with those students who scored 100% correct in Grade 3 and who did somewhat poorer in Grade 4.

Secondary school (ages 10;0–18;0)

It is important to include this age range, because it spans the time of puberty, which has loomed so large in the debate on age. Unfortunately, to date Berndt (1993) is still the only study of phonology in the late partial English IM program. It is a cross-sectional study of 13–14-year-old students at the end of Grade 7. Due to the structure of the program and the age of the students when tested, Berndt (1993) cannot be used to illustrate the beginnings of IM-based phonological acquisition at this age, because the L2 is introduced via LAS in Grade 5 and the IM component is not added until two years later. Also, this study does not provide any information as to the ultimate outcomes. What it does show is that the substitutions and the other phonological structures are the same as in LAS and as in the age groups considered above from the IM preschool and primary school programs.

Discussion

The findings above are consistent with the hypothesis that L2 phonological acquisition at age three is no different in terms of segments and their substitutions from older age ranges, probably up to age 18 and beyond. This appears to be so irrespective of whether the L2 is taught in school or acquired naturalistically and what kind of teaching is used, for example, whether LAS or IM. Of course, in the strict sense this can only be correct with respect to the acquisitional properties considered above. Note, however, that for them to be in evidence implies that the major phonological mechanisms are also in place, notably, categorical perception, equivalence classification, perceptual constancy and perceptuo-motor links.

Moreover, although not discussed in this chapter the above hypothesis also applies to other transfer phenomena, for example, syllable structure processes such as devoicing of final voiced obstruents, glottal stop insertion, or develarization of nonsyllable-initial /-l(-)/. That is, preschoolers and non-preschoolers alike devoice voiced syllable-final obstruents; they almost regularly insert a glottal stop before syllable-initial vowels; and their noninitial /-l/'s tend to be develarised most of the time.

Whereas the transfer evidence indicates that the mechanisms generally characterising L2 phonological acquisition are fully in place by age three, the evidence for the nontransfer based regularities needs to be viewed with some caution, because of gaps in the empirical evidence. This warning also pertains to the [w] substitute for the English /r/. On the one hand, the evidence from both types of children, that is, the four naturalistic learners and the IM preschoolers, was very clear and straightforward. [w] was their predominant substitute, but there were occasional occurrences of [ʁ] which were reminiscent of transfer from German. In BIR's case the source for her use of [ʁ] could be traced to transfer from German due to orthography. Whether any of the preschoolers' [ʁ]'s (Tables 13.4–13.5) are due to orthography cannot be decided, although this possibility should not be ruled out a priori given the fact that parents read stories to their children and/or even introduce their little ones to writing before they begin to go to school.

The major difficulty is the evidence for the English /r/ with school-age children and adults. The kind of evidence that is required is simply not available. What is needed are studies on the naturalistic, that is, noninstructed, L2 acquisition of the English /r/ by such learners. Such studies are likely to be next to impossible to find because of the impact of literacy and prevalence of English world wide. As highlighted by BIR's evidence, literacy provokes phonological transfer. It is quite telling, therefore, that in a very detailed study of a class of 11-year-olds at the end of their first year of English as LAS, Schröder (1979) found that the children used both [ʁ] and [w]. Since these children were taught according to LAS, the occurrence of [w] is no surprise in light of BIR's evidence. The surprise is the occurrence of [w] inspite of the emphasis on reading and writing in such programs.

Some Conclusions from the Teaching Point of View

The above evidence does not suggest that the demands imposed on the children by IM in preschool, primary school, or secondary school are beyond their abilities. On the contrary, the evidence clearly indicates that the children can cope with the task and that no particular language learning abilities are required that they do not otherwise already have. There is no psycholinguistic reason, therefore, to warn against continuing to teach foreign languages via IM. Moreover, the evidence from other countries, involving other languages than English and other sociocultural situations is such that this conclusion can be generalized to any language.

More specifically, the data reviewed above indicate that IM tends to produce highly satisfactory results for phonology without any remedial interventions on the basis of instructional techniques familiar from traditional LAS. Of course, as long as there are no pertinent experimental results we will not know whether and to what extent remedial exercises can improve L2 phonological development. No doubt, such studies need to be carried out, but from the point of view of the practationers in class, there is no need to feel obliged to go back to remedial phonetics. The students can be trusted to handle pronunciation on their own.

Whatever the reasons to deplore the fact that IM students tend not to reach native-like proficiency levels in school, as pointed out above, this is certainly not unique to IM. The reason why the above report was careful to compare IM results to other kinds of L2 settings, that is, naturalistic and LAS settings, was to show that the phonological learning abilities of human beings operate universally, that is, that they are made use of in any learning situation. It should, therefore, not come as a surprise that the structural properties of L2 phonological development are the same if a language is acquired in such diverse situations as reviewed in this paper. More than that, this explains why the phonological properties of contact varieties, for example, the many New Englishes, agree with those of L2 acquisition.

Just as in other kinds of foreign language teaching there is no way to predict which level a given child will reach in IM, no matter what his/her age of entry into the program. On the other hand, the many German exchange students who have spent a year in an anglophone country present the clearest evidence available to date that even post-puberty learners can hardly be prevented from approaching the local accent of their host community without anybody around to explicitly guide them. The extent to which they are likely to do so appears to be a matter of motivation (Piske *et al.*, 2001; Wode, 1981, 1988/93). Furthermore, in a series of experimental studies Bongaerts and his co-workers have shown that even post-puberty L2 learners can attain levels of proficiency so that they get mistaken as native speakers (see overview in Bongaerts *et al.*, 2000).

As for training IM teachers, if there is one thing they need to be familiar with in order to understand why learners at any age can develop high levels of pronunciation on their own, this is speech perception. There are two points in particular. One is the kind of development that occurs during the second half of the first year of life; the second is that the perceptual abilities do not vanish as a function of age, although they become increasingly difficult to access for processing input for the purpose of acquisition (see Wode, 1999 for references).

Notes

1. Canadian immersion has been particularly influential because for the past 40 years its various forms have been examined in a very large number of studies. The results of these studies have been documented in several thousand reports to school boards, articles, book chapters, and books. A well-researched experiment that began in a St Lambert, Quebec kindergarten in 1965 is often described as the origin of Canadian immersion (e.g. Wesche, 2002).
2. For details on IM in Germany/Europe see, for example, Wode (1995); on the IM network, Wode (1998, 2001a, 2002); on preschools, Wode (2001b, 2001c, 2006); on the primary school program, Burmeister and Pasternak (2004), Kersten *et al.* (2002), Wode (2004), Wode *et al.* (2002).
3. In fact, eventually BIR also developed the target-like /r/. Her developmental sequence, however, is interesting from the point of view of this chapter. She

did not go straight from [ʁ] to [r], but after [ʁ] she first reverted to [w] and then she developed the appropriate English /r/.

4. In Table 13.6 a third group of children, the V-(visiting) children, is distinguished. They also attended the IM preschool, but they were in one of the non-IM groups. Their teachers only spoke German. However, the V-children did have some exposure to English because they were allowed to visit the IM groups.

Glossary

All terms and concepts defined in this glossary appear in SMALL CAPS upon first mention in the different chapters of the book.

ACOUSTIC: Pertaining to the physical properties of sound waves.

ACOUSTIC ANALYSIS: Measurement of sound waves in terms of properties such as duration, frequency and amplitude.

ACOUSTIC VOWEL SPACE: Defined by the first and second formant frequencies (F_1 and F_2). In articulatory terms, F_1 roughly translates to tongue height; F_2 to the front/back position of the tongue.

ACQUISITION: The development of linguistic knowledge, either as a NATIVE LANGUAGE from early childhood, or through IMMERSION or LEARNING as a second language. Second Language Acquisition (SLA) is characterized by highly variable rates and levels of acquisition.

ADULT GRAMMAR: Generally taken to be synonymous with END (STEADY) STATE linguistic competence.

AFFECT: Attitudes, personality, motivation and other psychological variables that can influence second language acquisition (SLA).

AFFECTIVE ACTIVITIES: In processing instruction, activities for which only the respondent knows the answer – often involving an opinion, personal experience, and so on.

AFFECTIVE FILTER: A mechanism based on impact of affective factors (see, e.g. Krashen) claimed to prevent input from reaching the LANGUAGE ACQUISITION DEVICE. Negative affect such as boredom or tiredness is not held to influence the cognitive process of language acquisition, but to operate outside the language acquisition device.

AGE OF ARRIVAL/AGE OF ONSET (AOA/AO): The point at which a learner's exposure to or experience with the second language begins, either through immersion (by immigration, for example, as in AOA), by home exposure (through family members), or through foreign language classroom instruction (AO covers all these possibilities).

AKTIONSART (ACTION TYPE): Inherent aspects of different verb types (also known as LEXICAL ASPECT), commonly distinguished (see e.g. Vendler, 1967) as achievements, accomplishments, activities and states.

ALLOPHONIC REALIZATION: The realization (in linguistic terminology) of phones which are acoustically different, often because of different contexts, but based on the same underlying phonemic representation. For example, in Standard British English the phoneme /t/ is realized as [tʰ] if it occurs before vowels or approximants at the beginning of a stressed syllable (as in *tie* or *toe*), but it is unaspirated if it is preceded by /s/ at the beginning of a syllable (as in *steal* or *stop*).

ANECDOTAL EVIDENCE: Non-experimental evidence, gathered from everyday experience.

ANALYSIS OF VARIANCE: A statistical procedure used to explore the significance of different variables to explain observed differences between two (or more) groups, or between two (or more) treatments.

ANOVA: see ANALYSIS OF VARIANCE.

ARCHITECTURE: The underlying, mental representation or structure of language.

ARTEFACT: Co-occurring with but extraneous to the phenomenon in question. For example, to say 'affect is an artefact of age' means that it is confounded with the age construct (a by-product, so to speak), but is irrelevant to an investigation of the influence of maturation on SLA.

ASPECT HYPOTHESIS: The Hypothesis that LEXICAL ASPECT (or AKTIONSART) of the verb drives early acquisition of verbal inflection in L1 or L2. In other words, early verbs are predominantly affiliated with a prototypical inflection (e.g. -ing or -ed) depending on their inherent lexical aspect (Andersen & Shirai, 1994), rather than grammatical aspect such as the progressive.

ATTITUDES: Learner judgments of what is to be learned in positive, negative or neutral terms. Attitudes can be particularly informed by previous learning experiences.

AUDIO-LINGUAL METHOD (ALM): A language-learning methodology common from the 1940s to the 1960s in the West; the language is taught through frequent, intensive spoken repetition to memorize dialogs and target forms and through drill patterns.

AUDITORY (L2) INPUT: All the spoken second language (L2) a learner is exposed to, that is, all the L2 s/he hears.

AUTOMATIC PROCESSING: Processing that is fast, accurate, and can occur in parallel with other processing.

(THE) BASIC VARIETY: A second language learner's simple language system characterized by subject–verb–object word order and little or no inflectional morphology.

BIT RESOLUTION: The dynamic range of a digital audio recording (i.e. the difference between the loudest and the quietest point of the recording), usually measured in decibels (dB).

BOOTSTRAPPING: Mechanisms through which a simple system activates a more complicated system. In language acquisition these have been argued to be syntactic vs. semantic vs. pragmatic, referring to the specific system the child starts with to access the complexity of language.

/bVt/ FRAME: A syllable context in which the vowel (V) is placed between /b/ and /t/. For example, *bet* and *bite*.

CATEGORICAL PHONEMIC PERCEPTION: The underlying mental system that maps a specific language's phonemic system to ideal phoneme prototypes, allowing a listener to perceive a surface phone as a representative of the relevant underlying phonemic category.

CLITIC OBJECT PRONOUNS: Object pronouns that 'attach' themselves to verbs, as in Spanish *No lo tengo* '(I) don't have it.' vs. *No tengo el libro* '(I) don't have the book.'

COARTICULATED SPEECH: Running speech, sounds in speech context.

COARTICULATORY PATTERNS: Predictable changes to a speech sound caused by an adjacent speech sound, particularly affected by changes in place of articulation.

COGNITIVE PSYCHOLOGY: An approach to psychology that examines the range of internal mental processes that are hypothesized to underlie behavior, including problem solving and memory as well as language.

COMMUNICATIVE LANGUAGE TEACHING/COMMUNICATIVE APPROACH: An approach to teaching in which language acquisition is assumed to be driven by meaningful interactions with either native or non-native speakers. Most foreign-language classrooms in the Western world practice the 'weak' form of 'communicative language teaching' (CLT), supported by more 'traditional' approaches such as 'drilling', or sometimes comprehension-based activities. The 'strong' form of having learners work within *production*-based activities such as role-plays is usually reserved for more advanced learners.

COMMUNICATIVE COMPETENCE: Within the COMMUNICATIVE APPROACH, this serves as both the process and goal of language learning: the development of knowledge about how to use the target language appropriately. This includes not just intuitive knowledge of new grammar, but an awareness of how to interact with speakers, shift between different styles of speaking, how to clarify what is said, how to convey information clearly, and so on.

COMPETENCE (VS. PERFORMANCE): The term used by generative linguistics as in 'linguistic competence' to denote underlying, innately-driven knowledge of a specific language.

COMPLEXITY ARGUMENT: The complexity argument states that the system to be mastered is too complex to be taught and learned one item at a time: It must, therefore, be subconsciously acquired. The complexity argument has been applied to many aspects of language competence, including vocabulary (there are too many words to learn), syntax, phonics, and spelling (the rules are complex and have not been adequately described by grammarians).

COMPREHENSIBLE INPUT: Examples of the target language to which the learner is exposed which are taken to be readily understood through centext, prior experience, visual cues or the learners' interaction with the teacher or material.

COMPREHENSIBLE OUTPUT HYPOTHESIS: The hypothesis, developed by Merrill Swain, that language acquisition can occur when acquirers attempt to communicate, fail to do so, and then adjust their output to make it more comprehensible. Swain hypothesized that comprehensible output was necessary as a supplement to comprehensible input.

COMPREHENSION APPROACH (CPA): A system of instruction, associated, for example, with Harris Winitz, using picture-based language material, where the student uses implicitly-based (unconscious) strategies to understand the materials. (Based on Krashen's COMPREHENSION HYPOTHESIS.)

COMPREHENSION HYPOTHESIS: The hypothesis (also known as the INPUT HYPOTHESIS) that language is acquired through comprehension, when we understand what people tell us or what we read. Language is acquired via comprehension unconsciously, that is, we are not aware that we are acquiring while we are acquiring.

CONNECTIONISM: This theory (led by McClelland and Rumelhart) sees the brain in terms of neural or parallel distributed processing networks of interconnected units. These connections are either strengthened or weakened through activation or nonactivation. Connectionist approaches to language acquisition argue that language is learnt by learning rules from the input alone, with no involvement of an innate LANGUAGE ACQUISITION DEVICE.

CONSCIOUSNESS RAISING: A focus in teaching on certain problematic language features, with the intention of thereby helping the learner. (Based on Descartes' idea that language production – like all cognitive activity – is conscious.)

CONSONANTAL CONTEXT: The effect on a vowel of adjacent consonants.

CONSTRUCTION: In a very general sense, any sequence of units (e.g. morphemes or root words) that has some functional identity in the grammar of a language.

CONTENT AND LANGUAGE INTEGRATED LEARNING (CLIL): A primary focus on subject-based instruction where comprehension of subject-specific content is prioritized over grammatical rules.

CONTROLLED PROCESSING: Processing that requires attentional resources, and may therefore be slower as well as more error-prone than automatic processing.

CONVERGE: see NON-CONVERGENCE.

CORNER VOWELS: The vowels /i/, /u/, and /a/, which define the edges of the vowel 'space' (in the mouth/oral cavity) in which all vowels in all human languages are produced. In addition, the vowels /i/ and /u/ are the most closed vowels possible, and /a/ is the vowel with the most open vocal tract.

CRITICAL PERIOD: The limited age span thought to be the most advantageous for the acquisition of language, generally ending sometime before the onset of puberty because of decreased neurological plasticity, or flexibility. Some propose that a 'sensitive' period is more representative of this window since some individuals are able to reach a native-like level for some aspects of a new (second) language, including grammar and even phonology (rare) even beyond the presumed cut-off age. In addition, the concept of sensitive periods takes into consideration the observation that with increasing AGE OF ARRIVAL/AGE OF ONSET L2 learners show a gradual rather than a sudden decrease in the development of certain L2 abilities.

dB/OCTAVE PRE-EMPHASIS: A process designed to magnify some (usually higher) frequencies to improve the overall quality (signal-to-noise ratio) of the signal (to account for the fall-off in vowel spectrum of approximately 6 dB/octave).

DECLARATIVE KNOWLEDGE: Knowledge of facts ('knowing that ...'). In SLA often used to denote formally learnt language knowledge such as rules to explain verb forms.

DICTOGLOSS: An activity where students take notes of key words from a text that has been read aloud, then work in cooperative groups to recreate the text.

DIPHTHONGIZATION: A process through which one vowel quality changes to a second vowel quality within one syllable, as in [aɪ] ('I').

'DUAL-TASK' PARADIGM: A test technique in which participants perform two tasks simultaneously. Interference between the two tasks provides information about the automaticity of processing.

DURATION: Length of time involved in the articulation of sounds or syllables, usually measured in milliseconds (ms).

DYNAMIC SYSTEMS THEORY (DST): The science of the development of complex systems over time.

EARLY LEARNER/STARTER: A learner whose first exposure to a second language is before adolescence.

END (STEADY) STATE: An individual's final, fixed grammar, usually used in reference to syntax. In first language acquisition, this may also be referred to as the ADULT GRAMMAR, but without entailing that the speaker is of an adult age.

ENGLISH AS A SECOND LANGUAGE (ESL): Refers to situations in which immigrant learners (but also students) of English who are likely to stay in the English-speaking setting in which they are immersed learn English as an additional language. Distinguished by some authors from EFL (English as a Foreign Language) to describe situations in which English is learnt as an additional language in a formal classroom setting, particularly outside the target language country.

ENTRENCHMENT: Establishment of fixed non-target patterns, similar to FOSSILIZATION or 'stabilization'.

EPENTHESIS: Insertion of a phone, for example, an 'e' before the /s/ in 'Spain' and pronouncing it as 'Espain'. When the inserted phone is a vowel, it is called an 'epenthetic vowel'.

EQUIVALENCE CLASSIFICATION: In L2 acquisition some sounds of the new language may sound different from any sound in the L1 or any other language a given speaker may have learned already. In some cases these unfamiliar sounds are substituted in a highly systematic way by sounds from a language acquired before (see TRANSFER), because the former are perceived as equivalent to the latter. For example, speakers of German tend to perceive English /θ/ as [s] or

/æ/ as [ɛ]. Equivalence classification denotes the method of classifying sounds as to their equivalencies.

ERROR: A non-target form which represents a systematic stage of development.

EVENT PROBABILITIES: The likelihood that a situation occurs under one condition as opposed to another. In terms of verbs and events expressed by verbs, the likelihood that one noun as opposed to another represents the agent of the action. For the verb *correct* and the nouns *teacher* and *student*, either teacher or student can correct the other, but it is more likely that teachers correct students than the other way around. Thus, teachers correcting students has a higher event probability than students correcting teachers.

EXPLICIT KNOWLEDGE: Knowledge a person is aware of and can often articulate, whether in specialized terminology or everyday language.

EXTENDED CORE PROGRAMS: A Canadian term for a kind of program that combines traditional LANGUAGE AS SUBJECT (LAS) and a low dose of IMMERSION in a foreign language. Students are introduced to the new language via the core program which is a traditional LAS program. At some point in time the latter is extended by the addition of an immersion component in that some subjects are taught in the new language. Programs comparable to the Canadian extended core model exist in many parts of the world.

FOCUS-ON-FORM: A teaching approach where grammatical phenomena are not explained and taught explicitly in a one-by-one fashion (here defined as focus on form<u>s</u>, or FORM-FOCUSED – see below). Learners are guided to notice grammatical distinctions and particularities on their own, often through INPUT designed to be heavy in the target form (see INPUT FLOOD).

FORM-FOCUSED LANGUAGE LEARNING (also known as focus on forms): Used here to contrast with FOCUS ON FORM (see above). The primary focus is on correctness of grammatical forms in the learner's linguistic activity, designed to develop accuracy; emphasis is placed on the learner's awareness of the language 'rules'.

FORM-MEANING/FUNCTION MAPPINGS: The relationship between grammatical features and what they mean or what they do in a sentence (see also FORMAL ENCODING). For example, in English the meaning of plurality can be mapped onto -*s* (and its variants) when the latter appears at the end of a noun.

FORMAL ENCODING: How languages represent semantic information linguistically. For example, how languages do (or do not) represent temporal reference (past, present, future) on verbs.

FORMAL FEATURES: Any grammatical feature of a language, such as verb inflections, articles, or gender on nouns.

FORMANT FREQUENCY: Measurement of vocal cord resonances above the typical rate of vibration for age and gender (fundamental frequency = F_0). Specific sounds have emphasised resonances in multiples of the fundamental frequency, particularly first, second and third formant frequencies (F_1, F_2, F_3); also see ACOUSTIC VOWEL SPACE measurement. Measurements of these formant frequencies reveal patterns for specific speech sounds (seen as 'inherent' to that sound). Comparing these patterns reveals how different sounds, for example, vowels, can in certain contexts, show movement away from the inherent formant frequency ('vowel-inherent spectral change') and reveal how speakers vary slightly in producing those specific speech sounds.

FOSSILIZE: When a second language learner's GRAMMAR is not native-like yet does not progress further – known as FOSSILIZATION (Selinker, 1972).

GEMINATE: A long consonant. Geminate consonants can distinguish words in Italian, for example, *fato* means 'destiny' and *fatto* means 'done'. Actual length varies cross-linguistically; for instance in Italian geminates are (approximately) twice as long as 'singleton' (short) consonants. In alphabetic writing systems, geminate consonants can be represented by repeating the same consonant letter, as in the Italian word <fatto>. In others, for example, in Arabic, geminates are represented using a diacritic above the consonant. Phonetic transcription uses a triangular colon to represent geminates: /tː/.

GENERATIVE LINGUISTICS: Based on Noam Chomsky's ideas, the study of language from this perspective assumes abstract representation of language in the speaker's mind based on universals of human language.

GESTALT PSYCHOLOGY: The idea that the whole is greater than the sum of the parts, that the whole cannot be deduced from analysing the parts in isolation.

GRAMMAR: As in _a grammar_ or _the child's grammar_ in acquisition, this refers to stages of development where a child's (L1) or an L2 learner's is systematic and can be constrained by the same universal principles that apply to adult languages. Thus a stage represents the grammar of a possible (and sometimes attested) human language.

GRAPHEME: The smallest unit of a writing system, for example, a hanzi (character) in the Chinese writing system (corresponding to a morpheme), a letter or letter cluster in alphabetic writing systems, a syllable sign in a syllabic writing system.

GRAPHEME-PHONEME CONVERSION RULES: Rules that determine how a GRAPHEME is converted into the corresponding PHONEME(s) for each specific writing system or orthography. For instance, according to the English Grapheme-Phoneme Conversion rules, the grapheme or digraph <ch> corresponds to the phonemes /k/ in 'chord', /ʃ/ in 'chute', /tʃ/ in 'church'.

HEAD NOUN: In relative clauses, the noun or noun phrase the relative clause refers to. For example, in _John saw the woman who called last week_, _woman_ is the head noun for the relative clause _who called last week_.

HERMENEUTIC: Explanatory, interpretative.

HOMESIGN: Developed by deaf children not exposed to sign language input, a systematic gestural system that exhibits some of the same formal properties of attested languages.

HYPOTHESIS SPACE: All the hypotheses a language learner might consider.

HYPOTHESIS TESTER: A learner who uses positive evidence as well as negative evidence to acquire a language.

IMMERSION (IM): In a general sense, this term is often used to refer to an acquisition situation in which learners living in the target language country acquire a second language simply because they are 'immersed' in an L2-speaking environment. In a teaching context, the term refers to the use of the language to be learned as the medium of instruction to teach any subject. IM produces the best results if (a) the intensity of contact with the new language is high, that is, if at least 60–70% of the total teaching time is devoted to IM; (b) if IM is continued for at least six to seven years; and if the input for the new languge is structurally rich and not limited to selected structural areas only. Structural diversity can be achieved by including all subjects and all situations that may occur.

IMPLICIT KNOWLEDGE: Knowledge a person is not aware of and often cannot articulate; nevertheless, a person's behaviour shows that this knowledge is present.

INDIRECT NEGATIVE EVIDENCE: During communicative interactions, indications that a learner's production contains something non-native. Unlike error correction, which is direct negative evidence, the term indirect is used because the intent of the speaker is not to correct the learner but to confirm, query, and so on, as part of the communicative act and yet what the interlocutor says can act as evidence for how something should be said.

INDIVIDUAL VARIATION: How individuals vary from a group tendency or an observed phenomenon attributed to a group (e.g. teeth are white but there is individual variation as to whiteness).

INPUT: The term used in this book – unless otherwise specified – in a general sense to refer to the language a learner hears or sees (reads).

INPUT FLOOD: A pedagogical technique in which learners are purposely inundated with more examples than normal of a particular grammatical feature as they listen to or read material.

INPUT HYPOTHESIS (see also COMPREHENSION HYPOTHESIS): The hypothesis (introduced by Krashen) that second language acquisition is driven by COMPREHENSIBLE INPUT that is at a level just above the current level of the language learner (i+1).

INPUT-OUTPUT CYCLES: Teaching techniques to enhance language development through tasks incorporating both comprehension (input) and production (output).

INPUT QUALITY/QUANTITY: QUALITY focuses on the learner's opportunities to further develop L2 abilities through language use across a range of domains and situations, especially the personal/home domain. For phonology in particular, this contextual distinction appears to be significant.
QUANTITY refers to the amount of linguistic input available to the learner, usually measured in terms of hours, months, years, and so on, of exposure or experience (e.g. as time spent in-country, in the foreign language classroom, or more appropriately, time spent using the language for the negotiation of meaning).

INTAKE: The linguistic knowledge learners retain and process from the input.

INTERACTION HYPOTHESIS: The hypothesis that input which is modified through interaction (e.g. in a classroom setting) fosters the L2 acquisition process. Interaction occurs when comprehension breaks down in a communicative context and meaning needs to be negotiated.

INTERFACE: Instead of operating completely independently of each other as is often assumed in generative linguistics, subcomponents of the language (e.g. syntax, morphology, phonology) may reveal some interaction at, for example, a syntax-phonology interface.

INTERLANGUAGE: Coined by Selinker (1972), in its broadest sense, term referring to the underlying linguistic system a second language learner currently possesses (INTERLANGUAGE GRAMMAR); the mental representation for language of a second language learner (of syntax, of phonology, etc.). In its narrow sense, it refers to an indepedent system which displays features that are neither part of the target language nor derived from the learner's first language. This is the idea that the learner's innate predisposition for acquiring language can result in the creation of a unique interim system/grammar.

INTERNALIZATION/INTERNALIZE: The conversion of linguistic input into a linguistic representation, i.e. INPUT becomes INTAKE.

INTERPRETATION TASKS: Any classroom, pedagogical or research activity based on comprehension rather than production (e.g. 'Based on what you hear, select picture A or picture B').

ITERATION: Repeating a process or a procedure that leads to changes of the system.

KANA: An ORTHOGRAPHY consisting of two scripts, *hiragana* and *katakana*, used to explicitly indicate the pronunciation of Japanese alongside *kanji* (Chinese-derived characters), and to write words for which no characters exist in Japanese, such as foreign names and function words. Both consist of symbols representing 'moras', the units that organize Japanese rhythm; for example, *Nihon* 'Japan' consists of two syllables, but three moras: *ni, ho* and *n*, so is written with three symbols.

L1: Chronologically the first language acquired by a learner. Often used synonymously with NATIVE LANGUAGE (NL).

L2: Any language acquired after the first language (L1) or languages. Often used synonymously with with TARGET LANGUAGE (TL).

LANGUAGE ACQUISITION DEVICE: Coined by Chomsky, the hypothesised mechanism with which humans are innately 'wired' for the task of language acquisition.

LANGUAGE-AS-SUBJECT (LAS): The traditional way of teaching a new language where it is treated as the object of instruction, just as subject matter is in history, geography, math, etc. The teacher will explain things and decides what to learn and how to do it; the students are given grammar rules; errors are corrected; and the students are expected to produce grammatically correct sentences from the start. LAS is the opposite of IMMERSION, where the new language is acquired without recourse to any of the traditional teaching techniques.

LATE LEARNER/STARTER: A learner whose first exposure to a second language is in or after adolescence.

LEARNING: Frequently used to refer to the process of gaining language knowledge through explicit instruction, often seen as using different cognitive processes than implicit ACQUISITION.

LENGTH OF RESIDENCE (LOR): The time spent in the target language country, usually measured in years, and often found to be significant for attainment in the target language.

LEXICAL ASPECT: Synonymous with the term AKTIONSART.

LEXICAL FIELDS: Topics or themes used to present inter-related words and phrases to students.

LEXICAL PREFERENCE PRINCIPLE (LPP): The principle by which second language learners are said to rely on lexical items (words) to grasp a particular semantic intention when that same intention is also coded grammatically. Example: -s = third-person singular but so does *the dog* in *The dog barks a lot*. In this case, the LPP predicts that language learners get 'third-person singular' from *the dog* and not -s.

LEXICAL SEMANTICS: The study of word meaning. Word meanings may have various contextual effects. Consider, for example, the requirements that verbs impose on what can be the subject of an active sentence. For example, the verb *chew* requires that the subject be animate and have teeth (or something else to chew with) under most conditions.

LEXIS: Another term for vocabulary.

LOW PASS FILTER: A device to allow the transmission of relatively low frequency components in the signal while reducing higher frequency components.

MARKED/UNMARKED: In a pair of sounds, the marked sound is less natural or common, as determined by considering one or more of a variety of factors including frequency across languages and within a specific language, and early vs. late acquisition by children. The noun is 'markedness'.

MATCHED SUBGROUP TECHNIQUE: A statistical method of refining group results by analysing smaller groups within a large group, which differ for one specified variable factor (e.g. AOA) but which match for variables confounded with that factor.

MENTAL REPRESENTATION: The abstract and unconscious linguistic system in a person's mind (see also UNDERLYING REPRESENTATION).

MONITOR HYPOTHESIS: The claim that consciously learned aspects of language are only available in language production as a Monitor, or editor. Consciously learned language is held to make no contribution to fluency. It has been hypothesized that three necessary (but not sufficient) conditions must be met for the use of the Monitor: Knowledge of the rule, time to apply the rule, and a focus on forms.

MONOPHTHONG: A simple vowel with just one articulatory target, for example, the vowel in *bet* (/bɛt/. Unlike monophthongs, diphthongs are complex vowels with two articulatory targets, for example, the vowel in *bite* (/baɪt].

MORPHOSYNTAX: The relationship between the grammatical rules/functions underlying word order/sentence structure (syntax) and grammatical word forms/inflections that represent those functions (morphology).

MOVEMENT RULES: In syntactic theory, certain elements of a sentence are allowed to move from one spot to another under specified conditions. For example, the *who* of *Who did you see?* is said to be the object of the verb *see*, but normally objects come after verbs in English. Thus, *who* must have moved from its normal position and appears at the beginning of the sentence. The constraints on such movement are called movement rules.

NAÏVE REALISM: The idea of objective reality that exists, and we perceive reality as it exists.

NATIVE LANGUAGE (NL): A language acquired and used in the home from a very early age, before the age of five or six (contrasted with languages learnt in school) – see also TARGET LANGUAGE. Often used synonymously with L1.

NATIVE LANGUAGE MAGNET MODEL: The concept that an L2 learner initially perceives L2 phonemes in terms of the learner's L1 by the 'magnet' effect of the established L1 phonemic system. The Magnet Model also suggests that perception determines production, therefore L2 phonetic production will be affected by L1 TRANSFER until the L2 phonemic system is established.

NATIVE-LIKE: Using an L2 at a level similar to or indistinguishable from a NATIVE SPEAKER (NS) – see also TARGET-LIKE.

NATIVE SPEAKER (NS): Someone who speaks a language from very early childhood, and is thus expected to be fluent in the language without formal instruction.

NATURAL APPROACH: A comprehension-based classroom language-learning methodology developed by Stephen D. Krashen and Tracey D. Terrell which emphasizes the creation of a supportive, non-threatening environment in which understanding of COMPREHENSIBLE INPUT is prioritized.

NATURALISTIC: An acquisition situation in which the learner receives no instruction.

NEGOTIATED MEANING: Meaning that is arrived at by two or more people during an interaction because a miscommunication initially occurred.

NODE: In syntax, an invisible point at which two parts merge or join to make a syntactic unit or phrase.

NON-CONVERGENCE: A situation in which the level reached by the second language learner differs from the target language; is not TARGET-LIKE.

NON-TARGETLIKE: see TARGETLIKE

NULL-SUBJECT: In languages such as Spanish, the subject pronoun of a verb that has no visible or audible manifestation, as in *Juan vino temprano. Comió y se fue* 'John arrived early. He ate and left'. There is no visible pronoun produced before the verbs *comió* and *se fue* as is required in English.

OMISSION: Here, omission of a phone. For instance, second language learners or young L1 children can omit one consonant from consonant clusters which are difficult to articulate, pronouncing 'hold' as *[hol].

ONE-TO-ONE PRINCIPLE: The principle that in early L2 acquisition learners map one form to one function or concept, for example, -ing is first used to express progressive aspect or future tense, but not both functions at the same time.

ONSET: In a syllable, what precedes the vowel(s), for example, /k/ in /kæt/.

ORTHOGRAPHY: (1) a set of rules for representing a specific language with a script (i.e. a set of GRAPHEMES), including orthography-phonology correspondence rules and punctuation. For instance, the Italian orthography determines how the Roman alphabet (i.e. its script) is used to represent that language. (2) Sometimes used as synonym of WRITING SYSTEM.

ORTHOGRAPHIC INPUT: The written language a learner is exposed to.

OUTPUT HYPOTHESIS: As a response to the INPUT and INTERACTION HYPOTHESES, the Output Hypothesis (Swain, 1985) claims that learners' production is crucial to acquisition, primarily through raising consciousness of problems with certain structures and testing possible hypotheses in their output.

OUTPUT TASK: Any classroom, pedagogical or research activity that requires a language learner to produce that which is the target of instruction or investigation (e.g. 'Look at the picture and tell me what is happening').

PARAMETER SETTINGS: see UNIVERSAL GRAMMAR.

PARSING: The term used to refer to how listeners and speakers compute syntactic relationships as in the case of the ambiguous sentence, *John saw Robert after he returned from Europe.* The listener/reader must determine whether *he* refers to *John* or *Robert*, thus 'computing' the syntactic relationship between a pronoun and a possible antecedent.

PEAK-NORMALIZED: Peak-normalization is a procedure used to correct for differences in the intensity of speech samples. In a peak-normalized sample, the intensity of the whole sample is adjusted so that the most intense portion of the sample is amplified to peak just below the level of peak-clipping.

PERCEPTUAL CONSTANCY: Acoustic measurements of speech sounds show that no two sounds are completely identical. Yet listeners treat all variants as instances of a specific sound/phoneme, i.e. the perception is constant despite the difference in the speech wave.

PERCEPTUO-MOTOR LINK: In order to be able to develop the appropriate articulatory gestures for a given sound/language the learner needs to have peceivable input and/or feedback from the target language. Moreover, for perceptual information to have an impact on production it needs to feed into, hence be linked to whatever mechanisms may control the articulatory processes.

PERFORMANCE: The actual realisation of language through speech or writing, which can vary according to non-linguistic factors such as tiredness. Usually contrasted in UNIVERSAL GRAMMAR-based theories of language acquisition with COMPETENCE.

PHONE: The smallest concrete unit of sound. A phone is considered in terms of its articulatory character, without regard to its phonemic status. Phones are enclosed in square brackets: [ ].

PHONEME: The smallest abstract unit of a specific spoken language and part of the phonological system of a language. It is enclosed in slanted brackets: //. A phoneme contrasts with other phonemes, that is, it distinguishes words in that language: /p/ is a phoneme in English where it distinguishes 'pin' from 'bin'. However, the unaspirated /p/ in spin is not distinguished from the aspirated /p/ in 'pin'.

PHONETIC SYMBOLS: Internationally recognised representations of concrete language sounds (PHONE). The current version of the International Phonetic Alphabet (revised to 2005) is available at <http://www.arts.gla.ac.uk/IPA/IPA_chart_(C)2005.pdf>. Date last accessed 26 October 2008.

PHONOLOGICAL AWARENESS: The ability to reflect on and manipulate the contrastive units of a sound system including consonants and vowels as well as suprasegmental features such as syllables, stress and intonation. It is often measured with phonological awareness tasks, for instance where the test subject is asked to delete or substitute the first phoneme or the first syllable from a word.

PHONOLOGICAL TRANSPARENCY/OPACITY: The degree of regularity in the correspondence between graphemes and phonological units (phonemes, syllables, etc.) in a specific writing system. For instance, Italian is more phonologically transparent than English because in Italian one grapheme mostly corresponds to one phoneme and one phoneme mostly corresponds to one grapheme, for example, /p/ is spelled <p> and <p> is pronounced [p].

PIDGIN: A system of oral or signed communication that develops among adults who do not share a common language. A pidgin is thought to lack features that other human languages may share such as variable word order and inflections.

PINYIN: The standard modern romanization system for Chinese languages, that is, a writing system that uses the Roman alphabet to represent Chinese characters; hanyu pinyin represents Mandarin.

POSITIVE EVIDENCE: Utterances in the surrounding language heard by the learner which serve to inform the hearer/learner about what is possible in that language.

POVERTY OF THE STIMULUS: The idea that the input (the utterances heard by the learner) is impoverished relative to what it reveals about the underlying linguistic structure in the mind of the speaker who produces the utterances.

PRECURSOR: A model (see Van Geert, 1995) of dynamic growth in cognitive systems, where the relationship between growth rate and development is complex and non-linear.

PRESENT–PRACTICE–PRODUCE (PPP): A three-step teaching sequence, which involves presentation by the teacher, practice with the teacher (including perhaps drilling), and then less controlled production by the students.

PRIMARY LANGUAGE DATA (PLD) – see PRIMARY LINGUISTIC DATA.

PRIMARY LINGUISTIC DATA: Utterances produced by others in the learner's surroundings which are heard by the learner.

PROCEDURAL KNOWLEDGE: The knowledge of how to perform some task ('knowing how to …').

PROCESSABILITY THEORY: The theory (see Pienemann, 1998) that L2 linguistic structures are processed at different speeds; these structures are therefore acquired in predictable developmental sequences or stages as the learner's processing capacity increases. Forms such as, for example, third person singular -*s*, are only acquired at an advanced stage (stage 5 out of 6) because they are difficult to process.

PROCESSING: The act of PARSING a sentence and attaching meaning to all of its elements, including the function of MORPHOSYNTACTIC inflections mean (e.g. -ed means past temporal reference in *John called me*).

PRODUCTION: Speaking, writing or signing (in the case of sign language).

PROPERTY THEORY: A theory of language acquisition which seeks to account for a speaker's mental representation of that language at a given stage of development.

QUALITATIVE/QUANTITATIVE: Purely QUALITATIVE research in SLA focuses on questions of learner experience and orientation in the acquisition process. Here data are gathered through ethnographic means such as diaries, interviews, journal writing, surveys, and so on, where open-ended and semi-guided questions allow for individual responses. Such data (as well as spontaneous production data) can also be converted to QUANTITATIVE data. Quantifiable data are close-ended questionnaire responses such as scalar responses, multiple choice questions, and binary oppositions (e.g. yes/no). Quantitative data lend themselves to descriptive statistics such as range, mean, frequency and percentage as well as to inferential statistical tests such as correlation, factor analysis, regression and ANOVA. These tests seek to determine when relationships between background (independent) variables such as age of initial exposure to the L2 and outcomes (dependent variables) such as scores and ratings are not random, that is, when they are significant.

RECASTS: During conversation, repetition of what someone (e.g. a learner) says but in a more standard form (e.g. by a teacher, parent or other native speaker), usually as a way of confirming what a person has just heard.

REFERENTIAL ACTIVITIES: In processing instruction, activities that have a right or wrong answer.

RELATIVE CLAUSE MARKER: The grammatical device (usually a word) that begins a relative clause such as *that*, *who*, and *which* in English (e.g. John saw the woman *who* called last week).

RIME: All parts of a syllable except the ONSET, that is to say everything except the initial consonant(s). It is composed of the nucleus (vowel or vowels) and the coda (consonant or consonants that follow the nucleus). For instance, / æt/ in /kæt/.

ROOMAJI: An alphabet used to write the Japanese language in romanized form. Its use is primarily confined to teaching foreign learners of Japanese prior to introducing the actual Japanese writing systems, and giving examples of Japanese in academic texts.

[S]: A symbol for *sentence* in syntax.

SALIENT: In speech perception, the prominence of a sound, which is believed to result in the degree of ease with which the sound is perceived. Louder or longer sounds are easier to perceive, that is, more salient.

SAMPLING RATE: The rate at which a continuous sound signal is measured per second (or per other unit); usually measured in hertz (Hz).

SCARCITY ARGUMENT: The argument that some mechanisms cannot contribute much to language development because they occur so infrequently and the system to be acquired is so complex. The scarcity argument applies to the comprehensible output hypothesis, the hypothesis that we 'learn to write by writing', and views on the importance of error correction.

SECOND LANGUAGE ACQUISITION (SLA): The non-simultaneous acquisition of a language in addition to one's native language, regardless of whether it is the learner's second, third or *n*th language. When the distinction between the unconscious development of linguistic competence and general cognition-driven second language learning is important, authors use the term *acquisition*, with GENERATIVE linguistic theory as a point of departure. Terms such as SECOND LANGUAGE DEVELOPMENT, or nonnative language acquisition are also used.

SECOND LANGUAGE DEVELOPMENT (SLD): An alternative to second language acquisition (SLA), where language learning is seen as a number of dynamically interrelated processes in the mind of the second language/bilingual learner and involves both gain (acquisition) and loss (attrition).

SECOND LANGUAGE LEARNER (L2 learner): A neutral term typically used to refer to an individual acquiring a second language after the age at which the individual is assumed to have established the basics (syntactic and phonological competence) of their first language, held by many to be around age five. The term bilingualism is also used in reference to young children's acquisition of an additional language. However, application of this term varies, from its use only to refer to the simultaneous acquisition of two languages from birth, to its use to refer to the acquisition of an additional language at any age.

SHORT-TERM EFFECTS: In research, the effects of a given treatment immediately after the treatment is administered, or shortly thereafter (usually within days).

SILENT PERIOD: A period of time at the beginning of first or second language acquisition during which the learner does not speak much yet.

SKILL-BUILDING HYPOTHESIS: The hypothesis that we learn language and develop literacy by first mastering (consciously learning) the components or subskills (vocabulary and grammar for language learning, phonics for reading), by practising the subskills until they are automatic, and then gradually building up to larger units.

SPECTROGRAM: The most common form of the ACOUSTIC ANALYSIS of speech. A spectrogram is a printout from a (nowadays computer-generated) spectrograph showing frequency, duration, transition between speech sounds.

STANDARD DEVIATION (SD): In statistics, the measure of how widely spread data are around a group mean (average). The higher the standard deviation is, the greater the spread, indicating individual variation within a sample that the researcher typically assumes constitutes a homogeneous group.

STANDARD ERROR (SE): In statistics, a method of measuring the accuracy of an estimate.

STRUCTURALISM: As used in this volume, a theory of language dominant until the second half of the 20th century.

SUBJECT AND OBJECT RELATIVE: Subject and object relative refer to the syntactic function of a relative clause's head (e.g. *that, who, which*). A subject relative head behaves like the subject of a verb as in *John saw the woman who called last week*, where *who* functions as the subject of *called*. An object relative head noun behaves like the object of a verb as in *John talked to the man who Mary called last week* where *who* functions as the object of *called*.

SVO/SOV/OVS/VSO/OV/VO: The various permutations of subject (S), object (O), and verb (V) when referring to word order. Thus SVO = subject-verb-object word order.

SYNTACTIC PRIMING: The activation of the representation of syntactic structures in memory, which may result in speakers' tendency to repeat syntactic structures they have recently either produced or comprehended.

TARGET LANGUAGE (TL): The language in question in language acquisition research, for example, English is the target language for adult ESL learners. Used synonymously with SECOND LANGUAGE.

TARGETLIKE/NON-TARGETLIKE: More similar or less similar to the correct form in the target language. These terms can be used as a politically correct way of avoiding reference to errors or to an implied superiority of the native speaker.

TASK-BASED LEARNING: A methodology in L2 pedagogy which primarily focuses on communication-based activities and which downplays the role of language form; designed to enhance fluency.

TENSE: Here a type of vowel sound, usually defined in opposition to 'lax', often lasting longer than a lax vowel, but also articulated with greater muscular effort and a slightly higher tongue position.

TEXT ENHANCEMENT: A pedagogical technique in which grammatical features are highlighted in some way in written text to draw learners' attention.

TOTAL PHYSICAL RESPONSE: A method of language learning developed by James Asher (1977) starting with silent comprehension through physical demonstrations of words and phrases.

TRACE AND SHORTLIST MODELS: The TRACE model and its successor the Shortlist model are proposals to explain humans' perception of meaningful units from a continuous stream of speech sounds, whereby they gradually exclude possible competing lexical candidates using linguistic and acoustic cues until one meaningful unit (a word) is left.

TRANSFER (also referred to as 'interference'): The incorporation or influence of structural properties (e.g. phonological, syntactic) of a language already known into the new language during the process of acquisition. Transfer is an integral part of L2 acquisition and has been found to be highly systematic.

TRANSITION THEORY: Any theory of language acquisition which seeks to account for a learner's development from one stage to the next.

TRIGGER: Information in the input that results in the language learner revising his/her current linguistic system.

UNDERLYING REPRESENTATION: In syntax and in phonology, the shape of the sentence including word order, that is said to lie beneath what is actually spoken (or signed).

UNIVERSAL GRAMMAR (UG): The innate specifications for the nature of language that all humans bring to the task of language acquisition, proposed by Noam Chomsky. Often referred to in terms of hard-wired syntactic Principles (applying to all languages) and bi- or multi-valued PARAMETERS (cross-linguistically varying in terms of their settings).

[VP]: The symbol for *verb phrase* in syntax.

VOCALIC: Pertaining to vowels.

VOCALIC NUCLEUS: The vocalic center (peak) of a syllable.

VOICE ONSET TIME (VOT): The time which passes between the release of the closure of a consonant and the moment at which the vocal folds start vibrating.

WAVEFORM: Waveforms play an important role in the ACOUSTIC ANALYSIS of speech sounds. They are usually displayed as two dimensional graphs and show the pulses corresponding to each vibration of the vocal cords.

WILD CHILD/WILD CHILDREN: A rather colloquial term referring to children raised in exceptional circumstances, without exposure to any linguistic input at all, and in some celebrated cases by animals (hence the adjective 'wild').

WRITING SYSTEM: (1) the script and orthography of a specific language, that is, the set of GRAPHEMES and the rules used for writing a particular language. Sometimes called ORTHOGRAPHY. (2) The overall term for the ways in which graphemes connect to the language (e.g. phonemic writing system, syllabic writing system).

ZONE OF PROXIMAL DEVELOPMENT (ZPD): Term originally referring to how children can best respond to input or instruction (Vygotysky, 1978). The ZPD is defined as the distance between a child's real mental age and his or her ideal mental age after a period of learning. If that distance is too small or too large, no learning will take place. Optimal learning will only take place if the input or instruction is given within the child's ZPD.

References

Akita, M. (2001) The phonological development of adult Japanese learners of English: A longitudinal study of perception and production. Unpublished PhD thesis, Durham University.

Al-Zidjali, A.S.A. (2005) Lexical aspect: Its influence on the acquisition of tense and aspect morphology in L2 English. PhD thesis, University of Reading.

Andersen, R.W. (1993) Four operating principles and input distribution as explanations for underdeveloped and mature morphological systems. In K. Hyltenstam and Å. Viberg (eds) *Progression and Regression in Language* (pp. 309–339). Cambridge: Cambridge University Press.

Andersen, R.W. and Shirai, Y. (1994) Discourse motivations for some cognitive acquisition principles. *Studies in Second Language Acquisition* 16, 133–156.

Andersen, R.W. and Shirai, Y. (1996) Primacy of aspect in first and second language acquisition: The pidgin/creole connection. In W.C. Ritchie and T.K. Bhatia (eds) *Handbook of Second Language Acquisition* (pp. 527–570). San Diego: Academic Press.

Anderson, A. and Lynch, T. (1988) *Listening*. Oxford: Oxford University Press.

Anderson, J.R. (1983) *The Architecture of Cognition*. Cambridge, MA: Harvard University Press.

Anderson, J.R. (1993) *Rules of the Mind*. Hillsdale, NJ: Lawrence Erlbaum.

Anderson, J.R. (2005) *Cognitive Psychology and Its Implications* (6th edn). New York: Worth.

Anderson, J.R. and Fincham, J. (1994) Acquisition of procedural skills from examples. *Journal of Experimental Psychology: Learning, Memory, and Cognition* 20, 1322–1340.

Anderson, J.R., Fincham, J. and Douglas, S. (1997) The role of examples and rules in the acquisition of a cognitive skill. *Journal of Experimental Psychology: Learning, Memory, and Cognition* 23, 932–945.

Anderson, J.R., Fincham, J. and Douglas, S. (1999) Practice and retention: A unifying analysis. *Journal of Experimental Psychology: Learning, Memory, and Cognition* 25, 1120–1136.

Arnold, R. and Hansen, K. (1982) *Englische Phonetik*. München: Hueber.

Asher, J. (1969) The total physical response approach to second language learning. *Modern Language Journal* 53, 3–7.

Asher, J. (1977) *Learning Another Language Through Actions. The Complete Teacher's Guidebook*. Los Gatos, CA: Sky Oaks.

Asher, J.J. (1982) *Learning Another Language Through Actions: The Complete Teacher's Guidebook*. Los Gatos, CA: Sky Oaks.

Asher, J. (2000) *Learning Another Language Through Actions* (6th edn). Los Gatos, CA: Sky Oaks.

Asher, J. and Garcia, R. (1969) The optimal age to learn a foreign language. *Modern Language Journal* 53, 334–341.

Bahns, J. (1981) Der natürliche L2-Erwerb der englischen modalen Hilfsverben. Unpublished PhD thesis, University of Kiel.

Bahns, J. (1983) On acquisitional criteria. *International Review of Applied Linguistics* 21, 57–68.

Bailey, N., Madden, C. and Krashen, S. (1974) Is there a 'natural sequence' in adult second language learning? *Language Learning* 21, 235–243.

Baptista, L.F. and Petrinovich, L. (1984) Social interaction, sensitive phases and the song template hypothesis in the white-crowned sparrow. *Animal Behavior* 32, 172–181.

Barcroft, J. (2003) Effects of questions about word meaning during L2 Spanish lexical learning. *The Modern Language Journal* 87 (4), 546–561.

Barcroft, J. (2006) Can writing a new word detract from learning it? More negative effects of forced output during vocabulary learning. *Second Language Research* 22 (4), 487–497.

Bardovi-Harlig, K. (2000) *Tense and Aspect in Second Language Acquisition: Form, Meaning, and Use*. Oxford: Blackwell.

Bardovi-Harlig, K. (2002) Analyzing aspect. In R. Salaberry and Y. Shirai (eds) *The L2 Acquisition of Tense-Aspect Morphology* (pp. 129–154). Amsterdam: John Benjamins.

Barry, W.J. (1989) Perception and production of English vowels by German learners: Instrumental-phonetic support in language teaching. *Phonetica* 46, 155–168.

Bassetti, B. (2006a) Orthographic conventions and phonological representations in learners of Chinese as a foreign language. *Written Language and Literacy* 9 (1), 95–114.

Bassetti, B. (2006b) Pinyin orthographic input and CFL learners' pronunciation. Paper presented at the British Chinese Language Teachers' Seminar, Cambridge, 9–10 September 2006.

Bassetti, B. (2007) Effects of hanyu pinyin on pronunciation in learners of Chinese as a Foreign Language. In A. Guder, X. Jiang and Y. Wan (eds) *The Cognition, Learning and Teaching of Chinese Characters*. Beijing: Beijing Language and Culture University Press.

Bates, E. and MacWhinney, B. (1981) Functionalist approaches to grammar. In E. Wanner and L. Gleitman (eds) *Language Acquisition: The State of the Art* (pp. 173–218). Cambridge, UK: Cambridge University Press.

Bateson, G. (1981) *Ökologie des Geistes. Anthropologische, Psychologische, Biologische und Epistemologische Perspektiven*. Frankfurt: Suhrkamp. German edition of Bateson, G. (1972) *Steps to an Ecology of Mind, Collected Essays in Anthropology, Psychiatry, Evolution and Epistemology*. Chicago: University of Chicago Press.

Batstone, R. (2002) Making sense of new language: A discourse perspective. *Language Awareness* 11 (1), 14–29.

Bauer, J. (2006) *Das Gedächtnis des Körpers. Wie Beziehungen und Lebensstile unsere Gene Steuern* (6th edn). München: Piper.

Bauer, L. (1985) Tracing phonetic change in the received pronunciation of British English. *Journal of Phonetics* 13, 61–81.

Bax, S. (2003) The end of CLT: A context approach to language teaching. *ELT Journal* 57 (3), 278–287.

Beddor, P.S. and Gottfried, T.L. (1995) Methodological issues in cross-language speech perception research with adults. In W. Strange (ed.) *Speech Perception and Linguistic Experience* (pp. 207–232). Timonium, MD: York Press.

Benati, A. (2004) The effects of structured input activities and explicit information on the acquisition of the Italian future tense. In B. VanPatten (ed.) *Processing Instruction: Theory, Research, and Commentary* (pp. 207–225). Mahwah, NJ: Lawrence Erlbaum.

Benati, A. (2005) The effects of processing instruction, traditional instruction, and meaning-output instruction on the acquisition of the English past simple tense. *Language Teaching Research* 9, 87–113.

Benson, P. and Hjelt, C. (1978) Listening competence: A prerequisite to communication. *The Modern Language Journal* 62, 85–89.

Benson, P. and Lor, W. (1999) Conceptions of language and language learning. *System* 27, 459–472.

Berger, C. (1999) Pilotuntersuchungen zum Lauterwerb des Englischen in bilingualen Kindergärten am Beispiel der "roten Gruppe" in der AWO-Kindertagesstätte Altenholz. Mimeo, Kiel University.

Bernard, H., Killworth, P., Kronenfeld, D. and Sailer, L. (1984) On the validity of retrospective data: The problem of informant accuracy. *Annual Review of Anthropology* 13, 495–517.

Berndt, G. (1993) Phonologische Untersuchungen zum deutsch-englisch bilingualen Unterricht. MA dissertation, Kiel University.

Bertolo, S. (2001) *Language Acquisition and Learnability.* Cambridge, UK: Cambridge University Press.

Best, C.T. (1995) A direct realist view of cross-language speech perception. In W. Strange (ed.) *Speech Perception and Linguistic Experience* (pp. 171–204). Timonium, MD: York Press.

Best, C.T. and Bohn, O-S. (2002) Perception of American English glide consonants by Danish listeners. *Journal of the Acoustical Society of America* 112, 2388.

Best, C.T. and Tyler, M.D. (2007) Nonnative and second-language speech perception: Commonalities and complementarities. In O-S. Bohn and M.J. Munro (eds) *The Role of Language Experience in Second-Language Speech Learning: In Honor of James Emil Flege* (pp. 13–34). Amsterdam: John Benjamins.

Best, C.T., McRoberts, G.W. and Sithole, N.M. (1988) Examination of perceptual reorganisation for nonnative speech contrasts: Zulu click discrimination by English-speaking adults and infants. *Journal of Experimental Psychology* 14, 345–360.

Bickerton, D. (1981) *Roots of Language.* Ann Arbor, MI: Karoma.

Bildungsplan Gymnasium Baden-Württemberg (2004) Bildungsstandards für Englisch (1. und 2. Fremdsprache) – Gymnasien Klasse 10. On WWW at www.gymnasium-karlsbad.de/werwirsind/fachschaften/Englisch/bstdenglischinhalte10.pdf. Accessed 23.1.08.

Birdsong, D. (1992) Ultimate attainment in second language acquisition. *Language* 68, 706–755.

Birdsong, D. and Molis, M. (2001) On the evidence for maturational constraints in second language acquisition. *Journal of Memory and Language* 44, 235–249.

Bishop, D. and Mogford, K. (1988) *Language Development in Exceptional Circumstances.* London: Lawrence Erlbaum.

Blair, R. (ed.) (1982) *Innovative Approaches to Language Teaching.* Rowley, MA: Newbury House.

Bland, S.K. (1988) The Present Progressive in discourse. Grammar versus usage revisited. *TESOL Quarterly* 22 (1), 53–69.

Bleyhl, W. (1993) Nicht Steuerung, Selbstorganisation ist der Schlüssel. In K-R. Bausch, H. Christ and H-J. Krumm (eds) *Fremdsprachenlehr- und -lernprozesse im Spannungsfeld von Steuerung und Offenheit* (pp. 27–42). Bochum: Brockmeyer.

Bleyhl, W. (1996) Der Fallstrick des traditionellen Lehrens und Lernens fremder Sprachen. Vom Unterschied zwischen linearem und nicht-linearem Fremdsprachenunterricht. *Praxis des Neusprachlichen Unterrichts* 43 (4), 339–347.

Bleyhl, W. (ed.) (2000) *Fremdsprachen in der Grundschule. Grundlagen und Praxisbeispiele.* Hannover: Schroedel.

Bleyhl, W. (2001) Projekt 'Implizite und explizite Lernstrategien im fremdsprach-
lichen Anfangsunterricht' In A. Bonnet and P.W. Kahl (eds) *Innovation und
Tradition im Englischunterricht* (pp. 58–77) Stuttgart: Klett.

Bleyhl, W. (ed.) (2002) *Fremdsprachen in der Grundschule. Geschichten erzählen im
Anfangsunterricht – Storytelling.* Hannover: Schroedel.

Bleyhl, W. (2003a) Ist früher besser? – Die Bedeutung des frühen Lernens. In
C. Edelhoff (ed.) *Englisch in der Grundschule und darüber hinaus* (pp. 5–23).
Frankfurt: Diesterweg.

Bleyhl, W. (2003b) Psycholinguistische Grund-Erkenntnisse. In G. Bach and J-P.
Timm (eds) *Englischunterricht. Grundlagen und Methoden einer handlungsorienti-
erten Unterrichtspraxis* (pp. 38–55) (3rd edn). Tübingen: Francke.

Bley-Vroman, R. (1990) The logical problem of foreign language learning. *Linguistic
Analysis* 20, 3–49.

Bloom, L. (1970) *Language Development: Form and Function in Emerging Grammars.*
Cambridge, MA: MIT Press.

Bloom, L. (1973) *One Word at a Time: The Use of Single Word Utterances before Syntax.*
The Hague: Mouton.

Bloomfield, L. (1942) *Outline Guide for the Practical Study of Foreign Languages.*
Baltimore: Linguistic Society of America.

Blyth, C. (1997) A constructivist approach to grammar: Teaching teachers to teach
aspect. *The Modern Language Journal* 81 (1), 50–66.

Bohn, O-S. (2002) On phonetic similarity. In P. Burmeister, T. Piske and A. Rohde
(eds) *An Integrated View of Language Development. Papers in Honor of Henning
Wode* (pp. 191–216). Trier: Wissenschaftlicher Verlag Trier.

Bohn, O-S. and Flege, J.E. (1990) Interlingual identification and the role of foreign
language experience in L2 vowel perception. *Applied Psycholinguistics* 11,
303–328.

Bohn, O-S. and Flege, J.E. (1992) The production of new and similar vowels by
adult German learners of English. *Studies in Second Language Acquisition* 14,
131–158.

Bohn, O-S. and Munro, M.J. (eds) (2007) *The Role of Language Experience in Second-
Language Speech Learning: In Honor of James Emil Flege.* Amsterdam: John
Benjamins.

Bohn, O-S. and Steinlen, A.K. (2003) Consonantal context affects cross-language
perception of vowels. In M.J. Solé, D. Recasens and J. Romero (eds) *Proceedings
of the 15th International Congress of Phonetic Sciences* (pp. 2289–2292). Barcelona:
Futurgraphic.

Bolinger, D. (1960) *Instructor's Manual, Revised, for Modern Spanish.* New York:
Harcourt.

Bongaerts, T., Mennen, S. and van der Slik, F. (2000) Authenticity of pronunciation
in naturalistic second language acquisition: The case of very advanced late
learners of Dutch as a second language. *Studia Linguistica* 54, 298–308.

Bongaerts, T., Summeren, C., Planken, B. and Schils, E. (1997) Age and ultimate
attainment in the pronunciation of a foreign language. *Studies in Second Language
Acquisition* 19, 447–465.

Bosch, L., Costa, A. and Sebastián-Gallés, N. (2000) First and second language
vowel perception in early bilinguals. *European Journal of Cognitive Psychology* 12,
189–221.

Bowerman, M. and Brown P. (2006) Introduction. In M. Bowerman and P. Brown
(eds) *Crosslinguistic Perspectives on Argument Structure: Implications for Learnability*
(pp. 1–28). Mahwah, NJ: Lawrence Erlbaum.

Bradlow, A.R., Pisoni, D.E., Akahane-Yamada, R. and Tohkara, Y. (1997) Training
Japanese listeners to identify English /r/ and /l/: IV. Some effects of perceptual

training on speech production. *Journal of the Acoustical Society of America* 101, 2299–2310.

Brindley, G. (1987) Verb tenses and TESOL. In D. Nunan (ed.) *Applying Second Language Acquisition Research* (pp. 173–204). Adelaide: National Curriculum Centre.

Broad, D.J. (1976) Toward defining acoustic phonetic equivalence for vowels. *Phonetica* 33, 401–424.

Brown, C. (1954) *My Left Foot*. New York: Collins Educational.

Brown, C.A. (1998) The role of the L1 grammar in the L2 acquisition of segmental structure. *Second Language Research* 14 (2), 136–193.

Brown, R. (1973) *A First Language: The Early Stages*. Cambridge, MA: Harvard University Press.

Browning, S.R. (2004) Analysis of Italian children's English pronunciation. Unpublished report contributed to the EU FP5 PF STAR Project. On WWW at http://www.eee.bham.ac.uk/russellm/ItalianEnglishReport/ItalianEnglish_report_v2.htm. Accessed 29.1.08.

Buckmaster, R.A. (2003) The ELT Verb. Positive and Negative Grammar. Revised edition. On WWW at http://www.rbuckmaster.com/theeltverb.pdf. Accessed 23.1.08.

Burling, R. (1978) *Machine Aided Instruction in Aural Comprehension of Indonesian*. Final report to the US Office of Education.

Burmeister, P. and Pasternak, R. (2004) Früh und intensiv: Englische Immersion in der Grundschule am Beispiel der Claus-Rixen-Schule in Altenholz. Fachverband Moderne Fremdsprachen fmf, Landesverband Schleswig-Holstein (ed.) *Mitteilungsblatt*, August 2004, 24–30.

Burnham, D. (2003) Language specific speech perception and the onset of reading. *Reading and Writing* 16, 573–609.

Bybee, J.L. (1985) *Morphology: A Study of the Relation between Meaning and Form*. Amsterdam: John Benjamins.

Cadierno, T. (1995) Formal instruction from a processing perspective: An investigation into the Spanish past tense. *Modern Language Journal* 79, 179–193.

Canale, M. (1983) From communicative competence to communicative language pedagogy. In J.C. Richards and R.W. Schmidt (eds) *Language and Communication* (pp. 2–27). London: Longman.

Canale, M. and Swain, M. (1980) Theoretical bases of communicative approaches to second language teaching and testing. *Applied Linguistics* 1 (1), 1–47.

Caplan, D. and Waters, G. (2003) On-line syntactic processing in aphasia: Studies with auditory moving window presentation. *Brain and Language* 84, 222–249.

Carroll, S. (2001) *Input and Evidence. The Raw Material of Second Language Acquisition*. Amsterdam: John Benjamins.

Carroll, S. (2004a) Segmentation: Learning how to 'hear words' in the L2 speech stream. *Transactions of the Philological Society* 102, 227–254.

Carroll, S. (2004b) Commentary: Some general and specific comments on input processing and processing instruction. In B. VanPatten (ed.) *Processing Instruction: Theory, Research, and Commentary* (pp. 293–309). Mahwah, NJ: Lawrence Erlbaum.

Carter, R. and McCarthy, M. (2006) *Cambridge Grammar of English. A Comprehensive Guide*. Cambridge, UK: Cambridge University Press.

Castro-Caldas, A. and Reis, A. (2003) The knowledge of orthography is a revolution in the brain. *Reading and Writing* 16, 81–97.

Catford, J.C. and Pisoni, D.B. (1970) Auditory vs. articulatory training in exotic sounds. *Modern Language Journal* 54, 477–481.

Cato, T. and Hauser, M. (1992) Is there teaching in nonhuman animals? *Quarterly Review of Biology* 67 (2), 151–174.

Chaiken, M., Bohner, J. and Marler, P. (1993) Song acquisition in European starlings, Sturnus vulgaris: A comparison of the songs of live-tutored, tape-tutored, and wild-caught males. *Animal Behaviour* 46, 1079–1090.

Chaudron, C. (2001) Progress in the language classroom. Research evidence from *The Modern Language Journal*, 1916–2000. *The Modern Language Journal* 85, 58–76.

Cheney, D. and Seyfarth, R. (1990) *How Monkeys See the World*. Chicago: University of Chicago Press.

Chomsky, N. (1965) *Aspects of the Theory of Syntax*. Cambridge, MA: MIT Press.

Chomsky, N. (1966) Linguistic theory. *Northeast Conference on the Teaching of Foreign Languages, Working Committee Reports*. Reprinted in M. Lester (ed.) (1970) *Readings in Applied Transformation Grammar* (pp. 51–60). New York: Holt.

Chomsky, N. (1981) Principles and parameters in syntactic theory. In N. Hornstein and D. Lightfoot (eds) *Explanation in Linguistics: The Logical Problem of Language Acquisition* (pp. 123–146). London: Longman.

Chomsky, N. (1986) *Knowledge of Language, Its Nature, Origin, and Use*. New York: Praeger.

Christison, M.A. (1999) Brain Compatible Language Learning. Paper presented at the TESOL Convention. In W. Bleyhl (ed.) (2000) *Fremdsprachen in der Grundschule. Grundlagen und Praxisbeispiele* (p. 132). Hannover: Schroedel.

Clahsen, H., Meisel, J. and Pienemann, M. (1983) *Deutsch als Zweitsprache: Der Spracherwerb ausländischer Arbeiter*. Tübingen: Narr.

Clark, E. (2003) *First Language Acquisition*. Cambridge: Cambridge University Press.

Collentine, J. (1998) Processing instruction and the subjunctive. *Hispania* 81, 576–587.

Collentine, J. and Freed, B. (2004) Learning context and its effects on second language acquisition. *Studies in Second Language Acquisition* 26, 153–171.

Comenius, J.A. (1654) *Orbis Sensualium Pictus*. On WWW at http://www.grexlat.com/biblio/comenius/index.html. Accessed 26.10.08.

Comrie, B. (1976) *Aspect*. Cambridge: Cambridge University Press.

Comrie, B. (2000) Language contact, lexical borrowing, and semantic fields. In D. Gilbers, J. Nerbonne and J. Schaeken (eds) *Languages in Contact* (pp. 73–86). Amsterdam: Rodopi.

Cook, V.J. (1999) Going beyond the native speaker in language teaching. *TESOL Quarterly* 33, 185–209.

Cook, V.J. (2001) *Second Language Learning and Language Teaching*. London: Arnold.

Cook V.J. (2005) Second language writing systems and language teaching. In V.J. Cook and B. Bassetti (eds) *Second Language Writing Systems* (pp. 424–441). Clevedon: Multilingual Matters.

Cook, V.J. and Bassetti, B. (2005) Introduction to researching second language writing systems. In V.J. Cook and B. Bassetti (eds) *Second Language Writing Systems* (pp. 1–67). Clevedon: Multilingual Matters.

Cook, W. (1912) Should we teach spelling by rule? *Journal of Educational Psychology* 3, 316–325.

Coppieters, R. (1987) Competence differences between native and near-native speakers. *Language* 63, 544–573.

Corder, S.P. (1967) The significance of learner's errors. *IRAL* 4, 161–170.

Cornman, O. (1902) *Spelling in the Elementary School*. Boston: Ginn.

Costamagna, L. (2000) *Insegnare e Imparare la Fonetica*. Torino, Italy: Paravia.

Coulmas, F. (2003) *Writing Systems: An Introduction to their Linguistic Analysis*. Cambridge: Cambridge University Press.

Cox, F. (1999) Vowel change in Australian English. *Phonetica* 56, 1–27.

Cox, F. (2006) The acoustic characteristics of /hVd/ vowels in the speech of some Australian teenagers. *Australian Journal of Linguistics* 26 (2), 147–179.

Croft, W. (1991) *Syntactic Categories and Grammatical Relations*. Chicago: University of Chicago Press.

Crystal, T.H. and House, A.S. (1988) The duration of American-English vowels: An overview. *Journal of Phonetics* 16, 263–284.

Csikzentmihalyi, M. and Larson, R. (1987) Validity and reliability of the experience-sampling method. *Journal of Nervous and Mental Disease* 175, 526–536.

Curtiss, S. (1982) Developmental dissociations of language and cognition. In L. Obler and L. Menn (eds) *Exceptional Language and Linguistics* (pp. 285–312). New York: Academic Press.

Damasio, A.R. (1994) *Descartes' Error. Emotion, Reason and the Human Brain*. New York: Putnam.

Davidsen-Nielsen, N., Færch, C. and Harder, P. (1982) *The Danish Learner*. Kent: Taylor.

Davies, N. (1980) Putting receptive skills first: An experiment in sequencing. *Canadian Modern Language Review* 36, 461–467.

Davies, R.J. and Ikeno, O. (eds) (2002) *The Japanese Mind: Understanding Contemporary Japanese Culture*. North Clarendon, VT: Tuttle.

De Bot, K. (1996) The psycholinguistics of the output hypothesis. *Language Learning* 46, 529–555.

De Bot, K., Lowie, W. and Verspoor, M. (2005) *Second Language Acquisition, an Advanced Resource Book*. London: Routledge.

De Bot, K., Verspoor, M. and Lowie, W. (2007) A dynamic systems theory approach to second language acquisition. *Bilingualism, Language and Cognition* 10 (1), 7–21.

De Jong, N. (2005a) Can second language grammar be learned through listening? An experimental study. *Studies in Second Language Acquisition* 27, 205–234.

De Jong, N. (2005b) Learning second language grammar by listening. Unpublished PhD thesis, University of Amsterdam.

Deevy, P. (2000) Agreement checking in comprehension: Evidence from relative clauses. *Journal of Psycholinguistic Research* 29, 69–79.

Dehaene-Lambertz, G. and Dehaene, S. (1994) Speed and cerebral correlates of syllable discrimination in infants. *Nature* 370, 292–295.

DeKeyser, R. (1997) Beyond explicit rule learning: Automatizing second language morphosyntax. *Studies in Second Language Acquisition* 19, 195–221.

DeKeyser, R. (2000) The robustness of critical period effects in second language acquisition. *Studies in Second Language Acquisition* 22, 499–534.

DeKeyser, R. (2001) Automaticity and automatization. In P. Robinson (ed.) *Cognition and Second Language Instruction* (pp. 125–151). Cambridge, UK: Cambridge University Press.

DeKeyser, R. (2003) Implicit and explicit learning. In C.J. Doughty and M.H. Long (eds) *The Handbook of Second Language Acquisition* (pp. 313–348). Malden, MA: Blackwell.

DeKeyser, R. and Larson-Hall, J. (2005) What does the critical period mean? In J. Kroll and A. DeGroot (eds) *Handbook of Bilingualism, Psycholinguistic Approaches* (pp. 88–108). Oxford, Oxford University Press.

DeKeyser, R., Salaberry, M.R., Robinson, P. and Harrington, M. (2002) What gets processed in processing instruction? A response to Bill VanPatten's 'Update'. *Language Learning* 52, 805–823.

DeKeyser, R. and Sokalski, K. (1996) The differential role of comprehension and production practice. *Language Learning* 46, 613–642.

Derwing, B.L. (1992) Orthographic aspects of linguistic competence. In P. Downing, S.D. Lima and M. Noonan (eds) *The Linguistics of Literacy* (pp. 193–210). Amsterdam: John Benjamins.

Derwing, T. and Rossiter, M. (2003) The effects of pronunciation instruction on the accuracy, fluency and complexity of L2 accented speech. *Applied Language Learning* 13, 1–17.

D'Eugenio, A. (1985) *Manuale di Fonologia Contrastiva Italiano-inglese*. Foggia, Italy: Atlantica.

Diaz-Campos, M. (2004) Context of learning in the acquisition of Spanish second language phonology. *Studies in Second Language Acquisition* 26, 249–273.

Dickerson, W. (1991) Orthography as a pronunciation resource. In A. Brown (ed.) *Teaching English Pronunciation* (pp. 159–172). London: Routledge.

Diehl, E., Christen, H., Leuenberger, S., Pelvat, I. and Studer, T. (2000) *Grammatikunterricht: Alles für die Katz? Untersuchungen zum Zweitsprachenerwerb Deutsch*. Tübingen: Niemeyer.

Diessel, H. and Tomasello, M. (2000) The development of relative clauses in spontaneous child speech. *Cognitive Linguistics* 11 (1/2), 131–152.

Diller, K. (1971) *The Language Teaching Controversy*. Rowley, MA: Newbury House.

Disner, S.F. (1978) Vowels in Germanic languages. *UCLA Working Papers in Phonetics 40* (pp. 1–79). Los Angeles: University of California.

Doughty, C. and Williams, J. (1998) *Focus on Form*. Cambridge: Cambridge University Press.

Doughty, C.J. (2003) Instructed SLA: Constraints, compensation and enhancement. In C.J. Doughty and M.H. Long (eds) *Handbook of Second Language Acquisition* (pp. 256–310). Oxford: Blackwell.

Dowty, D.R. (1979) *Word Meaning and Montague Grammar*. Dordrecht: Reidel.

Dretzke, B. (1998) *Modern British English and American English Pronunciation*. Paderborn: Schöningh.

Dudley, R. (2004) Natural language learning. *English Teaching Professional* 34, 28–30.

Dulay, H. and Burt, M. (1973) Should we teach children syntax? *Language Learning* 23–24, 245–258.

Dulay, H. and Burt, M. (1974a) Natural sequences in child second language acquisition. *Language Learning* 24, 37–53.

Dulay, H. and Burt, M. (1974b) A new perspective on the creative construction process in child second language acquisition. *Language Learning* 24, 253–278.

Dulay, H., Burt, M. and Krashen, S. (1982) *Language Two*. New York: Oxford University Press.

Eckert, H. and Barry, W. (2002) *The Phonetics and Phonology of English Pronunciation*. Trier: Wissenschaftlicher Verlag Trier.

Eckman, F. (2004) From phonemic differences to constraint rankings: Research on second language phonology. *Studies in Second Language Acquisition* 26 (4), 513–549.

Ehri, L. and Wilce, L. (1980) The influence of orthography on readers' conceptualization of the phonemic structure of words. *Applied Psycholinguistics* 1, 371–385.

Eimas, P., Siqueland, E., Jusczyk, P. and Vigorito, J. (1971) Speech perception in infants. *Science* 171, 303–306.

Elliott, A. (1997) On the teaching and acquisition of pronunciation within a communicative approach. *Hispania* 80 (1), 95–108.

Ellis, N. (2002) Frequency effects in language processing. *Studies in Second Language Acquisition* 24 (2), 143–188.

Ellis, N. (2005) Measuring implicit and explicit knowledge of a second language. *Studies in Second Language Acquisition* 27, 141–172.

Ellis, R. (1985) *Understanding Second Language Acquisition.* Oxford: Oxford University Press.

Ellis, R. (1990) *Instructed Second Language Acquisition.* Oxford: Blackwell.

Ellis, R. (1992) On the relationship between formal practice and second language acquisition: A study of the effects of formal practice on the acquisition of German word order rules. *Die Neueren Sprachen* 91 (2), 131–147.

Ellis, R. (1994) *The Study of Second Language Acquisition.* Oxford: Oxford University Press.

Ellis, R. (2002) A metaphorical analysis of learner beliefs. In P. Burmeister, T. Piske and A. Rohde (eds) *An Integrated View of Language Development. Papers in Honor of Henning Wode* (pp. 163–179). Trier: Wissenschaftlicher Verlag Trier.

Ellis, R. (2003) *Task-based Language Learning and Teaching.* Oxford: Oxford University Press.

Ellis, R. (2005) Principles of instructed language learning. *System* 33, 209–224.

Elman, J., Bates, E., Johnson, M., Karmiloff-Smith, A., Parisi, D. and Plunkett, K. (1996) *Rethinking Innateness: A Connectionist Perspective on Development.* Cambridge, MA: MIT Press.

Erdener, V. and Burnham, D. (2005) The role of audiovisual speech and orthographic information in nonnative speech production. *Language Learning* 55 (2), 191–228.

Erlam, R. (2004) Evaluating the effectiveness of structured input and output-based instruction in foreign language learning. *Studies in Second Language Acquisition* 25, 559–582.

European Commission (2004) *Promoting Language Learning and Linguistic Diversity: An Action Plan 2004–06.* Luxemburg: Office for Official Publications of the European Communities.

Farley, A.P. (2001) Authentic processing instruction and the Spanish subjunctive. *Hispania* 84, 289–299.

Farley, A.P. (2004) Processing instruction and the Spanish subjunctive: Is explicit information needed? In B. VanPatten (ed.) *Processing Instruction: Theory, Research, and Commentary* (pp. 227–239). Mahwah, NJ: Lawrence Erlbaum.

Farley, A.P. (2005) *Structured input: Grammar Instruction for the Acquisition-Oriented Classroom.* New York: McGraw-Hill.

Fathman, A. (1975) The relationship between age and second language productive ability. *Language Learning* 25, 245–253.

Felix, S. (1985) More evidence on competing cognitive systems. *Second Language Research* 1, 47–72.

Felix, S. and Weigl, W. (1991) Universal Grammar in the classroom: The effects of formal instruction on second language acquisition. *Second Language Research* 7, 162–180.

Fennell, B. (1997) *Language, Literature, and the Negotiation of Identity.* Chapel Hill: University of North Carolina Press.

Fernández, C. (2005) The role of explicit information in instructed SLA. Unpublished PhD thesis, The University of Illinois at Chicago.

Ferreira, F., Henderson, J.M., Anes, M.D., Weeks, P.A. and McFarlane, D.K. (1996) Effects of lexical frequency and syntactic complexity in spoken-language comprehension: Evidence from the auditory moving-window technique. *Journal of Experimental Psychology: Learning, Memory, and Cognition* 22, 324–335.

Finegan, E. (1999) *Language: Its Structure and Use* (3rd edn). New York: Harcourt Brace.

Fischer-Jørgensen, E. (1972) Formant frequencies of long and short Danish vowels. *Annual Report of the Institute of Phonetics, University of Copenhagen 7*, 49–57.

Fisiak, J.E. (1980) *Theoretical Issues in Contrastive Linguistics*. Amsterdam: John Benjamins.

Flege, J.E. (1987) A critical period for learning to pronounce foreign languages? *Applied Linguistics 8*, 162–177.

Flege, J.E. (1988) The production and perception of foreign language speech sounds. In H. Winitz (ed.) *Human Communication and Its Disorders* (pp. 224–401). Norwood, NJ: Ablex.

Flege, J.E. (1995) Second-language speech learning: Theory, findings, and problems. In W. Strange (ed.) *Speech Perception and Linguistic Experience: Issues in Cross-language Research* (pp. 229–273). Timonium, MD: York Press.

Flege, J.E. (1996) English vowel productions by Dutch talkers: More evidence for the 'similar' vs 'new' distinction. In A. James and J. Leather (eds) *Second Language Speech. Structure and Process* (pp. 11–52). Berlin: Mouton de Gruyter.

Flege, J.E. (2003) Assessing constraints on second-language segmental production and perception. In A. Meyer and N. Schiller (eds) *Phonetics and Phonology in Language Comprehension and Production, Differences and Similarities* (pp. 319–355). Berlin: Mouton de Gruyter.

Flege, J.E., Birdsong, D., Bialystok, E., Mack, M., Sung, H. and Tsukada, K. (2006) Degree of foreign accent in English sentences produced by Korean children and adults. *Journal of Phonetics 34*, 153–175.

Flege, J.E., Bohn, O-S. and Jang, S. (1997) The effect of experience on nonnative subjects' production and perception of English vowels. *Journal of Phonetics 25*, 437–470.

Flege, J.E. and Davidian, R. (1984) Transfer and developmental processes in adult foreign language speech production. *Applied Psycholinguistics 5*, 323–347.

Flege, J.E. and Eefting, W. (1987) The production and perception of English stops by Spanish speakers of English. *Journal of Phonetics 15*, 67–83.

Flege, J.E. and Eefting, W. (1988) Imitation of a VOT continuum by native speakers of English and Spanish: Evidence for phonetic category formation. *Journal of the Acoustical Society of America 83*, 729–740.

Flege, J.E. and Fletcher, K. (1992) Talker and listener effects on degree of perceived foreign accent. *Journal of the Acoustical Society of America 91*, 370–389.

Flege, J.E. and Liu, S. (2001) The effect of experience on adults' acquisition of a second language. *Studies in Second Language Acquisition 23*, 527–552.

Flege, J.E., MacKay, I. and Piske, T. (2002) Assessing bilingual dominance. *Applied Psycholinguistics 23*, 567–598.

Flege, J.E. and MacKay, I. (2004) Perceiving vowels in a second language. *Studies in Second Language Acquisition 24*, 1–34.

Flege, J.E. and Munro, M. (1994) The word unit in L2 speech production and perception. *Studies in Second Language Acquisition 16*, 381–411.

Flege, J.E., Munro, M. and MacKay, I. (1995a) Effects of age of second-language learning on the production of English consonants. *Speech Communication 16*, 1–26.

Flege, J.E., Munro, M. and MacKay, I. (1995b) Factors affecting strength of perceived foreign accent in a second language. *Journal of the Acoustical Society of America 97*, 3125–3134.

Flege, J.E., Schirru, C. and MacKay, I. (2003) Interaction between the native and second language phonetic subsystems. *Speech Communication 40*, 467–491.

Flege, J.E., Takagi, N. and Mann, V.A. (1996) Lexical familiarity and English-language experience affect Japanese adults' perception of /ɹ/ and /l/. *Journal of the Acoustical Society of America 99*, 1161–1173.

Flege, J.E., Yeni-Komshian, G. and Liu, S. (1999) Age constraints on second-language learning. *Journal of Memory and Language* 41, 78–104.

Fourcin, A. (1975) Language development in the absence of expressive speech. In E. Lenneberg and E. Lenneberg (eds) *Foundations of Language Development* (pp. 263–268). New York: Academic Press.

Fouts, R. (1997) *Next of Kin.* New York: William Morrow.

Fox, R.A. and McGory, J.T. (2007) Second language acquisition of a regional dialect of American English by native Japanese speakers. In O-S. Bohn and M.J. Munro (eds) *The Role of Language Experience in Second-Language Speech Learning: In Honor of James Emil Flege* (pp. 117–134). Amsterdam: John Benjamins.

Fuller, J. (1966) *The Interrupted Journey.* New York: Berkley Publishing Corporation.

Garan, E. (2002) *Resisting Reading Mandates.* Portsmouth, NH: Heinemann.

Gardner, R. and Lambert, W. (1972) *Attitudes and Motivation in Second-Language Learning.* Rowley, MA: Newbury House.

Garey, H.B. (1957) Verbal aspect in French. *Language* 33, 91–110.

Gary, J.O. and Gary, N. (1981) Comprehension-based language instruction: Theory. In H. Winitz (ed.) *Native Language and Foreign Language Acquisition* (pp. 332–342). New York: New York Academy of Sciences.

Gass, S. (1988) Integrating research areas: A framework for second language studies. *Applied Linguistics* 9, 198–217.

Gass, S.M. (1997) *Input, Interaction, and the Second Language Learner.* Mahwah, NJ: Lawrence Erlbaum.

Gass, S. and Madden, C. (eds) (1985) *Input in Second Language Acquisition.* Rowley, MA: Newbury House.

Gass, S. and Selinker, L. (2001) *Second Language Acquisition. An Introductory Course* (2nd edn). Mahwah, NJ: Lawrence Erlbaum.

Gavis, W.A. (1998) *Stative Verbs in the Progressive Aspect: A Study of Semantic, Pragmatic, Syntactic and Discourse Patterns.* Downloadable doctoral thesis. On WWW at http://digitalcommons.libraries.columbia.edu/dissertations/AAI9839066/. Accessed 30.1.08.

Gavruseva, E. (2002) Is there primacy of aspect in child L2 English? *Bilingualism: Language and Cognition* 5, 109–130.

Gibbons, J. (1985) The silent period: An examination. *Language Learning* 35, 255–267.

Giglioli, P. (ed.) (1972) *Language and Social Context.* London: Penguin.

Gilhooly, K.J., Logie, R.H. and Wynn, V. (1999) Syllogistic reasoning tasks, working memory, and skill. *European Journal of Cognitive Psychology* 11, 473–498.

Gleick, J. (1987) *Chaos: Making a New Science.* London: Viking Penguin.

Gleitman, L. (1990) The structural sources of verb meanings. *Language Acquisition* 1 (1), 3–55.

Goad, H., White, L. and Steele, J. (2003) Missing surface inflection in L2 acquisition: A prosodic account. In B. Beachley, A. Brown and F. Conlin (eds) *Proceedings of the 27th Annual Boston University Conference on Language Development* (pp. 264–275). Somerville, MA: Cascadilla Press.

Goh, C.M.C. (2000) A cognitive perspective on language learners' listening comprehension problems. *System* 28, 55–75.

Goldin-Meadow, S. (2005) *The Resilience of Language. What Gesture Creativity in Deaf Children can Tell Us about How All Children Create Languages.* Hove: Psychology Press.

Goodman, K. and Goodman, Y. (1979) Learning to read is natural. In L.B. Resnick and P.A. Weaver (eds) *Theory and Practice of Early Reading, Volume 1* (pp. 137–154). Hillsdale, NJ: Lawrence Erlbaum.

Goodman, K. and Goodman, Y. (1982) Spelling ability of a self-taught reader. In F. Gollasch (ed.) _Language and Literacy: The Selected Writings of Kenneth S. Goodman, Volume 2_ (pp. 135–142). London: Routledge.

Gopnik, A., Meltzoff, A.N. and Kuhl, P.K. (1999) _The Scientist in the Crib. Minds, Brains, and How Children Learn._ New York: Morrow.

Gottfried, T.L. and Bohn, O-S. (2002) Duration and rate effects on American English vowel identification by native Danish listeners. _Journal of the Acoustical Society of America_ 112, 2250.

Gradman, H. and Hanania, E. (1991) Language learning background factors and ESL proficiency. _Modern Language Journal_ 75, 39–51.

Granger, C.A. (2004) _Silence in Second Language Learning: A Psychoanalytic Reading._ Clevedon: Multilingual Matters.

Gray, P. and Leather, S. (1999) _Safety and Challenge for Japanese Learners of English._ London: First Person Publishing.

Greenfield, S. (2000) _Brain Story. Unlocking Our Inner World of Emotions, Memories, Ideas and Desires._ London: BBC.

Grimshaw, J. (1981) Form, function and the acquisition device. In C. Baker and J. McCarthy (eds) _The Logical Problem of Language Acquisition_ (pp. 165–182). Cambridge, MA: MIT Press.

Grønnum, N. (1998) _Fonetik of Fonologi: Almen og Dansk._ Copenhagen: Akademisk Forlag.

Haggan, M. (1991) Spelling errors in native Arabic-speaking English majors: A comparison between remedial students and fourth year students. _System_ 19 (1,1), 45–61.

Halbach, A. (2000) Finding out about students' learning strategies by looking at their diaries: a case study. _System_ 28, 85–96.

Halliday, M.A.K. (1990) _Spoken and Written Language._ Oxford: Oxford University Press.

Hammill, D., Larson, S. and McNutt, G. (1977) The effect of spelling instruction: A preliminary study. _Elementary School Journal_ 78, 67–72.

Han, Z. (2004) _Fossilization in Adult Second Language Acquisition._ Clevedon: Multilingual Matters.

Han, Z-H. (2007) Pedagogical implications: Genuine or pretentious? _TESOL Quarterly_ 41 (2), 387–393.

Harmer, J. (2003) Popular culture, methods and context. _ELT Journal_ 57 (3), 288–294.

Harrington, M. (2004) Commentary: Input processing as a theory of processing input. In B. VanPatten (ed.) _Processing Instruction: Theory, Research, and Commentary_ (pp. 79–92). Mahwah, NJ: Lawrence Erlbaum.

Hauser, M. (1996) _The Evolution of Communication._ Cambridge, MA: MIT Press.

Hawkins, R. (2001) _Second Language Syntax: A Generative Introduction._ Oxford: Blackwell.

Hazan, V. and Barrett, S. (1999) The development of phonemic categorization in children aged 6–12. _Journal of Phonetics_ 28, 377–396.

Haznedar, B. (2001) The acquisition of the IP system in child L2 English. _Studies in Second Language Acquisition_ 23, 1–39.

Henton, C.G. (1983) Changes in the vowels of received pronunciation. _Journal of Phonetics_ 11, 353–371.

Herschensohn, J. (2007) _Language Development and Age._ Cambridge: Cambridge University Press.

Hillocks, G. (1986) _Research on Written Composition. New Directions for Teaching._ Urbana, IL: ERIC.

Højen, A. (2002) Detection of Danish accent in English by native speakers of Danish. In J. Leather and A. James (eds) _New Sounds 2000. Proceedings of the 4th_

International Symposium on the Acquisition of Second-Language Speech (pp. 80–86). Amsterdam: Amsterdam University Press.

Hopper, P. (1998) Emergent grammar. In M. Tomasello (ed.) *The New Psychology of Language: Cognitive and Functional Approaches to Language Structure* (pp. 155–176). Mahwah, NJ: Lawrence Erlbaum.

Horwitz, E.K. (1999) Cultural and situational influences on foreign language learners' beliefs about language learning: A review of BALLI studies. *System* 27, 557–576.

Housen, A. (2002) The development of tense-aspect in English as a second language and the variable influence of inherent aspect. In R. Salaberry and Y. Shirai (eds) *The L2 Acquisition of Tense-Aspect Morphology* (pp. 155–197). Amsterdam: John Benjamins.

Hua, Z. (2002) *Phonological Development in Specific Contexts: Studies of Chinese-Speaking Children.* Clevedon: Multilingual Matters.

Huang, J. (2005) A diary study of difficulties and constraints in EFL learning. *System* 33, 609–621.

Hyams, N. (1986) *Language Acquisition and the Theory of Parameters.* Dordrecht: Reidel.

Hyltenstam, K. and Abrahamsson, N. (2003) Maturational constraints in SLA. In C. Doughty and M. Long (eds) *Handbook of Second Language Acquisition* (pp. 539–588). Malden, MA: Blackwell.

Hymes, D.H. (1972) On communicative competence. In J.B. Pride and J. Holmes (eds) *Sociolinguistics* (pp. 269–293). Harmondsworth: Penguin.

Iivonen, A.K. (1995) Explaining the dispersion of single-vowel occurrences in an F1/F2 space. *Phonetica* 52, 221–227.

Ioup, G. and Weinberger, S. (1987) *Interlanguage Phonology.* Rowley, MA: Newbury House.

Ioup, G., Boustagi, E., El Tigi, M. and Moselle, M. (1994) Re-examining the critical period hypothesis: A case study of successful adult SLA in a naturalistic environment. *Studies in Second Language Acquisition* 16, 73–98.

Iverson, P., Kuhl, P., Akahane-Yamada, R., Diesch, E., Tohkura, Y., Kettermann, A. and Siebert, C. (2003) A perceptual interference account of acquisition difficulties for non-native phonemes. *Cognition* 87, B47–B57.

Iwashita, N. (2001) The effect of learner proficiency on interactional moves and modified output in nonnative-nonnative interaction in Japanese as a foreign language. *System* 29, 267–287.

Izumi, S. (2003) Processing difficulty in comprehension and production of relative clauses by learners of English as a second language. *Language Learning* 53, 285–323.

Izumi, S. and Bigelow, M. (2000) Does output promote noticing and second language acquisition? *TESOL Quarterly* 34 (2), 239–278.

Izumi, S., Bigelow, M., Fujiwara, M. and Fearnow, S. (1999) Testing the output hypothesis: Effects of output on noticing and second language acquisition. *Studies in Second Language Acquisition* 21 (3), 421–452.

Jacobs, D. (1998) *The Threat.* New York: Simon and Schuster.

Jacoby, L. and Hollingshead, A. (1990) Reading student essays may be hazardous to your spelling: Effects of reading correctly and incorrectly spelled words. *Canadian Journal of Psychology* 44, 345–358.

Jenkins, J. (2000) *The Phonology of English as an International Language: New Models, New Norms, New Goals.* Oxford: Oxford University Press.

Jespersen, O. (1904) *How to Teach a Foreign Language.* London: G. Allen.

Jia, G. and Aaronson, D. (1999) Age differences in second language acquisition: The dominant language switch and maintenance hypothesis. *Proceedings of* the Annual Boston University of Conference on Language Development 23, 301–312.

Jia, G. and Aaronson, D. (2003) A longitudinal study of Chinese children and adolescents learning English in the United States. *Applied Psycholinguistics* 24, 131–161.

Jia, G., Aaronson, D. and Wu, Y. (2002) Long-term language attainment of bilingual immigrants: Predictive variables and language group differences. *Applied Psycholinguistics* 23, 599–621.

Johnson, J. and Newport, E. (1989) Critical period effects in second language learning: The influence of maturational state on the acquisition of English as a second language. *Cognitive Psychology* 21, 60–99.

Jordan, G. (2004) *Theory Construction in Second Language Acquisition*. Amsterdam: John Benjamins.

Jordens, P. (1996) Input and instruction in second language acquisition. In P. Jordens and J. Lalleman (eds) *Investigating Second Language Acquisition* (pp. 407–449). Berlin: Mouton de Gruyter.

Juffs, A. (1998) Some effects of first language argument structure and morphosyntax on second language sentence processing. *Second Language Research* 14, 406–424.

Jusczyk, P. (1993) From general to language-specific capacities: The WRAPSA model of how speech perception develops. *Journal of Phonetics* 21, 3–28.

Kandel, E. (2006) *In Search of Memory: The Emergence of a New Science of Mind*. New York: W.W. Norton.

Kecskes, I. and Papp, T. (2000) *Foreign Language and Mother Tongue*. Mahwah, NJ: Lawrence Erlbaum.

Kempen, G. (1998) Comparing and explaining the trajectories of first and second language acquisition: In search of the right mix of psychological and linguistic factors. *Bilingualism, Language and Cognition* 1, 29–30.

Kennison, S.M. (2002) Comprehending noun phrase arguments and adjuncts. *Journal of Psycholinguistic Research* 31, 65–81.

Kenworthy, J. (1987) *Teaching English Pronunciation*. London: Longman.

Kersten, K., Imhoff, Ch. and Sauer, B. (2002) The acquisition of English verbs in an elementary school immersion program in Germany. In P. Burmeister, T. Piske and A. Rohde (eds) *Integrated View of Language Development: Papers in Honor of Henning Wode* (pp. 473–497). Trier: Wissenschaftlicher Verlag Trier.

Klein, W. (1986) *Second Language Acquisition*. Cambridge: Cambridge University Press.

Klein, W. and Perdue, C. (1997) The basic variety (or: couldn't natural languages be much simpler?) *Second Language Research* 13, 301–347.

Klieme, E., Eichler, W., Helmke, A., Lehmann, R.H., Nold, G., Rolff, H-G., Schröder, K., Thomé, G. and Willenberg, H. (2006) *Unterricht und Kompetenzerwerb in Deutsch und Englisch. Zentrale Befunde der Studie Deutsch-Englisch-Schülerleistungen-International (DESI)*. Frankfurt: DIPF.

Kohler, K.J. (1981) Contrastive analysis and the acquisition of phonetic skills. *Phonetica* 38, 213–226.

Kohler, K.J. (1995) *Einführung in die Phonetik des Deutschen* (2nd edn). Münster: Schmidt.

Konieczny, L. (2000) Locality and parsing complexity. *Journal of Psycholinguistic Research* 29, 627–645.

Köpke, B. (2004) Neurolinguistic aspects of attrition. *Journal of Neurolinguistics* 17, 3–30.

Kramsch, C. (2003) Second language acquisition, applied linguistics and the teaching of foreign languages. *Language Learning Journal* 27, 66–73.

Krashen, S. (1973) Lateralization, language learning and the critical period: Some new evidence. *Language Learning* 23, 63–74.

Krashen, S. (1976) Formal and informal linguistic environments in language acquisition and language learning. *TESOL Quarterly* 10, 157–168.

Krashen, S. (1981) *Second Language Acquisition and Second Language Learning.* New York: Prentice-Hall. On WWW at http://www.sdkrashen.com. Accessed 29.1.08.

Krashen, S. (1982a) *Principles and Practice in Second Language Acquisition.* Oxford: Pergamon.

Krashen, S. (1982b) Theory versus practice in language teaching. In R. Blair (ed.) *Innovative Approaches to Language Teaching* (pp. 15–30). Rowley, MA: Newbury House.

Krashen, S. (1984) *Writing: Research, Theory and Applications.* Torrance, CA: Laredo.

Krashen, S. (1985) *The Input Hypothesis: Issues and Implications.* London: Longman.

Krashen, S. (1988a) Do we learn to read by reading? The relationship between free reading and reading ability. In D. Tannen (ed.) *Linguistics in Context: Connecting Observation and Understanding* (pp. 269–298). Norwood, NJ: Ablex.

Krashen, S. (1988b) Comprehensible output? *System* 26, 175–182.

Krashen, S. (1989) We acquire vocabulary and spelling by reading: Additional evidence for the input hypothesis. *Modern Language Journal* 73, 440–464.

Krashen, S. (1991) Sheltered subject matter teaching. *Cross Currents* 18, 183–188. Reprinted in J. Oller (ed.) *Methods That Work* (pp. 143–148). Boston: Heinle and Heinle.

Krashen, S. (1994) The input hypothesis and its rivals. In N. Ellis (ed.) *Implicit and Explicit Learning of Languages* (pp. 45–77). London: Academic Press.

Krashen, S.D. (1996) The case for narrow listening. *System* 24 (1), 97–100.

Krashen, S. (2000) What does it take to acquire language? *ESL Magazine* 3 (3), 22–23.

Krashen, S. (2002a) The NRP comparison of whole language and phonics: Ignoring the crucial variable in reading. *Talking Points* 13 (3), 22–28.

Krashen, S. (2002b) The comprehension hypothesis and its rivals. In *Selected Papers from the Eleventh International Symposium on English Teaching/Fourth Pan-Asian Conference* (pp. 395–404). English Teachers Association/ROC.

Krashen, S. (2002c) Defending whole language: The limits of phonics instruction and the efficacy of whole language instruction. *Reading Improvement* 39 (10), 32–42.

Krashen, S. (2003) *Explorations in Language Acquisition and Use: The Taipei Lectures.* Portsmouth, NH: Heinemann.

Krashen, S. (2004) *The Power of Reading.* Portsmouth, NH: Heinemann.

Krashen, S. (2005) Is in-school free reading good for children? Why the National Reading Panel Report is (still) wrong. *Phi Delta Kappan* 86 (6), 444–447.

Krashen, S. and White, H. (1991) Is spelling acquired or learned? A re-analysis of Rice (1897) and Cornman (1902). *ITL: Review of Applied Linguistics* 91–92, 1–48.

Krashen, S. and Terrell, T. (1983) *The Natural Approach.* Oxford: Pergamon.

Kuhl, P.K. (1998) The development of speech and language. In T.J. Carew, R. Menzel and C.J. Shatz (eds) *Mechanistic Relationships between Development and Learning* (pp. 53–73). New York: Wiley.

Kuhl, P.K., Williams, K.A., Lacerda, F., Stevens, K.N. and Lindblom, B. (1992) Linguistic experience alters phonetic perception in infants by 6 months of age. *Science* 277, 606–608.

Ladefoged, P. (1990) Some reflections on the IPA. *Journal of Phonetics* 18, 335–346.

Ladefoged, P. (2005) *Vowels and Consonants.* Malden, MA: Blackwell.

Lado, R. (1957) *Linguistics Across Cultures*. Ann Arbor, MI: University of Michigan Press.

Lado, R. (1964) *Language Teaching: A Scientific Approach*. New York: McGraw-Hill.

Lambacher, S.G., Martens, W.L, Kakehi, K., Marasinghe, C.A and Molholt, G. (2005) The effects of identification training on the identification and production of American English vowels by native speakers of Japanese. *Applied Psycholinguistics* 26, 227–247.

Landau, B. and Gleitman, L.R. (1985) *Language and Experience: Evidence from the Blind Child*. Cambridge, MA: Harvard University Press.

Largo, R.H. (2001) *Babyjahre. Die Frühkindliche Entwicklung aus Biologischer Sicht. Aktualisierte Neuausgabe*. München: Piper.

Larsen-Freeman, D. (1976) An explanation for the morpheme acquisition order of second language learners. *Language Learning* 26, 125–135.

Larsen-Freeman, D. (1997) Chaos/complexity science and second language acquisition. *Applied Linguistics* 18 (2), 141–165.

Lee, J. (2004) L1 transfer in L2 variation: The case of "disappearing /w/" in the English of Korean learners. *University of Wisconsin Linguistics Students Organization Working Papers in Linguistics* 4 (1), 53–64. On WWW at http://ling. wisc.edu/lso/wpl-main.html. Accessed 17.7.07.

Lee, J.F. and VanPatten, B. (2003) *Making Communicative Language Teaching Happen* (2nd edn). New York: McGraw-Hill.

Lee, S.Y. (2005) Facilitating and inhibiting factors in English as a foreign language writing performance. A model test with structural equation modeling. *Language Learning* 55 (2), 335–374.

Lenneberg, E. (1962) Understanding language without ability to speak: A case report. *Journal of Abnormal and Social Psychology* 65 (6), 419–425.

Lenneberg, E. (1967) *The Biological Foundations of Language*. New York: Wiley.

Lenzing, A. (2004) Analyse von Lehrwerken für den Englischunterricht in der Grundschule. FMF-SH Mitteilungsblatt, August 2004, 36–41.

Lewin, R. (1999) *Complexity: Life at the Edge of Chaos*. Chicago: University of Chicago Press.

Lewis, M. (1993) *The Lexical Approach. The State of ELT and a Way Forward*. Hove: Language Teaching Publications.

Lightbown, P.M. (1985) Great expectations. Second language acquisition research and classroom teaching. *Applied Linguistics* 6, 173–189.

Lightbown, P.M. (1992) Can they do it themselves? A comprehension-based ESL course for young children. In R. Courchêne, J. St. John, C. Thérien and J. Glidden (eds) *Comprehension-based Language Teaching: Current Trends* (pp. 353–370). Ottawa: University of Ottawa Press.

Lightbown, P.M. (2000) Anniversary article: Classroom SLA research and second language teaching. *Applied Linguistics* 21, 431–462.

Lightbown, P.M. (2004) Commentary: What to teach? How to teach? In B. VanPatten (ed.) *Processing Instruction: Theory, Research and Commentary* (pp. 65–78). Mahwah, NJ: Erlbaum.

Lightbown, P.M. and Spada, N. (2006) *How Languages are Learned* (3rd edn). Oxford: Oxford University Press.

Lightbown, P.M. and White, L. (1987) The influence of linguistic theories on language acquisition research: Description and explanation. *Language Learning* 37, 483–510.

Lightbown, P.M., Halter, R.H., White, J.L. and Horst, M. (2002) Comprehension-based learning: The limits of 'Do It Yourself'. *Canadian Modern Language Review* 58 (3), 427–464.

Lindblom, B. (1963) Spectrographic study of vowel reduction. *Journal of the Acoustical Society of America* 35, 1773–1781.

Lindsay, P. and Norman, D. (1972) *Human Information Processing*. New York: Academic Press.

Linell, P. (1982) *The Written Language Bias in Linguistics*. Sweden: University of Linkoeping.

Little, D., Devitt, S. and Singleton, D. (1994) The commuicative approach and authentic texts. In A. Swarbrick (ed.) *Teaching Modern Languages* (pp. 43–47). Routledge: London.

Livbjerg, I. and Mees, I.M. (2000) *Practical English Phonetics. Ny Kontrastiv Fonetik*. Copenhagen: Schønberg.

Long, M. (1990) Maturational constraints on language development. *Studies in Second Language Acquisition* 12, 251–285.

Long, M. (1991) Focus on form as a design feature in language teaching methodology. In K. De Bot, R. Ginsberg and C. Kramsch (eds) *Foreign Language Research in Cross-Cultural Perspective* (pp. 39–52). Amsterdam: John Benjamins.

Long, M. (1996) The role of linguistic environment in second language acquisition. In W. Ritchie and T. Bhatia (eds) *Handbook of Second Language Acquisition* (pp. 413–468). New York: Academic Press.

Long, M. (2005) Problems with supposed counter-evidence to the Critical Period Hypothesis. *International Review of Applied Linguistics* 43, 287–317.

Lust, B. and Foley, C. (2004) *First Language Acquisition: The Essential Readings*. Oxford: Blackwell.

Lyster, R. (1987) Speaking immersion. *Canadian Modern Language Review* 43, 701–717.

Lyster, R. and Ranta, L. (1997) Corrective feedback and learner uptake: Negotiation of form in communicative classrooms. *Studies in Second Language Acquisition* 19, 37–66.

MacDonald, M., Badger, R. and White, G. (2001) Changing values: What use are theories of language learning and teaching? *Teaching and Teacher Education* 17, 949–963.

MacIntyre, P., Baker, S., Clément, R. and Donovan, L. (2003) Sex and age effects on willingness to communicate, anxiety, perceived competence, and L2 motivation among junior high school French immersion students. In Z. Dörnyei (ed.) *Attitudes, Orientations and Motivations in Language Learning* (pp. 13–165). Malden, MA: Blackwell.

MacIntyre, P., Dörnyei, Z., Clément, R. and Noels, K. (1998) Conceptualizing willingness to communicate in a L2: A situational model of L2 confidence and affiliation. *Modern Language Journal* 82, 545–562.

MacKay, I., Flege, J.E. and Imai, S. (2006) Evaluating the effects of chronological age and sentence duration on degree of perceived foreign accent. *Applied Psycholinguistics* 27, 157–183.

MacKay, I., Flege, J.E., Piske, T. and Schirru, C. (2001a) Category restructuring during second-language (L2) speech acquisition. *Journal of the Acoustical Society of America* 110, 516–528.

MacKay, I., Meador, D. and Flege, J.E. (2001b) The identification of English consonants by native speakers of Italian. *Phonetica* 58, 103–125.

MacWhinney, B. (2002) Language emergence. In P. Burmeister, T. Piske and A. Rohde (eds) *An Integrated View of Language Development: Papers in Honor of Henning Wode* (pp. 17–42). Trier: Wissenschaftlicher Verlag Trier.

Major, R. (1993) Sociolinguistic factors in loss and acquisition of phonology. In K. Hyltenstam and Å. Viberg (eds) *Progression and Regression in Language:*

Sociocultural, Neuropsychological and Linguistic Perspectives (pp. 463–478). Cambridge: Cambridge University Press.

Marchman, V.A. and Bates, E. (1994) Continuity in lexical and morphological development: a test of the critical mass hypothesis. *Journal of Child Language* 21, 339–366.

Marcus, G. (1993) Negative evidence in language acquisition. *Cognition* 46, 53–85.

Marler, P. (2004) Science and birdsong: The good old days. In P. Marler and H. Slabbekoorn (eds) *Nature's Music: The Science of Birdsong* (pp. 1–38). New York: Elsevier.

Marler, P. (1970) Birdsong and speech development. Could there be parallels? *American Scientist* 58, 669–673.

Marx, H. and Jungman, T. (2000) Abhängigkeit der Entwicklung des Leseverstehens vom Hörverstehen und grundlegenden Lesefertigkeiten im Grundschulalter. Eine Prüfung des Simple View of Reading-Ansatzes. *Zeitschrift für Entwicklungspsychologie und Pädagogische Psychologie* 32 (2), 81–93.

Mason, B. (2004) The effect of adding supplementary writing to an extensive reading program. *International Journal of Foreign Language Teaching*, Winter, 2–16.

Mason, B. (2006) Free voluntary reading and autonomy in second language acquisition: Improving TOEFL scores from reading alone. *International Journal of Foreign Language Teaching* 2 (1), 2–5.

Matthews, J. and Brown, C. (2004) When intake exceeds input: Language specific perceptual illusions induced by L1 prosodic constraints. *International Journal of Bilingualism* 8, 5–28.

Maule, D. (1991) *The Naked Verb. The Meaning of the English Verb Tenses.* London: Macmillan.

Mayer, M. (1969) *Frog, Where Are You?* New York: Pied Piper.

McAllister, R. (1995) Perceptual foreign accent and L2 production. In K. Elenius and P. Branderud (eds) *Proceedings of the XIIIth International Congress of Phonetic Sciences* (Vol. 4) (pp. 570–573). Stockholm: KTH and Stockholm University.

McCandless, P. and Winitz, H. (1986) Test of pronunciation following one year of comprehension instruction in college German. *Modern Language Journal* 70 (4), 355–362.

McClelland, J. and Rumelhart, D. (1985) Distributed memory and the representation of general and specific information. *Journal of Experimental Psychology: General* 114 (2), 159–188.

McDonough, K. (2005) Identifying the impact of negative feedback and learners' responses on ESL question development. *Studies in Second Language Acquisition* 27 (1), 79–103.

McGraw, K.O., Tew, M.D. and Williams, J.E. (2000) The integrity of web-delivered experiments: Can you trust the data? *Psychological Science* 11, 508–512.

McKenna, T. (1991) *The Archaic Revival.* New York: HarperCollins.

McQueen, J.M. and Cutler, A. (2001) Spoken word access processes: An introduction. *Language and Cognitive Processes* 16 (5), 469–490.

Mees, I.M. and Collins, B. (1996) *Sound English. A Practical Pronunciation Guide for Speakers of Danish.* Copenhagen: Schønberg.

Meng, Z. (1998) Duiwai hanyu yuyin jiaoxue zhong shiyong 'hanyu pinyin fang'an' de jige wenti [Some issues related to using hanyu pinyin in the teaching of Chinese as a Foreign Language]. In J. Chao and Z. Meng (eds) *Yuyin yanjiu yu duiwai hanyu jiaoxue* (pp. 322–329). Beijing: Beijing Yuyan Wenhua Daxue Chubanshe.

Meyer, R.J. (2002) *Phonics Exposed: Understanding and Resisting Systematic Direct Intense Phonics Instruction.* Mahwah, NJ: Lawrence Erlbaum.

Missaglia, F. (1999) Contrastive prosody in SLA – An empirical study with adult Italian learners of German. *Proceedings of the 14th International Congress of Phonetic Sciences* (Vol. 1), 555–558.

Mitchell, R. and Myles, F. (2004) *Second Language Learning Theories* (2nd edn). London: Arnold.

Moneta, G. (1996) The effect of perceived challenges and skills on the quality of subjective experience. *Journal of Personality* 64, 275–310.

Moulton, W. (1962) *The Sounds of English and German.* Chicago: University of Chicago Press.

Moyer, A. (1999) Ultimate attainment in L2 phonology: The critical factors of age, motivation and instruction. *Studies in Second Language Acquisition* 21, 81–108.

Moyer, A. (2004a) *Age, Accent and Experience in Second Language Acquisition. An Integrated Approach to Critical Period Inquiry.* Clevedon: Multilingual Matters.

Moyer, A. (2004b) Accounting for context and experience in German (L2) language acquisition: A critical review of the research. *Journal of Multilingual and Multicultural Development* 25, 41–61.

Moyer, A. (2005) Formal and informal experiential realms in German as a foreign language: A preliminary investigation. *Foreign Language Annals* 28, 377–387.

Moyer, A. (2006) Language contact and confidence in L2 listening comprehension: A pilot study of advanced learners of German. *Foreign Language Annals* 39, 255–275.

Moyer, A. (2007) Empirical considerations on the age factor in L2 phonology. *Issues in Applied Linguistics* 15, 109–127.

Moyer, A. (2008) An investigation of experience in L2 phonology: Does quality matter more than quantity? Unpublished manuscript, University of Maryland at College Park.

Munby, J. (1978) *Communicative Syllabus Design.* Cambridge: Cambridge University Press.

Muneaux, M. and Ziegler, J.C. (2004) Locus of orthographic effects in spoken word recognition: Novel insights from the neighbour generation task. *Language and Cognitive Processes* 19, 641–660.

Munro, M. (1993) Production of English vowels by native speakers of Arabic: Acoustic measurements and accentedness ratings. *Language and Speech* 36, 39–66.

Munro, M. and Mann, V. (2005) Age of immersion as predictor of foreign accent. *Applied Psycholinguistics* 26, 311–341.

Myles, F. (2004) From data to theory: The over-representation of linguistic knowledge in SLA. *Transactions of the Philological Society* 102, 139–168.

Nagy, W. and Herman, P. (1987) Breadth and depth of vocabulary knowledge: Implications for acquisition and instruction. In M. McKeown and M. Curtiss (eds) *The Nature of Vocabulary Acquisition* (pp. 19–35). Hillsdale, NJ: Lawrence Erlbaum.

Nation, P. (2001) *Learning Vocabulary in Another Language.* Cambridge: Cambridge University Press.

National Institute of Child Health and Human Development (NICHD) (2000) Report of the National Reading Panel. (NIH Publication No. 00–4754). Washington, DC: U.S. Government Printing Office.

Nearey, T.M. and Assmann, P.F. (1986) Modeling the role of spectral change in vowel identification. *Journal of the Acoustical Society of America* 80, 1297–1308.

Newmeyer, F. (1982) On the applicability of transformational generative grammar. *Applied Linguistics* 3, 89–120.

Newmeyer, F. and Weinberger, S. (1988) The ontogenesis of the field of second language learning research. In S. Flynn and W. O'Neil (eds) _Linguistic Theory in Second Language Acquisition_ (pp. 34–46). Dordrecht: Kluwer.

Newport, E., Gleitman, L. and Gleitman, H. (1977) Mother, I'd rather do it myself: some effects and non-effects of maternal speech style. In C. Snow and C. Ferguson (eds) _Talking to Children_ (pp. 109–149). Cambridge: Cambridge University Press.

Nicolis, G. and Prigogine, I. (1989) _Exploring Complexity. An Introduction._ New York: Freeman.

Nida, E.A. (1958) Some psychological problems in second language learning. _Language Learning_ 6, 1.

Nisbet, S. (1941) The scientific investigation of spelling instruction: Two preliminary investigations. _British Journal of Educational Psychology_ 11, 150.

Nizegorodcew, A. (2007) _Input for Instructed L2 Learners: The Relevance of Relevance._ Clevedon: Multilingual Matters.

Nobuyoshi, J. and Ellis, R. (1993) Focused communication tasks and second language acquisition. _ELT Journal_ 47, 203–210.

Nord, J.R. (1980) Developing listening fluency before speaking: An alternative paradigm. _System_ 8, 1–22.

Nord, J.R. (1981) Three steps leading to listening fluency: A beginning. In H. Winitz (ed.) _The Comprehension Approach to Foreign Language Instruction_ (pp. 69–100). Rowley, MA: Newbury House.

Nunan, D. (1998) Teaching grammar in context. _ELT Journal_ 52 (2), 101–109.

O'Grady, W. (2003) The radical middle: Nativism without universal grammar. In C.J. Doughty and M.H. Long (eds) _The Handbook of Second Language Acquisition_ (pp. 43–62). Oxford: Blackwell.

O'Grady, W., Lee, M. and Choo. M. (2003) A subject-object symmetry in the acquisition of relative clauses in Korean as a second language. _Studies in Second Language Acquisition_ 25, 433–448.

Ohde, R.N. and Sharf, D.J. (1975) Coarticulatory effects of voiced stops on the reduction of acoustic vowel targets. _Journal of the Acoustical Society of America_ 58, 923–927.

Okada, T. (2005) Spelling errors made by Japanese EFL writers: With reference to errors occurring at the word-initial and the word-final position. In V.J. Cook and B. Bassetti (eds) _Second Language Writing Systems_ (pp. 164–183). Clevedon: Multilingual Matters.

Oller, J. (2005) Common ground between form and content: The pragmatic solution to the bootstrapping problem. _Modern Language Journal_ 89 (1), 92–113.

Olson, L. and Samuels, S. (1982) The relationship between age and accuracy of foreign language pronunciation. In S. Krashen, R. Scarcella and M. Long (eds) _Child-Adult Differences in Second Language Acquisition_ (pp. 67–75). Rowley, MA: Newbury House.

Ortega, L. (2007) Second language learning explained? SLA across nine contemporary theories. In B. VanPatten and J. Williams (eds) _Theories in Second Language Acquisition: An Introduction_ (pp. 225–250). Mahwah, NJ: Erlbaum.

Oxford, R.L. (1990) _Language Learning Strategies: What Every Teacher should Know._ New York: Newbury House.

Oyama, S. (1976) A sensitive period for the acquisition of a nonnative phonological system. _Journal of Psycholinguistic Research_ 5, 261–283.

Palmer, H. (1917) _The Scientific Study and Teaching of Languages._ Yonkers-on-Hudson: World Book Company.

Patkowski, M. (1980) The sensitive period for the acquisition of syntax in a second language. _Language Learning_ 30, 449–472.

Pearlmutter, N.J., Garnsey, S.M. and Bock, K. (1999) Agreement processes in sentence comprehension. *Journal of Memory and Language* 41, 427–456.

Peltzer-Karpf, A. and Zangl, R. (1998) *Die Dynamik des frühen Fremdsprachenerwerbs.* Tübingen: Narr.

Pennington, M.C. (1996) Cross-language effects in biliteracy. *Language and Education* 10 (4), 254–272.

Petit, J. (2002) Acquisition strategies of German in Alsatian immersion classrooms. In P. Burmeister, T. Piske and A. Rohde (eds) *An Integrated View of Language Development: Papers in Honor of Henning Wode* (pp. 433–448). Trier: Wissenschaftlicher Verlag Trier.

Petrinovich, L. and Baptista, L. (1987) Song development of the white-crowned sparrow: Modification of learned song. *Animal Behaviour* 35, 961–974.

Pfaff, C. (1992) The issue of grammaticalization in early German second language. *Studies in Second Language Acquisition* 14, 273–296.

Pfandl-Buchegger, I. (2005) Rezension: H. Eckert and W. Barry, The Phonetics and Phonology of English Pronunciation. A Coursebook with CD-ROM and B. Collins and I.M. Mees, Practical Phonetics and Phonology. A Resource Book for Students. *Arbeiten aus Anglistik and Amerikanistik* 30, 267–271.

Piaget, J. (1970) *Epistémologie Génétique.* Paris: Presses Universitaires de France.

Piatelli-Palmarini, M. (ed.) (1979) *Language and Learning: The Debate between Jean Piaget and Noam Chomsky.* Cambridge, MA: Harvard University Press.

Pica, T. (1988) Interactive adjustments as an outcome of NS-NNS negotiated interaction. *Language Learning* 38, 45–73.

Pica, T. (1994) Research on negotiation: What does it reveal about second-language learning conditions, processes and outcomes? *Language Learning* 44, 493–527.

Pica, T. (2003) Second language acquisition research and applied linguistics. *Working Papers in Educational Linguistics* 18, 1–26.

Pica, T., Doughty, C. and Young, R. (1986) Making input comprehensible: Do interactional modifications help? *ITL, Review of Applied Linguistics* 72, 1–25.

Pickering, M.J., Branigan, H.P., Cleland, A.A. and Stewart, A.J. (2000) Activation of syntactic information during language production. *Journal of Psycholinguistic Research* 29, 205–216.

Pienemann, M. (1998) *Language Processing and Second Language Development: Processability Theory.* Amsterdam: John Benjamins.

Pienemann, M. (2006) Was in den Köpfen von Kindern vor sich geht. In M. Pienemann, J-U. Keßler, and E. Roos (eds) *Zweitsprachenerwerb in der Grundschule* (pp. 33–63). Paderborn: UTB.

Pienemann, M., Keßler, J-U., Roos, E. (eds) (2006) *Englischerwerb in der Grundschule.* Paderborn: Schöningh.

Piller, I. (2002) Passing for a native speaker: Identity and success in second language learning. *Journal of Sociolinguistics* 6, 179–206.

Pinker, S. (1984) *Language Learnability and Language Development.* Cambridge, MA: Harvard University Press.

Pinker, S. (2003) The semantic bootstrapping hypothesis. In B.C. Lust and C. Foley (eds) *First Language Acquisition: The Essential Readings.* Oxford: Blackwell.

Piske, T. (2007) Implications of James E. Flege's research for the foreign language classroom. In O-S. Bohn and M.J. Munro (eds) *Language Experience in Second Language Speech Learning. In Honor of James Emil Flege* (pp. 301–314). Amsterdam: John Benjamins.

Piske, T. (2008) Phonetic awareness, phonetic sensitivity and the second language learner. In: J. Cenoz and N.H. Hornberger (eds) *Encyclopedia of Language and Education* (2nd edn), *Vol. 6: Knowledge about Language* (pp. 155–166). Berlin: Springer.

Piske, T., MacKay, I. and Flege, J.E. (2001) Factors affecting degree of foreign accent in an L2: A review. *Journal of Phonetics* 29, 191–215.

Piske, T., Flege, J.E., MacKay, I. and Meador, D. (2002) The production of English vowels by fluent early and late Italian-English bilinguals. *Phonetica* 59, 49–71.

Pöppel, E. (1985) *Grenzen des Bewußtseins*. Stuttgart: Deutsche Verlags-Anstalt.

Postovsky, V. (1970) The effects of a delay in oral practice at the beginning of second language teaching. Unpublished PhD dissertation, University of California at Berkeley.

Postovsky, V. (1977) Why not start speaking later? In M. Burt, H. Dulay and M. Finocchiaro (eds) *Viewpoints on English as a Second Language* (pp. 17–26). New York: Regents.

Postovsky, V. (1981) The priority of aural comprehension in the language acquisition process. In H. Winitz (ed.) *The Comprehension Approach to Foreign Language Instruction* (pp. 170–186) Rowley, MA: Newbury House.

Postovsky, V. (1982) Delayed Oral Practice. In R. Blair (ed.) *Innovative Approaches to Language Teaching* (pp. 67–76). Rowley, MA: Newbury House.

Prigogine, I. (1996) *The End of Certainty. Time, Chaos and the New Laws of Nature.* New York: Free Press.

Purcell, E. and Suter, R. (1980) Predictors of pronunciation accuracy: A re-examination. *Language Learning* 30, 271–287.

Pytte, C. and Suthers, R. (2000) Sensitive period for sensorimotor integration during vocal motor learning. *Journal of Neurobiology* 42, 172–189.

Quirk, R., Greenbaum, S., Leech, G. and Svartik, J. (1985) *A Grammar of Contemporary English.* London: Longman.

Rast, R. (2008) *Foreign Language Input: Initial Processing.* Clevedon: Multilingual Matters.

Rice, J. (1897) The futility of the spelling grind. *Forum* 23, 163–172, 409–419.

Richards, J.C. (2006) *Person to Person: Communicative Speaking and Listening Skills* (3rd edn). Oxford: Oxford University Press.

Rischel, J. (1968) Notes on the Danish vowel pattern. *Annual Report of the Institute of Phonetics, University of Copenhagen* 3, 177–205.

Robinson, B. and Mervis, C. (1998) Disentangling early language development: Modeling lexical and grammatical acquisition using and extension of case-study methodology. *Developmental Psychology* 34 (2), 363–375.

Robison, R.E. (1990) The primacy of aspect: Aspectual marking in English interlanguage. *Studies in Second Language Acquisition* 12, 315–330.

Robison, R.E. (1995) The aspect hypothesis revisited: A cross-sectional study of tense and aspect marking in interlanguage. *Applied Linguistics* 16, 344–370.

Rochet, B.L. (1995) Perception and production of second-language speech sounds by adults. In W. Strange (ed.) *Speech Perception and Linguistic Experience: Issues in Cross-Language Research* (pp. 379–410). Baltimore, ML: York Press.

Rohde, A. (1996) The aspect hypothesis and emergence of tense distinctions in naturalistic L2 acquisition. *Linguistics* 34, 1115–1137.

Rohde, A. (1997) *Verbflexion und Verbsemantik im natürlichen L2-Erwerb.* Tübingen: Narr.

Rost, M. (1990) *Listening in Language Learning.* London: Longman.

Roth, G. (2001) *Fühlen, Denken, Handeln. Wie das Gehirn unser Verhalten Steuert.* Frankfurt: Suhrkamp.

Rumelhart, D.E. and McClelland, J.L. (1986) On learning the past tense of English verbs. In J.L. McClelland and D.E. Rumelhart (eds) *Parallel Distributed Processing: Explorations in the Microstructure of Cognition. Volume 2: Psychological and Biological Models* (pp. 216–71). Cambridge, MA: MIT Press.

Sagarra, N. and Alba, M. (2006) The key is in the keyword: L2 vocabulary learning methods with beginning learners of Spanish. *The Modern Language Journal* 90 (2), 228–243.

Sakui, K. (2004) Wearing two pairs of shoes: Language teaching in Japan. *ELT Journal* 58 (2), 155–163.

Sakui, K. and Gaies, S.J. (1999) Investigating Japanese learners' beliefs about language learning. *System* 27, 473–492.

Salaberry, M.R. (1997) The role of input and output practice in second language acquisition. *Canadian Modern Language Review* 53, 422–451.

Salaberry, M.R. (1998) On input processing, true language competence, and pedagogical bandwagons: A reply to Sanz and VanPatten. *Canadian Modern Language Review* 54, 274–285.

Salaberry, R. and Shirai, Y. (2002) L2 acquisition of tense-aspect morphology. In R. Salaberry and Y. Shirai (eds) *The L2 Acquisition of Tense-Aspect Morphology* (pp. 1–20). Amsterdam: John Benjamins.

Sanz, C. and Morgan-Short, K. (2004) Positive evidence versus explicit rule presentation and explicit negative feedback: A computer assisted study. *Language Learning* 54, 35–78.

Sanz, C. and VanPatten, B. (1998) On input processing, processing instruction, and the nature of replication tasks: A response to M.R. Salaberry. *The Canadian Modern Language Review* 54, 263–273.

Sato, K. and Kleinsasser, R.C. (1999) Communicative language teaching (CLT): Practical understandings. *The Modern Language Journal* 83 (4), 494–517.

Savignon, S.J. (1997) *Communicative Competence: Theory and Classroom Practice* (2nd edn). New York: McGraw-Hill.

Savignon, S.J. (2003) Teaching English as communication: A global perspective. *World Englishes* 22 (1), 55–66.

Savignon, S.J. and Wang, C. (2003) Communicative language teaching in EFL contexts: Learner attitudes and perceptions. *International Review of Applied Linguistics* 41, 223–249.

Scherer, G. and Wollmann, A. (1986) *Englische Phonetik und Phonologie*. Berlin: Schmidt.

Schmidt, R.W. (1990) The role of consciousness in second language learning. *Applied Linguistics* 11, 129–158.

Schmidt, R.W. (1994a) Deconstructing consciousness in search of useful definitions for applied linguistics. *AILA Review* 11, 11–26.

Schmidt, R.W. (1994b) Implicit learning and the cognitive unconscious: Of artificial grammars and SLA. In N.C. Ellis (ed.) *Implicit and Explicit Learning of Languages* (pp. 165–209). London: Academic Press.

Schmidt, R.W. (1995) Consciousness and foreign language learning: A tutorial on the role of attention and awareness in learning. In R.W. Schmidt (ed.) *Attention and Awareness in Foreign Language Learning* (pp. 1–48). Honolulu: Second Language Teaching and Curriculum Center, University of Hawai'i.

Schmidt, W.C. (2001) Presentation accuracy of Web animation methods. *Behavior Research Methods, Instruments, and Computers* 33, 187–200.

Schröder, A. (1979) Aussprachefehler bei Sextanern im Englisch-Anfangsunterricht im Lichte des natürlichen L2-Erwerbs. *Arbeitspapiere zum Spracherwerb* 23. Kiel: English Department, Kiel University.

Schröder, K., Harsch, C. and Nold, G. (2006) DESI – Die sprachpraktischen Kompetenzen unserer Schülerinnen und Schüler im Bereich Englisch. Zentrale Befunde. *Neusprachliche Mitteilungen* 59 (3), 11–32.

Schulz von Thun, F. (2005) *Miteinander reden* (Vol. 1) (44th edn). Störungen und Klärungen/Reinbeck: Rowohlt.

Schumann, J. (1978) *The Pidginization Process. A Model for Second Language Acquisition.* Rowley, MA: Newbury House.

Schwab, G. (2002) Die Vielschichtigkeit des Lernprozesses beim frühen Fremdsprachenunterricht der Grundschule. Unpublished MA dissertation, Pädagogische Hochschule Ludwigsburg.

Schwartz, B.D. (1993) On explicit and negative data effecting and affecting competence and linguistic behavior. *Studies in Second Language Acquisition* 15, 147–163.

Schwartz, B.D. (1999) Let's make up your mind. 'Special nativist' perspectives on language, modularity of mind, and nonnative language acquisition. *Studies in Second Language Acquisition* 21 (4), 635–655.

Schwartz, B.D. and Gubala-Ryzak, M. (1992) Learnability and grammar reorganization in L2A: Against negative evidence causing the unlearning of verb movement. *Second Language Research* 8, 1–38.

Schwarz, M. (1996) *Einführung in die Kognitive Linguistik* (2nd edn). Tübingen: Francke.

Schweyer, D.H. (1996) *Consonant-to-Vowel Coarticulatory Effects in English and French.* Ann Arbor, MI: UMI Dissertation Services.

Scovel, T. (1988) *A Time to Speak. A Psycholinguistic Inquiry into the Critical Period for Human Speech.* Cambridge, MA: Newbury House.

Scovel, T. (2000) A critical review of critical period research. *Annual Review of Applied Lingustistics* 20, 213–223.

Scrivener, J. (2005) *Learning Teaching* (2nd edn). Oxford: Macmillan.

Sebastián-Gallés, N. and Soto-Faraco, S. (1999) Online processing of native and non-native phonemic contrasts in early bilinguals. *Cognition* 72, 111–123.

Segalowitz, N. (2003) Automaticity and second languages. In C.J. Doughty and M.H. Long (eds) *The Handbook of Second Language Acquisition* (pp. 382–408). Malden, MA: Blackwell.

Segalowitz, N. and Hulstijn, J.H. (2005) Automaticity in second language learning. In J.F. Kroll and A.M.B. De Groot (eds) *Handbook of Bilingualism: Psycholinguistic Approaches* (pp. 371–388). Oxford: Oxford University Press.

Selinker, L. (1972) Interlanguage. *International Review of Applied Linguistics* 3, 209–231.

Senghas, A., Kita, S. and Özyürek, A. (2004) Children creating core properties of language: Evidence from an emerging sign language in Nicaragua. *Science* 305, 1779–1782.

Sharwood Smith, M. (1993) Input enhancement in instructed SLA: Theoretical bases. *Studies in Second Language Acquisition* 15, 165–179.

Sharwood Smith, M. (1994a) *Second Language Learning.* London: Longman.

Sharwood Smith, M. (1994b) The unruly world of language. In N. Ellis (ed.) *Implicit and Explicit Learning of Languages* (pp. 33–43). London: Academic Press.

Sharwood Smith, M. and Truscott, J. (2005) Full Transfer Full Access. A processing-oriented approach. In S. Unsworth, T. Parodi, A. Sorace and M. Young-Scholten (eds) *Paths of Development in First and Second Language Acquisition* (pp. 201–216). Amsterdam: John Benjamins.

Shehadeh, A. (2001) Self- and other-initiated modified output during task-based interaction. *TESOL Quarterly* 35 (3), 433–457.

Shehadeh, A. (2002) Comprehensible output, from occurrence to acquisition: An agenda for acquisitional research. *Language Learning* 52 (3), 597–647.

Shirai, Y. and Kurono, A. (1998) The acquisition of tense-aspect marking in Japanese as a second language. *Language Learning* 48, 245–279.

Sieg, A. (2004) Die Entwicklung der Phonologie von der dritten zur vierten Klasse des ersten immersiv auf Englisch unterrichteten Jahrgangs der Claus-Rixen-Schule. MA dissertation, Kiel University.

Silver, R.E. (2000) Input, output, and negotiation: Conditions for second language development. In B. Swierzbin, F. Morris, M.E. Anderson, C.A. Klee and E. Tarone (eds) *Social and Cognitive Factors in Second Language Acquisition* (pp. 345–371). Somerville, MA: Cascadilla Press.

Singer, W. (1990) Ontogenetic self-organization and learning. In J.L. McGaugh, N.M. Weinberger and G. Lynch (eds) *Brain Organization and Memory, Cells, Systems, and Circuits* (pp. 211–233). New York: Oxford University Press.

Singer, W. (2001) Was kann ein Mensch wann lernen? Vortrag, Werkstattgespräch Initiative McKinsey, Frankfurt, 12 June 2001. On WWW at http://www.mpih-frankfurt.mpg.de/global/Np/Pubs/mckinsey.pdf. Accessed 23.1.08.

Singleton, D. (2001) Age and second language acquisition. *Annual Review of Applied Linguistics* 21, 77–89.

Skinner, B. (1957) *Verbal Behaviour*. New York: Appleton-Century-Crofts.

Smith, F. (1988) *Joining the Literacy Club*. Portsmouth, NH: Heinemann.

Smith, F. (1994) *Writing and the Writer* (2nd edn). Hillsdale, NJ: Lawrence Erlbaum.

Smith, F. (2004) *Understanding Reading*. Mahwah, NJ: Lawrence Erlbaum.

Smith, K. (2006) A comparison of "pure" extensive reading with intensive reading and extensive reading with supplementary activities. *International Journal of Foreign Language Teaching* 2 (2), 12–15.

Smith, K., Kirby, S. and Brighton, H. (2003) Iterated learning: A framework for the emergence of language. *Artificial Life* 9 (4), 371–386.

Smith, N. and Tsimpli, I-M. (1995) *The Mind of a Savant*. Oxford: Blackwell.

Smith, R. and Supanich, G. (1984) *The Vocabulary Scores of Company Presidents*. Chicago: Johnson O'Conner Research Foundation Technical Report 1984–1.

Snow, C. (1999) Social perspectives on the emergence of language. In B. MacWhinney (ed.) *The Emergence of Language* (pp. 257–276). Mahwah, NJ: Lawrence Erlbaum.

Snow, C.E. and Hoefnagel-Höhle, M. (1978) The critical period for language acquisition: Evidence from second language learning. *Child Development* 49, 1114–1128.

Sorace, A. (2000) Syntactic optionality in non-native grammars. *Second Language Research* 16, 93–102.

Speck, B.P. (2001) Markedness and naturalness in the acquisition of phonology. In C. Munoz and L. Celaya (eds) *Trabajos en Lingüística Aplicada* (pp. 179–185). Barcelona: Universibook.

Spitzer, M. (2000) *Geist im Netz. Modelle für Lernen, Denken und Handeln*. Heidelberg: Spektrum.

Spitzer, M. (2002) *Lernen. Gehirnforschung und die Schule des Lebens*. Heidelberg: Spektrum.

Spitzer, M. (2004) *Selbstbestimmen. Gehirnforschung und die Frage: Was sollen wir tun?* Heidelberg: Spektrum.

Spolsky, B. (1970) Linguistics and language pedagogy – applications or implications? In J. Alatis (ed.) *Report of the 20th Annual Round Table Meeting on Linguistics and Language Sciences* (pp. 143–155). Washington, DC: Georgetown University.

Sprang, K. (2006) Can monolingualism be cured? In E.M. Rickerson and B. Hilton (eds) *The 5-Minute Linguist: Bite-Sized Essays on Language and Languages* (pp. 128–131). London: Equinox.

Steele, J. (2005) Assessing the role of orthographic versus uniquely auditory input in acquiring new L2 segments. Paper presented at *7èmes Journées Internationales du Réseau Français de Phonologie (RFP2005)*, Aix-en-Provence, 2–4 June.

Steinlen, A.K. (2005) *The Influence of Consonants on Native and Non-native Vowel Production. A Cross-Linguistic Study*. Tübingen: Narr.

Steinlen, A.K. and Bohn, O-S. (2002) How phonetic context affects cross-language comparisons of vowels and L2 production accuracy. In J. Leather and A. James (eds) *New Sounds 2000. Proceedings of the 4th International Symposium on the Acquisition of Second-Language Speech* (pp. 325–334). Amsterdam: Amsterdam University Press.

Stern, E. (2002) Wie abstrakt lernt das Grundschulkind? Neuere Ergebnisse der entwicklungspsychologischen Forschung. In H. Petillon (ed.) *Handbuch Grundschulforschung. Bd 5: Individuelles und soziales Lernen* (pp. 27–42). Leverkusen: Leske and Budrich.

Stevens, K.N. and House, A.S. (1963) Perturbation of vowel articulations by consonantal context: An acoustical study. *Journal of the Acoustical Society of America* 6, 111–128.

Strange, W. (1992) Learning non-native phoneme contrasts: Interactions among subject, stimulus, and task variables. In Y. Tohkura, E. Vatikiotis-Bateson and Y. Sagisaka (eds) *Speech Perception, Production and Linguistic Structure* (pp. 197–219). Tokyo: Ohmsha.

Strange, W. (2007) Cross-language phonetic similarity of vowels: Theoretical and methodological issues. In O-S. Bohn and M.J. Munro (eds) *The Role of Language Experience in Second-Language Speech Learning: In Honor of James Emil Flege* (pp. 35–55). Amsterdam: John Benjamins.

Strange, W. and Bohn, O-S. (1998) Dynamic specification of coarticulated German vowels: Perceptual and acoustical studies. *Journal of the Acoustical Society of America* 104, 488–504.

Strange, W., Bohn, O-S., Nishi, K. and Trent, S.A. (2005) Contextual variation in the acoustic and perceptual similarity of North German and American English vowels. *Journal of the Acoustical Society of America* 118, 1751–1762.

Strange, W., Bohn, O-S., Trent, S.A. and Nishi, K. (2004) Acoustic and perceptual similarity of North German and American English vowels. *Journal of the Acoustical Society of America* 115, 1791–1807.

Sumdangdej, S. (2007) Input and the acquisiton of suprasegmental phonology in English by Thai school children. Unpublished PhD thesis, Durham University.

Swain, M. (1985) Communicative competence: Some roles of comprehensible input and comprehensible output in its development. In S.M. Gass and C.G. Madden (eds) *Input in Second Language Acquisition* (pp. 235–253). Rowley, MA: Newbury House.

Swain, M. (1995) Three functions of output in second language learning. In G. Cook and B. Seidlhofer (eds) *Principle and Practice in Applied Linguistics: Studies in Honor of H.G. Widdowson* (pp. 125–144). Oxford: Oxford University Press.

Swain, M. and Lapkin, S. (1995) Problems in output and the cognitive processes they generate: A step towards second language learning. *Applied Linguistics* 16, 371–391.

Tahta, S., Wood, M. and Loewenthal, K. (1981) Foreign accents: Factors relating to transfer of accent from the first language to the second language. *Language and Speech* 24, 265–272.

Tarone, E. (1978) The phonology of interlanguage. In J.C. Richards (ed.) *Understanding Second and Foreign Language Learning* (pp. 15–33). Rowley, MA: Newbury House.

Tarone, E. and Bigelow, M. (2005) Impact of literacy on oral second language processing: Implications for SLA research. *Annual Review of Applied Linguistics* 25, 77–97.

Tesch, F. (1993) Der Erwerb morpho-syntaktischer Strukturen bei Fremdsprachenlernern. In C. Küper (ed.) *Deutsch als Fremdsprache* (pp. 55–80) *Arbeitspapiere zur Linguistik* 29. Berlin: Universitätsbibliothek.

Tesch, F. (2000) *Das englische Präsens in der gesprochenen Sprache: Tempus – Kookkurrenz – Signalgrammatik.* Augsburg: Wißner.

Teschner, R.V. and Whitney, M.S. (2004) *Pronouncing English: A Stress-Based Approach with CD-ROM*. Washington, DC: Georgetown University Press.

Thelen, E. and Smith, L.B. (1994) *A Dynamic Systems Approach to the Development of Cognition and Action*. Cambridge MA: MIT Press.

Thompson, I. (1987) Memory in language learning. In J. Rubin and A. Wenden (eds) *Learner Strategies in Language Learning* (pp. 43–56). London: Prentice Hall.

Thompson, I. (1991) Foreign accents revisited: The English pronunciation of Russian immigrants. *Language Learning* 41, 177–204.

Thornton, R. and MacDonald, M.C. (2003) Plausibility and grammatical agreement. *Journal of Memory and Language* 48, 740–759.

Tomasello, M. (1999) *The Cultural Origins of Human Cognition*. Cambridge, MA: Harvard University Press.

Tomasello, M. (2000) First steps towards a usage-based theory of language acquisition. *Cognitive Linguistics* 11 (1/2), 61–82.

Toth, P.D. (2000) The interaction of instruction and learner-internal factors in the acquisition of L2 morphosyntax. *Studies in Second Language Acquisition* 22, 169–208.

Towell, R. and Hawkins, R. (2004) Empirical evidence and theories of representation in current research into second language acquisition: Introduction. In R. Towell and R. Hawkins (eds) *Special Issue. Transactions of the Philological Society* 102, 131–137.

Tracy, R. (2000) Sprache und Sprachentwicklung: Was wird erworben? In H. Grimm (ed.) *Sprachentwicklung* (pp. 3–39). Göttingen: Hogrefe.

Trapp, N.L. and Bohn, O-S. (2002) Training Danish listeners to identify word-final /s/ and /z/: Generalisation of training and its effect on production accuracy. In J. Leather and A. James (eds) *New Sounds 2000. Proceedings of the 4th International Symposium on the Acquisition of Second-Language Speech* (pp. 343–350). Amsterdam: Amsterdam University Press.

Truscott, J. (1996) The case against grammar correction in L2 writing classes. *Language Learning* 46 (2), 327–369.

Truscott, J. (1998) Noticing in second language acquisition: A critical review. *Second Language Research* 14 (2), 103–135.

Tsui, A. (1996) Reticence and anxiety in second language learning. In K.M. Bailey and D. Nunan (eds) *Voices from the Language Classroom: Qualitative Research in Second Language Education* (pp. 145–167). Cambridge: Cambridge University Press.

Tyler, M.D. (2001) Resource consumption as a function of topic knowledge in non-native and native comprehension. *Language Learning* 51, 257–280.

Uber Grosse, C. (1991) The TESOL methods course. *TESOL Quarterly* 25, 29–49.

Vainikka, A. and Young-Scholten, M. (1994) Direct access to X'-Theory: Evidence from Korean and Turkish adults learning German. In T. Hoekstra and B.D. Schwartz (eds) *Language Acquisition Studies in Generative Grammar:* Amsterdam: John Benjamins.

Vainikka, A. and Young-Scholten, M. (1996) Gradual development of L2 phrase structure. *Second Language Research* 12, 7–39.

Vainikka, A. and Young-Scholten, M. (1998) Morphosyntactic triggers in adult SLA. In M-L. Beck (ed.) *Morphology and its Interfaces in Second Language Knowledge* (pp. 89–113). Amsterdam: John Benjamins.

Vainikka, A. and Young-Scholten, M. (2005) The roots of syntax and how they grow: Organic Grammar, the Basic Variety and Processability Theory. In T. Parodi, A. Sorace, S. Unsworth and M. Young-Scholten *Paths of Development* (pp. 77–106). Amsterdam: John Benjamins.

Van Boxtel, S., Bongaerts, T. and Coppen, P. (2003) Native-like attainment in L2 syntax. In S. Foster-Cohen and S. Doehler (eds) _Eurosla Yearbook. Volume 3_ (pp. 157–181). Amsterdam: John Benjamins.

Van Dijk, M. and Van Geert, P. (2005) Disentangling behavior in early child development: Interpretability of early child language and the problem of filler syllables and growing utterance length. _Infant Behavior and Development_ 28 (2), 99–117.

Van Ek, J. (1975) _The Threshold Level_. Strasbourg: Council of Europe.

Van Geert, P. (1991) A dynamic systems model of cognitive and language growth. _Psychological Review_ 98 (1), 3–53.

Van Geert, P. (1994) _Dynamic Systems of Development: Change between Complexity and Chaos_. New York: Harvester.

Van Geert, P. (1995) Dimensions of change: A semantic and mathematical analysis of learning and development. _Human Development_ 38, 322–331.

Van Geert, P. (1998) A dynamic systems model of basic developmental mechanisms: Piaget, Vygotsky and beyond. _Psychological Review_ 5, 634–677.

Van Geert, P. and Van Dijk, M. (2003) Ambiguity in child language, the problem of interobserver reliability in ambiguous observation data. _First Language_ 23 (3), 259–284.

Van Gelder, T. and Port, R. (1995) It's about time: An overview of the dynamical approach to cognition. In R. Port and T. Van Gelder (eds) _Mind as Motion: Exploration in the Dynamics of Cognition_ (pp. 1–45). Cambridge, MA: MIT Press.

VanPatten, B. (1987) On babies and bathwater: Input in foreign language learning. _The Modern Language Journal_ 71 (2), 156–164.

VanPatten, B. (1988) How juries get hung. Problems with evidence for a focus on form in teaching. _Language Learning_ 38, 243–260.

VanPatten, B. (1989) Can learners attend to form and content while processing input? _Hispania_ 72, 409–417.

VanPatten, B. (1993) Grammar instruction for the acquisition-rich classroom. _Foreign Language Annals_ 26, 433–450.

VanPatten, B. (1996) _Input Processing and Grammar Instruction: Theory and Research_. Norwood, NJ: Ablex.

VanPatten, B. (1998) Perceptions and perspectives of the term "communicative". _Hispania_ 81, 925–932.

VanPatten, B. (2002a) Processing instruction, prior awareness and the nature of second language acquisition: A (partial) response to Batstone. _Language Awareness_ 11 (4), 240–258.

VanPatten, B. (2002b) Processing instruction: An update. _Language Learning_ 52, 755–803.

VanPatten, B. (2004a) Input processing in SLA. In B. VanPatten (ed.) _Processing Instruction: Theory, Research, and Commentary_ (pp. 1–31). Mahwah, NJ: Lawrence Erlbaum.

VanPatten, B. (2004b) Several reflections on why there is good reason to continue researching the effects of processing instruction. In B. VanPatten (ed.) _Processing Instruction: Theory, Research, and Commentary_ (pp. 325–335). Mahwah, NJ: Lawrence Erlbaum.

VanPatten, B. (2007) Input processing in adult SLA. In B. VanPatten and J. Williams (eds) _Theories in SLA: An Introduction_. Mahwah, NJ: Lawrence Erlbaum.

VanPatten, B. and Cadierno, T. (1993) Explicit instruction and input processing. _Studies in Second Language Acquisition_ 15, 225–243.

VanPatten, B. and Fernández, C. (2004) The long-term effects of processing instruction. In B. VanPatten (ed.) _Processing Instruction: Theory, Research, and Commentary_ (pp. 273–289). Mahwah, NJ: Lawrence Erlbaum.

VanPatten, B. and Oikkenon, S. (1996) Explanation versus structured input in processing instruction. *Studies in Second Language Acquisition* 18, 495–510.

VanPatten, B. and Sanz, C. (1995) From input to output: Processing Instruction and communicative tasks. In F. Eckman, D. Highland, P.W. Lee, J. Mileham and R.R. Weber (eds) *Second Language Acquisition Theory and Pedagogy* (pp. 169–85). Mahwah, NJ: Lawrence Erlbaum.

VanPatten, B. and Williams, J. (2007) Early theories in second language acquisition. In B. VanPatten and J. Williams (eds) *Theories in Second Language Acquisition: An Introduction* (pp. 17–35). Mahwah, NJ: Erlbaum.

Vendler, Z. (1967) *Linguistics in Philosophy*. Ithaca: Cornell University Press.

Verspoor, M. and Winitz, H. (1997) Assessment of the lexical-input approach for intermediate language learners. *International Review of Applied Linguistics* 35 (1), 61–75.

Verspoor, M., de Bot, K. and Lowie, W. (2004) Dynamic Systems theory and variation: A case study in L2 writing. In H. Aertsen, M. Hannay and R. Lyall (eds) *Words in their Places. A Festschrift for J. Lachlan Mackenzie* (pp. 407–421). Amsterdam: Free University Press.

Vygotsky, L. (1978) *Mind and Society*. Cambridge, MA: Harvard University Press.

Weinberger, S.H. (1987) The influence of linguistic context on syllable simplification. In G. Ioup and S. Weinberger (eds) *Interlanguage Phonology*. Rowley, MA: Newbury House.

Weinberger, S.H. (2006) What causes foreign accents? In E.M. Rickerson and B. Hilton (eds) *The 5-Minute Linguist: Bite-Sized Essays on Language and Languages* (pp. 120–123). London: Equinox.

Wells, J.C. (2000) *Longman Pronunciation Dictionary*. Harlow: Pearson.

Wells, J. (1962) A study of the formants of the pure vowels of British English. Unpublished MA, University of London.

Wells, J. (1982) *Accents of English. Volumes 1–3*. Cambridge: Cambridge University Press.

Wenden, A.L. (1999) An introduction to *Metacognitive Knowledge and Beliefs in Language Learning*: Beyond the basics. *System* 27, 435–441.

Werker, J., Gilbert, J., Humphry, I. and Tees, R. (1981) Developmental aspects of cross-language speech perception. *Child Development* 52, 349–355.

Werker, J. and Tees, R.C. (1984) Cross-language speech perception: Evidence for perceptual reorganization during the first year of life. *Infant Behavior and Development* 7, 47–63.

Wesche, M. (1994) Input and interaction in second language acquisition. In C. Gallway and B. Richards (eds) *Input and Interaction in Language Acquisition* (pp. 219–249). Cambridge: Cambridge University Press.

Wesche, M. (2002) Early French Immersion: How has the original Canadian model stood the test of time? In P. Burmeister, T. Piske and A. Rohde (eds) *An Integrated View of Language Development: Papers in Honor of Henning Wode* (pp. 357–379). Trier: Wissenschaftlicher Verlag Trier.

West, M.J., King, A. and Goldstein, M. (2004) Singing, socializing, and the music effect. In P. Marler and H. Slabbekoorn (eds) *Nature's Music: The Science of Birdsong* (pp. 374–387). New York: Elsevier.

Weyerts, H., Penke, M., Münte, T.F., Heinze, H-J. and Clahsen, H. (2002) Word order in sentence processing: An experimental study of verb placement in German. *Journal of Psycholinguistic Research* 31, 211–268.

White, C. (1999) Expectations and emergent beliefs of self-instructed language learners. *System* 27, 443–457.

White, L. (1987) Against comprehensible input: The input hypothesis and the development of second language competence. *Applied Linguistics* 8, 95–110.

White, L. (1989) *Universal Grammar and Second Language Acquisition.* Amsterdam: John Benjamins.

White, L. (1996) Universal Grammar and second language acquisition. Current trends and new directions. In W. Ritchie and T. Bhatia (eds) *Handbook of Second Language Acquisition* (pp. 85–120). London: Academic Press.

White, L. (2003) *Second Language Acquisition and Universal Grammar.* Cambridge: Cambridge University Press.

White, L. and Genesee, F. (1996) How native is near-native? The issue of ultimate attainment in adult second language acquisition. *Second Language Research* 12, 233–265.

Wilde, S. (1990) A proposal for a new spelling curriculum. *Elementary School Journal* 90, 275–290.

Wilkens, K. (2006) Das Babylabor. *Die Zeit Wissen* 1/2006. On WWW at http://www.zeit.de/zeit-wissen/2006/01/Striano.xml. Accessed 23.1.08.

Wilkins, D. (1972) *Notional Syllabuses.* Oxford: Oxford University Press.

Williams, J.N. (1999) Memory, attention, and inductive learning. *Studies in Second Language Acquisition* 21, 1–48.

Winitz, H. (1981a) A reconsideration of comprehension and production in language training. In H. Winitz (ed.) *The Comprehension Approach to Foreign Language Instruction* (pp. 101–140). Rowley, MA: Newbury House.

Winitz, H. (1981b) Input consideration in the comprehension of first and second language. In H. Winitz (ed.) *Native Language and Foreign Language Acquisition* (pp. 296–308). New York: The New York Academy of Sciences.

Winitz, H. (1981c) Nonlinear learning and language teaching. In H. Winitz (ed.) *The Comprehension Approach to Foreign Language Instruction* (pp. 1–13). Rowley: Newbury.

Winitz, H. (1981d) *The Learnables. English.* Kansas City: International Linguistics Corporation.

Winitz, H. (1996) The comprehension approach: Methodological considerations. In *Fremdsprachen Lehren und Lernen: FLuL* (pp. 13–37). Tübingen: Narr.

Winitz, H. (2002) *The Learnables, Book 1* (5th edn). Kansas City, MO: International Linguistics Corporation.

Winitz, H. (2003) *The Learnables, Book 1* (6th edn). Kansas City, MO: International Linguistics Corporation.

Winitz, H. and Reeds, J. (1973) Rapid acquisition of a foreign language (German) by the avoidance of speaking. *International Review of Applied Linguistics* 11 (4), 295–317.

Winitz, H. and Verspoor, M. (1991) The effectiveness of comprehension instruction. Unpublished manuscript, Kansas.

Winitz, H. and Yanes, J. (2002) The development of first year, self-instructional university courses in Spanish and German. In P. Burmeister, T. Piske and A. Rohde (eds) *An Integrated View of Language Development: Papers in Honour of Henning Wode* (pp. 517–535). Trier: Wissenschaftlicher Verlag Trier.

Winitz, H., Gillespie, B. and Starcev, J. (1995) The development of English speech patterns in a 7-year-old Polish-speaking child. *Journal of Psycholinguistic Research* 24, 117–143.

Wittgenstein, L. (1963) *Tractatus Logico-philosophicus.* Frankfurt: Suhrkamp.

Wode, H. (1976) Developmental sequences in naturalistic L2 acquisition. *Working Papers in Bilingualism* 11, 1–31.

Wode, H. (1981) *Learning a Second Language: An Integrated View of Language Acquisition.* Tübingen: Narr.

Wode, H. (1988/1993) Einführung in die Psycholinguistik: Theorien, Methoden, Ergebnisse. Ismaning: Hueber. Reprinted as *Psycholinguistik: Eine Einführung in die Lehr- und Lernbarkeit von Sprachen.*

Wode, H. (1994a) Nature and nurture and age in language acquisition: The case of speech perception. *Studies in Second Language Acquisition* 16, 325–345.

Wode, H. (1994b) Speech perception and the learnability of languages. *International Journal of Applied Linguistics* 4, 143–168.

Wode, H. (1994c) *Bilinguale Unterrichtserprobung in Schleswig-Holstein. Bericht zur Entwicklung eines Kommunikativen Tests für die Überprüfung des Englischen einer 7. Jahrgangsstufe, Band. 1: Testentwicklung und holistische Bewertung.* Kiel: L & F.

Wode, H. (1995) *Lernen in der Fremdsprache: Grundzüge von Immersion und Bilingualem Unterricht.* Ismaning: Hueber.

Wode, H. (1998) A European perspective on immersion teaching: The German scenario. In J. Arnau and J.M. Artigal (eds) *Els Programes d'Immersió: una Perspectiva Europea – Immersion Programmes: A European Perspective* (pp. 43–65). Barcelona: Edicions Universitat de Barcelona.

Wode, H. (1999) On the perceptual basis of sound systems: The case of VOT. In K. Grünberg and W. Potthoff (eds) *Ars Philologica: Festschrift Prof. Panzer* (pp. 211–224). Frankfurt: Peter Lang Verlag.

Wode, H. (2001a) Kerncurriculum Englisch: Früher Beginn – Mehrsprachigkeit – neue Inhalte. In H-E. Tenorth (ed.) *Kerncurriculum Oberstufe: Mathematik – Deutsch – Englisch* (pp. 271–285). Weinheim: Beltz.

Wode, H. (2001b) Mehrsprachigkeit durch Kindergarten und Grundschulen: Chance oder Risiko? *Nouveaux Cahiers d'allemand* 19, 157–178.

Wode, H. (2001c) Multilingual education in Europe: What can preschools contribute? In S. Björklund (ed.) *Language as a Tool: Immersion Research and Practices* (pp. 424–446). Vaasa: University of Vaasa.

Wode, H. (2002) Fremdsprachenvermittlung in Kita, Grundschule und Sekundarbereich: Ein integrierter Ansatz. In C. Finkbeiner (ed.) *Perspektiven Englisch* 3 (pp. 33–42). Hannover: Schroedel Verlag.

Wode, H. (2003) 'Young age' in L2 acquisition: The age issue in reverse in phonology. In L. Costamagna and G. Stefania (eds) *La Fonologia dell'Iinterlingua: Principi e Metodi di Analisi* (pp. 71–92). Pavia: Francoangeli.

Wode, H. (2004) *Frühes Fremdprachen lernen: Englisch ab Kita und Grundschule – Warum? Wie? Was bringt es?* Kiel: Verein für frühe Mehrsprachigkeit an Kindertageseinrichtungen und Schulen e.V. On WWW at http://www.fmks-online.de. Accessed 23.1.08.

Wode, H. (2006) Mehrsprachigkeit durch immersive Kitas: Ziele und Umsetzung. In H. Rieder-Aigner (ed.) *Zukunfts-Handbuch Kindertageseinrichtungen* (16 pp.). Regensburg: Walhalla.

Wode, H., Devich-Henningsen, S., Fischer, U., Franzen, V. and Pasternak, R. (2002) Englisch durch bilinguale Kitas und Immersionsunterricht in der Grundschule: Erfahrungen aus der Praxis und Forschungsergebnisse. In B. Voß and E. Stahlheber (eds) *Fremdsprachen auf dem Prüfstand: Innovation – Qualität – Evaluation* (pp. 139–149). Berlin: Pädagogischer Zeitschriftenverlag.

Wong, W. (2004a) The nature of processing instruction. In B. VanPatten (ed.) *Processing Instruction: Theory, Research, and Commentary* (pp. 33–63). Mahwah, NJ: Lawrence Erlbaum.

Wong, W. (2004b) Processing instruction in French: The roles of explicit information and structured input. In B. VanPatten (ed.) *Processing Instruction: Theory, Research, and Commentary* (pp. 187–205). Mahwah, NJ: Lawrence Erlbaum.

Wong, W. (2005) *Input Enhancement: From Theory and Research to the Classroom.* New York: McGraw-Hill.

Wong, W. and VanPatten, B. (2003) The evidence is IN: Drills are OUT. *Foreign Language Annals* 36, 403–423.

Wright, R. (1966) *Black Boy.* New York: Harper and Row.

Ye, J., Cui, L. and Lin, X. (1997) *Waiguo xuesheng hanyu yuyin xuexi duice* [Chinese phonetics for foreign students]. Beijing: Yuwen Chubanshe.

Young-Scholten, M. (1995) The negative effects of 'positive' evidence on L2 phonology. In L. Eubank, L. Selinker and M. Sharwood Smith (eds) *The Current State of Interlanguage* (pp. 107–122). Amsterdam: John Benjamins.

Young-Scholten, M. (1996) A new research programme for L2 phonology. In P. Jordens and J. Lallemann (eds) *Investigating Second Language Acquisition* (pp. 263–292). Berlin: Mouton de Gruyter.

Young-Scholten, M. (1998) Second language syllable simplification: Deviant development or deviant input? In J. Allan and J. Leather (eds) *New Sounds '97* (pp. 351–360). Amsterdam: University of Amsterdam.

Young-Scholten, M. (2002) Orthographic input in L2 phonological development. In P. Burmeister, T. Piske and A. Rohde (eds) *An Integrated View of Language Development: Papers in Honour of Henning Wode* (pp. 263–279). Trier: Wissenschaftlicher Verlag Trier.

Young-Scholten, M. (2004) Longitudinal naturalistic data: Treasures out of Pandora's Box. In G. Holzer (ed.) *Voies vers le Plurilinguisme* (pp. 195–209). Besançon: Presses Universitaires de Franche-Comté.

Young-Scholten, M., Akita, M. and Cross, N. (1999) Focus on form in phonology: Orthographic exposure as a promoter of epenthesis. In P. Robinson and N.O. Jungheim (eds) *Pragmatics and Pedagogy. Proceedings of the Third PacSLRF* (Vol. 2) pp. (227–233). Tokyo: Aoyama Gakuin University.

Zampini, M.L. (1994) The role of native language transfer and task formality in the acquisition of Spanish spirantization. *Hispania* 77 (3), 470–481.

Zimmermann, G. (1992) Zur Funktion von Vorwissen und Strategien beim Lernen mit Instruktionstexten. *Zeitschrift für Fremdsprachenforschung* 3 (2), 57–79.

Zobl, H. (1992) *SLA as an Academic Discipline Colloquium*. Utrecht. LARS meeting, 20 August.

Author Index

Subject Index

All terms and concepts that appear in SMALL CAPS in this index are defined in the glossary.